# PARTICULAR PASSIONS

# PARTICULAR

**Talks with women who have shaped our times**

# PASSIONS

**by Lynn Gilbert and Gaylen Moore**

**CLARKSON N. POTTER, INC./PUBLISHERS · New York**
**Distributed by Crown Publishers, Inc.**

To Ronnie

Inquiries should be addressed to Clarkson N. Potter, Inc.,
One Park Avenue, New York, New York 10016

Printed in the United States of America

Published simultaneously in Canada by
General Publishing Company Limited

Acknowledgments: Barbara Walters interview © 1981, Barbara Walters


Library of Congress Cataloging in Publication Data
Main entry under title:

Particular passions.

   Includes index.
   1. Women—United States—Biography.   2. Success.
I. Gilbert, Lynn.   II. Moore, Gaylen.
HQ1412.P34   1981        920.72′0973        80-27045
ISBN: 0-517-543710 (cloth)
        0-517-545942 (paper)

Designed by Dennis J. Grastorf

10   9   8   7   6   5   4   3   2

# Contents

# Preface BY LYNN GILBERT

IN 1976 WHEN I was asked to photograph Louise Nevelson for the Pace Gallery, I went to her studio to meet her and was dazzled. Her house on Spring Street was very spare but very ordered. One can see the disciplined structure that dictates the way she lives. Surrounded by the amazing work of her own hands, she creates her own atmosphere, her own environment. That day she had an extraordinary outfit on—a Chinese robe over an American couture gown. A silver African necklace around her neck, a black velvet riding hat, those clodhopper space shoes. The effect was bizarre, yet right. Feeling the tremendous energy and focus of her personality, I was deeply moved.

Back home after the session, I said to myself, there are other women like her who have created something extraordinary and enriched life for themselves and others. Who are they? How were they able to develop themselves and make their astonishing contributions to society? The idea of photographing them and doing brief profiles took form in my mind.

My first task was deciding whom I would include. Who's Who was the logical place to start but I found, in leafing through, that the entries only provided information on positions held and awards won. It was impossible to assess the real contributions and far-reaching effects of the subjects. I knew I was in for a lot of research. Plunging in, I used the Readers' Guide to Periodical Literature and began reading any and every article on a woman or women I could lay my hands on. When an article mentioned another woman who I thought might be considered, I would follow up on that. Eventually I found lists of outstanding women that had been compiled in popular magazines and realized that the lists themselves were new to arrive on the scene. Only in the early seventies did the almanacs, of which there are many, begin to compile lists of distinguished women. In the mid-seventies Fortune magazine wrote its first full-scale article on women in finance and industry, followed by one in Business Week. The most thoroughly researched list to appear in any of the women's magazines was published in 1971 by the Ladies' Home Journal. According to the author The 75 Most Important Women were the "women who had made the greatest impact on our civilization within the last five years and would continue to affect us significantly for the next five years." The author added, it is a "representative list that speaks highly for the quality of feminine leadership in America." But it was interesting to see that a number of women on this list were women whose positions were predicated on their relationships to men of national or international importance. Included were Rosemary Woods, "Executive Secretary to President Nixon since he became senator," Jacqueline Kennedy Onassis, "widow of President Kennedy and wife of a Greek near billionaire—the woman most other women would like to be" and Rose Kennedy. I wanted my list, in contrast, to include only women whose contributions had come out of their own energies and endeavors. My criterion would be women who had done pioneer work in their field that had significantly changed society and/or opened up a new field for women.

When I had exhausted the *Readers' Guide,* I consulted experts in the fields of art, medicine, science, law and so forth, and asked them for their recommendations. I finally created a master list of women, with a second column consisting of the writers, editors and experts who could help me make the assessment of the subject's contributions. I decided each subject would need at least three referrals by solid sources in order to be included.

Throughout the selection process, I tried to be receptive to the information I was being given. When I was compiling a list of black women for instance, the women who were repeatedly suggested to me were almost exclusively in the field of civil rights. I checked my own impulse to find a black writer, a black scientist. Any list is necessarily arbitrary finally. But by feeling my way, I tried to be true to the names that continued to emerge with the most insistence. I finally arrived at a list of over fifty women. Several of the women, among them Marian Anderson, Martha Graham, Susan Sontag and Susan Langer who indisputably should have been included in such a book, preferred not to be. There were several others including Jane Jacobs, the architect and city planner, whom I was not able to reach. Lillian Hellman agreed to be photographed for the book but not interviewed. I photographed three women, Margaret Mead, Cecelia Helena Payne-Gaposhkin and Aileen Osborn Webb but they were not interviewed before their deaths. Dorothy Height and Dede Allen could not be included for reasons beyond our control. Therefore, the forty-six women included here do not represent a definitive list but rather a sampling of the scope and significance of women's contributions to American society over the last fifty years.

At this point I envisioned the book as portraits of the women, each accompanied by a brief text. I hoped my photographs could portray each woman with dignity and I hoped to catch a gesture, a glint in the eye or some small detail that would enable me to go beyond the public and sometimes well-known image and capture an essential inner quality. In order to put my subjects at ease during the photography sessions, I prepared by reading published interviews and profiles and their own books and articles and as we talked many of the women told me stories I had not seen in print. I went home and wrote down everything I could remember, but it was not long before I realized that these stories were more compelling than the primarily visual book I had planned. I felt that if I could understand these women, how they function in our society, it would not only help me understand my own life but perhaps help others.

I wanted the text accompanying the photographs to reflect the style of my portraits: to be revealing, yet written with honesty, dignity and kindness. As the book evolved I needed a writer who would go back to the women, gain their trust, listen to the stories I had heard and go beyond. Again, I relied on research—this time interviews and profiles—to find a journalist with a sensibility compatible with mine.

*Particular Passions* turned into a collaboration when I read an interview by Gaylen Moore on Elsa Perretti for the *New York Times Magazine.* I said to myself, This is the first writer of profiles who knows what a person is really about. We proceeded slowly and surely, coping with the difficult logistics of interviews, writing, editing. This idea of mine took five years to fulfill, and with the collaboration of Gaylen Moore has resulted in a book far richer than any I could have imagined.

I hope that our book will not only add to the feminist literature of our time but will inspire women everywhere to pursue their own particular passions.

# Preface BY GAYLEN MOORE

THE FIRST TIME I talked to Lynn Gilbert was the morning she called from a pay phone to ask me if I wanted to write the text accompanying her photographs of distinguished American women; she had already been through four writers, and her ambitions for the text had grown from brief biographies that documented each woman's achievement to full-length profiles that would be no less probing than her photographs. Lynn had read several profiles I had written for the *New York Times Magazine* and thought I might be able to do what she wanted.

I was interested in taking on the project if I could find a way to make the book compelling. The book as a whole would have to tell a story and each woman would be a chapter. The broader story they would tell would emerge as I interviewed them.

As I read over the research that Lynn had gathered, I realized that most of the women she had chosen for the book had been profiled dozens of times. The profiles contained similar information and even many of the same quotations. They were either straightforward biographies or upbeat success stories. How could we get a more revealing look at these women? Would we be able to discover what it was that drove them?

We came up with two ideas. First, the format. Our editor suggested that instead of writing a profile of each woman, I should do oral histories. I would tape my interviews with them, make transcripts and then edit them. This format would give the text an immediacy; each woman would have the opportunity to tell her own story. The texture of their voices might add a revealing dimension to the information they were communicating. Second, the focus. We decided that I would focus my interviews not so much on what the women had done, or how, but on why they had done what they did. In that way we hoped to find the thread that would tie all of these women together.

When I began interviewing, what was immediately apparent was not the similarities among the women but the differences. Women like Frances Steloff, the founder of the Gotham Book Mart who nurtured and promoted the generation of avant-garde writers in the twenties and thirties, belong to the tradition in which women dedicated themselves to helping others realize their talents and gain recognition. The younger women, like architect Denise Scott Brown and television producer Lucy Jarvis, have made their contributions to society by nurturing their own talents to become powerful figures in their fields.

I realized that this contrast represented the two ends of a spectrum within which fell the forty-six women in the book. Right in the middle of the spectrum were the women of both generations whose efforts to transform society made the evolution of woman as nurturer to woman as a power in her own right a possibility—women like Maggie Kuhn of the Gray Panthers, Eleanor Holmes Norton of the Equal Employment Opportunity Commission, family court judge Justine Wise Polier and politician Bella Abzug, who have fought for and defended the rights of the aged, minorities, children and women.

When all the interviews were finished, Lynn and I recognized that together they provided an historical perspective of the last fifty years in this country. The story the women were telling was the story of the emergence of modern woman. In the interview that concludes the book, Betty Friedan points out that while many women today have achieved power and even celebrity, the price has sometimes been an ambivalence about themselves and what they have accomplished. Perhaps, she suggests, women today are discovering that without a vision of the world, the achievement of power for its own sake is meaningless.

What distinguishes the women in this book is that their goal was not power but a search for the truth, and what motivated their search was not personal success but passion—the passion that comes from the effort to transform reality according to their particular vision of the world.

# Acknowledgments

THERE ARE many people whom I wish to acknowledge for having made this book possible. First I want to thank the subjects themselves, who gave of their time and encouraged us to complete this book, and their secretaries or assistants, who were more than gracious in providing requested information.

Second, I want to thank the experts in many fields, whose advice made it possible to make the final selection of the subjects. Among the more than one hundred people there were a number whose knowledge and helpfulness were especially important in shaping this book.

In women's studies: Elizabeth Norris, librarian and YWCA historian; Ellen Sweet, formerly public education director at the Women's Action Alliance; Jan Mason, assistant editor of *Life* and head of research of the "Remarkable American Women" issue; Irene Arnold, formerly executive director of Retarded Infants Service; Margaret Adams, senior editor national affairs department, *Good Housekeeping;* Annette Baxter, Adolph S. and Effie Ochs Professor of History at Barnard College; Maralyn Boll, formerly IBM public relations consultant to the United Nations.

In civil rights and African-American studies: Jewell Jackson McCabe, president of the Coalition of 100 Black Women and director of government/community affairs at WNET; Anna Hedgemann, consultant on African-American studies; Jean Blackwell Hutson, formerly chief of the Schomburg Center; Ruth Ann Stewart, formerly assistant chief of the Schomburg Center; Mildred Roxborough, director of operations, NAACP; Althea Simmons, director of Washington bureau, NAACP; Evelyn Cunningham, formerly special assistant to President Ford.

In the sciences: Joan Warnow, associate director of the Center for the History of Physics of the American Physical Society; David Dvorkin, research associate of the American Institute of Physics; Dr. Sylvia Frank, Mount Sinai School of Medicine; Dr. Ann Briscoe, Association for Women in Science.

In religion: Beverly Harrison, professor of Christian social ethics at Union Theological Seminary.

In the arts: Paul Cummings, formerly director of oral history at the Archives of American Art, New York; Rose Slivka, former editor in chief, *Craft Horizon;* Jack Frizzelle, manager of public information at the Metropolitan Museum; Rona Roob, Museum of Modern Art.

In architecture: Pershing Wong, fellow of AIA, designer with I. M. Pei; Suzanne Stephens, senior editor, *Progressive Architecture.*

In computer technology: Dr. Carl Hammer, director of computer sciences at Sperry Univac.

In astronomy: Dr. Charles Whitney and Dr. Owen Gingrech, professors of astronomy at the Center for Astrophysics at Cambridge, Massachusetts.

There were many others whose input helped create this book. Arnie

Glimcher, whose children I photographed, asked me to photograph Louise Nevelson for the Pace Gallery, which provided the particular experience out of which this book evolved. My aunt and uncle, Red and Pick Heller, arranged for me to photograph several of the first subjects. Audrey Adler, a literary agent, liked the portraits and was encouraging in the early stages of the book.

*Acknowl-edgments*

Among the most helpful in finding the proper writer were Michael and Ann Loeb, and their friend Dick Brickner; Arthur Loeb of the Madison Avenue Bookshop; Harriet Lyons of *Ms.*; Richard De Combray, who kept the project going when it might have come to an end and Martha Saxton, who generously suggested that Gaylen Moore might be perfect for the job.

Sylvia Porter suggested I get the finest legal advice and I did, thanks to my lawyer Nancy Wechsler, suggested by Jimmy Adler, and Jerry Chazen, all of Greenbaum, Wolff and Ernst.

My friends were always supportive. Lila Bader, an excellent listener, helped me overcome many hurdles. Edward Merrin exhibited my portraits, while the book was in progress, at the Edward Merrin Gallery in New York City.

My only experience with a publisher has been a happy one. Our editor, Carol Southern, determined the book's form, gave the book its title, did a superb job of editing and with the publisher, Jane West, was responsible for the book being published. It was their faith in my idea that enabled me to pursue the task of finding a writer. Anne Goldstein, assistant editor, worked diligently checking progress and details with us almost daily. She believed in our manuscript and it helped her decide to leave publishing, change her life and follow her own particular star.

Without the encouragement of Ronnie, my husband, our boys, Paul and George, our housekeeper Lessie Freeman and their faith in my ability to accomplish whatever I set out to do, I'm not sure I could have tolerated the seemingly endless obstacles and difficulties in the five years that it took to complete this book.

Each of these people played a special role in the evolution of this project, but it is to Gaylen Moore I owe my deepest gratitude. Our collaboration has enriched my life immeasurably and given me the opportunity to work with a skilled writer where the development of an idea was our shared goal.

L.G.

# Frances Steloff

*Frances Steloff (born 1887, Saratoga Springs, New York) founded the
Gotham Book Mart in New York City in 1920. She played a unique and
instrumental role in the literary world of the 1920s and 1930s when she
helped launch the work of Henry Miller, James Joyce, Gertrude Stein, E.
E. Cummings, Anaïs Nin and Ezra Pound. Because of her faith in these
and other unknowns, the Gotham became a haven for the literati and a
setting for their gatherings. Today the Gotham Book Mart with its stock
of approximately 100,000 books has the most complete collection of
twentieth-century literature and poetry in the country.*

IT WASN'T ANYTHING SUDDEN. It was my attitude toward my work that
made the Gotham Book Mart a success. I felt that writers were very
important and I wanted to do all I could for them. My way of doing it was
buying their books, always having them on hand, showing them in the
window, listing them in the catalog and taking advertising in the *Times*
and *Herald Tribune*. That's my job and I thought I'd do it the best way I
could, and that's what endeared me to these people. If I'd been married all
this time, if my husband hadn't died six years after we were married,
things probably would have been different. I probably would have found
it easy to accept the invitations that were offered to us, all the dinners.
Consequently, I wouldn't have given all my love and devotion to the
Gotham. I never did anything that wasn't for the good of the shop.

My customers were book people. They were all interested in the
welfare of the shop and they all wanted to contribute something. They
had good ideas and I immediately put them into action. When somebody
came in and said, "Oh, you must read this wonderful book," even if I
didn't read it, I'd order it and tell others about it. At one time, every book
in the shop was a recommended book. When my customers came in and
saw their advice put into practice, they were pleased. It was simple, a
simple thing, but it turned out to be very useful.

My customers liked first editions. Authors that I had faith in, even if
the book wasn't on the best-seller list, I'd order a larger quantity than we
needed so as to have first editions for future customers. Sometimes my
enthusiasm for certain books was temporarily mistaken, and we often
had to wait until they went out of print or the authors became recognized
or died. This happened with John Steinbeck and William Faulkner and
many others whose early books were all remaindered. We kept them in
the basement along with all our other unsold books, which in those days
were not returnable to the publisher. Someone would always ask for
them eventually. It turned out to be a very famous basement.

My first book job was at Loeser's department store in Brooklyn. I was
working in the corset department. One day in November, the floorwalker

came up to me and said, "We need someone to work at the Christmas book table, so learn all you can about these books." Oh, I was in heaven. People would jumble up the books, take them out of boxes and out of tissues, and I'd put them back properly and sell them. I never ran when the closing bell rang. I wanted to stay working.

One day, the man who replaced the stock said to me, "If you like these books so much, why don't you ask the buyer to keep you on in the book department." "Do you think he might?" I said. "Ask Mr. Peck," he said. "He comes up here every day to see how things are going and he wears a black derby." I watched the next day and, sure enough, he appeared. He looked very forbidding. I said to myself, I'll wait until tomorrow. But tomorrow I felt the same way.

Finally it got to be Christmas and I thought, Wouldn't it be awful if I lost my job. They won't have this table and they won't want me back in the corset department. So I went downstairs and found Mr. Peck. I was trembling. "Would it be possible for me to work in the book department?" I asked. "We have all we can do to keep our own staff busy," he said. He had a growly voice. "It gets very dull after Christmas." All I could think of was, This is my last chance. How can I leave his office? Just as I was turning to go, he said, "Wait a minute. Do you know anything about magazines?" "No, but I'd learn quickly," I said. He took me over to the magazine counter and introduced me to the girl there. "She'll teach you how to take subscriptions."

There was nothing between that magazine counter and the outdoors except a swinging door. It was cold. At home, I laid out scarves and sweaters, all the extra clothes I had. I wasn't going to get sick and miss work.

I'd been working there a year and a half. I was getting seven dollars a week. Mr. Mischke, who was in charge of the old and rare books, no matter what time it was when he left in the evening, he always saw me there working. He often stopped by at my counter to see how I was getting on. One day he invited me to lunch. He asked me if I'd gotten a raise. "Oh no," I said. "Well, you ask them for a raise," he said. "Don't ask Mr. Peck. Go right up to Mr. Cooper, the superintendent, on the fourth floor." I was afraid again. Every time Mr. Mischke came by, he asked me if I'd done what he told me to do. "No, but I will," I'd say.

Finally I took courage. Mr. Peck had gotten a card from Crowley, the magazine man. It said, "Congratulations on your splendid order clerk." That was me. It was this card that prompted me to go up. I took the card up with me and showed it to Mr. Cooper, along with my sales figures. I had doubled the sales. "Seven dollars is all the job pays," he said, I went back and told Mr. Mischke. He said, "I'm going to talk to my friend at Schulte's Bookstore about a job for you." I wished he wouldn't because I liked my work at the magazine counter.

Well, I got the job at Schulte's. I had charge of the circulating library and the Sunday school supplies. One day, a customer, Mrs. Wilson, came in with a long list of titles she wanted that were out of print. I found them for her. When she was leaving, she said, "If you ever think of making a change, call me." She had a bookshop, the McDevitt-Wilson Bookshop, in the Hudson Terminal Building. I went down there one day and, sure enough, it was one of the most beautiful bookshops I'd ever been in. It had the feminine touch. It had little mottoes all over the walls. A book fitly chosen is a lifelong friend, was one of them, I remember. It was, oh, so very inviting and homelike, so cozy. That appealed to me. Besides, she was going to give me a dollar raise. So I made the change.

McDevitt-Wilson was a real bookstore. They had nothing but books, no Sunday school supplies or circulating library or anything but wonderful books. They had all the books you could love, the best of poetry, fiction, travel. I'd been there for a while when Mr. Wilson had to go to California for a library convention. He talked to me about taking charge of the store while he was gone. "Just run it as if it were your own shop," he said. When he came back he was so pleased by the way I took care of it. I was very happy there. I stayed over three years and I really learned about what it takes to run a bookstore.

Later I went to work at Brentano's. I began to know enough about drama and the theater to know what books were going to be called for, and I worked myself up to being in charge of the drama department. People came in all the time asking for books on the theater that were out of print. Four blocks away, on Twenty-third Street, there were about a dozen secondhand bookshops. I used to spend my lunch hours there. When I saw an out-of-print book that I'd been asked for at Brentano's, I'd buy it and tell the manager that a certain customer had been asking for it. If the customer didn't come back for it, I'd keep the book. I started my own collection in a little bookcase at home.

One day I was going over to see one of my half-sisters. She was working in the office at the Astor Hotel. I don't know what prompted me to cross on West Forty-fifth Street, but halfway between Sixth and Seventh Avenues, I saw a little window, about a yard square, and it had a homemade sign in pencil that said Space for Rent. This was in 1919, right after the First World War when there was no space to be had anywhere. I was thirty-two years old. I went over to the door. There was a ragged old curtain at the window. Inside, I could see girls working at sewing machines. I pointed to the sign and they pointed to Claire's Dress Shop next door.

I went in to inquire. Claire took me out the back way and led me into what had been the kitchen of an old brownstone. She stood in the doorway between the living room and dining room and said, "All this, and the rent is seventy-five dollars a month." It was very cheap. Oh, it was a very cute room. It had a fireplace, a marvelous fireplace, and there was a settee under the window.

Well, that room kept burning in my mind. I thought, Wouldn't it make a cute bookshop. The feeling came over me that this was the thing to do. That evening I got my friend David Moss, the head of stock at Brentano's who later became my husband, to come with me to look at it. We peeked through the torn curtain. "Oh yes," he said. "That'd make a cute bookshop. But I think you ought to wait a year or so until you're better prepared." "But this cute little shop won't be here then," I wailed. He wasn't very much help.

Then I called Mr. Mischke from Loeser's. He was then working at an old and rare bookshop near Brentano's. I felt sure he'd encourage me. Well, he didn't discourage me, but he didn't hold out any great hopes. He asked me about my finances. I said I had a hundred-dollar Liberty Bond, almost a hundred dollars in cash, and about a hundred out-of-print books on the theater. He thought about it, then said, "It would be worth trying. But if you do take it, make sure your first customer is a young person." I didn't know why, but I didn't ask.

The next morning I went to the bank and drew out all my money and went right over to Claire's Dress Shop to rent the space. The next thing I did was get a carpenter to build shelves on one side of the room. I thought I could put my little bookcase from home next to the mantel on the other side.

When David Moss and Mr. Mischke heard that I'd decided to take the place, they both wanted to know how they could help. On New Year's Day in 1920, they came to my apartment on Sixteenth Street and helped me pack up my books. Besides the bookcase, I had a desk, a rocking chair, a kitchen chair and a long table that I wanted to take over to the shop too. David said he knew a man on Second Avenue with a horse and wagon. He went down and got him to come up. We loaded the wagon and we drove up Sixth Avenue in the snow to the first Gotham Book Mart.

We worked until midnight that night, putting the finishing touches on the shop. The walls were terribly disfigured. There were gaping holes in the plaster, so we covered them up with burlap. When everything was ready, I arranged my books on the shelves. I put them with their covers facing front so you could see the whole book. It made the shelves look fuller. Then I brought out everything I had that I thought would look good in a bookshop—all my prints and all my photographs. I arranged all my nice little knickknacks that I loved on the mantel, and I had an old clock. It was just like a little home. And people loved it.

The next day the snow was thick and heavy. I waited and waited for a customer and, pretty soon, I saw a tottering old man coming down the stairs. He asked for a book that I didn't have. I didn't know whether to be glad or sorry because of what Mr. Mischke had said. Nobody else came in that day. The next day I saw this handsome young man looking in the window. Oh, I thought, if he'd come down and buy a book . . . I no sooner had the thought than he came tripping down the stairs. "How much is that costume book in the window?" he asked. I was afraid to tell him. It was the most expensive book in the shop and the only costume book I had. "Fifteen dollars," I said. He took some money out of his pocket. "Here's ten. I'll be back after the matinee with the rest." He gave me a little narrow card—Mr. Glenn Hunter, it said—and he flew out the door. I went out without hat or coat to see where he'd gone to and I saw him disappear into the stage entrance of the Hudson Theater, a few doors down the street. Outside the theater, the poster read Billie Burke and Glenn Hunter in *Clarence* by Booth Tarkington. I looked at the card he'd given me and danced around the table. I had made my first sale and it was to a young person!

Sure enough, after the matinee, Glenn Hunter came back with a friend and paid the five dollars. He came back many times after that. After he came in, many Broadway theater people began coming into the shop. The whole cast from *The Goldiggers*—Ina Claire was the leading lady—all came over in the evenings after the performance. And they kept coming. They loved all my little things and they always found something they wanted to buy. I started staying open until midnight.

When I'd been open for a while I began to see there was a call for books with colored plates. In those days, theaters didn't have their own stage designers. The directors would adapt illustrations from Dulac or Rackham and others. They came into the shop all the time looking for colored illustrations. I knew a bookseller in Leipzig and I would write to him for books with plates that could be adaptable for stage sets. Fortunately he trusted me. I didn't have to pay him for the books until I'd sold them. Otherwise I couldn't have afforded to stock them. That's the way I kept the shop going for the first few years.

In 1940 we published a catalog of our experimental literature called "We Moderns." "We Moderns" put the Gotham Book Mart on the literary map. It was reviewed in the *New York Times* and the *San Francisco Chronicle,* just like a book would be. It sold books too. People knew just where to come to find the new authors, the hippies you'd call them now. The public called them the nuts. They certainly wouldn't have been known by so great many people if it hadn't been for the catalog.

It came about by chance. One day in 1938, my friend Christopher Morley, an author and an editor at the *Saturday Review,* came in and said, "A friend of mine has just graduated from college and needs a job desperately." It was still the Depression and we could barely pay our bills. And yet I didn't want to turn a deaf ear to anything Chris wanted. He'd been so good to the shop. I kept thinking, What can I do? when the words came out without my even knowing it. "I suppose he could make a good catalog."

The young man came in the next morning and I tried to teach him the art of cataloging in one lesson. Finally I said, "Instead of describing each book and telling people why they should have it, why don't you introduce the author and then just list his books and the prices." I'd never seen it done that way, but I liked to experiment. He produced a catalog called "The Book-Collector's Odyssey, or Travels in the Realms of Gold." Well, it was a great success. Everybody liked it. They came in and complimented us on having done it.

Two years later, in 1940, we were going to celebrate our twentieth anniversary. We always did something special for our anniversaries. One year it was a bookmark that had a ruler and a calendar with astrological signs. I tried to think, maybe a paper knife, but that would be too expensive. Everything I thought of seemed to have a drawback. Finally, I said to Miss Steele, my assistant, a very able assistant, "Well, since they liked that catalog so much, why don't we do it for the experimental writers."

The first person who came into the shop after I had this idea was Carl Van Vechten, and knowing his friendship with Gertrude Stein, I thought he could write something about her. I showed him the first catalog and said, "Something like this, but you can say anything you like, and make it as long or short as you like." He thought that was quite an assignment. In a few days he called up and said, "How do you like this?" and he read me what he had written.

> Gertrude Stein rings bells, loves baskets and wears handsome waistcoats. She has a tenderness for green glass and buttons have a tenderness for her. In the matter of fans you can only compare her with a moving picture star in Hollywood and three generations of young writers have sat at her feet. She has influenced without coddling them. In her own time she is a legend and in her own country she is with honor. Keys to sacred doors have been presented to her and she understands how to open them. She writes books for children, plays for actors, and librettos for operas. She writes fiction and autobiography and criticism of painters. Each one of them is one. For her a rose is a rose and how!

Well, I didn't think it made much sense, but since he knew Gertrude Stein so well, I thought it was safe to accept it. I thought, maybe when I see it in type it will sound different. The next day I got it in the mail and I still couldn't make head or tail out of it, so I referred to Miss Steele. She said, "Well, they'll all understand it."

So we made a list of all the people who were to go into this catalog, and the likely people to write about them. As people came into the shop, we asked them for their suggestions. They all had someone to suggest and sent them in. People who had never been to the Gotham before came. Conrad Aiken came in and wanted to know if there was any special slant or number of words. Everybody was begging to write something for this catalog. I didn't know . . . I didn't realize it was going to be so interesting and unusual, but they seemed to be aware of it.

I think people who write books and poems are special. They have something to say and know how to say it. They can say it in a way that imparts knowledge to others. The best of the author is between the two covers of a book. I never read enough to get the benefit of the inside of books. I always hoped to read. When I was fifty I began putting books aside on my shelf and saying, When I retire, this is what I'm going to read. But I never retired. Now that I have all the books in the world and ought to have time, my eyes won't take it. But just having them, just seeing them there is consoling. I have this wonderful feeling I'm in the presence of greatness.

Oh how grateful I've been. I would have been nothing, nothing but a sassy little brat if it hadn't been for books. I was born in 1887 and grew up in Saratoga Springs, a fashionable, elegant resort where rich people came. It had one of the finest racetracks in the world and they came up there for sport and for their health because of the springs and mineral baths. In the midst of all that wealth and beauty, my mother died when I was three years old and we immediately got a stepmother. She was all that a stepmother implies. She was brought up in poverty and she was well-meaning, but she had a very bad temper and I guess she was sorry she walked into a house with five young ones. She was young and deserved better.

My father was a very poor provider. He was a scholar, a student of the Bible and religious books, and that was what he was mainly interested in. There was no way of earning money in Saratoga except during the racing season and that only lasted a month, so my father ordered things from the Sears, Roebuck catalog and took them way out to the country, where they didn't have stores, to sell them. I didn't see much of him. He came home only on weekends.

We lived right near the railroad roundhouse, just a few yards away. There was a high picket fence that shut out the tracks. I used to look through the knotholes and cracks and watch them filling the engines with coal and turning them around. I always wished I was on one of those trains going anywhere; it didn't matter which direction, just away.

During the racing season, I sold flowers. Our neighbors had a beautiful garden. They'd make bouquets and I'd sell them on Broadway. One day when I was twelve, I was hurrying to get to the hotels in time for the people coming back from the races. It was midsummer, August. I had a little brother, one of my stepmother's children. He'd been playing in the sand. All he had on was a little shirt. When he caught sight of me with my tray of flowers, he began to cry. He wanted to come along. I knew that if I went off without him he'd follow and get hurt. He was only three years old. There was no time to wash and dress him, so there was nothing for me to do but slip a little dress over his muddy shirt and take him along.

Well, he was quite a handsome child. He had golden curls and big blue eyes. Some people at the hotel fell in love with him. They were from Boston and they didn't have any children of their own. They wanted to know if they could take him home with them. I said, "Well, you'll have to ask his mother." They came over to the house and asked my stepmother if they could adopt this little boy. Of course she wouldn't part with him. When they couldn't have him, they wanted to know if they could have me. That was an answer to my prayers. I thought anything was better than what I had. It was arranged that I'd go back to Boston with them.

It was like jumping from the frying pan into the fire.

The woman I went to live with was an alcoholic. She was ill-tempered and cruel. She loved to go out driving with her horses and trap. Soon after I went to live with them, they moved out into the country to Wakefield—it was about an hour out from Boston—because she wanted to take care of the horses herself. She didn't trust the people at the stables. In Wakefield there was a country school with two classes in one room, but unfortunately the woman wouldn't let me attend regularly. She wanted me to stay home and do things for her. The house had to be kept clean. You might say my schooling ended before finishing the seventh grade.

I never had any idea what this woman was going to do next. To give you an idea how cruel she could be . . . We had dogs. I was crazy about animals, always have been. We had four dogs at one time, all different sizes. One was a fox terrier. He was a cute little dog. She trained him to follow her carriage. One day, poor little Maxie saw another dog and forgot all about the carriage. It made her very angry. She turned the carriage around and went after him. By that time Maxie had had enough of the other dog, so he came. She brought him home. She held him by the collar, and with a horse whip, she whipped him . . . and . . . my poor little dog . . . he choked. I was crying and she said, "If you don't stop, I'll do the same thing to you." She was capable of doing it and I knew it. The next morning Maxie was dead.

Well, Bunker Hill Day is on the seventeenth of June. In Boston it's a legal holiday. I took courage. Her husband was home that day. They were going out driving in the afternoon. She always did the driving, but sometimes he wanted to drive and she wouldn't let him have the reins, so they quarreled. I didn't feel comfortable with that quarreling, so I preferred to stay home and do something I wanted to do. I was hurrying to make the beds so I wouldn't have that to do after they left, when she called out, "Come downstairs." I said, "I'll be down as soon as I finish." Well, she came upstairs in a rage, a perfect rage.

I grabbed my china piggy bank and ran out of the house. I didn't know where I was going. I had a sister in New York. I knew she lived in Harlem but I wasn't sure of her address. I ran to the railroad station at the foot of the street. I was known there, of course, and I borrowed a commutation ticket. That took me into Boston. I emptied the piggy bank into my lap on the train and I had two dollars and something. That was enough to go to New York on the Fall River Boat Line.

I arrived in New York just as I was, with no hat or coat, a few pennies, not enough to buy a cup of coffee or anything. I walked from the Battery all the way to Harlem. I was afraid every time I saw a policeman that he knew I was running away. It was getting dark. I looked up at a window that said Employment Agency. I went up there to find out if there was anything I could do. The woman was very kind. I told her my predicament. "Well, you can sleep on the couch if you want to," she said. "But you have to be up at eight because that's when I open."

The next morning people began coming in, employers looking for help, but she didn't ever tell them about me. I looked at the newspaper the agency had and saw there was someone wanted to take care of a baby.

Oh, I thought, that's my specialty. I went and answered the ad. It was a nice home and a nice family and the most beautiful baby. I thought it was a living doll with red hair and blue eyes. When I was settled, I wrote to the man in Wakefield at his office, not to his wife, and I sent him back the commutation book I had borrowed. He was very nice and very kind. He wanted me to come back. I said, "No, I never want to see that woman again."

I used to feel cheated, cheated by having my mother die, cheated by having my stepmother beat me, and a stranger too, that's even worse, cheated because I never had books. I never read the juveniles and classics and the others as they came along. There are references to them everywhere. I missed all that. It used to hurt, but I've come to feel that all the cruelty I've suffered was for a reason, and it doesn't hurt anymore. Perhaps if I'd had a college education I might not have been so hungry for books. I would have thought I knew it all, and I wouldn't have been so humble. I wouldn't have been so eager to do for my customers, to please them, or love them and be grateful to them for buying my books.

I remember one day I went to my aunt's house but she wasn't home. I waited and waited. My grandmother was always so concerned when she saw us children. She made a beeline for the kitchen to get me some cookies. While she was in the kitchen I noticed some books on the marble-top table in the corner of the living room. I was drawn to those books like a magnet. I went over to them. They were children's books. I hadn't seen any other books than schoolbooks and religious books. These books had pictures in them and I could read them. I thought every one of them was so wonderful, I could not leave them behind. I finally selected two that I thought I couldn't live without. Without waiting for Grandmother to bring the cookies, I started for home.

When I got to the end of the path and onto the sidewalk, I thought I was safely home with them, when I heard my grandmother calling, "I can't let you take those books. Your aunt would be very cross with me if I let you take them. They belong to your cousins." If she had stabbed me with a knife, it wouldn't have hurt any more. I gave her the books and went home. I had no place else to go. I never went back.

I can't bear to see books abused. Books have feelings. See, my father was a booklover. He kept his books on a shelf in the attic, high up near the ceiling. Even if I stood on a chair, I couldn't reach them. If he ever dropped one of his books on the floor, he picked it up and kissed it.

# Tatyana Grosman

*Tatyana Grosman (born 1904, Ekaterinburg, Russia) revived lithography as a fine art in this country when she set up her print workshop called Universal Limited Art Editions in 1957 in West Islip, Long Island. She also introduced the European idea of the livre de luxe, the special edition of a book illustrated by an artist. Among the artists who have discovered the print through her enthusiasm and encouragement are Jasper Johns, Robert Rauschenberg, Helen Frankenthaler, Robert Motherwell, Jim Dine, Larry Rivers, James Rosenquist, inventor R. Buckminster Fuller and poet Andrei Voznesensky. Her studio has a reputation for perfectionism that is unmatched anywhere else.*

WHEN MY HUSBAND had his first heart attack in 1955, I knew I had to make a living. I remember one night, it was about two o'clock in the morning, and I was thinking What shall I do? I hadn't learned anything, I had no craft. So I said to myself, I have to start something. Probably it will be something I will do for the rest of my life, so it has to be worth while for me. I would like to contribute something. Whatever I start, I have to put in it everything, all my life experience, all that I love, and all that I am interested in. I decided I would like to publish. I would like to combine words and images and only words and images that I like.

I came actually from a city named Ekaterinburg, called Sverdlovsk now, on the other side of the Ural Mountains that divide Europe and Asia. We lived on the Siberian side. It was not typical of Russia, no traditional family estates passed down through generations. It was surrounded by emerald and platinum mines and became a wealthy industrial city which was built very fast and grew very fast. The population was mostly adventurers, deportees, miners and people who had been political prisoners in Siberia and had lost touch with central Russia. These people with imaginations came to the Urals to begin new enterprises.

My father was sent to Ekaterinburg by the Russian government because he was a typographer and they wanted him to start a newspaper so they would know what was happening in Siberia. First, he had the problem of finding typographers to work for him. The men he hired came to work with their families, the wife, the children, and of course there was the goat and the cow. Some of these men who were willing but illiterate, he had to teach. The journalists my father hired had certain kinds of opinions and conceptions, otherwise they would not have ended in Siberia. The paper was a pioneering effort for a young man who was twenty-one. It was lively and well read and very successful.

We led a bourgeois life. We had a nice house and we had many servants.

In the kitchen we had eleven people, but there was only one room for them. It was piled to the ceiling with pillows and mattresses. In the evening the maids would take their mattresses and pillows and run around to find a place to sleep. They slept just anywhere, in the den, the dining room and salons. My brother's *nannya* slept in the same room with him, and my governess slept in the room next to me.

Winter lasted at least eight or nine months so there was a big to-do for heat. Between every two rooms there was a stove and it had to be fed with wood. There was one person to chop the wood for each stove and one person to put it in.

My education was the same as for most people of this class. The first years, up to seven or eight, you were privately taught. At nine, you went to the gymnasium where Latin and Greek were included and work was assigned like it is in a university—in two weeks you had to read this and that. It was demanding, so we all had tutors.

School was from nine until two o'clock, when the family ate dinner together. Then came the tutors. I had to work until five or six o'clock. After the tutors left, instead of being cosy on the bear rug in my room with my books, my mother, who was German educated, said I had to go to sports. This meant to her shoveling snow even though it was getting dark. It was so cruel. Even today, I remember how my hands were frozen, my legs were frozen, my nose was frozen. But I had a solution. We had a big dog, Bobka, and when I was shivering, I crawled in the hut with Bobka and Bobka kept me warm and licked my face. Then I came home for my music lesson. Somewhere in between sports and my piano lesson I had to do exercises on the piano for half an hour.

My greatest relief was that every year, after the Christmas parties where I ate too much sweets, I got ill. Then I could stay in bed and read. I waited for this moment, always. From the beginning I loved all kinds of books and had read all of Tolstoy, Dostoevski, Turgenev and all our classics before I was fifteen.

We left Russia in 1918, because of the revolution and uncertainties. We left everything and went through Siberia to Vladivostok and awaited the events. But the events didn't settle. We had expected to go back. That was the moment when money began to be of no value, so my father invested in platinum, gold, emeralds and pearls which were easy to carry.

When we went from Vladivostok to Japan the emeralds were sewn into the hems of our dresses. I had a sailor skirt with big pockets and I had bars of gold in them which were very heavy. I was always afraid the pockets would tear, so I kept my hands inside the pockets and held the fabric very tightly. We went to Japan in order that we could go to school, because my parents were conscientious about education. They put me in a boarding school, the Convent of Sacré Coeur, in Tokyo. My parents didn't mind my being at a convent because they never felt Jewish. They converted to Calvinism, I suspect, because in Russia there were restrictions where Jews could live and work. In Russia, being Jewish was only a religion. It was much later that Hitler established Jews as a race.

The convent had great style, mystique. We wore black veils and went to church three times a day. Certain days we had to contemplate and were not permitted to talk at all. Actually I liked it very much.

We were in Japan just waiting to see what was happening in Russia, but after a year my parents decided we had to have a better education. In my father's mind the schools in Switzerland were the best, but we were only able to get transit visas to Italy. When we got off the boat in Venice my parents still hoped to go to Switzerland. It was apparent that the visas would be very difficult to get. As my mother's family lived in Dresden, we decided to visit them and see what was doing in Switzerland. We went to Dresden and never left.

Life was very difficult for me in Dresden, very difficult. It was too petit bourgeois, too small, too narrow. Strangely enough, what I learned at the convent in Tokyo, the silence, was very close to my nature. I stopped talking for two years. I don't mean I didn't ask anybody to pass me the tea sometimes, but I was not interested in talking to anyone. There was nobody to talk to so I just read.

In Dresden there was always vacation time when I traveled with my mother. She was addicted to spas. When spring came we had to go to the spas in Czechoslovakia to rinse the liver. Three times a day you went to the source to drink. You drank this kind of water and that kind of water. You walked around and then at four o'clock you changed your clothes.

My father felt I was too curious, too controlled and my mother felt this inhibited her spirit. I was an introvert and it irritated her terrifically. She was very frivolous, very coquette, very pretty, very small and round and had blond hair. Every time we were on the train on a trip, my mother found a gentleman who was interested in her. For my mother it was embarrassing that I was so silent, so tall and thin, but I accepted her. I didn't know another mother.

When I graduated from the Lyceum in Dresden, I went to the Academy of Applied Arts. I studied art there and at the botanical gardens, where I went to draw flowers. It was very satisfying. It was very pleasant to be alone in the sun with the flowers and plants. Today I still have very strong feelings about botanical gardens.

While I was at the Academy I met Maurice Grosman, an artist who had finished the school, but had his studio there. I had seen him before at the Café Zunz which had a few tables in the back and was a place where artists and intellectuals met. I saw him again at a ball. Every year in Dresden there was the famous Jester's Ball. Everyone dressed up in costumes and there was good music. People came from all over Germany. The very wealthy, society and industrial people were there and I was dragged by my mother. I always felt misplaced. When I danced with Maurice there, for the first time, it was so natural, there was never any doubt. I knew that he would be my husband.

What my parents felt about Maurice is a long sad story. They didn't want him to be my husband. I left home because my mother was quite rude to me when she talked about him, and I didn't want to be exposed to

those scenes. He belonged to a group of artists who were very, very
bohemian, who had no money, only friends and admirers. When I
married my husband in 1931, they never accepted him at all. Ever. It
wasn't only that they didn't accept him, but my mother made life very
difficult for us. A certain family offered us an apartment, the little
servants' quarters in their big house. It was very comfortable and nice,
but we never got it because my mother said to them, "With every
newspaper it will be known that you have a Jew in your house and an
awful person." We went to live in Paris. We made friends in the cafés of
Montparnasse with painters—Lipchitz, Chaim Soutine, Ossip Zadkine.

In certain ways perhaps I found my life liberated. There was no more
etiquette and demanding traditional life at home. I had no servants and
had decided never to have any. I didn't like the way they were treated. It
was simpler just to make my own omelet. But I still didn't fit into this
bohemian life. My husband's artist friends resented me. They felt an artist
who marries a girl from a wealthy family should not have a spoiled wife
who had no money. Life should be for the better. But my husband always
felt we were better off than anybody else, no matter how poor we were.
With his great generosity and camaraderie, he always helped others.
When we didn't even have a piece of bread or a penny, he would say,
"Tomorrow will take care of itself."

In 1933, Larissa, our daughter, was born. When I had to leave the
hospital, I sat bundled up on the steps of the hospital with my baby, while
my husband went running around trying to borrow money. He finally
collected money he was owed from a friend in a café and we were able to
take a taxi home.

When Larissa was still a baby, my husband's younger brother, who
was in such fragile health he could hardly walk, wanted to get out of
Poland to study. Well, he succeeded. He came to us, but I couldn't take
care of a baby and a sick boy. My husband took him to a doctor, but he
was too ill and the doctor wouldn't take care of him, so my husband
brought him to the hospital and he died. I suppose I felt I would be
punished because I didn't take care of another mother's child.

When Larissa was sixteen months old, I decided I wanted to leave her
for a few hours a day in one of those homes where the mothers who work
could leave the children. I wanted her to be among other children, and I
wanted to be free to help my husband in his work. She needed a
vaccination to be admitted. The vaccination was given one morning and
in the evening we were having dinner . . . she had just fallen asleep and
suddenly I heard a kind of scream. We ran into the bedroom, and I saw
she had a kind of cramp. I picked her up, but she was unconscious. We
took her to the children's hospital and they said leave her here and come
back tomorrow. I would have preferred to take her to a doctor, but it was
very difficult to have your own doctor in Paris. You had to pay and pay,
to cultivate your own doctor. You couldn't just call a doctor from the
telephone book, or use the next-door neighbor's doctor. So I left her in the
hospital. Early the next morning we rushed there. Maurice had wanted to

take a toy, but I said, "Come. Later you will take a toy." When we got there she didn't exist anymore.

When Larissa died it was a great void. I remember I had to physically hold something, because she was still very small and I was used to carrying her around. I reproached myself and felt perhaps we should have kept her at home. You never quite get over the death of a child. The loss is not just for the child itself. Sometimes I think how old would she be, how would it feel to have a daughter of that age. I feel I am ageless now. I have no measure of comparison. I have only my work, That is what interests me, and what I do for people and also what they do that I would like them to do.

When Larissa was born, my parents should have helped me, but I didn't want them to because they would have wanted to take me home. I also couldn't go back to Germany because I foresaw the Nazis. I knew it. War did come and because we were Jews, we had to leave Paris. We were trying to go to America and had reached Marseilles and were living near there when Maurice was arrested. I didn't know where he was. Suddenly I received an envelope, it was a little note from him saying, "I am with this boat." The boat was in Marseilles being painted and it was used as a jail because the prisons were too full and couldn't hold the six thousand Jews who had been arrested. He was kept in the hold of the boat with the rest of the people and I don't know how he came out on deck. He said to one of the painters, "My wife doesn't know where I am, would you kindly give her a note." The painter, continuing to paint, stretched out his leg and said, "Put it in my shoe." My husband bent over and slipped it in.

I learned that the people on the boat would be sent to a camp, or, if you had fifty thousand francs, to an assigned residence where you were free but had to report to the police every day. Maurice didn't have the money but said he did. A sculptor friend offered all his money if Maurice was asked by the authorities to show it, but he wasn't. He was sent to Alzon, a very small place, maybe a hundred people. In the meantime I was promised visas for the United States and we had to report to the American consulate in Marseilles. On that basis I got a permit that said Maurice could pass through all the little towns on the way there. When we got to the consulate, a man there said, "Well, we have all the papers but one. We need a paper from Paris that says you never had a criminal record." I had never heard of such a thing. Paris was already occupied and I felt it was dangerous to wait any longer. I said, "Maurice, we will leave without the papers, just as citizens of the world." I wasn't going to give up my life because a paper wasn't there.

After that we had many narrow escapes from the police and the Gestapo. Sometimes I didn't think we would be able to get away. Some friends helped us to get to the Spanish border. We knew if we could get to Spain we might be able to get visas, but first we would have to cross the Pyrenees on foot. My husband did not want to go, but I felt this was something we had to do. Maurice carried his easel and paint box so we would not look suspicious, and I wore my fur coat. Everything else was

**15**

left behind. Our only document was a copyist's permit Maurice had gotten from the French Ministry, to copy art in museums. Once a *guardia civil* stopped us, but Maurice had seen him coming, gotten out his sketch pad and begun drawing a tree. Maurice just held up his copyist's permit and the guard went on. Somehow we always found food to eat, places to sleep. I was happy during our walk. I was never afraid. I felt free.

In Barcelona we finally got visas to the United States. When we arrived in New York in 1943 many of our friends were already there— Lipchitz, Zadkine. Ossip Zadkine helped us find our studio apartment on Eighth Street. Maurice painted, and gave lessons in drawing and painting to make money. He taught himself to make silk-screen prints—he made prints after well-known modern paintings and we sold them to Marlboro Book Shops.

We lived in the studio on Eighth Street, but we had friends on Fire Island who in the summer would invite us for weekends. One day we were standing at the ferry in Bay Shore. It was so lovely and nice. I said to Maurice, "Why don't we come out here—perhaps we can find a room with kitchen privileges for the summer." So one day we took the train for Bay Shore but we got off at Babylon, the stop before. We looked all around for a room with kitchen privileges, but there were too many dogs and children and ladies cooking. My husband said, "Let's go home. You see this is not for us. It's also too expensive."

I said, "Listen, we are already here for the day. Let's spend this one day in the country. We're here and we can't afford to come again. This will be the only day we have here, so let's stay and see it through." We walked out on the road near here—Montauk Highway—and my husband was grumbling, "I want to go home. Why are you dragging me here?" I started to walk, determined.

After just a few steps, a car pulled up and stopped. It was a big limousine. A man dressed in a blue suit opened the door and said, "I cannot see people walking on the road. Kindly get in and take a seat." So we got in. Then he asked, "Where can I take you?" I said, "To the next bus stop." "What are you doing here?" And we told him. In the meantime we passed a big white mansion and he pointed and said, "I live here." He took us to the bus stop, let us out, and started to turn the car around. Then he stopped and said, "Listen, if you don't find anything by this evening, come and see me. Perhaps I can help you." And he drove off.

That evening we took a bus to the gentleman's house, and he was outside, working on the rose arbors. He said, "Oh, there you are. You didn't find anything?" We answered no, and he said, "Wait." He went into the house and came back out with a little key and said, "Follow me." He took us here, to this little house. It was the gardener's cottage. Upstairs he showed us the bedroom. We looked out the window at the garden and the woods—it was all so lovely. He asked, "Do you like it?" We did, but we were afraid it was going to be too expensive. Sensing this, the man said, "Would fifteen dollars a month be too much?" "No," we answered, "that we could afford."

It turned out that the mansion belonged to the Dominican Order and that the gentleman was a Dominican brother. The house became 5 Skidmore Place and we came here in the summers and invited our friends. Then, in 1955, Maurice had a heart attack and was very ill. It was very serious for a while and he couldn't go out and he couldn't walk. I brought him out to Long Island and we gave up the studio on Eighth Street. I put a Do Not Disturb sign on the door and then went out to try and get the five dollars for the next day somewhere.

My husband was a painter, and a very good painter, and through most of our life together it was his work that interested me, that was my life. So what was I to do? I sold some of his paintings and then later he did silk-screen reproductions of certain artists, Picasso, Miró. . . . But I didn't really like the silk-screen process—maybe it was just the smell—and then one day William Lieberman, the curator of prints at the Museum of Modern Art, explained to me the difference between work made without the artist's collaboration—reproductions—and original prints, in which the artist himself creates the image on the stone or plate.

I thought, It takes so much time and it's only a reproduction. Why do a reproduction? Why not try to do original work? After that I knew what I really wanted was for the artist to work personally.

Then, by some miracle, somebody said to me, "Mrs. Grosman, the stones in front of your house are lithographic stones. If you take them out, you will see." I found them and I had the idea that I could use these stones to make a book. My real passion had always been books, books with visual images. I had just read a book that inspired me very much, Monroe Wheeler's *Modern Painters and Sculptors as Illustrators*. Wheeler told about artists doing graphic work to illustrate books of poetry. Many French artists had done that. He wrote that the ideal thing would be for the artist and a poet to work *together* on a book, and that seemed like a wonderful idea.

Soon afterward, Maurice and I drove out to Southampton to see Larry Rivers. We had known him since 1950, when we met on a ship going to Europe. I talked to Larry about my idea of a book that would be a real fusion of poetry and art. Larry listened very carefully and then called out, "Hey, Frank," and down the stairs came this nice young man in blue jeans. It was the poet Frank O'Hara. And so it was decided on the spot that we would do a book together, artist and poet working together on the same surface. That is how things have happened to me in my life: they just work out somehow.

Some neighbors had an old lithography press they were not using anymore and they sold it to me for fifteen dollars. After finding the lithographic stones in our yard, we found more in many other places, including a former bullet factory on Greene Street in New York; it was a place that had changed hands many times. Probably once it had been a lithography plant, because there were so many stones lying around. The present owners were happy to get rid of them.

Frank and Larry started to work and, after two years, we published a

portfolio of lithographs called "Stones." But Larry was very impatient
and if Frank were not around he would draw on stones that were not part
of the portfolio. I would have the printer do small editions of these stones,
and that's how I started to do single editions. Originally I had thought of
doing only books.

It was really the lithographic stones themselves that gave me the idea
of using lithography to make books. I like stone—it is a natural element. I
like to see something drawn on stone. It does not have the coldness of a
metal plate.

The technical aspects of printing are not really important to me. Even
today I don't know anything about lithographic techniques. The way we
work is very simple. The artist makes his drawing on the stone, the
printer makes a proof, and then the artist decides what he likes or doesn't
like and then makes changes. I might make some suggestions, and we
select the paper. The most important thing is that the print be alive. It
must have the heartbeat of the artist in it.

The stone itself imposes, inspires, limits. The grain is always slightly
different, one is rough and one is gentle. Some stones are gray like granite,
some more sand-colored and one has beaten edges, another smooth. No
two stones are alike. The stone is given to the artist in the studio—
Rauschenberg likes to work in the living room at a specific table, Jasper
likes to work in a little patio, where he sits on the floor.

The artist is the author of the image on the stone. Rauschenberg in
particular has a special feeling for the surfaces and the edges of the
stones, the elements he works with. When he is working, Rauschenberg is
very inventive and always brings something new to the medium. He
spends one day and leaves a month's work. Jasper, on the other hand, is
meticulous but he never knows what he wants until it is there.

The printers are the interpreters and can interpret the stones in
various ways. It takes two years for the people who work here to
understand how we work. There is no rush. Most of the printers who
work here were just drifting along from one job to another, searching for I
don't know what. But here they have the feeling they are growing and
participating. That's very important. You see, each print from the artist is
a new question to be solved, a new challenge to be faced, a new
adventure. We don't repeat ourselves, so it is very exciting for them. The
printer must know exactly what he is doing, he must feel the print. He
must have the technical knowledge, like a dancer, to know when to jump
and when he has to be very light. Sometimes I say to the printer be very
gentle and delicate here, but here make it strong and sparkle. I don't like a
print to smell of sweat, hard work. It is hard work, perhaps, but it
shouldn't show.

Paper is the fabric of the print. It can be rough or smooth, white or off-
white; it can have big margins or narrow margins. It can be a great
inspiration.

Then we have the mission of the image. A print is not a drawing or a
poster. A poster has a message that you have to see in a split second,

sometimes passing by car, on the way to the train. The message has to be clear. But a print is very intimate; it is the rapport between the artist and the stone. Always between the idea and the execution of a print something happens. I don't know what. Sometimes you see that the artist does not realize that between making a drawing and making a print there is a difference. It must not be rushed. Sometimes it is good just to let an edition sit for a while and maybe the artist will add something or take something away. I think it is my responsibility to make sure that the artist should never have any reason to regret what he has done. Once an edition is out, it cannot be recalled. It is an example of an artist's work that is in many places at once, all over the world, so it is usually seen by more people than one painting or one drawing.

All these years I have worked only with people I wanted to work with, people I was interested enough in and I felt I could introduce to a different medium. I observed their work for a while because I never jump into an adventure. I watched Jasper Johns for two years before I had the courage to approach him. I saw his show at the Modern and twice at Castelli. His work was irresistible, so I wrote him a letter. I assumed I would have an answer in three days. One day from here to New York, one day he would reflect and another day I would have my answer. I waited and waited and felt every ship was burned. I was completely lost. It had to be Jasper Johns or my life was ended, finita!

Perhaps a week later he called from South Carolina to say he had received my letter and that as soon as he came back to New York he would see me. A few days later he called to say he would come at this and this time. So I was sitting at that time waiting for Jasper Johns. I didn't know how he looked. Suddenly in dashed this adolescent boy who says, "Can you tell me where I can find 5 Skidmore Place?" I thought, Oh God, what does he want from me? I wait for Jasper Johns. I said, "This is 5 Skidmore Place." He looked at me and said, "My name is Jasper Johns." I couldn't believe it, this kid was Jasper Johns.

It is interesting to work always with the same artists. They grow and develop and give me a part of their life and development. That's what my life is about. I never thought in terms of making money, but I wanted what I did to have a solid base, and then to build step by step. When there is a crisis, I always do the same thing. I do nothing. I wait and then life picks up. I can't say, "It is better to do that, no matter what." That doesn't exist. It is very strange, but something comes along that gives me courage. It is like an invisible hand and it guides me. Then I hold on to that and I feel that is the way to follow. Then the responsibility comes. In my case there are the artists, the printers, the curators of the museum who exhibit, the journalists who have to write. There is a complete company, an army of people who have to be stimulated, supported, so whatever happens then, it has to be right, it must work by itself.

a very wonderful man, a practical visionary and a great librarian whose innovations placed the Newark Museum Library ahead of many other institutions with its range and ability to serve the public. I was never sure he really understood art, but he knew it was important. During the 1920s, he put on many exhibitions and raised funds for a collection of modern American painting and sculpture. In addition, he made sure his apprentices were well exposed to art.

In New York at that time the only way to see modern artists' work was by going to their studios. A man named Holger Cahill, who was helping teach our class how to be museum workers, knew all the current crop of American artists, so he would take us to New York and we'd meet those wonderful people in their studios. Cahill could see which ones were breaking new ground. Some of them had studied in Paris, but what he saw was a movement beginning here in New York. It was very exciting to meet those artists and listen to them talk. Here was the real thing, all these experiments going on, the sort of work we'd never heard of in college. I might not understand what I was looking at, but I didn't have any doubt that it was important because Cahill knew it was important and wanted us to see these things.

The Newark Museum class lasted about ten months. Then because the museum was expanding and needed a staff, they hired all nine of us apprentices. We had a deadline a few months away to create a brand new museum, with three floors, a garden, a junior museum and a library—all open to the public. The museum had very varied collections, not only modern art but a huge nineteenth-century American painting collection and all sorts of ethnological collections—Tibetan, American Indian, Oriental, early American. They had acquired these over the years, often by donation, sometimes by purchase. It was great fun for us apprentices because we got such a smattering of everything.

The first job I was given was to set up two empty galleries in the new building. All over the floor were boxes of African Negro art and South Sea Islands material that had been recently acquired. It was wonderful stuff. The director told me, "Here, read about this, then install it and write the labels." Most of the things written about African Negro art were written by French collectors, and in this country by Dr. Alfred Barnes. He had bought a big collection in Paris, the Paul Guillaume collection, and he exhibited it and wrote about it. The only trouble was that Barnes wouldn't allow anyone into his museum!

When the Newark Museum opened, after a few hectic months, they began using us as models for the costume collection. We were constantly dressing up in Tibetan or Chinese or Victorian clothes and posing for photographs for the newspapers. The newspapers loved the Newark Museum and every week there was a story about its collections, its director or its apprentices dressed up in costumes. Then we were assigned a special task of "docenting"—guiding school classes, ladies' clubs and other groups through the galleries and lecturing to them. We were taking as many as three or four big school classes through the museum every day. The groups were really very responsive. They'd never seen a museum like this, or any of this kind of material, but the museum kept us at it so long that we almost died of exhaustion. We begged for mercy and asked them to hire full-time docents, so we could finish our training in the other fields of museum work. But it was a very exciting year because they really didn't have time to train us; they just had to say, "Here, get to work and install these galleries." So that was the way we worked, and *fast*.

I stayed at the Newark Museum for four years. While I was there, the founding of the Museum of Modern Art was announced in the summer of 1929. My best friend at the Newark and I looked at each other and said, "That's where we must go." We knew it instantly. I felt I'd been at Newark long enough, so I deliberately gave up a perfectly good job—during the Depression—and went to New York without work. I didn't have a steady job for several years. I did odd jobs, such as cataloging an American folk art collection (now at Williamsburg), cataloging and installing a huge American Indian collection for the Montclair, New Jersey, Museum, jobs that would take a few weeks or sometimes years. I never regretted leaving the Newark Museum because it was so great being in New York.

Alfred Barr was the director of the new Museum of Modern Art. Even though he was only twenty-seven years old, he was the unquestioned expert in the field. He had had a fellowship and had spent a year in Europe, going to talk with the famous artists and see their work, which had not yet reached the museums or even the private galleries here. Barr knew everybody; he was unique at that moment.

In 1932–33 he took a leave of absence because of illness and Holger Cahill was asked to run the museum and its exhibitions while Barr was away. Cahill called me and said, "Come and help me." So I became a part-time, dollar-an-hour worker at the Museum of Modern Art.

In the beginning, the staff was very small. It was the director and his assistant, the business manager and his assistant, a carpenter, the guards. Then in 1932, Philip Johnson started the architecture department. He financed it himself. He and Barr put on the first exhibition of modern architecture in this country, "The International Style."

Nothing could have been more different from the Newark Museum. The Modern was devoted to modern painting, sculpture, drawings, prints, architecture and industrial design. I worked on a big American show of paintings and sculpture from the Civil War to the present, then on an American folk art show, then on Cahill's great show, "American Sources of Modern Art."

I had never met Alfred Barr. When he returned in 1934, I said, "Do you think I could work here?" or something timid like that. And he said, "Yes, I'd like to have you, but I have to get permission from the trustees to hire another staff member." He later told me that he wanted me because, by then, I'd had ten years of museum experience and he thought it would be nice to get someone who had experience instead of somebody just out of college. So I finally got the job that I'd wanted for so long.

The museum really was a terribly exciting place then. There was nothing else like it in New York, or anywhere for that matter. Alfred Barr had the most extraordinary mind I had ever come in contact with, and his ideas were very different from those of museum directors of that period. For instance, he realized that if you have a committee choose a show you get a committee exhibition. It doesn't have a point of view, an individual's point of view. His first exhibitions at the museum had to be committee jobs, selected by the Board of Trustees, and he knew that they resulted only in compromises. He firmly believed that one person should be chosen to do each show, and that person should have complete responsibility for it. That was the principle behind the exhibition program of the museum, including the series of American shows I did later.

The first show I did alone was the WPA (Work Projects Administration) Federal Art Project show late in 1936. It was in a way a report on the first year of the project. The museum trustees decided that I should do the show and should have complete and final choice of inclusions.

Holger Cahill, then my husband, was running the WPA Federal Art Project. I traveled all over the country. In each city every good artist would be on the project, and a great many new, young artists were being discovered. In addition to saving actual lives of artists and turning up many unknown talents, the WPA was extremely important in creating a new public for art. The government projects set up community art centers in cities and towns that had no other form of art activity. In 1935–36, the first year of the projects, over a hundred of those community art centers were established all over the country. That was the kind of man Cahill was—he could make an extraordinary thing like that happen.

Then, about 1942 the museum's exhibition committee decided to have an all-American show that would exclude New York artists. We all knew the New Yorkers, at least those who were showing in the galleries and museums. But we didn't know about the people who had developed out of the WPA art projects elsewhere. So they let me do that show and let me travel all over the country again to see the projects. There's nothing more exciting to me than looking at all the art activities in this country. I saw there were many regional trends and a general level of great work, some of which had been shown in New York, but most of which was new.

To me, perhaps the most striking regional trend, one of the most successful and most different from any other, was in Seattle, where Mark Tobey was the "old master" and Morris Graves and others of his young age were all on the WPA Project. Seattle had a flavor of its own which was quite different from, say, Chicago. I knew already about Mark Tobey; he had once been in a big group show selected by Barr. Also he was an old friend of my husband's; they had lived in the same house in New York years before. So I went to Seattle and immediately looked up Mark Tobey and saw his work. Then I told him that I'd heard about a new painter on the WPA and I'd seen his work in Washington. That was Morris Graves. I said, "Morris won't answer my letters. I've written to him and begged to see him." Mark said, "I'll get him for you. He was my student." So, sure enough, he set up an appointment.

Morris was really, genuinely reluctant to be "discovered." Without Mark, I probably couldn't have got to Morris at all. Morris arrived from his country shack in an old Ford truck. Our meeting place was the basement of the Seattle Museum. In the back of the old Ford truck he had about a hundred of those wonderful pictures, unframed, unmatted, on tracing paper, just thrown in a heap in the truck. He took them out and he was very cross. He reluctantly spread them out all over the floor of the basement. I didn't have to think. One look at all those wonderful birds in the moonlight . . . a quick glance and then I went to work to try and persuade him to send them to New York. "I'm not ready to show," he said. "I'm just beginning." I did my best for fifteen minutes, trying to convince him. Then I said, "All right, let's forget about exhibiting. Won't you just send them to the museum so that I can show them to Alfred Barr and the trustees? They'd be awfully pleased and delighted."

I told him, "I'll be able to sell a lot of these for you," which he could hardly believe, and I said, "How much do you want for them?" He said, "A hundred dollars each." It was a fair price at that time. Then I turned to another young artist, Kenneth Callahan, who worked in the Seattle Museum, and I said, "Do you think you can make him do it? Will you pack them and send them?" He said, "Well, I'll do my best but he'll probably change his mind." But they came. I had to wait six weeks. I thought I'd never get those things to New York.

When I opened the package with Alfred Barr, and there were all those marvelous pictures, well, everybody in the office just died. Some of our trustees who were on our painting and sculpture committee came rushing in to look at them. There were eighty pictures and we spread them out on the sixth-floor rug before teatime. The trustees and staff all wanted to buy, but Alfred said, "The museum gets the first choice, then Dorothy gets the next choice because she succeeded in getting them here." Alfred chose ten for the museum, then I chose one and then the staff and trustees went to work on them. By the time we got through I'd sold all eighty paintings.

Graves was absolutely stunned, and at last he was pleased. He wrote me a marvelous letter saying, "The grocer here is very much surprised to have my bill paid in full. The bill has been running for eight months." He cited other things like that. After that he was very responsive to us. I think he was convinced that somehow he was ready to exhibit after all and didn't know it. So he was in my 1942 American show.

The museum let me do another American show in 1946, and then one in 1952. Clyfford Still exhibited in the 1952 show. He was a very strange and difficult man. At the time he was with the Betty Parsons Gallery where he'd had three shows by 1950. My husband went to see the last show and called me at the museum and said, "Get right over here quick and see this work." So I ran over. It seemed then very rough, tough, but very sophisticated. It wasn't smooth and elegant like Rothko's. It seemed the rugged expression of a person who'd grown up in the wilds of the West. It was turbulent and eloquent at the same time.

I was selecting people to be in my 1952 show and I'd selected Mark Rothko who had shown before, quite a lot, and was much better known than Still; of course, Jackson Pollock was in the show and Pollock had become quite famous, but Still—I knew he'd refuse to be in the show. He was against a lot of things, like exhibiting in New York, but I asked him one day, "Would you be in this show? You can write whatever you want in the catalog." He said, "You mean I can really write whatever I want to?" I said, "Yes, you can, but I can't send the catalog through the mail if there's anything obscene in it!"

He was terribly nice. He let me go again and again to his studio where he had rolls and rolls of huge paintings and he unrolled them. I looked at maybe a hundred paintings, and together he and I chose about thirty or thirty-five which we took to the museum so we'd have a broad choice in arranging them. We hung his gallery in the show together one evening. He seemed very pleased and I was very pleased. The show was called "Fifteen Americans" and it was impressive. Of all my shows this one had the biggest impact because so much that was new and radical had happened in the six years since my previous show in 1946. Pollock and everybody had blossomed . . . the whole Abstract Expressionist movement. I had about forty artists and I was going mad trying to choose, there were so many very, very good people. Some of them I put in my next show four years after that. It was a terribly exciting moment in New York. I haven't been conscious of any time since then that has been that exciting.

I have a tremendous passion for making a good exhibition. You've got fifteen artists, who's going to be in the first gallery? The order in which you place the artists, that's so important. What you look for and what you try to achieve are climaxes—introduction, surprise, going around the corner and seeing something unexpected, perhaps several climaxes with very dramatic things, then a quiet tapering off with something to let you out alive. There has to be an element of drama in it, at least for me . . . keeping up the interest as you go through seventeen galleries, don't let the interest flag, something new is coming around the corner, it's going to knock your eyes out.

In those old days at the museum, you could do it any way you wanted. You had the whole great third floor of the museum. You'd decide first on the sequence of artists and how to get that drama into it, and then how you could best design the floor plan around the demands of each artist's presentation. With the high cost of everything now, I'm sure they have to use a space that's already there without redesigning special galleries. I could always move the walls and I had my choice of colors.

There was a very tight, rigid schedule, three weeks or even less between the big shows. There'd be four days to reposition the walls, three days plus a weekend for repainting them, and at the end there'd always be two days and two nights for making the final arrangement of paintings and sculptures, then two more days for the actual hanging. We had marvelous teams of trained men to do all this, our own painters, our own carpenters and our own hangmen, as we called them, who could just read your mind. "I was sure you were going to put that there," they'd say to me. There was nothing more fun for me than arranging a big exhibition. That was my only small claim to creativity.

A lot of the artists we showed had never shown in a museum although some had shown in galleries, which have a smaller attendance. That was one of the purposes of our shows, to bring new work that we thought was excellent before our huge museum public. Sometimes I was scared. "Fifteen Americans" was supposed to be a very far-out show. I was ready to stick behind my choices, but I didn't know how it would be accepted. I had a twenty-foot wall filled with one big Pollock. I think some of our trustees were worried about what the critics would say. Some of them came and looked at the show the morning before the preview. The president of the board was brought through by Rene d'Harnoncourt, director of the museum, to break it to him gently. I remember this trustee came up to me afterward. I was putting up labels and getting it ready for the preview that night. He said, "Dorothy, it's a wonderful show. I'm crazy about it," and he bought several things from it. Our trustees were a wonderful group anyway, eager to accept new things and to support the staff.

It turned out to be one of the most successful shows of that period. Margaret Barr, Alfred's wife, came rushing up to me at the preview and said, "It's a colossal success." I said, "How do you know?" She said, "The air is electric." It's very funny when you look at those paintings today. This work was shocking to many people. It was too rough and tough. I used to walk through the galleries at crowded hours just to listen to the reactions. People were saying "Outrageous! Shocking!" as they walked from one gallery to another. It's hard to believe things moved so fast then. By putting these paintings in the museum, I think we may have changed the minds of some experienced collectors. As for the general public, I think they always expected the museum to do things they weren't going to approve of.

One of my chief satisfactions at the museum was this series of American shows. These exhibitions involved some artists who were already known but little appreciated. They also aimed at discovering new people and selling their work to collectors and the museum. I'd say that was the most satisfying thing about my work. One of my most "radical" artists, Clyfford Still, has had a big exhibition at the Metropolitan Museum of Art—the final accolade.

The idea of going any higher on the ladder at the museum did not occur to me. I always felt it a great privilege to work with Alfred Barr and the other brilliant people there. I'd had a lot of good training. I was also lucky because I worked with two people who had the best eyes for art that I have ever known, Cahill and Barr. My husband taught me a lot, and there were many things he was quicker at than I was. I'd say, "No, I don't get it yet." But we did agree on a great many things that we liked. We also had a healthy amount of disagreement.

Year after year, Barr and I used to wind up at exhibitions in New York on Saturday afternoons. He'd walk into a gallery full of paintings and say, "Let's each decide which one we like best and then we'll compare." Well, he'd go just like a bee to the best picture. He proved that over and over again. I might not think it was the best then, but in the end somehow he'd always picked the best.

In the late 1950s, there was a group show at Castelli's, and there was a little tiny painting of an American flag. I said to Leo, "Who did that?" He said, "Oh, he's wonderful, that's Jasper Johns." Sometime later Castelli gave Johns his first one-man show. I remember it was a Saturday morning, it was opening day but it was raining. Alfred Barr got there before I did because he lived uptown. He called me and said, "How fast can you get here?" I said, "Twenty minutes if I take a taxi." When I got there he was alone in the gallery. The great variety of Jasper's works was impressive. There were the numbers, the letters, the targets, all sorts of things.

Leo Castelli was very considerate. He left us alone to discuss which ones the museum should buy. We knew we should buy several, the only way to get the range of the work. They were very inexpensive. After much discussion we decided on four that we should bring before our Collections Committee. We could not give any assurance that they would be bought, but we called Leo out and said, "These are the ones we'd like to have. Will you send them over?" He said, "Fine, would you like to meet the artist?" And poor Jasper had been sitting in a little inner room no bigger than a closet hearing everything we'd said for an hour. He was twenty-six and dressed in a neat business suit, hair cut well, not at all a bohemian New York artist, which he wasn't, of course; he was from South Carolina. He was too shy to talk to us. Alfred kidded him about something and he couldn't respond. It was a memorable meeting.

Even at that time, the late 1950s, modern art was still new enough so you felt you could show people something they'd never seen before. You don't feel that anymore. Everybody's seen everything, because there's so much more activity, more dealers, more publicity, more artists, maybe three times as many artists today as there were thirty years ago—that's just a guess. There are thousands more collectors, too. When I first started at the museum, we knew most of the collectors. There were about twelve of them in New York—the big names, Stephen Clark, the Lewisohns, Mrs. Rockefeller; we felt we knew them all. They were all interested in the museum and our board, but it wasn't until later, I'd say the 1940s, that the vast number of new collectors developed. One might almost say that an enormous mania for collecting developed.

Nobody could possibly count the collectors in New York today. Every house you pass has a collector in it. Some of it had to do with the great increase in the numbers of artists and dealers, as well as with the extraordinary rise in the value of art. I had a lot of fun just buying what I liked, for a few hundred dollars; the Nevelsons, the folk art, the Jasper Johns, the Gorky. I bought a Franz Kline for a thousand dollars and now it's so valuable I shouldn't have it here in my apartment, but I just forget about all that and keep on living in my dear little firetrap. It amuses me that they've increased so much in value, but I'm never tempted to sell them, I just want to look at them.

I know there is still the possibility of discovering artists today, but you have to weed through an awful lot of stuff you don't want to see because there's so much being made and shown.

I have done a good deal in helping private collectors to buy art and I have been fortunate in that they have all bought because they love art. Once in a while someone has called me on the telephone to say, "I'd like to buy something that's going to be eight times as valuable . . ." I say, "Well, I'm not interested. I only buy things myself because I'm crazy about them and I advise other people to do the same. If it becomes more valuable, that's just good luck." I don't help anybody who says he wants to buy for investment purposes, I don't like that as a reason for buying.

There were too many things about my career that were luck, luck that I happened to get the job at the Museum of Modern Art and that there were such wonderful people there to teach me and help me along. It was a great staff. I did make a risky decision to leave a perfectly good job at the Newark Museum in the depths of the Depression, but New York was always a mecca to me. Even when I was a tiny kid, my first conscious aim was to get to New York because it meant so much excitement, the Natural History Museum, the Metropolitan Museum, the lights of Broadway, the Bronx Zoo, all these things. My parents used to tell me that when I was three or four years old, and was angry at something, I would stamp my foot and say, "I will take my suitcase and go to New York."

I used to get offered directorships or other good jobs in other cities, but I never considered them because I knew the only place where I wanted to be was New York. Here's where it's cooking. There's no other place like it. I wouldn't live anywhere else. People say, "Don't you want to retire to your little country house?" I say, "Oh, I'm not leaving New York, good God, no, I wouldn't dream of it."

# Aileen Osborn Webb

Aileen Osborn Webb (born 1892, New York City, died, Garrison, New York, 1979) was a central figure in the modern crafts movement that began in the 1930s and was instrumental in raising crafts to the level of an art recognized around the world. During the Depression she organized a project to help rural peoples market their crafts. In the forties, with seed money from an inheritance, she helped found America House, which marketed crafts in a metropolitan area for the first time, and launched the magazine Craft Horizon. Over the next twenty years she was instrumental in founding the American Crafts Council to educate both craftsmen and the public, the Museum of Contemporary Crafts in New York City, the first crafts school at the University of Rochester and the World Crafts Council.

# Ellen Stewart

*Ellen Stewart (born Alexandria, Louisiana) is founder of La Mama, the
off-off-Broadway theater and a pioneer in experimental theater in
America in the early 1960s. La Mama has launched more composers and
presented more foreign artists than any other contemporary theater in
America: composers Elizabeth Swados, Philip Glass and William Elliot,
American directors Wilford Leach and Tom O'Horgan, foreign directors
Andre Serban, Peter Brook, Tadeusz Kantor. Stewart was the first artistic
sponsor for Polish director Jerzy Grotowski. Between its inception in 1961
and 1980, La Mama produced more than 900 plays here and around the
world.*

**M**Y PASSION HAS ALWAYS BEEN for people. Some people I was interested
in wanted to do theater and so that's how I got into it.

I grew up in Chicago. When I came to New York in 1950, I came to go
to Traphagen, the school of design. That was my intent. In my day, if you
were colored you were not allowed to enter the fashion school in
Chicago. There was one school in San Francisco that a colored could go
to, and a colored could go to Traphagen in New York. I tossed a coin. It
was heads for San Francisco and tails for New York. It came up tails and
that's why I came to New York.

When I got to New York, a woman named Edith Lances gave me a job
at Saks Fifth Avenue, trimming threads from custom-made brassieres and
corsets, and doing little menial tasks as needed. I didn't know anyone in
New York, so every Sunday I would ride the subway and get off
someplace.

One Sunday I got off on Delancey Street. I had never seen anything
like it. This was the Jewish area where people set up stalls to sell things.
There used to be a lot of stalls all along both sides of the streets. I was
looking at the fabrics and things and a little man came out of his store and
tried to sell me something. I didn't have any money. I went into his store
and I was adopted that day into his family. This man was Abraham
Diamond. He was the founder of Orchard Street. He came from Rumania
when he was eleven years old and he put the first pushcart on Orchard
Street. I went to visit him every Sunday, and each Sunday night when I
would leave he would give me a little packet. When I'd go home I'd open
it and it would be a piece of fabric. I'd take the fabric and make
something; I would wear it back there the next Sunday. I was his
daughter, the designer.

At Saks Fifth Avenue, colored had to always wear blue smocks. You
could take the smock off at lunchtime when you would go out to lunch.
When I took the smock off I would be wearing what I had made out of the
fabric that Papa Diamond gave me. Women in the store who saw me

**33**

assumed that I was a model wearing Balenciaga clothing. From that, I got to be one of the executive designers at Saks Fifth Avenue, which I was for almost eight years.

I was a crackerjack designer. Few people know that.

I stopped working at Saks and up until about 1961, I was doing free-lance designing. I free-lanced for Bergdorf Goodman, Henri Bendel. Then I decided to go to Morocco on a vacation—I like to take long vacations—just work enough to make some money. So in the Hotel Momorrah, which is in the Casbah in Morocco, I ran into a friend, Teresa Klein, who even today has a little café called The Open on Lexington Avenue, which many people don't know about. When Teresa wants to open her doors she just marks in chalk on the outside, OPEN. She serves marvelous teas, she collects fabulous things, she's an incredible painter. It's a salon kind of thing.

I was in her hotel room, the morning of my fate, feeling very sorry for myself because I didn't know what I wanted to do. People don't believe in the idea of a dybbuk. Jewish people know what a dybbuk is, it's some other soul that manifests itself through another human being. My Papa Diamond used to always tell me that the important thing in life was to have a pushcart and that if I had a pushcart and I pushed it, not for myself but for other people, it would take me where I wanted to go. So there in her room, my Papa Diamond spoke from Teresa's mouth. This is really true. She was talking to me and trying to make me feel better and all of a sudden her voice changed into his voice. "You go get a pushcart." The next day I left.

When I got back to New York I decided what the pushcart would be. I was going to try to make a little theater, because my brother and his friend Paul Foster, a playwright, wanted to do theater. I was not interested in theater, but anything my brother and his friends wanted to do, that's what I would have been doing because I was interested in them. Not knowing anything about theater, I thought it's like playing house. I would continue to do free-lance designing, I thought. I could always make money. I would have this little theater and they would write plays and all their friends would be in them and live happily ever after. So that's how La Mama started.

I rented this little basement at 321 East Ninth Street. The people in the building had great objection to my being there because they didn't want to be living with a nigger or near where a nigger was, and they tried to make me get out. What happened was this. I had many friends who were modeling for *Women's Wear Daily* and they had friends. If they were between gigs they would come over all dressed up, change clothing, and work for as much time as they had to spare, helping me fix this basement. The tenants would see these white men coming in and out, and they used this as an excuse to ask the Health Department to give me a summons for prostitution.

The inspector that was sent to serve me the summons turned out to be

someone who had worked in vaudeville years ago, and when he learned
that we were trying to make a little theater, he was very sympathetic. In
those days, the license required by the city authorities for any location
presumably doing theater was impossible to get. Since I didn't have a
license, I would get a summons for breaking the law. I would be convicted
and have to spend the night or several hours in the Women's House of
Detention. The inspector suggested that rather than a theater, why didn't I
have a coffeehouse and in the coffeehouse I could do theater. "But," he
said, "you have to have a restaurant license to be a coffeehouse, and I'll
get you one."

Now everybody called me Mama. When he wanted to know what I
was going to call the coffeehouse, somebody said, "It's Mama." And then
Robert Paulsen, one of my friends helping me, said, "No, La Mama."
That's where the name came from, and so our little coffeehouse became
La Mama.

The tenants finally did make me leave, even though Mr. Slywotski,
who was from the Ukraine and had recently bought the building, tried to
keep me there. He championed me. He told them they could leave but I
was staying. However, they made his life miserable by vandalizing their
own apartments in order to get me out. He and his wife both told me that
even if the tenants burned the building down they wanted me to stay, but
I did not want him to suffer like this on my behalf. It got to be too much. I
left. That was the beginning of the moves.

The theater didn't have any identity then. Playwrights like Leonard
Melfi, Paul Foster, Sam Shepard, Lanford Wilson, Jean-Claude van Itallie,
were just beginning to write. Michael Locascio wrote our first original
play in 1962. I liked Harold Pinter's play *The Room*, and so we proceeded
to do it. It was 1962. Not knowing anything about the theater, we didn't
know you had to have rights or anything. You find a play, you just do it.
Pinter had not fared well in England. He was not appreciated as a
playwright there, so he had come to America and was in the midst of
getting his first American production. They had just started rehearsals at
the Cherry Lane, I think it was. But our play was ready to open. The night
before it opened this very elegant man, a beautiful man—I can see him
now, you know, he had on a white shirt with broad black stripes in it, and
a beautiful tailored suit—he came into our little basement coffeehouse
with two women. One had on a little white mink shrug, and the other one
had on tweeds and brogan shoes. That one was his wife, a very nice
human being, and the other one was his agent.

I was wiping off our coffee bar that we had made out of old shoeshine
stands and he comes down and says, "I say there. Who is and where is
this Mama woman?" And I said, "Who wants to know?" He says, "I'm
Harold Pinter and I want you to give her a message that if she dares to put
on my play in this little hole tomorrow, that she is no longer going to
exist," or something like that, because he had been told by his friends that
our little theater was illegal and if he reported it, we would be closed

immediately. How dare I put on his play in this little hole! He was Harold Pinter. He raged and raged until finally I said, "Well, Mr. Pinter, I'm the Mama woman. I love your plays and I had planned to do all of them."

He stood there with his mouth open. Then this lady—not the one with the tweeds, she never said a word but the one with the mink shrug—pushed him aside and said, "I am Mr. Pinter's agent. I hereby tell you if you do this piece . . ." And then he tried to interrupt, and she told him to shut up. Then he stepped in front of her and told her, "No one tells me to shut up!" And he said, "Mama woman, you do this play as long as you want to, and until it gets a commercial production, it's your play, from this time on. You do it as much as you want." She screamed at him, "You can't do that!" and he said, "I most certainly can and furthermore I'm going to come to see it. When does it open?"

He didn't come to see it because he got a cable to return to England immediately and he really did leave. It wasn't an excuse or something. Years later, in 1967, when we were playing in England at the West End, we didn't fare so well but we did get a West End production of Paul Foster's *Tom Paine,* and there were interviews and all that. Pinter was at a party where they were talking about these American off-off-Broadway people who had come to London and how we caused quite a stir with our ways. "Well," he says, "that's quite all right. I'm a La Mama playwright also." So he told it, I didn't, and the papers talked about it.

By 1965 I thought that some of our playwrights should be published because they had begun to write new plays which were, in my terms, excellent. I would send the plays to publishers and they would send them back saying they would not read plays that had not been reviewed, and critics rarely came to see our plays.

Now what happened next is such a complex thing to explain. Paul Foster, who had written a play before, wrote a play called *Hurrah for the Bridge.* He had a friend, Edgar Negret, who is a sculptor in Bogotá, Colombia. When Edgar returned home to Colombia in 1964, he took Paul's play with him. Some students there were going to participate in a theater festival. They liked Paul's play. The play was translated into Spanish. Their student production won the prize. The prize was an invitation to participate in a theater festival in Erlangen, Germany. Then at the Erlangen festival, a theater group from Arhus, Denmark, directed by Jens Okking, saw Paul's play, contacted me, and asked if we had any others. I said yes, if they could get us some reviews. They said they could.

In the meantime, in 1964, Tom Eyen wrote a play, a little curtain raiser which was all of ten or fifteen minutes long, called *The White Whore and the Bit Player.* It was written for Marie-Claire Charba and Jacqueline Colton, and it was based on Marilyn Monroe. The play since has become a classic. This play was shown with Tom's main play, *My Next Husband Will be a Beauty,* which was about forty-five minutes long. You see, there was an unwritten law that whatever went on the stage had to be at least an hour long. These playwrights were just beginning and it was difficult for them in those days to write beyond, or even as much as, an hour. Lanford Wilson wrote our first full-length play in 1965 or 1966. It was called *No Bomb in Gilead.*

At around Christmastime, the two girls in *The White Whore* got the opportunity through their parents to go to Paris. They performed the play there in the English bookstore. There was an electrical strike, the critics came through the streets with candles, and they saw the play.

So I thought, if I can get reviewed in Paris and if I can get reviewed in Denmark, then maybe I ought to take as many plays as I could to Europe, which is exactly what I did. I went to Europe first to search out everything and then I took twenty-two plays over there in September 1965. In Paris, David Davis allowed us to convert a large ballroom in the Centre Américaine for students and artists on Boulevard Raspail into a theater which, by the way, it still is today. And we rented a little theater in Copenhagen called the Comedie-Heuset. On the one hand, I was given twenty-four hours to get out of Paris because I put on Jean-Claude van Itallie's *America Hurrah* in the Centre Américaine, and in Copenhagen, the Danes welcomed us with open arms, and through our productions there we met Elsa Gress-Wright, a critic and writer, who gave us great assistance in those early years.

In Paris we got terrible critiques. They didn't like what we were doing at all. In Denmark, the critics called us lovable little puppies. They said we didn't know how to act, they certainly didn't understand our plays, but they liked us and we were invited to come back the following year. Also some Yugoslavians who saw us invited us to come there, and several theater groups in Sweden, in Malmö and Stockholm, invited us to come there, and we were also invited to come to Nottingham, England.

We would have gone to Timbuktu, anywhere to get critiques so that the plays could be published. Then from our going there, theater troupes from these countries came here and performed their plays at La Mama, and we became an international theater. Even in the early 1960s, Koreans, East Indians, Israelis, Latin Americans, the French, British and many others were participating in our productions.

I don't know what would have happened if I had been allowed to stay in that basement which was about half the size of my living room, but I wasn't, or if the critics had come to see the plays, but the circumstances literally made me decide I had to find a way to do what I like doing. I don't call it helping people, it's not helping people, it's helping myself because it gives me a way of life too, you see. I don't have anything to eat either if there's nothing on the table. This way we all sit down and whatever it is, that's what we have. It's a making together. I never expected to be doing all the things that we did. The objective was never that but to do everything we could possibly do and do it as well as we could.

We got away from the lovable little puppy stage because a dear friend of mine, Brice Howard, who was then the executive director of National Education Television, NET, was going to put on three plays from La Mama. In 1966 he put on *Fourteen Hundred Thousand* by Sam Shepard, *The Recluse* by Paul Foster, and *Pavane,* which later was to be called *Interview* by Jean-Claude van Itallie. He said he couldn't use many of the La Mama actors because they were terrible, they couldn't act, and I'd have to understand that. The one concession that he made, he would let Tom O'Horgan direct or try to direct one piece, to start. If it looked like he could do it, he would let him be the artistic director, which worked out. It was called "Three Plays from La Mama," I think, and it is now considered one of Channel 13's prized accomplishments. However, they fired Brice Howard at the time for doing that program.

What came from that—I decided I should try to do something to make our actors better. It was standing in the way. So I went to the Actors Studio and I went up that little stoop that you go up. They have a large reception room. There's a desk, somebody was sitting at the desk, and there's couches and there are actors lounging around on the couches. I went up to the desk and said I was Ellen Stewart and I came from Café La Mama and I had come there to get somebody to teach us how to act. I said it like that. I didn't even know this was Lee Strasberg's studio. And the actors and the people sitting around made fun of me and I went out crying.

But I said, Okay, then I have to make up my own way, so I told Tom O'Horgan, "We've got to make our actors." And that's what helped. So Tom started our very first workshop. This began the first troupe of La Mama and he began to evolve methods to teach our actors which were exemplified in his staging of the Broadway production of *Hair,* which was La Mama's all-time success. That pot has been seasoned by many other directors such as Joe Zwick, Andrei Serban, Wilford Leach, John Braswell, Julie Bovasso and John Vaccaro. We have this huge pot now and we have wonderful actors. We did and we have had and we do have a group that would be a repertory company if I could sustain them here but it's impossible. That's the Great Jones Repertory Company.

La Mama stayed a coffeehouse until we moved into the present building in 1969. The playwrights wanted space to play. They didn't want all those tables and chairs. (We had the tables and chairs, we bought them, but I never used them.) Each time I got kicked out of one place, the next place I found by accident happened to be larger, so the playing area got larger and so they had to write larger plays. That was the growth that gave rise to our epic dramas. It's only in much more recent years, I'd say since about 1972 until now, that we really have begun to be noticed here.

Things have changed now in the playwriting genre. I tell you truthfully, I haven't found many playwrights today who particularly interest me. And I'll tell you why. I've always been interested primarily in people, a kind of oneness with people—communication. Going to Europe and being in Europe every year since 1965, I began to realize that we could best establish the oneness with people that I am so intensely interested in by being able to communicate through our theater. If a play is entirely dependent on one's comprehension of the language that's being spoken, it is impossible to communicate its intent to persons not familiar with the language. And so there is an immediate barrier to oneness. This doesn't mean that a text isn't valid, but it does mean that I feel that a text should show itself as well as speak itself. As Wilford Leach says, "Playwrighting for me is playmaking."

So I have tried to encourage artists working in the theater to find ways to express a literal text through visuals—music, dance and video. Most playwrights don't want music to be a part of their show because they feel music might take away from what they have to say. Whereas I feel that music can say it for you and you don't necessarily need the text at some points. Music or dance can certainly communicate beyond words.

What amazes me is that playwrights in particular don't seem to be able to perceive what is the great genius of Shakespeare. His great strength to me is so apparent because although his text is so abundant, it's so visual, and that is why from 1600 until now he can be loved and appreciated all over the world. It would seem to me that any playwright would perceive this for himself and try to apply Shakespeare's techniques to his own work. Peter Brook's *Midsummer Night's Dream* shows you that; Serban's *As You Like It,* which we're doing in Germany, does too. Not one word of the text was cut. Germans came over to see it and they want it there in the Stuttgart Festival because they feel that everybody can appreciate Shakespeare the way we do it, even though we're speaking the text in English. We also produced a Korean *Hamlet* that many people felt was the best *Hamlet* that they had ever seen in their lives. The whole text was spoken in Korean. But the way it was done, so exquisitely, the visuals and things, the audience was sitting hanging on every word in Korean.

Since I clearly don't have financial remuneration for what I do, the only satisfaction that I have is liking what I'm doing and so I do what I like. People whose names are synonymous with La Mama, so to speak, are working in the genre that I've tried to explain. There are few playwrights today who are willing to work like that.

I'm now in serious financial trouble. The National Endowment for the Arts which has supported us consistently over the years says two things: One, that there are now hundreds of theaters all over America like La Mama, that La Mama is no longer as relevant or as needed as it used to be because all these theaters are doing exactly the same work as we are— which, of course, is not true. I personally do not think there is any theater in the U.S. that is doing the work that we are doing and have been doing for the past nineteen years. The National Endowment says that they don't have much money and we can't get what we used to get because the monies have to be disseminated to all these hundreds of theaters.

And part two, they say they are not trying to censor La Mama. It is simply that they are not interested in what La Mama does. The panel funds theaters that do productions they are interested in, and these productions reflect Americana for Americans. Many of my productions will not be Americana for Americans. We have been international since we began in 1961 and we shall remain so.

But the National Endowment says that if an American taxpayer buys a ticket to see a foreign performance then that foreign performance is using American taxpayers' dollars. And I said, "Well, does this mean that the National Endowment is dictating what the American audience should spend their money for?" No, they say, they're not dictating but if the foreign performance isn't here, then the American audience cannot spend their money for it, and if they want to see theater, they will see Americana. So they cut over half of our operating budget. We used to get $150,000 from the National Endowment. We have been cut to $70,000.

The exception to this arrangement is monies given to us specifically for foreign performances by the Rockefeller Foundation and the monies that we have always been allowed to apply to our productions by the New York State Arts Council. I want to say that the New York State Arts Council has always helped me in whatever I want to do. These monies cover about one quarter of the necessary expenditures. The rest of the monies have been raised by the participating theater companies from their governments, sponsors and other sources.

When Peter Brook's Center for International Theater Research came to La Mama this year (and many other foreign troupes have come and played upon our stage) the only funds that we were able to offer them were box-office receipts. When you think of twenty-five or fifty persons from another country and all I can do is offer our stage, the facilities and the box office, everything else, hotel rooms, per diems, salaries, travel, production monies must somehow be taken care of—what they receive from La Mama is almost nothing. Peter Brook could have played on Broadway, anywhere in New York, but he elected to play at La Mama. I didn't have a quarter but he said, don't worry about it. He was going to play here with me and he was going to get the money. I thought, Oh, Con Ed, don't embarrass me when Peter Brook comes and turn the lights off.

We have four theaters. We will probably go bankrupt in this situation. If I was in my right mind, I'd go down and close the doors right now, tell everybody to go home and just pray that the marshals don't come in, but I'm not going to do that. I think I'll just let them come and carry me out, that's all. It's nip and tuck every day.

The Ford Foundation used to help us a great deal, but since their arts program has been severely cut they can no longer do this. But from time to time we do receive small amounts of monies from them. Foundations, as it appears, are turning more and more to ethnic situations, to minority things. I'm a black woman but I'm not considered a black woman since La Mama is not a "black" theater. So we are not considered a minority situation, not by any means, so there you are.

I have not had to struggle because I was black or because I was a woman. Rather it is because I have always wanted to do what I believed in and what I believed in isn't necessarily what one is supposed to do. I could perhaps do a switch now and do plays and philosophies that bore me and maybe I would get money to do that, and maybe I might be of some service to the persons involved in these plays, and I would have a better life and there wouldn't be two people here trying to run four theaters. Neither one of us has been paid since January. Or I could become a black theater and maybe that would make my road a little easier. Maybe. I guess I have many alternatives, none of which appeals to me. I have great faith that as long as I believe in what I am doing, I can do what I want to do and if it doesn't work, I accept that. I certainly think that our presentation of foreign troupes has contributed to the growth of theater in America as it exists today.

Joseph Papp, the director of the Public Theater in New York, has always been a radical, he's always been political, and he's very much a person whose whole identity is America first. What he does is largely Americana, with the exception of Shakespeare, for which he gets enormous funding and support because he's doing exactly what the American taxpayer, I guess, and the NEA and other foundations want, and he has an enormous patronage. Now he's worked very hard for all that he receives. His success just didn't roll into his life, and he deserves all that he has. He just happens to fit into the right thing to do.

I don't fit. I have never fit. Because in the beginning, with the playwrights, I couldn't get a critic to come to see them, I couldn't get them published. There was no recognition. But Lanford Wilson and Sam Shepard are now Pulitzer Prize winners. I was outside in the beginning and I'm still outside. No matter what, I'm still outside.

I have no pension. I have no savings. I have nothing but my Social Security. That's what I'll have when this thing is over, but this is also my life, I love what I'm doing and I'm certainly not going to quit.

When I began I didn't know anything about theater. I was only interested in some people that I came to know, and it just so happened that the people I was interested in happened to be some of the ones that the world is interested in today. I never read their plays. I don't know how to read a play, really, to tell the truth. I don't know because I don't have an academic education in theater. But I do know a little bit how to read a person. My mind tells me this person *must*. The "must" of this person is a valuable contribution that I feel somehow must be gotten, and make it possible for others to benefit from that contribution. This is my pushcart.

# Rosalyn Yalow

*Rosalyn Yalow (born 1921, New York City) is a nuclear physicist who, with her colleague Solomon A. Berson, developed a sensitive biological analytic technique called radioimmunoassay, considered to be one of the most important advances in basic research directly applicable to clinical medicine of the last twenty years. The test, now used in labs around the world, detects quantities of biological substances so infinitesimal they had previously eluded measurement. The Nobel Committee made an exception to its rule and in spite of the fact that her collaborator was deceased, awarded her the Nobel Prize for Medicine in 1977.*

IF YOU EVER HAVE a new idea, and it's really new, you have to expect that it won't be widely accepted immediately. It is a long hard process. Till my dying day I will remember Greer Garson and Walter Pidgeon, in the film *Marie Curie*, coming back to the laboratory at night and seeing the glowing that meant they had discovered radioactivity. That was exciting! They knew they had it, but it was the culmination of a long process of blood, sweat and tears. It was followed by a good deal more blood, sweat and tears. You don't suddenly come out of your bath and say "Eureka!" Science is only in part like that.

I'm a morning person. When I'm stewing about something I'm working on in the laboratory, I'll wake up at two or three in the morning and by daybreak everything will fall into place and I know the experiment that has to be done the next day. Usually there are a lot of experiments that have to be done. You try the critical experiment the next day, and somebody drops the tube or it's broken in the centrifuge or the refrigerators stop working. You know you have a great idea but until you've built in the many controls or verified and reverified the results, you're not completely certain. Perhaps theoretical physicists say "Eureka!" but we experimental physicists need a lot of hard work and luck. It isn't blind luck. Part of it is being in the right place at the right time, but recognition is important.

For instance, somebody made the same observation as we did at the time . . . that labeled insulin disappeared more slowly from diabetics than nondiabetics. They made the same observation but we discovered radioimmunoassay. Now would you call it luck that we made the discovery? If so, they had the same luck, but we knew what to do with it. We thought the slower disappearance of the insulin was due to antibodies. They thought it was due to something wrong with diabetics. They simply made the wrong interpretation.

Once we demonstrated that the slow disappearance was due to

**43**

antibodies, we had to quantitate the concentration of the antibodies. Once we'd quantitated the concentration of antibodies, we appreciated that we could quantify the antigen. Now it was luck for both sets of investigators to discover that insulin disappears more slowly from one group of patients than from another. The rest was science. That's what you mean by discovering something by accident. You make an observation. But it isn't by accident that you interpret the observation correctly. That's creativity. Thirty-three years later, I still think discovery is the most exciting thing in the world.

Radioimmunoassay was a very important discovery. If one considers that for many years half the papers from the Endocrine Society and many from other medical society meetings were dependent on radioimmunoassay, it is evident that the Nobel Prize in 1977 was appropriate. What delayed our getting the Nobel for so long was the fact that it took a while to catch on that this was a very basic tool for investigation in many areas of medicine.

It was in fact three years from the time my colleague Sol Berson and I had the idea until we made it practical. The possibility for radioimmunoassay was in our 1956 paper. It was 1959 before we applied it to the measurement of plasma insulin in man, and it was another five or six years before it caught on in the scientific community, because in the scientific community, like any community, there's dogma. Dogma means it is known, it is believed, it is right! Scientific discovery changes dogma and people are resistant to accepting highly original ideas that bring about change. However, all good highly original scientific ideas eventually catch on. The progress of science is not held back forever because of dogma. During those years Sol Berson and I gave courses to train people in radioimmunoassay. We were our own public relations people. Within five years it took off exponentially. Radioimmunoassay is now dogma. This is really how progress in science is made.

Two things contributed importantly to my success. I have long felt that the trouble with discrimination is not discrimination per se but rather that the people who are discriminated against think of themselves as second-class. They believe the propaganda and this in a sense keeps them from succeeding. Even in the periods when I felt discrimination, and that was a long time ago, I never felt second-class. There was something wrong with the discriminators, not something wrong with me. I think this kind of belief keeps people going when they're having a hard time of it.

Secondly, I accept the fact that there has been discrimination against women. I appreciate it, but the way to upward mobility is not by playing games with a dictionary. I have never been a "chairperson" if I can avoid it. As long as I'm a member of the human race, not the "huperson" race, and as long as I'm a woman and not a "woperson," I'm perfectly prepared to be a "chairman." We can stop playing these games. I think it's important to spend time not with words but with real issues.

More particularly, the concerns I have are as to whether or not the current activist movement for women's rights is related not so much to women's rights as it is to women's need to work. It is very evident now when more than half of women with children under six are working, that they work because they have to and that the money they make is very important. Even now, at every level of education, women are earning about two-thirds of what men are earning. This is in part due to the fact that they have chosen or have been forced into jobs that are considered women's work. Since the jobs are considered women's work, then the salaries for the jobs are correspondingly lower.

Another factor that has been important to my success relates to the kind of commitment I've made. If for one reason or another—particularly because they are mothers and have had the responsibility for child care—women drop out for too many years, then one should compare their salaries to their input. They should not be compared to people their age but to people with the same number of years of career work behind them.

Women's admission rates to medical school are now about 25 percent, a rate quite comparable to their ratio in applications. However, women must accept that if they ask for part-time residencies instead of full-time residencies, then they will continue to be looked upon as second-class citizens. If the community is going to invest in a professional person's career—and all of us who go to school are supported by the community—the community has a right to expect first-class work, because it costs as much to send a woman through medical school as a man. The community has every right to expect the woman to put in full-time effort, equal to that of the man.

What are we going to do with the children? I believe it would be a great loss to the community as well as to women if talented women did not have children. They should have at least as many, if not more, children than less talented women. And therefore, dating back almost twenty years, since the time I got the Federal Woman's Award, I was much more concerned not with women's supergrade positions in government, since this is relatively unimportant for most, but with the need for universities, industry and particularly government to take the initiative in providing for expert high-quality day-care for children.

It is time we rejected the notion that those who can't do anything else should take care of children. This is a serious mistake. It will hurt the children and it will hurt the community. It is important for the community, in one of its various guises, to provide absolutely first-class care for children, starting, when necessary, at a very young age. It is not necessary to wait until children are two or three; it's possible to provide excellent care even for infants. Even in the nursery of a hospital one nurse can do a good job of taking care of six or seven infants. There are people who are expert in child care, even as there are people who are expert in physics or science or politics or anything else. The work is just as important and should be just as well paid.

If we did this, we'd be far better off in the quality of child life. We would probably not see the decline in reading scores and other intellectual scores that we're now finding, and we'd all be better off.

I did have sleep-in help when the children were small but my mother came over every day to make sure they were read to, that they had the proper cultural exposure. My mother had never gone to high school but she appreciated the kinds of things that bright children should know and did, in fact, help to expose my children to them. I think that if the schools are having trouble, it's not that the kids are stupid but that they haven't learned early in life that the way up is through reading and writing and living in an intellectual atmosphere. By the time they come to formalized school learning, they are psychologically unprepared for a very strong learning experience.

I grew up in a community in which most of the parents were not educated beyond sixth grade. Some finished eighth grade, a few even high school. In my immediate community we did not have many parents who were professionals. Perhaps there was an occasional schoolteacher, but there were no scientists, doctors or other professionals. We didn't have books in my house, but there was never a week that went by from the time I was four or five years old that I wasn't going to the library to pick up books. I remember the rules for being able to join the library. You had to be able to read a statement and sign your name. Every one of my friends aspired to do this as early as possible. By the time we were five or six, most of us joined the library.

When I was in college it was abundantly clear that women weren't getting fellowships to go to medical school, so I could not afford to have gone to medical school. I chose physics. Physics was very exciting, and I had the good fortune to have had teaching assistantships all the way through graduate school.

When I went into nuclear physics, in the middle forties, it was a "mom and pop" operation. Read the biographies of the physicists of the thirties and forties and you see that nuclear physics was mostly small science. A few people would sit around and talk to each other. One of them would have a great idea, go to the laboratory and work for days or weeks and make the discovery worthy of a Nobel Prize. It was absolutely a fantastic time. At the end of World War II, largely because of the atom bomb and the fact that the field underwent a transition to high-energy physics which requires bigger and bigger machines, it became big science. Now scientific papers in this field can have twenty-seven authors! It was time for me to get out of that field.

It was accidental that, at the same time nuclear physics was going in a way in which I would not have felt comfortable, the use of radioisotopes in medicine began to increase, which permitted my involvement in a small scientific field which I was really to enjoy.

In 1947 I was teaching at Hunter College in the Bronx. It is now

Lehman College. My husband, who is a physics professor, doesn't like to hear me say it, but teaching fifteen hours a week seemed to me to be only a halftime job, therefore I was looking for some research to do on the side. I heard through my husband about the application of radioisotopes in medicine and I went to see Dr. Edith Quimby, who was the leading woman in the field in the country. She took me to see Dr. G. Failla, who was the major medical physicist in the country and senior consultant at the Bronx Veterans Administration hospital. After talking to me for a little while, fifteen or twenty minutes, he called the hospital and told them, "If you want to get involved with radioisotopes, you have to hire her." And that's how I began. For two years, while setting up the laboratory at the VA, I continued teaching at Hunter. Two and a half years later, when the laboratory was beginning to flourish, I had the good fortune to be joined by Sol Berson, after he completed his residency at our hospital. This laboratory soon became a research center for the Veterans Administration.

Radioimmunoassay is big business now. We don't have a patent on it. Perhaps it could have been patented. What would we have done with the money, except pour it into research? I'm not sure that any individual should have too much money for research. If I had five million dollars a year for research it would be necessary for me to supervise a hundred scientists. It would be impossible for me to talk to each of them every day. I chose not to be an administrator but a scientist. If I'm to remain a scientist, I must exchange ideas, not paperwork, with people. A minimum amount of money is necessary: you have to have equipment; you have to have some supplies and people. However, I'm not certain that too much isn't worse than too little. I'm psychologically adjusted to "mom and pop" science. I like to have the one-on-one interaction that I have in this laboratory with the younger people, and I don't like to have a big empire.

Over the last three years, I haven't done as much routine laboratory work as I did before. I have been involved in a lot of public relations, talking about science, writing review articles. I'm involved in science policy, so I no longer do the pipetting I once did. I start my writing at about six in the morning. Once my research fellows are in, I try to get around to everyone every day. I share my laboratory now with Dr. Eugene Straus, who has been with me for eight years and whom I consider to be a partner in the same sense that Sol Berson and I were partners.

This laboratory is as productive as it ever was. I doubt if our work will again be worthy of a Nobel Prize, for such a discovery is an occasional accident. However, our laboratory has a continuing record of being in the forefront of science. Our experiments still employ the original tools, either radioimmunoassay per se or receptor assays which are based on it. The versatility of this tool permits us to apply it to many different areas and these applications are important in medicine. We are now setting up a second laboratory at Montefiore Hospital. One of the reasons for doing it is because they have a very bright house staff. I don't want to train a thousand people; I want to find one or two or three young physicians each year and teach them the joys of investigation. I'm hoping that this new laboratory will give me an opportunity to do that.

I'm one of fifteen scientists who have been asked to write a chapter for a book in honor of Claude Bernard, who was a great nineteenth-century French physiologist. In the chapter I quote Bernard who wrote, "The fundamental problem of critical importance is how to identify the few who make the breakthroughs which permit their horizons to open, from the many who attempt to build on these breakthroughs, often without imagination." Claude Bernard dealt realistically with that problem by stating, "There are indeed two sides to science and evolution. On the one hand, what is acquired already, on the other hand, what remains to be acquired. In the already acquired, all men are more or less equal, and the great cannot be distinguished from the rest. Mediocre men often have the most acquired knowledge. It's in the darker regions of science that great men are recognized. They are marked by ideas which light up phenomena hitherto obscure, and carry science forward."

He essentially makes the very important point that one can be very bright and know everything but this isn't the same as having scientific imagination. People can look at the same data and some people simply describe the data, but others see beyond the data itself. I do not know how to train people to be perceptive. I think all you can do is find and identify those who have the potential to light up the darker regions of science. I've trained a goodly number of people in my laboratory. Some of the brightest and most skilled have been encouraged to return to clinical medicine because being the brightest and most skilled isn't enough. It's necessary to be imaginative. The talent of a research director is to find and encourage those with a potential for creativity.

This is true in other fields. There are people who write music but there are few Mozarts. It is possible for one to be a genius in a particular field and still not succeed. There may be personality problems; one can find himself in the wrong atmosphere or be turned aside for one reason or another. But you can't make a creative scientist from one without innate talent and perception.

One starts with young people who are obviously bright and knowledgeable and talented. They are usually scared about their abilities as investigators. If, after a nurturing period, they start to see things that nobody else saw before, then I know I have found someone with talent and I nurture it. It've very exciting.

I have a commitment to developing a cadre of young medical investigators in a laboratory, which I still find exciting. That's why I come to work at six o'clock every morning. People come to see me and they say, "Don't you have any hobbies?" I say, "What hobbies?" What am I going to do? Ride a horse? Play tennis? This is where the excitement is.

Everyday you hope there's something new. This is it! We may never again discover radioimmunoassay but there are enough new things going on in this laboratory all the time to excite me. After x years of playing tennis, do you really feel the next day there will be a dramatic change and you will revolutionize tennis? If there is no excitement it isn't a hobby, it's drudgery.

# Helen B. Taussig

*Helen B. Taussig (born 1898, Cambridge, Massachusetts) is a pediatric cardiologist whose pioneer work on the heart provided a significant impetus to open-heart surgery. In the early 1940s she conceived an operation, developed with surgeon Dr. Alfred Blalock, at Johns Hopkins hospital that alleviated an often fatal condition in children, commonly known as blue-baby syndrome, caused by a malformation of the heart. This procedure saved the lives of thousands of children.*

I STARTED MEDICAL SCHOOL in a casual way. I had transferred from Radcliffe College to the University of California where I received my B.A. degree. I came back to Cambridge and I considered studying medicine. The Harvard Medical School did not accept women. My father was a distinguished economist and a liberal man; he thought that public health was a woman's field and surely the Harvard School of Public Health, opening that fall (1922), would admit women. My father urged me to consider public health. I went up to see the dean and asked him, "What are you doing for women?" He said, "Oh, we thought about it and we decided that all students must have two years of medicine. Women will be permitted to study public health but not admitted as candidates for degrees." I said, "Who'd be such a fool as to spend two years studying medicine and two more years studying public health and not get a degree?" He answered, "No one, I hope." I replied, "I will not be the first one to disappoint you. Good afternoon."

So I decided on medicine. Women were permitted to take some courses at Harvard, but it depended entirely on whether or not the professor wanted to have women in his class. It seems absurd now, but the only two courses in the Harvard Medical School from the mid-1920s until 1945 that did not admit women were obstetrics and gynecology! Those were subjects that women should know nothing about! I took bacteriology and then histology. I had to sit up in the far corner of the lecture room by myself, and when I studied the slides I had to do it in a separate room and I wasn't allowed to speak to any of the men, but the professor was very kind and helpful.

When I finished the course in histology, my professor said, "It's foolish for you to be taking these courses here and not getting any credit for them. You should go over to Boston University and get a year of credit." So I went.

At B.U. I took gross anatomy. The professor gave me an ox heart in order to study the muscle bundles. It was difficult, so I decided to approach the problem through physiology. I isolated strips of heart

51

muscle and set them up in Ringer's solution, as had others who had tested skeletal muscles. I ran oxygen through the solution and the muscle started to contract rhythmically, to beat. I didn't know it but others had tried similar experiments with heart muscle and failed. Having no idea it couldn't be done, I just tried and it worked. I was not hampered by being told it was impossible.

My professor was very impressed. He suggested I ought to go to Johns Hopkins Medical School. He said he understood one good letter would get a student in, and he asked me, "Who do you know at Harvard who would recommend you?" He was very generous and anxious to get me accepted at Hopkins even though he was dean of Boston University. I asked the professor of physiology at Harvard to recommend me. I think he knew better than I the value of my work at Boston University. That was what gave me my start in my work on the heart, which I continued in medical school and, indeed, throughout my life.

Johns Hopkins had admitted women to their medical school from the word go, thanks to Mary Elizabeth Garrett. She was a wealthy woman interested in women's education. Johns Hopkins had left his money for a university and a medical school. The university was established first, but with the depression of the 1880s, there was not enough money to complete the medical school. There are several versions of the story about Miss Garrett's generous contribution to the medical school. The following tale was told to me by Dr. William Sidney Thayer, who sat as a junior member of a committee to draw up plans for a medical school.

The university approached Miss Garrett, asking her for help in raising the funds necessary to open the medical school. She replied, "Draw up your plans for an ideal medical school and I'll consider it." The committee decided that, among other things, everyone admitted to the school should have a college degree and a reading knowledge of French and German, and then to please Miss Garrett, they added, "women should be admitted on the same terms as men." Miss Garrett studied the requirements. She liked them. She immediately gave a generous amount and offered to help raise the rest. When they failed to raise the $500,000, she put in the balance. In all, she offered and gave over $300,000 of the $500,000 needed for the medical school to open, *provided* they would have their ideal medical school.

Then the medical school said, "That which is ideal and that which is practical are two different things. No students would come if we required a college degree, and what would we do with the women?" She replied, "If you want an ideal medical school, you'll have my money, and if not, I'll put my money elsewhere." So the doctors decided to accept the agreement, thinking that if no medical students applied, Miss Garrett would see the futility of it and the medical school would have its pie and be able to eat it too.

Lo and behold, in their first class, 1883–84, they got their full quota of medical students, all with college degrees, some of the brightest in the country, and they got four women. They didn't take as many women as men; usually they took about 10 percent. When they had very good applications from women, they took more women. After graduation, women couldn't get hospital appointments as easily as the men, but at least they got a good medical education.

Upon graduation from medical school, almost all students applied for internships. There's no question that a good internship gives you a good start in medicine. Surgery very seldom took women. Obstetrics occasionally took a woman; medicine only took one each year.

When we were waiting to hear about our internships, I was taking an elective in pediatric cardiology. While I was working in the pediatrics dispensary one day, the instructor called us in to look at a baby with chicken pox. It was a black baby. He said, "Take a good look at that lesion and you'll know that lesion when you see it next." I took a good look and wondered what it would look like on a white person.

The day before Christmas vacation, the internships were announced. I wanted a medical internship but was refused because another woman stood two tenths of a point ahead of me. I felt awful that evening, and I was surprised that I was so wrought up about not getting my internship. I felt just plain miserable. When I undressed that night I looked at my abdomen and the words flashed back to me, "You'll know that lesion when you see it next." I spent my entire Christmas vacation as a patient on the ward with chicken pox.

I had worked in the adult heart station during my medical school years. When I was refused my internship, I was offered a fellowship in cardiology. Years later, when introducing me at a lecture, my host said, "She was so brilliant she was given a fellowship and not an internship." I replied, "That's a lovely interpretation, but I was given my fellowship because I wasn't worth an internship." My professor of pediatrics said, "That which is a disappointment in time may prove to be one's good fortune." My first good fortune was that I couldn't get into the School of Public Health. The second was that the Harvard Medical School did not admit women and I went over to Boston University and got involved in studying the heart, and the third was that I was denied a medical internship and got a fellowship in cardiology.

That year, 1927, Dr. Edwards A. Park came to Johns Hopkins Hospital as chief of pediatrics. He immediately started four special clinics. One was the cardiac clinic. Before starting that clinic, he sought the advice of Dr. Carter, under whom I had the fellowship. Dr. Carter arranged for one of his senior fellows to run the pediatric clinic one morning a week, and I tagged along.

The next year I interned in pediatrics, and the following year Dr. Park put me in charge of the cardiac clinic. My friends said, "Why go into such a narrow field as pediatric cardiology?" To me it was a golden opportunity to combine my two great interests, pediatrics and cardiology. Often success is a matter of luck, being in the right place at the right time to take advantage of what comes along. Therefore I say: Don't neglect a good opportunity in a stimulating environment.

A scientific discovery comes to people in many different ways. Somebody asked me once about what I had discovered: Did I dream it? I said, "No, it was a gradual process." When Dr. Park obtained a fluoroscope for the pediatric department, he told me that I would learn congenital malformations of the heart. The idea did not appeal to me. But many blue babies were referred to me because nothing could be done for them. No treatment was known.

A blue baby is a baby who has an abnormally blue tinge to the skin. This color is called cyanosis. It is visible when the blood is not fully oxygenated. The less oxygen in the blood, the bluer the baby is. In the case of most blue babies, the cyanosis is due to the failure of an adequate amount of blood to pass through the lungs where it can pick up oxygen.

As a result of carefully examining blue babies during their lives and studying their hearts after they died, I realized that many blue babies died from a lack of oxygen because the structure of the heart was defective in such a way that very little blood could reach the lungs. I devised an operation which bypassed the obstruction in the heart, allowing more blood to reach the lungs, thereby giving the baby an adequate amount of oxygen and a normal pink color.

Therefore when the surgeon Dr. Robert Gross, working at Children's Medical Center in Boston, showed that it was possible to tie off a vessel (*ductus ateriosus*) which allowed too much blood to reach the lungs, I immediately thought it must be possible for a surgeon to "build" a vessel to increase the circulation to the lungs. I went to Boston to see Dr. Gross and asked if he could build such a vessel. He said yes, he had built many, but he was not in the least interested in my idea when I said it would help a cyanotic child. I think the reason he was not interested in the idea was because he was in the full flush of success. It was a very remarkable thing he had done and everybody was congratulating him, so why try to do the reverse?

In 1940, Dr. Alfred Blalock came to join the staff at Johns Hopkins Hospital. I knew that he was a thoracic surgeon and I knew he had operated to close the ductus as Dr. Gross had done. Blalock was anxious to do something better. So I said to him, at the end of his first operation in Baltimore in which he performed Dr. Gross's operation, "I stand in awe and admiration of your surgical skill, but the truly great day will come when you will build a ductus for a child dying from lack of blood reaching the lungs and not when you tie off a ductus for a child who has a little too much blood going to the lungs." I think that when I said it had to be something greater than what Dr. Gross had done, it appealed to Dr. Blalock. Surgeons are great rivals. They all want to do something the other fellow hasn't done.

**54**

Dr. Blalock went to work in the laboratory and quietly tried, first to create the condition, to make a malformed heart in a dog, then to build the ductus. You can't do that overnight. For two years he worked; he worked on about two hundred dogs, perfecting the operation. If I was convinced the operation would help, at the end of those two years he was convinced he knew how to do it. So we started.

The first child we operated on was a little bit of a baby, fourteen months old, and she weighed less than ten pounds. She'd been living in an oxygen tent for three months. Dr. Blalock felt very strongly that this type of very sick child was the right one for a new operation. The family and doctors were keen to have something done. The child couldn't live without an operation.

The vessel was very small and Dr. Blalock thought he felt blood going to the lungs, but he didn't get a sufficiently good flow to feel that blood was going *through* the lungs. That disappointed Dr. Blalock. The baby lived to go home for Christmas. She lived six months more and then they tried a second operation and she died. Many people think our first operation was a failure and I don't. It wasn't a failure. The baby lived and was improved by the operation. You can't take a tube the size of a matchstick and put the two ends together and hope it will stay open indefinitely. If you take a vessel the size of a finger and do it, you've got a considerably better chance of success.

The second child was an eleven-year-old child and she couldn't walk across the room without stopping for breath and squatting down. She frequently lost consciousness. Her family was desperate for the operation. At the operation, Dr. Blalock found a large vessel and things went well. She was better after the operation but it wasn't a dramatic improvement. We did not appreciate how much she'd improved until three weeks later when she walked quietly down the length of the hall to meet her father.

The third child was a six-year-old boy who was miserably unhappy and who could no longer walk. At the end of the operation when Dr. Blalock first released the clamps, the child had a tremendous hemorrhage. I had been told that some day I was going to have to go down and talk to the parents. I thought this was it. But Dr. Blalock quickly controlled the hemorrhage, replaced the clamps and sewed up the bleeding point. He gave the child plasma to compensate for the loss of blood. When he again released the clamps he said he felt a lovely thrill—blood going through the lungs, and almost simultaneously the anesthesiologist said, "He's a lovely color now." I walked to the head of the table and the child had bright pink cheeks and cherry-red lips! I had suggested we might see a change in color but I never expected to see anything as dramatic as that.

Indeed, the fact that anyone who saw a blue baby before and immediately after operation could see the color change to pink was what made the operation appeal to the public. As soon as the success of the blue-baby operation reached the press, hordes of little children were referred to me. If a community raised money to send a blue child to Baltimore and he returned bright and happy and with normal pink cheeks and was able to run and play, that seemed wonderful.

A skillful surgeon is essential for a successful operation. Fortunately I had one. As all blue babies could not be helped by the operation, it was my responsibility to select the patients who could be helped and take the most incapacitated children first. I was responsible for their care after surgery.

Dr. Blalock and his associates did more than a thousand operations during the first six years and I saw more than three thousand children in my clinic during those years. We had a slew of work to be done and patients to be cared for. We had opened up treatment for the entire field of malformation of the heart and we learned fast. The Children's Bureau and the National Institutes of Health each gave me four fellowships to train doctors in the diagnosis and care of children with cardiac malformations. I usually had four American and four foreign doctors training with me each year.

Over the years I've gotten recognition for what I did, but I didn't at the time. It hurt for a while. It hurt when Dr. Blalock was elected to the National Academy of Arts and Sciences and I didn't even get promoted from an assistant to associate professor. Subsequently, I have been elected to the National Academy of Arts and Sciences. I didn't get my professorship until 1959. Dr. Park always said, "It's not your rank, it's work you do that counts," and he was right. A distinguished microbiologist is reputed to have said, "Thank heaven we voted her a full professorship before we knew Harvard was giving her an honorary degree." Both came the same year, but I was still an associate professor when I received my degree from Harvard.

Surgeons seldom do the blue-baby operation today. They do open-heart surgery and use a pump and an oxygenator so that they can open the heart and correct the malformation. Our operation was outside the heart. It was only palliative. Nevertheless, it gave a tremendous spurt to heart surgery. When surgeons realized that you could operate on a deeply cyanotic child, they felt they could operate on almost anyone.

Pediatrics is a natural field for women because they have more understanding of the mother's problem. They don't ask the impossible, whereas many male pediatricians think the woman has nothing to do but take care of a child all day.

I have long thought one can do anything but not everything. Raising a family is probably a great experience. I never married or had children of my own but I've had other experiences and other satisfactions that other women haven't had. If a woman marries and wants a career, she must have an understanding husband. I doubt that she could do it without that and without help at home. I couldn't have done what I did, even without children, without help at home. I had a remarkable black woman who was my housekeeper and we became devoted friends. She took care of me; she kept the house beautifully; she planned the meals and ordered the food; she cooked and served the dinner. I could work all day and get home just in time to change for dinner and be hostess at a party that night.

Basically I am a scientist. A good research doctor has curiosity, persistence and a willingness to work hard. There is nothing leisurely in that occupation. You take a problem and mull it over until you see what can and needs to be done first and do that. Usually that opens up the next obvious thing to do, and you do that and continue until suddenly the problem is solved. You can't try to eat the whole cake at once or you'll choke on it.

# Grace Murray Hopper

*Grace Murray Hopper (born 1906, New York City) is a mathematician who while working with the world's first digital computer in the 1940s, developed the concept of automatic programming with a compiling system using words instead of mathematical symbols. From this concept she developed the computer language called COBOL (Common Business Oriented Languages), used today in data processing. She is presently serving as head of the Navy Programming Languages Section in the Pentagon.*

I WAS BORN WITH CURIOSITY. I always claim that I had a strong resemblance to the elephant's child in Kipling's *Just So Stories* who pokes his nose into everybody's business. Finally the alligator latches onto his nose and the elephant's child is pulled away and his nose gets stretched.

I remember when I was about seven, we had seven bedrooms up at our summer home for all the cousins to come visiting. Each room had an alarm clock, one of those round ones with two feet and a bell up on top that rings like crazy when the alarm goes off. When we were going on a trip, Mother would always go around at night and set all the alarm clocks. One night she went around to set them and they had all been taken apart. What had happened was that I'd taken the first one apart and I couldn't get it together so I opened the next one. I ended up with all seven of them apart. After that I was restricted to one clock. It's that kind of curiosity: How do things work?

I was very fortunate in that my father believed his daughters should be given the same opportunities as his son, so my sister and I both went to Vassar. It was a little unusual back in those days. I was class of '28 and my sister was class of '30. Mostly the only people who went to college then were going to be schoolteachers. But my father had seen the panics of 1893 and 1907 and he said he might or might not be able to leave us any money, but he could see that we were trained.

I loved mathematics all the way through school, especially geometry. I used to draw pretty pictures with it. It's not really unusual for a woman to have an interest in mathematics. Actually I think you'll find an equal number of girls have it as boys. They just get discouraged when they're younger. They hit a hard problem and somebody's apt to say, "Oh, girls can't understand that." They're not encouraged by teachers or parents. That didn't happen to me. As a matter of fact, my sister made all A's in math too, though she was an economics major.

During World War II, and right after the war, when the men came back, they were all busy going to college and getting their degrees, so the women got in on the very beginning of the computer field and they've stayed there. It's probably one of the best fields there is for women to move up in. Women turn out to be very good programmers for one very good reason: They tend to finish up things, and men don't very often finish. After men think they've solved a problem, they want to go off and get a new one, whereas a woman will always wrap it up in a neat package and document it. I think that's because you don't half-cook a dinner, you finish it and put it on the table, or you put the snappers and buttons on a dress. We're sort of used to finishing things.

I was an associate professor of mathematics at Vassar when I went into the navy. I joined the navy because there was a war on and everybody was going into something. I'd had a grandfather who was a rear admiral and I would have loved to have been in the navy from the beginning but at the time when I was growing up they didn't take women.

The navy assigned me to the Bureau of Ordnance Computation Project and sent me to Harvard to work on the first computer in the United States, the Mark I. Nobody knew anything about computers then. That was the first one. The Mark I computer was fifty-one feet long; today a computer with similar powers is about three eighths of an inch, a chip, an integrated circuit.

When we started programming computers we had to write all the programs in octal code (that's base 8 instead of base 10). When you start doing that, you can sure make mistakes. So what I had done over time was to collect pieces of code to compute a sine or a logarithm or some such function that I knew was checked out and knew was correct so that I could use them again in another program. I kept them in a notebook. But to put them in a new program I still had to copy them and add them to all the addresses. Copying and adding them to addresses is a very dull occupation and I found I made mistakes. And there sat the big computer. It would do it. So I decided to make a library of all these pieces of code and I'd give them each a name and then I'd tell the computer to put them together, copy them and add them to the addresses.

So I built the first compiler. It was a mathematical compiler. It translated mathematical notation into machine code. Manipulating symbols was fine for mathematicians but it was no good for data processors who were not symbol manipulators. Very few people are really symbol manipulators. If they are they become professional mathematicians, not data processors. It's much easier for most people to write an English statement than it is to use symbols. So I decided data processors ought to be able to write their programs in English, and the computers would translate them into machine code. That was the beginning of COBOL, a computer language for data processors. I could say "Subtract income tax from pay" instead of trying to write that in octal code or using all kinds of symbols. COBOL is the major language used today in data processing.

No one thought of that earlier because they weren't as lazy as I was. A lot of our programmers liked to play with the bits. I wanted to get jobs done. That's what the computer was there for. When I started with the first compiler, nobody really believed it. I went to a meeting and gave a paper on it, but everybody said, "You can't do that." It took two years before they began to accept that concept. They had to because it worked.

Right after the war there was a tremendous surge of innovative development in computers. Everything was changing. In weaponry, where you used to fire shells you now fired rockets and missiles. We were talking about guided missiles, about airplanes, and they all needed a tremendous amount in the way of design and computation; the need for computers was very great.

Then when we started with the space effort, it became even greater because you had to plot the courses for things and you had to put computers on board. They had to be smaller and lighter. There was tremendous support for innovation in all areas.

I think one of the reasons we're not getting those kinds of innovations today is that government support has almost totally disappeared, and with inflation, companies themselves have cut back on the amount they spend on research. They may spend the same amount but because of inflation it doesn't have as much effect. You'll notice that much of the equipment we're using today is the result of the work done right after World War II—the forties and early fifties.

That hasn't affected my work because I'm concerned with using the computers to do things. Most people don't know much about the microcomputers, the chips; they don't quite understand them and it's hard to believe that what used to be in a big blue box can all be on one chip. It's a little hard to explain it to people. Sometimes, you have to prove it. What we're up against is people's resistance to change. I have a clock on the wall in my office that runs counterclockwise. That's so nobody in the office can ever say we've always done it this way. It tells perfectly good time. It just shows there was never any good reason why clocks had to go clockwise. What bothers me is the number of people who can't change, who say, "We've always done it this way, don't make waves."

When I was young, I was already on my way to take off. I don't know why, I just was. My family had a lot of confidence in me. After the war I worked for UNIVAC. I worked there from 1949 until 1967 when I became a senior staff scientist. I can remember once I went to the general manager of UNIVAC to get some money or people, I've forgotten what I was trying to get. He said no, and I said, "O.K., I'll quit, I'll clean out my desk and leave this afternoon." He beckoned me to come back and said, "Wait a minute, Grace, you've already done that once this year, you can't do it again." I always figured I could get a job as a waitress. It would have been temporary. You must stand on your own two feet. That's half the fun.

The contemporary malaise is the unwillingness to take chances. Everybody is playing it safe. We've lost our guts. It's much more fun to stick your neck out and take chances. But you see, we've provided for everything. Everybody's wrapped in cotton batting. It used to be if you lost your job, you went out and got another one or you didn't eat. Now you get unemployment insurance. Don't eat saccharin, don't do this, take care of that, fasten your seat belt. The whole attitude is protect yourself against everything, don't take chances. But we built this country on taking chances. Instead of going to higher echelons and saying, "Can I try this on my computer?" I do it. If it works, I get a pat on the back; if it doesn't work, I try to explain why it didn't; but I don't wait for somebody to tell me to do it.

Safety, security, no change, that's what a lot of people have been taught to value. It's the old pioneer spirit that's lacking. I had an ancestor who lived in Newbury, Massachusetts, and got tired of it. There were about three hundred families and he thought it was getting too crowded so he piled his family and possessions into a wagon and went up and founded Boscawen, New Hampshire. How about the people who came over here in the beginning who were dissatisfied with things the way they were in Europe? They embarked on little tiny boats and came three months across the North Atlantic looking for something better. How many people would do that today? We could start settling in space, couldn't we? There were people in Europe when the early ones set sail who said the same thing: "Really, is that possible?"

The most important thing I've accomplished, other than building the compiler, is training young people. They come to me, you know, and say, "Do you think we can do this?" I say, "Try it." And I back 'em up. They need that. I keep track of them as they get older and I stir 'em up at intervals so they don't forget to take chances. Once in a while I've had to tell somebody that they were falling into a rut, that they had greater capabilities than that and why didn't they get a move on . . . you know, hold a small conference and give 'em a little boot in the rear. People in a way are very much waiting for someone to express confidence in them, and once you do it, they'll take off.

I never thought about what I wanted to accomplish in life. I had too many things to do. I was so deeply involved in things, I just kept on going. Then something came along and changed the direction. I went off with it. I didn't know where it was going to lead me. It just keeps on leading me.

I'm still on the CODASYL committee that monitors the COBOL language, but I've gone off into this business of trying to build systems of computers instead of one big computer. Now that we have the chips, instead of using one big computer to do all the jobs, we can use separate computers for each job and have them all running parallel and talking to each other.

I've gotten away from the mathematical side of computers. I'm over on the data processing side, the business side, because that's more exciting. You don't have equations, you're dealing with people and they don't obey equations. I'm working with computers to run the navy now. We use computers to supply petroleum, ammunition, people—send orders for training, move 'em around the country. You don't do anything in the navy without a piece of paper, and they all come out of computers. Same thing's true of your big companies. If those computers stopped, this whole country would come to a screeching halt. If we didn't have computers, we'd be solving these problems on paper and some that we do in an hour would take three hundred years. Computers are tools; they can be misused by people. If I have a wrench in the garage to fix the kitchen sink, someone can come and hit someone over the head with it, but it wouldn't be the wrench that did it, it would be the person. So when we write laws, they shouldn't be laws about computers, but laws about the people who use them. We're developing very good techniques for keeping unauthorized people from plugging into the computer system.

My vision of a world with computers is a world in which people have a lot more time to do what they like, to do what they want to do and read the books they want to read. It won't make books obsolete, it's too tiring to read on computers. Playing tennis, jogging . . . they'll have plenty of time to go to the shore. I'd go over to the library and start digging through books. I could do my work at home. I could have a computer at home and talk to my office. I could live up on top of a nice mountain in New Hampshire and smell pine trees and it would be the same as if I were here in the sub-sub-subbasement of the Pentagon. I think that would be much better. I'm not afraid to live in a world like that. I would hate to go back to wearing cotton knitted stockings; I like nylon. I wouldn't go back for anything. Change is slow. You have to see the contrast. I think you have to live seventy years before you get to see it.

The navy retired me from the reserves on December 31, 1966, and recalled me to full active duty on August 1, 1967. I'm seventy-three years old. Now I'm very much interested in genealogy. When I can sneak a few minutes, I go to the library. My interest in genealogy started with my own family because when Mother died, I'd found she'd gotten part way and I thought I'd finish it, but now I'm ending up studying early American history. My mother's family goes way back to before the American Revolution. When I started tracing these things I realized that in school they taught us that the Pilgrims landed in 1620 and in 1773 we had a Boston Tea Party, and I discovered I didn't know anything that had happened in between, which was the time of the development of town meetings and our political system. So I started finding out how our system developed.

I told you, I have insatiable curiosity. It's solving problems. Every time you solve a problem, another one shows up immediately behind it. That's the challenge. Nothing ever stays the same, it's always new and different. Anybody who's been bitten by the computer bug and had the fun of making those things do things in the fraction of the time you used to take doing them and make them do all sorts of things you never had any chance to do otherwise, why you can't let go of that, you want to keep on doing it. I'll never finish my work with computers, anymore than I'll ever finish the genealogy because the generations double with every step. Wouldn't it be dull to do things that ended? I'm having a heck of a good time and contributing a little bit here and there to solving problems.

# Cecelia Helena Payne-Gaposhkin

Cecelia Payne-Gaposhkin (born 1900, England, died Massachusetts, 1979) was an astronomer whose pioneering studies of the spectra of the stars in the 1920s gave the first convincing evidence that the stars are similar to the sun in their chemical makeup. She demonstrated that their apparent differences are due to differing surface temperature. Her later work, classifying stars of variable brightness, enabled astronomers to understand the history of stellar development and led to a knowledge of the structure of our galaxy. In 1956, she became the first woman to be advanced to the rank of Professor at Harvard University.

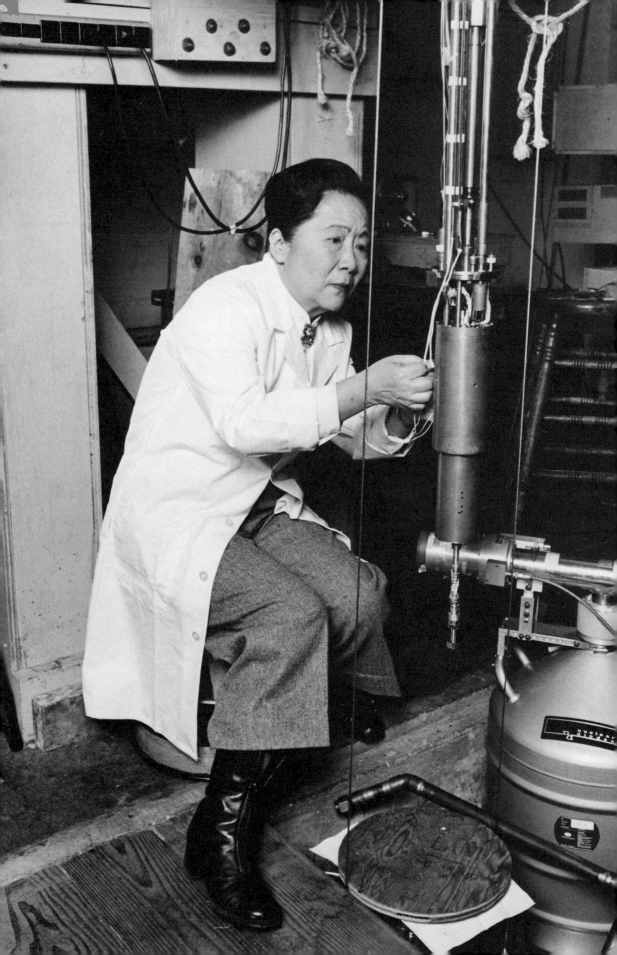

# Chien-Shiung Wu

*Chien-Shiung Wu (born 1912, Liu Ho, China) is an experimental physicist and a professor at Columbia Uiversity. In 1956, her most celebrated experiment overturned one of the basic laws of physics, the law of conservation of parity, which held that a phenomenon of nature is symmetrical and looks the same whether observed directly or in a mirror with left and right reversed. Dr. Wu devised the experiment for theoretical physicists Tsung-Dao Lee and Chen Ning Yang, who suggested that the parity principle would not apply when dealing with weak interactions of subatomic particles. Drs. Lee and Yang were awarded the Nobel Prize for this work.*

I WAS BORN AND BROUGHT UP in China and came to this country in 1936 after I completed my college education. I had a totally different family upbringing than the young girls have in this country. My father was educated in the old Chinese tutorage fashion. He taught himself algebra, geometry and general sciences and he became interested in Western cultures by reading and studying. He believed very strongly in democratic systems and women's emancipation. While I was in grade school he devoted his time and energy to establishing a girls' school in our region which later became very well known. Our family led a very simple life. We had an intimate and congenial family environment. We enjoyed studying and playing together. My father encouraged us to ask questions and taught us to solve problems. He wanted us all to be independent and to lead interesting, happy lives.

The events which led me to major in the sciences make a very dramatic story. One afternoon in the summer after I graduated from the girls' Normal School in Soochow where I was studying to be an elementary schoolteacher, a letter came from my school informing me that I had been selected from the graduating class to enter the National Central University with highest honors. Of course my parents were delighted and asked what I would like to study there. I said I would like to study physics, but unfortunately the normal school gave us very little scientific training. If I went, I would probably have to study education. When my father heard me, he disagreed. He said there was ample time to prepare myself in mathematics before the university opened.

Later that day he came home with one textbook on high algebra and a textbook each on physics and chemistry as well. I was elated to receive these books all at once. I studied them that summer at home. In the fall I went to one of the best universities in China and registered as a freshman in mathematics. In my sophomore year, I became more confident in myself and transferred to the physics department. Imagine what a near miss it had been. If it hadn't been for my father's encouragement, I

**67**

wouldn't have had the courage to select physics as a major field and I
would be teaching grade school somewhere in China now.

I came to this country in 1936 because the quality of education in the
United States, particularly its higher education, was well known in China.
I was very, very lucky. I was supposed to go to a university somewhere in
the Midwest, but when I arrived in San Francisco, a friend took me to
Berkeley to visit and when I saw the University of California, I just loved
it and I changed my mind. I stayed on at Berkeley until 1942.

That was the golden age for the physics department at Berkeley.
Berkeley was at the top of the world. Professor Ernest Lawrence, who
was my thesis director, had just been awarded a Nobel Prize for his
invention of the particle accelerator known as the cyclotron or atom
smasher. Physicists all over the world came to visit the famous cyclotron
laboratory. It was the mecca, the holy land for atom smashing. Professor
Robert Oppenheimer was heading the theoretical group and gathered
around him a group of young and talented theoretical research associates.
I worked closely with Professor Ernest Segrè on nuclear fission.

In 1942, during the war, I got married in Pasadena, California. My
husband is also a physicist. He had been at Cal Tech but had to move
east. I remembered the dean of Smith College, who had visited Berkeley,
and had said to me, "When you have your doctorate degree, I hope you
will come to Smith." I wrote to her and she said, "Yes, come," and so I
came east to join the faculty at Smith College. I really had a pleasant time
teaching at Smith, but when Dr. Lawrence saw me at a physical society
meeting, he said, "What at you doing at Smith?" He knew I had no
opportunity to do research there. He wrote me letters of recommendation
to several leading universities and I got appointments from them all. I
accepted Princeton's appointment for a year, then I came to Columbia in
1944 to join the war work here, the Manhattan Project. Most of the major
work on the Manhattan Project was done at Oak Ridge, Tennessee, and
Los Alamos, New Mexico. Here at Columbia they worked on how to
enrich uranium 235. We were working on uranium enrichment right here,
but we also carried on neutron research.

I have always been interested in scientific study because of its very
objective way of looking at things. Science is actually a way to study the
nature of matter, and when you understand the nature of matter, then you
also try to use that to explain all the phenomena around you. So therefore
it is a very broad and intimate subject.

Scientists are generally dedicated to search for new knowledge and to
formulate new understanding. Broad and penetrating insights into the
interdisciplinary relations between different sciences will certainly help a
great deal in finding interesting and important subjects to study and in
adopting versatile new tools to solve the problems. For example,
traditionally in biology and in life sciences the emphasis in learning was
put on the description and classification of things in groups. Prior to the
biomolecular age, scientists were not even sure whether the forces

encountered in the life sciences were the same as the ones that occurred in physics and chemistry. When Watson and Crick discovered DNA in the late 1950s, they began to explain the genetic relations in terms of biomolecules. From then on, not only physicists and chemists but also biologists, botanists and medical scientists all became aware of and were indoctrinated in biomolecular terms. The atomic and molecular structure developed in physics which once seemed so remote and irrelevant to biologists has now been miraculously adopted to explain phenomena observed in biology and life sciences. So at the present moment, we are entering an age in which interdisciplinary study plays a very important role.

In the last few years, our small research group in the Physics Department at Columbia University has focused its interests on an area called nuclear orientation. We built an ultra-low-temperature laboratory in the basement of the Pupin building so that we can carry out experiments to study "symmetry principles and nuclear structure." At zero degrees Kelvin, which is 273.17 degrees below zero centigrade, the thermal motions of atoms or molecules are greatly reduced, like in a drowsy state. This is the way we set up the now famous experiment which overthrew the law of parity in 1957.

Early in 1956, Tsung-Dao Lee of Columbia and Chen Ning Yang of the Institute of Advanced Study had taken up a serious new question: Why did two newly discovered atomic particles called K-mesens, with the same mass and other properties, produce different particles when they decayed? The two theorists proposed that nature might not be symmetrical in such weak interaction. This hypothesis challenged a "conservation of parity" law that was considered a cornerstone of physics. I had devoted most of my research life up to 1956 to the study of beta decay and weak interaction. I immediately proposed a way to test the theory.

The test was to take radioactive cobalt 60, place it in a magnetic field, supercool it, and watch where its electrons went. It was a rather simple experiment in conception, but we had to use an ultra-low-temperature facility to perform the experiment and only one or two existed in this country at that time. We were fortunate to have the wholehearted cooperation of several low-temperature-nuclear physicists at the National Bureau of Standards.

Many things worried me. Very often in doing these experiments, something goes wrong. Most physicists thought we would find nothing exciting. The odds were one million to one in their favor that the law of parity in beta decay was conserved. In fact, many famous physicists bet on it. It was a horrible position to be in.

Our cobalt 60 experiment found that a majority of tens of thousands of electrons emitted by the cobalt every second were ejected primarily in one direction—the one opposite the direction in which the nucleus of each atom was spinning. This unexpected discovery stunned world scientists. It revealed that nature is not always symmetrical with respect to left and right. The behavior of the cobalt nucleus was proven to be left-handed, and the law of parity, which is derived from left-right symmetry, could not hold.

I did the experiment two or three times with different conditions and they all showed the same thing. After the discovery I couldn't sleep for about two weeks. Why should the Lord want to tell this secret through me? When I received the Research Corporation Award in 1958, I remarked that it was probably the first ever given "not for establishing a law, but for overthrowing it." This taught us a lesson never to take the so-called self-evident laws for granted. With this discovery, nature gives us a new tool to pry into the phenomena of weak interactions.

The Committee of Women Physicists of the American Physical Society has worked very hard to encourage more women to go into the field of physics. Unfortunately there are still only about 2 percent women in physics. When our former secretary of education, Shirley Hufstedler, went to visit some classrooms in a Washington high school, one of the classes she attended was a chemistry class. I think that gives a great deal of encouragement to young girls for someone in her position to be so interested in science. I think the reason why women are so far behind is because the guidance counselors in high schools and colleges don't really give correct guidance to young girls. They don't encourage them.

If you don't take basic courses in mathematics or sciences, then how can you select more advanced science as your major? You won't. I have two cousins. They wanted so much to study science, or medicine. They asked me, "Well, what do we take?" But they then ended up taking all those soft sciences. I asked, "Why? How can you take all this soft science and expect to major in the physical sciences?" One of them said, "Oh, I don't like the teachers of the other courses." That's very bad. If you don't have a proper mathematical and physical sciences background by the time you are a junior or senior, you are not properly prepared to go into physical or natural sciences, no matter how interested you are.

I think the social scientists in this country really don't do justice to women. In 1965 at an M.I.T. symposium on women in science and engineering, Bruno Bettelheim told a story about a young Russian girl who worked in the engineering field. He said, "She loved her work with a womanly embracing of her tasks rather than a masculine conquering of them." Then he quoted Balzac about a woman who has the advantages of a *man's* education. He said that bringing a woman's point of view may be an advantage in some areas of education and social sciences but not in physics and mathematics where we strive always for objectivity. I doubt that the tiny atoms and nuclei or the mathematical symbols or the DNA molecules have any preference for either masculine or feminine treatment.

Women in physics have always had a very good record, beginning with Madame Curie who won the Nobel Prize twice for her discovery of radioactivity and the isolation of radium and plutonium. No man could compete with that at that time. Her elder daughter, Irene Curie Joliot, and her husband were also awarded a Nobel Prize for their discovery of artificial radioactivity. Dr. Lise Meitner contributed to our understanding of the alpha and gamma radiations. In 1963 another woman physicist, Dr. Maria Mayer, was awarded the Nobel Prize for her important contribution to the nuclear shell model.

My husband and my son are also physicists. My husband works at Brookhaven which is in Upton, Long Island. He comes home for the weekend and goes back early Monday morning. It's nice to revisit that way. There are many possible ways to ease the conflict between career and family. Managing a home together with a full-time job is not really a problem if both husband and wife contribute. Somehow, in order to bring up children normally, it is more natural to have both parents care for the child. Actually in this country, fathers love their children dearly but choose to do as little as possible at home. Why? I had such a good relationship with my father. I always remember the talks we had and how we played together. I think a child's upbringing is incomplete if you only have a father's influence or a mother's.

Also the young family, if both husband and wife work, has to spend some of their income to have a part-time or full-time helper or housekeeper. I had a lovely lady who looked after my son when he was an infant. Now this lady is eighty-eight years old and has remained a close friend of the family. On the other hand, is it too much to ask in this age of science and technology for the society to provide excellent professional child-care centers during the day so that women can work in their chosen fields?

I teach one course three times a week. I enjoy teaching. I love these young students. The research I do is also a part of the teaching, because I have young Ph.D. candidates working with me. Without them I think the academic life would be on the dull side. With them it is so stimulating and inspiring. They are young, energetic and work extremely hard.

Nobody really goes out looking for the secrets of nature, but then maybe something small might turn out to be something very big and important. Really science is very mysterious and you have to understand it. What is the word? You have to have an insight. Sometimes it appears very unimportant. Actually it is a very important clue. That clue can lead you to some more important things.

Every experiment, if it comes out beautifully, I'm always excited. I remember once I was doing an experiment late in the night, four o'clock in the morning, and something was not right. It turned out the error was mine because I was calculating wrong. Finally I put the right number in the formula, then it came out exactly as I expected and I couldn't believe it. It seemed that the electrons know better than I. That's the kind of joy one frequently experiences in experimentation. I don't know how to convey it to people. It is esthetic and fantastic!

# Louise Nevelson

*Louise Nevelson (born 1900, Rockland, Maine) is one of America's most distinguished living sculptors whose work helped to elevate sculpture to a place of prominence in our culture. She is best known for her sculpture "environments" in which she uses carved pieces and found objects painted a uniform black. Assembled individually or stacked to form sculptural walls, these pieces, rather than standing in space, contain space. She also makes use of new developments in technology to create large, free-standing metal sculptures for public spaces.*

I THINK BASICALLY the whole thing in my life was that I wanted to see the world with more awareness and more harmony. I've been able to do that almost as much as is human.

I knew that I was gifted because from the day you go to school, your teachers know what you have. At least they did in my school. In Maine, over seventy years ago, they felt I was an artist. They just knew it. Something about me projected it, even as a child, and I knew it. Some people are born a certain way. They really are, no doubt about it. Caruso had a voice when he was born. Well, others had voices but he had the combination. Then he built on it. You have something, then you devote your life to building on it. Now I evidently came from a place, maybe it was the home and the environment and all that. It made me feel like a high-powered engine. I had energy. So it does mean that some of us are born with these constitutions from birth. We're born a certain way.

Then also I think being an artist is a state of mind. There were a great many frustrations in my life, too. But the only thing I can say is that I was looking for harmony and I think my long suit was that I was able to remember things and externalize them. I wanted harmony within myself so I externalized it in my work.

I never used a yardstick to measure anything. It would embarrass me. If I had to measure this to this and I had to stop to measure it with a yardstick, there would already be a question in my mind. My mind would have already gone through something that I don't want. I know where I want it to be. Consequently, I just knew what I wanted out of life. It wasn't easy but I didn't know you could live another way. I didn't know.

When I was about seventeen or eighteen, it was during World War I, I was the most exciting girl in my whole town. I was already studying voice and dramatics and modern dance. I was captain of the high school basketball team, so I wasn't what you call an academic student, but I was out in front in these things. Well, if you were as active as I, you couldn't be an old maid at the time.

The Nevelson brothers had a shipping firm down on Wall Street in New York and they had ships for the government, for Woodrow Wilson.

They were playing a big role in the war. They came to Maine because we had shipyards in Maine. And they came for repairs because their ships had been shot at. Anyway, we got acquainted. I was pretty young. I didn't go out much with boys. I was already pretty mature and I wasn't going to go around with those local kids.

I think I was caught. I never solved it but I knew that when the older Mr. Nevelson said his younger brother was coming up, I smelt that they were already figuring things out, and so was I. I had told my mother I wasn't going to get married because I was going to go to Pratt Art Institute in New York and that I'd be an artist. I wanted to go there so I could teach art and be self-supporting. Then I got a phone call, "Mr. Nevelson is coming." Before he even came I said, "You know, Mother, Mr. Nevelson is coming and he's going to propose to me this evening and I'm accepting him." I don't think the poor woman knew what I was even talking about, but it happened that way. He came and he proposed, and said, "Well, you can still go to art school," and he was very sympathetic with me. I've always thought I just superimposed the whole thing on him. See, you want something badly enough, you can just somehow make it happen.

I made a beeline in my life for art. I went to art school all my life. I went to Europe and studied with Hans Hofmann in 1931 before he came to America. It's like the people who swim in the ocean. There are some who swim and some who drown. I never had any problems. When I came to New York I went to the Art Students League. The first week I was there, they put my drawings on the wall. I had 100-plus wherever I went. There's something about me. . . . See, you have to have an awareness of where you want to go, who you want to associate with, then you work toward projecting that.

I was the only American artist that Karl Nierendorf showed in his gallery in the thirties. He said, "Look, Nevelson, with your sensibilities, you'd be great in Paris. That's where Picasso and all the boys, Matisse . . ."—he knew them all. And I said no. I was brought up in this country, this pioneer country, it's still a young country, and I like the feeling of being a pioneer in this country and I am. I think I made some rather good choices. Right along they worked for me. New York was right for me, because I had all this energy.

I didn't go away summer or winter. I happen to like warm weather here so I never went away, I never went to an art colony to stay. I didn't want that because, well, I'd already lived in a very expensive way and they were struggling, and it just didn't fit me. When I first came to New York, if you were an artist you lived in Greenwich Village and you were a bohemian. That meant free. What did you do? You lived down there and you put on a beret. Wasn't that a uniform? That didn't appeal to me. I did it my way, I guess. I didn't want to be part of a community of artists. It didn't interest me.

I dressed like a queen. Even then. I always dressed, and my family always saw that I could have very beautiful clothes. People thought if you looked like that and you already had expensive and gorgeous, expensive clothes and jewelry and everything, how could you use old woods in your work? There probably wasn't one person on earth that understood what I was doing. At the time, you see, the work was different, old wood, nails, mirrors and glass, all the goddam things.

After my first exhibition was over I destroyed all the work I'd done. What else could I do? I didn't have a nickel. I had no place to store it, I never sold anything, so what was I to do? Kill myself? I had no choice at that time. I guess it was nearly forty years ago. I never would ask anyone for anything so it was a struggle. Anyway I did destroy them. All I have are a few photos of the work.

It wasn't too long after that that I began showing at Nierendorf. I still struggled. No one knows how much I struggled. The work was all right. I could do that but, yes, there were depressions . . . "At sea, at sea, what can it be that I remain so long at sea?" Yes, but I pulled out. I hunted and found a few notes that have sustained me for the rest of my life.

I had a son. The agonies were economic, guilts about motherhood . . . I think the greatest guilt of all is having children without thinking too much. I was thinking but we didn't have the Pill. I did everything . . . but I think I was too healthy. And you pay a price. Some of us are not ready to be mothers. I've never been ready. My son is fifty-six and I still feel guilty, but I've done a great deal to overcompensate him for this. I was young. I hadn't had any experience with sex. Well, it was just difficult for me to confront this. I wouldn't and I had a cesarean because I couldn't face it. The point is that even to this day, who has the courage to really give life to another person? Don't you think that's a great responsibility? People have said to me, "Well, aren't you glad that you were born?" and I'll say, "Well, if I wasn't I wouldn't know the difference."

What I see about humanity makes me a pessimist. But in my work I'm an optimist. Look at humanity, look at what's happening on this earth. I think anyone who takes the attitude that they can do something that will change the world is very naive. For instance, I've taught art. I'll say to my students, "Well, what do you want?" "I want perfection," they say. I say, "Well, who in the hell do you think you are that you can demand perfection?" It's nonexistent anyway.

Words like *ruthless* and *sacrifice* are kind of false judgments. You don't do it that way. When you have labor pains, you don't say, Could I have done it this way or that way? You go into labor. Those words belong to what we call three dimensions. I didn't think like that. Living the way I did . . . see, I broke all the traditions. If I wanted a lover, I had a lover. I didn't have to get married again. So I had courage to live as I understood it. I thought that art was more important than other things. I work for myself. It was only because I had so little confidence in the world that I wanted to build my own world, not *the* world, *my* world.

When I found the cube, it stabilized me. I didn't have to flounder. And really it's not fashionable at this moment to give credit to the cube, but having studied metaphysics, and recognizing the cube, it gave me my terra firma because I can understand the cube in space. It has been said that Picasso discovered the cube. Now, if you study metaphysics, it has its own symbols. And the cube is the highest form that the human being has come to. First in consciousness you have a dot, then you have a line, then you have the square. Then you project it into a cube. That is as far as the human species can go.

So Picasso, maybe without even knowing metaphysics, still was brilliant enough to move into the cube. Beethoven uses the octave and out of those eight notes he makes a world of sound. Now that's harmony. And that's what "environment" meant to me. I don't need eight notes. Give me one or two notes and I can work on it and I'm satisfied. That gives me my structure. There is no limit to those one or two notes, because there's variation on a theme, unlimited variations on a theme. I can go back to the variation of one theme and that's my consciousness. So I stand on the strength of that. Nothing has been able to shake me. I don't think anything could have stopped me from doing my art. I stopped working for a little while and I'd get abcesses and boils, I'd get sick. See, the machinery—if you're a Rolls-Royce, you can't be walking, you've just got to be riding.

I can't say it's possible to do what I've done without going through periods of despair. I only know I drank and I also knew that somewhere when I would come out, it sensitized me. It often gave me a kind of moment of rest. I don't say that you have to drink all the time but I think without it I would have gone off a little crazy. So it was like you'd fall and there was like a clothesline that kind of kept you from going down.

We hear so much about the material and the spiritual, the soul and the body. I do not want to make a division. I feel it's all one. In oriental philosophy, they say there isn't a world, that we project a world. I needed this philosophy to live or I'd kill myself. I don't give a damn if it's right or wrong. It suits me and I like it. That's enough for me.

Now I don't make moral distinctions like this is a lie and this is the truth. If a lie is going to sustain me I will kiss it and welcome it. I read that Napoleon said, "You stoop to conquer." I always felt like a nice American wooden Indian. My knees wouldn't give. I always thought it would be easier to steal than beg. That's where your pride comes in. So I got a few keys that have been able to sustain me, and helped. Anyone who's in such despair, I'm sure they will hunt for them. Some people go to religion, some to analysis, some to medicine; I don't care what they go to but if they need it, fine. If it will help them, what's the difference?

So, looking back, I saw that I knew what I wanted and I felt that I had the tools to fulfill it. The work I do I've done basically for me. Why? Because I wanted to give meaning to my life. It's the very best way I know how to live my life. How else could I live it?

I live pretty much as I want to. I don't want to have a lot. I've had all kinds of jewelry, I had diamond bracelets before I was twenty. I've had great collections—American Indian pottery, African art. I've tasted of almost everything on earth. It has not changed my life because it all came at a certain time when I was ready. Do you realize how few rich people create? They don't have to. Art is a struggle. I call it a spiritual labor pain.

When I did the series of etchings called *Essences*, I was already in my late seventies. I went to the studio for two weeks. I was just going to make one or two etchings. I was so excited I stayed probably a year and made thirty-six editions. And if someone had come and given me the world, I wouldn't have taken it. It was so exciting to me.

I called them *Essences* because I didn't use the technique of drawing, of painting or any technique. First I had the materials. I've used laces for forty years, but it was the weight and the placement that were new. So in other words, my technique had nothing to do with the concept of what has been done in the past with drawing and painting and sculpture.

I feel that the *Essences* are like a breath. Now, darling, we have our body but it's the breath . . . you know, people die because their lungs get filled with water and they can't breathe and that is the end. The *Essences* gave me probably the closest feeling of where I wanted to go. It's like perfume. Think of what we have to do to get an ounce of perfume. That is what these *Essences* are to me. They're as close . . . it's almost all consciousness, and you see . . . it's kind of a bouquet to myself. Did I take this breath yesterday or a minute ago? Look. It's a new breath, it's always new, and you do add, from minute to minute, you do add a little more awareness, yes, as long as you live. Otherwise we'll cease living.

In those *Essences*, I wanted to get a quality, something like ethereal, and I did to a point. Now I want to carry it to a whisper. Because I think a whisper can be stronger, an atom can be stronger than a whole mountain.

Now when you're eighty, no matter how you slice it, things have happened. I'm living my life pretty much as I wanted to. Nevertheless, you know nature is very bright, and when you get to be this age, it plays its part, too. Nature is still a mystery.

I didn't see too much happiness. I lived alone almost my whole adult life. Now that doesn't mean *alone*. I've always had help around me. But I mean marriage, it's difficult without that. It's a partnership. Of course, one always has friends and the older I got the more interesting friends I had, still have. I really don't regret too much. I've been too busy. It's been constructive so how can I regret anything? I give myself a 100-plus for the way I've lived my life, the choices I've made, what has come out of it. Every day I've lived I wanted to flower more and more and more.

We don't have everything. I thought my mother was the most beautiful woman on earth but she shouldn't have been married. She was totally misplaced. She used rouge in Rockland, Maine, when no one rouged. She used to wear feather hats when no one wore them. She was misplaced and unhappy. I thought, when I was growing up, with my abilities and appearance and everything, that I should have a place that would suit me. It's like a setting you want. It's the harmony I'm looking for. Well I never had that. I've never lived in a place that I really want, even now. Now it's too late and I don't want to bother. So I made *Mrs. N's Palace*. I just projected that and I created my world.

# Mary Lou Williams

*Mary Lou Williams (born 1910, Atlanta, Georgia, died 1981) was a pianist, composer and arranger who played a central role in every era of jazz since the 1920s. She was the only musician to employ the form of each era—rhythm and blues, swing, bebop—and still retain her own style. Many of her four hundred compositions have become classics. The* Zodiac Suite, *which she played with the New York Philharmonic in 1946, was the first jazz work to be commissioned and performed with a symphony orchestra.* Mary Lou's Mass, *which she performed at St. Patrick's Cathedral in 1975, was the first to be commissioned for liturgical services. She taught jazz at Duke University in North Carolina.*

I THINK PEOPLE SHOULD do their work. If they're talented, then whatever's coming to them, they'll get it. Things happened to me that I never realized. You see, I'm so involved with the music that sometimes I forget about the outside world and what's happening. I'm just in a little world by myself.

I was born in Atlanta, Georgia. My mother played the organ by ear for the church, and all of a sudden she couldn't hear. Her pitch left her—relative pitch, perfect pitch, whatever she had—and she couldn't improvise anymore. One day, I was about three, she was holding me on her lap and she was pumping this organ. My little fingers beat her fingers to the keys. Because she dropped me on the floor and ran and got the neighbors, I must have been playing something pretty good. After that I never left the piano. She wouldn't allow a teacher near me; she had professional men come in and play for me.

Kids would come to call for me, my half-brother would come over, he was about two years younger, he'd come over to play with me, but I'd be busy at the piano. Sometimes I'd stop and go out and play with him a little while, and then come back in to the piano, getting my own sounds, and I've been doing that all my life. I didn't know what I was doing. I didn't even know where C, A or any of the notes were, but the piano played for my fingers. I was born with perfect pitch, and I was hearing what I wanted to hear. If somebody hummed something, I played it.

I started playing the piano professionally when I was between six and eight years old. Sometimes a man would hold me on his lap so I could reach the keys. I've been with men all my life. It was normal. I guess that's the reason I feel so differently about women. There's something about a woman. She cannot fill a trumpet or trombone the way she should, and these woman are out there trying to do it, and not doing things right. I never even thought about being a woman or man, because the musicians never allowed me to feel that I was inferior to them. It was strength of thinking. I'm feminine but I think more or less like them. Thelonius Monk was here one day with his wife and he said to her, "Mary's the only woman that I'll pay attention to, because the others don't even know what they're talking about."

When I was five or six we moved to Pittsburgh. I used to play regularly for the Mellon family. This very elegant woman had little bridge parties and she used to send a chauffeur for me. The chauffeur never even realized that somebody that tiny could play. The Mellons' house was set up so that I was in one room playing the piano and they were playing bridge in another room. I took two girls with me to dance, and Mrs. Mellon said, "I don't want to see them dance, the little girls, you just play." So I played and when I finished she gave me a check for a hundred dollars, and gave them twenty-five dollars each. When I got home, everybody almost fainted because that was like five thousand dollars, you know. My mother said, "Are you sure that she didn't make a mistake?" We stayed up until the banks opened the next day.

How did people know about me? Well, everybody knew because I did home talent shows and people began to pay me one dollar an hour for their socials and teas and for graduations. After a while, my reputation became so great in Pittsburgh that they began to call me "the little piano girl." This vaudeville show came to Pittsburgh one day. A little Western Union boy delivered a telegram to the manager at the theater and after he read it he said to the boy, "I'm so disgusted, I have no piano player." The Western Union boy said, "Well, let's go out to East Liberty Street. The 'piano girl' is out there. Man, she can really play."

This manager, he drove out to East Liberty and I happened to be outside playing hopscotch with the kids. When the car drove up, the little boy said, "There she is." And the man said, "Oh my goodness, I spent all of my time coming out here and I should be looking for a pianist. That kid can't play." "Well, take her in the house," said the boy. And he took me in the house.

I don't know how old I was, I must have been ten or twelve years old, and so he sat there. He heard me play and it was so fabulous to him, he almost went out of his mind. He said, "Where's your mother?" He ran around and found her and said, "I'd like to sign her up." She said, "No, she's going to school. This is summer vacation now." So he sat there and hummed all the tunes in the show to me and I memorized them and went downtown and played the whole show that night. Memorizing, that's what I was used to doing, memorizing, because I couldn't read music at all then. And I played all the show; everything that he hummed to me, I played. My mother allowed me, accompanied by a woman, to go out on tour with the man and his vaudeville show until it was time to go back to school in the fall.

After that, musicians would come in from New York and ask my mother if they could take me out on gigs with them, and she allowed me to go. I went out with the Cotton Pickers, I used to jam with Chu Berry later on. It never seemed strange to me to be a little girl among all these men. It was something that I had to do. I did it. They treated me so very well that their wives would get jealous. After I had played the show, the trumpet player threw me up in the air and kissed me. They had a habit of doing that. I never liked anybody to hug or kiss me, not even my mother. I had to kiss them first. This guy threw me up in the air and when I came down, his wife had a knife, and I fainted. Another time a woman started to hit me. I was just taking all her blows. But suddenly I put my hand out to protect myself and accidentally made her nose bleed. Seeing the blood frightened her and she left me alone after that.

I went to a great high school. It produced people like Erroll Garner, Billy Strayhorn and Ahmad Jamal. Earl Hines is also from Pittsburgh. You see what happened in jazz, there were certain cities that produced piano players, like Pittsburgh, and other cities trumpet players, like St. Louis, and the reason why Kansas City was so great was that everyone gathered there—piano, drums, saxophones, though both Ben Webster and Charlie Parker were actually born in Kansas City. Maybe one man, eighty years ago, was a great musician in the city and everybody copied and wanted to play trombone or whatever instrument he played. Pittsburgh happened to be a city of great piano players that became well known later on. This teacher at the high school, Miss Alexander, I think she's still alive, she would tell Erroll Garner about me, and when Ahmad Jamal went to school, she told him about Erroll Garner and Mary Lou and so forth. I was there a few years ago and I said to the principal, "Why don't you put up pictures of all the great people who were here? That would inspire the kids to do something." He didn't know what to do. He said he needed somebody like me to think of things like that.

Well, I married at an early age. When I married, I married instruments. A guy playing a crazy instrument, I'd fall in love with the instrument and I didn't even know it. My first husband was the first baritone sax in the world, and he played a terrific baritone, and I fell in love with his instrument because I've never had what you'd call a deep, deep love. My love was always in the music and I wondered about that. I'd be in love for about a month, heavy. One boyfriend I had, if he saw a beautiful girl, I'd introduce him to her. Everyone said I paid my girl friend to take my husband away from me. I wanted to pay her because he really wasn't too kind to me. And then I discovered they'd been going together all along anyway, which got me off the hook. I could never make it with a boyfriend or being married because I'm too independent and I didn't stay in love long enough. After two months I'd be back playing my music again and forget all about him.

My husband joined the Andy Kirk band. I wasn't working with them. They had a regular pianist, but I'd travel with them. Sometimes when they got stuck, when the band wasn't going over too big, they'd call me in

**81**

to play "Froggy Bottom." One night when they were playing at the Savoy in New York, they got me to come in to play and the audience went wild because I must have only weighed 110 pounds, and for a woman to be up there swinging like a man, playing hard like Fats Waller, they never heard of it.

I'm the type of person, I think, who was sort of born with the music. I didn't even realize that I was being spoiled. I worked for everything, but I never in my life have wanted for anything, even when we didn't have anything and I was starving and out traveling, doing one-nighters, it didn't even bother me. Nothing.

It was worse than a hard life. I've been out with the Andy Kirk Band, stranded in a city. One time, we were in the back of a farm, and I went and ate raw corn. I ate it almost up to the farmer's back door. This was in Greeley, Colorado. We were starving. It was after the bank crash, the Depression. We'd play at places and nobody would come in because people were too poor. They didn't have money. Sometimes when we were in Kansas City, we had a place we'd play for food, fried chicken or frogs' legs. One time everybody got so hungry, a professional baseball team came to town, I think it was in Greeley, and we booked ourselves with the team, playing night ball, and the guys were falling out. I was carrying water for them. It was really funny. They thought they could make some money like that, you know.

They were wonderful guys and they stuck together more or less. There was an awful lot of love there, and protection of one another. We kept going. We stayed together. But I've been on the road. . . . There were towns down South that we couldn't stay in. They lynched an eighteen-year-old kid in Arkansas somewhere, and we had to move on. We were in New Orleans and the place was jammed and packed and the police shot their pistols up in the air and made the people go home, 'cause they were having a ball. But it *was* fun.

Finally the Andy Kirk band began to hit because they began to record, for Jack Kapp, on Decca. He'd heard about the band and sent for them to come to Chicago to record. He'd heard me sit in and when the band got to Chicago, he said, "Well, where's the girl with the band?" Andy said, "She doesn't play regular. She's in Kansas City." He said, "Well, send for her." So they sent for me. They put me on the train and I went to Chicago, and I recorded with them.

My first record under my own name was "Nite Life" in 1929. Jack Kapp asked to hear me play. I usually compose something new when I play in situations like that and I didn't know they were recording me. They put out "Nite Life" on Brunswick with "Drag 'Em" on the other side.

I didn't join the band then, but we began to record and I recorded with the band. Later on when we went to a theater in Philadelphia called the Pearl Theater, I played for Ethel Waters. Ethel Waters's regular pianist was Pearl Wright, who had to go home because I believe her mother had died. So Ethel asked me to play for her during her engagement at the Pearl Theater. Things like, "Eili Eili" and "Am I Blue?" Ethel said to me, "Sing it out, baby." I timidly replied in a small voice "I can't sing." Ethel just screamed—she meant for me to make the piano sing out and match her own energy. She was a great and brilliant woman. I also played for Bill Bailey. Bill was Pearl Bailey's brother and a great tap dancer who taught me how to tap-dance, and Pearl at that time was a chorus girl in the show. Moms Mabley, she was on the scene then, too.

We were there I don't know how long, six months or a year. We were stationed there and the band played for many of the acts. Then what happened: they had a little upright piano for me, and for the other pianist they had a Steinway. I guess he got sick of me sitting there too, so one day he didn't come in. I jumped over to the Steinway and played and so Mr. Stieffel, who owned the theater, happened to be there. He said, "You don't need that man. You keep her." And that's how I got the job with the band. Otherwise they'd still've been using me as a sit-in.

After I joined Andy Kirk's Band, I had ideas for arrangements but I couldn't write them down. Andy Kirk used to come to the house at eleven in the morning and write until midnight. So what I did, he came back one day and I'd written an arrangement by just watching him and asking questions and the only thing that was out of range was the trombone and the tenor. He showed me what to do about that and I began writing music. He taught me my chords in fifteen minutes. I had fabulous ideas and he'd sit there with me all night.

Jack Kapp recorded us then and we came to New York. By that time I was writing music. I'd leave the recording studio and I'd sit in the hotel in New York down at 118th Street, and the boys would bring me food, and I wrote twenty hits in one week, but I didn't know they were going to be hits. I'd just sit there and write music. We'd record it the next day. That's the way I am. Like I was sitting here last night with a girl and something came to me and I wrote it on a piece of music paper so I could finish it off later after she left. If she hadn't been there, I would have finished it off right then and there.

Whenever I play nightly I compose, but playing, you also have to play something that people know. I've been playing "Caravan" for thirty years and I can change it, I can switch it, but I have to have a bass player with me who can hear. Sometimes if I'm playing with a really good bass player, often he'll play a really good deep note, and that'll inspire me to compose or create. I work as a team with everybody, and I work as a team with the bass player. If he's no good, I know I'm on the spot. There won't be too much creativity or anything happening, I'll just be playing and the mind will stop. But if he's playing well, he'll open you up and you can do things like Stravinsky and everybody in jazz. That's the reason why it's so interesting.

My last record I recorded for Norman Granz. He wouldn't allow anybody to play with me. "I don't want a bass player to mess her up," he

said. "Let her create." So practically everything I did on the record was
something new, or if I played anything old, it was done differently. I
create while I play.

I would never play anything but jazz because it's so inspiring to play.
It gives you a lift inside. If you've had a very bad day, put your hands on
your instrument and play—it's all gone. You're ready for something new
to happen and you feel like working again.

I've had doubts. If you had doubts in jazz, you'd say, "I'm going down
to Birdland and listen to Dizzy," and you'd come home hyped up again
and there you'd go writing. You're never failing in anything you're doing,
because there's somebody out there to hype you up again, to stimulate
you. Most of the musicians like Bud Powell and Thelonius Monk would
come up here every day and write their music. Benny Goodman and
Dizzy have been here, and all the original boppers, they used to come
here every day, and Erroll Garner. They said I inspired them. We became
friends. Art Tatum, I used to hang out with him every night in Cleveland,
and I'd say, "Ooh, show me how you do that," and he'd say, "Watch."
That's what you have to do, listen and watch. I was trained right. I've
been around the greatest musicians all my life. They taught me everything
I know.

There have been four great eras of jazz—spirituals, ragtime, Kansas
City swing and bop. And the blues have been there all along. I was there
at the beginning of each era. How that happened, if someone wanted me
to play ragtime, he showed me how to play it. And when I moved to
Kansas City, oh, that was a fabulous era, the musicians showed me how
to play that, and the bop era; I'm the only living musician, I hate to say
that, who's played through all the eras. Other musicians never changed,
they kept the same style until they died. But I was thrown into it through
playing with various groups that would come and get me to play with
them, see, and I'd have to learn their style. It was kind of forced on me.

What I teach from is a diagram I drew called the Tree of Jazz. Jazz
came out of the first early suffering of the black slaves. It has nothing to
do with New Orleans or Africa. It was born out of the experience of what
happened here in America. The slaves were taken to church and were
taught the spirituals and they began to write their own spirituals. They
used this same music but put different lyrics to it for their parties and
what not.

The strange thing is, blacks at one time thought jazz was the devil's
music. But in fact, if you go to a Baptist church, or any of those churches,
they dance when the spirit hits them, and it was all right as long as the
slaves were dancing in front of the church, but when they gave parties
and danced on the outside, it was called the devil's music. Isn't that
strange? God gives you a talent and people try to block it by saying that
what you're playing isn't acceptable, that you're bad and the music is bad.
That's a stupid thing about the world. All through my career I was

fighting that separation between spirituals and blues or jazz; it's all spiritual music, every bit of it, all of it.

The next era we move onto is the blues. That's your spiritual feeling and healing. It grew out of the roots of the spiritual. Now the blues was also connected with the suffering. Slaves, when they were depressed, they'd sing whatever was happening to them. It was good therapy.

The twenties era was very short. During the twenties, the musicians were active, more or less like the rockers today, but it was still jazz. Somebody with us, probably the trombone player, would play the trombone with his foot instead of his hand. I've never seen anybody do that since, nor have I heard of anybody that could do it, who could really play. You see when they clowned during that period they were still playing good notes. They were playing something—good music.

Then jazz moved into Kansas City. Kansas City was very prejudiced. We had to ride on the back of the streetcars and buses when I first went there to live in the twenties and thirties. They didn't allow blacks into nightclubs there to even play. That didn't bother me at all because I'm writing my music and everything and I'm not thinking about people being prejudiced. When I decided to go someplace, I got there. Ben Pollack's band came to town and please forgive me, I'm living there in a black neighborhood, and Jack Teagarden and all those white musicians—Benny Goodman, Tommy and Jimmy Dorsey—came out and got me and took me downtown to a nightclub. The owner said, "You can't bring her in here." The band said, "We won't be back." The club opened the doors and let me in. See how I got in? Doing my work.

I've always gotten ahead by experimenting. Even when I was a little girl, I'm telling you, I was really trouble for my mother. She said I was a nervous kid. The reason why she held me on her lap at the organ was both to keep me out of trouble and because I had to see things for myself. I wouldn't ask questions. I'd take a clock or something apart and put it back together again; I wanted to see how it worked. Even when I was in grade school. In history class we read about anthracite coal and I didn't believe a word about it until I played the same city in Pennsylvania where they actually mined the coal. I had to go there and see it for myself.

So in the thirties when there was three-part harmony, I'd play an extra note on the piano, like the sixth of the chord. Musicians like Guy Lombardo, during that era, would play a major chord, but I'd add a note. Andy Kirk said to me, "Mary, you can't use that note, that's against the rules." "Rules?" I said. "That's what I hear." That came about through experimenting. I'd get a sound and say, "Gee, that sounds good." I wrote "Walkin' and Swingin'" in four-part harmony. We only had three saxophones so I gave the fourth note to a trumpet in a hat, and all the musicians wanted to play that arrangement because musically it was different for that time.

If I passed out an arrangement to the band that was wrong, the guys would laugh. I played an introduction to a song once and my husband said, "Don't do that again, Mary, that's terrible." And I said, "I'm going to do it," and boom! he knocked me off the piano stool and on the floor I went. I would cry, but I'd go back and do it over. They'd give me a chance. Musicians like something different when they're playing the same tunes every night, and they knew that I was going to feed 'em something different.

Sometimes there was a mistake and I'd say, "Oh my goodness, I got sleepy and I copied the wrong parts." So once Duke Ellington said, "Let's try it the way it is." And it would work out. It didn't matter what I wrote, he said, "Mary, you're a genius," and he'd hype me up to write something else. He knew how to do it, you know. He talked me into it. He'd play anything that I gave him while I was traveling with them. For years and years afterward, he played "Trumpet No End" which I wrote for the Ellington band.

Everything I write comes from the head, the mind. The piano would slow me up. I discovered that instruments are limited. You get some avant-garde guys who put pins in the piano, or clothespins, to get those weird sounds and harmonies. But the instrument, as far as sounds, is limited, so you have to work with that limitation. Yet I was rehearsing a band and I told the alto player to play a high G. He looked at me as though I didn't know what I was talking about. He said, "Why would you tell me a note that isn't on this instrument?" I said, "I've heard it. I've heard Coltrane and Charlie Parker play it." The alto player next to him showed him how to do it. It's kind of a freak fingering. Sometimes when a piano is out of tune, if I feel like fooling with it, I can work, play it in tune with my fingers. Things like that. That's what jazz is.

In the thirties we never used music stands on the stage. We memorized everything. To us, it didn't look good for musicians to be reading from a stand, not unless it was a show and they had to learn it in a day. But in a day or two, they'd memorize it. Music flows from music that has been memorized. It frees a musician to play whatever comes to his mind, because it comes from the mind, heart, fingertips, as fast as lightning.

I don't have anyone to contradict me or not allow me to do what I want to do. I could be out now doing something to inspire myself to write again or play better. It inspires me to help the poor. It inspires me to run away from everybody and come back fresh again. Those two things are important. If you hold me you can drown me. I've been a loner all my life, even with the band. I'd leave the band and drive down to the river. I like flowers and water and things like that. Like if anybody wanted to trick me or get me going on something that they wanted me to do, they'd send me flowers. A guy did that down in Durham and really did get me in trouble. I was listening to his story, you know, and forgetting my own. So I have to watch that.

But my inspiration comes from helping someone who really needs help, not a phony, 'cause I usually discover it before I get too far into it.

The world's full of that. Someone who really needs it will just inspire me to write and play madly, if I think I've done good. I always worked with somebody that was *bad*. Say, for instance, if you were drinking too much, you were a drug addict or something, I always thought that I could help you, and maybe I did. I don't know. I got a lot of good results. You have to give 'em a lot of talk. There were some musicians I knew. When one of them needed his injection, I said, "Wait a minute. Look at this thing I wrote." And he'd just sit back down at the drums and it would go away. He'd be perspiring and doing everything and I'd be using this music. I played with him awhile and thought, "Well, I'll see what happens. I'll go fix something to eat." And he said, "Well, Mary, I think I've got to go down and . . ." I said, "Wait a minute, I just thought of something else!" You know? That's what I did, I kept him on his drums. I'd do that all day from eight o'clock in the morning until eleven or twelve at night. Then another one would come in and they'd meet, then I'd have something on my hands, but I'd deal with it.

At one point I had to stop helping people because the musicians were coming up here, they were writing and I wasn't. I was feeding them, you know and I wasn't doing anything. That can happen, you have to be very careful of it. That was during the forties. They couldn't get started, so I said to my brother, I said, "I'm going to have to help these musicians out. I'm going to start a bop era." He said, "How are you going to do that?" I said, "You just wait and see, I'm going to do it, the Dizzy Gillespie era. I'm going to help them because they should be working."

So I thought of this: During that period, publishers always got me to record a tune. I was very popular in New York then. If I recorded something, the musicians would follow me, and once, twice, the musicians paid me to record something of theirs. And so I struck upon this idea. I said, "If I go around to all the record companies and ask them to record Dizzy or Bud Powell or somebody like that, it won't happen." So I just went to this company and recorded "modern music." It was a little different because it was some of the bop harmonies that I had learned from the guys. I said, "That's called modern music. Put it on the record sleeve." I had them play it on the radio. After that you should have seen the companies that recorded bop. The guys got big breaks then, and everybody started going modern. I wrote the first bop tune with a lyric, "In the Land of Oo-Bla-Dee."

I stopped playing music in 1954. I just stopped. One thing, I was in England too long. During that period I was used to moving on to concerts and things, and I accepted an eleven-day engagement. I didn't want to be there so long. I went there to break a ban of thirty years between two unions. English musicians were not allowed to enter America to play gigs and vice versa with Americans. The unions had this thing going on and they sent me over to break this ban by playing with all the English musicians. The queen's cousin gave a party for me and some musicians. There was a little black GI there, and I had two Scotches and I was acting so funny. He said, "You're nervous. My grandmother said to always read the ninety-first Psalm." I was so drunk off those two drinks I went home and I stayed up all night and read *all* the Psalms.

Something happened to me then and I got into praying and praying. After London, I went to Paris and I was working on two jobs, in the theater and a nightclub. I was making more money than I'd ever made in my life, and all of a sudden I walked off and left my salary. A little French boy who liked me there, he went back and got my money from the club, and he took me out to his grandmother's house and all I did was sit there and pray. Then when I got ready to come back home, they wanted me to go on the Sarah Vaughan tour. I toured with her all over Europe and then came back to America. After that, I wouldn't play anymore.

That's how I became Catholic. I used to sit in the Catholic church and pray because it's very quiet and you can meditate there and it's open all day. What got me was the serenity that I felt in this church around the corner from my house, Our Lady of Lourdes. I could have become a fanatic. Then the priests came on. You see, really truthfully speaking, those that know about music are concerned about this music. They know what I spiritually know about it. This is a heavy one because it came out of suffering. You see this makes it a true art. It's a true art because a race of people was involved, you see, and they know this. When I asked Cardinal Cooke if I could do a jazz concert in St. Patrick's, you know what he said? "That's what we need."

Before I went into this religious phase I was aware of something special about this music . . . for instance, I was in California playing and this woman ran in. She had known me from the Andy Kirk days. She was an elderly woman, she was very, very sick, and she made them bring her to the club to hear me play. When I was finished, I was talking to the bass player and she ran back to where I was and said, "Look, I'm completely healed. Here, look at me, I've been sick for a year." I looked at my bass player and said, "She's healed because she sat and listened to the music and got all her worries off her mind." So I got rid of her as fast as I could because if it was known there were certain people that were healed when I played, you know like these quacks, immediately they think you're greater than God. Just leave it alone. I've used it with Dizzy and somebody I know like that, but not publicly. But people have been healed when there's good jazz, just listening to the music.

The whole world would have dropped jazz if this priest, Father Peter O'Brien, hadn't brought me out and protected me from becoming a fanatic. He was in California. I was in retirement again, 'cause I had given it up. The music that I heard was so disgusting. Everything is false now in music. You don't get any good musicianship. Musicians are playing maybe one chord for six to four bars. They don't move at all. They scream and make a lot of noise.

Commercial musicians of today stopped the growth of jazz. You wonder why I said that? Because if a guy playing in the era after bop is going to create a new sound for you, a new word, and he listens to what's happening on records, and radio, TV, that stops his creativeness. Jazz stopped. I know many young musicians think they've found something new and they haven't. They're good musicians, but the sounds and things they're playing are nowhere, nowhere. They've been played before. The new era hasn't come along.

I'm so happy that Frank Tirro came up here to New York to book me down to Duke University. He called me from the airport, this man that I didn't know, and he said to me, "May I have an appointment to see you?" I says, "Yes." He came up to the house and he was sitting there and said, "We want you at Duke." I said, "Duke what?" "Duke University," he said, "to teach." I said, "I don't think I should be teaching." "To save jazz," says Frank. I owe Frank Tirro something, many thanks, for taking me down to Duke because it's opened me up as to the truth of the music. See, jazz will never die. I must tell you that because it's God's music.

# Lillian Hellman

Lillian Hellman (born 1905, New Orleans, Louisiana) is a writer and playwright who has been a literary force in this country for the past fifty years. Her plays The Children's Hour, produced in 1934, The Little Foxes (1939), Watch on the Rhine (1941) and Toys in the Attic (1959) established her as the first woman to become a major American playwright. With The Dark Angel, a screenplay written in 1935, she became one of the first major women screenwriters in Hollywood. Her memoirs were published in 1969 under the title An Unfinished Woman, followed by Pentimento in 1973, Scoundrel Time in 1976 and Maybe: A Story in 1980.

# Agnes de Mille

*Agnes de Mille (born New York City) is a dancer, choreographer, director and writer whose skill as a storyteller has enriched dance and contributed to its growth in this country as a respected and popular art form. In 1942, she developed a style of dance singularly her own in the ballet* Rodeo *and became one of the first Americans to contribute to the standard repertoire of classical ballet. Her choreography for Rodgers and Hammerstein's* Oklahoma! *in 1943, followed by* Carousel *in 1945 and* Brigadoon *in 1947, made dance an integral part of the plot and ushered musical theater into its golden age. She was instrumental in the passage of legislation to improve working conditions for dancers. She is the author of ten books that are considered among the finest body of literature on dance. Among them are* Dance to the Piper *(1952),* To a Young Dancer *(1962),* The Book of the Dance *(1963) and* Speak to Me, Dance with Me *(1973).*

**W**HAT I WANT TO SAY is this, I've never had any theories. I don't have any favorite kind of dancing, I don't have any favorite subject, anything like that. As Martha Graham says, and has said often, there are two kinds of dancing: good and bad. And I subscribe to that. A good work of art is a good work of art and I don't care if it's made out of jackstraws, marble or gesso. And what makes a good work of art is a very subtle subject. I'm not going into that now, that's aesthetics. But I hate vagueness, I hate flummery. I think there is a very great deal of it and imagine there always has been. People get away with murder if they possibly can. Not artists, they don't want to.

The difference between an artist and a nonartist, I think, is that the artist will not settle for anything less than the truth as far as he can sense it, or feel it, or perceive it, whatever the medium. He doesn't *know* what the truth is ever—he senses it. He has to feel toward it. If he knew what it was, he'd say it. Or somebody else would have said it. Now, art always has an element of personality, of involvement, of passion, of sincerity, and the individual gives into it and gets out of it the best that he can.

What I wanted to do was to feel toward my statement, and my statement would have to be what moves me, and what intrigues me.

I think it is a miracle that I turned into anything of worth because I had an amateur background. It was Edwardian. I was the petted daughter in a fairly wealthy household, in which being a lady was *the* thing. It was like being a knight, a Southern gentleman, or like an officer in the American army used to be. My father thought my wanting to dance was an aberration, just like little boys wanting to be firemen. He always wanted me to write. Several of my teachers wanted me to write, but I felt

deeply, and I can't explain this, but I felt I could only write when I had a
child and a husband.

Ballet dancing excited me. I had seen Anna Pavlova. In ballet
technique in the case of women it is the *pointe* work and the leg. In the
case of the men, it's elevation, being able to jump the way they do. They
are superb athletes. I was only allowed to dance one hour a day. I pined
and wept and carried on, but I never disobeyed. I cheated. "Well now,"
I'd say, "I've thought about something else for five minutes, so I'll put
another five minutes on the end." I think it would have been smarter of
Father to let me be a dancer, a good dancer.

Even though I had so little opportunity to dance in the early years, I
had a sense of drama. My father was a playwright, which affected me
enormously. From him I learned story continuity and dramatic tension. I
read the books he wanted me to: complete Balzac, complete Victor Hugo,
complete Dickens. He got me to read books with a very strong story line.
He didn't read Henry James; I was out of college before I read Henry
James. My father was a brilliant man. To hear him talk about literature or
theater was a treat. He had total influence in training my mind.

My life with my parents was very happy. I was repressed as a dancer,
but my God, we had the most marvelous time as children. My adolescence
was a ball. It was later that I suffered.

I was interested in school and I was absolutely fascinated by college. I
went to UCLA and had marvelous teachers. It was the most stimulating
intellectual challenge I had ever met in my life. I used to get absolutely
intoxicated when I saw the names of the courses. I always signed up for
more than I could possibly take.

I was in love with all of my professors but I fell deeply in love with
two of them. One was a man and that was rather serious. My mother was
so worried about it that she enrolled in one of my courses. She could do
that because it was a state college. She took the course with me and kept
an eye on me. I didn't deal very well with my mother keeping tabs on me.
I was smothered. She didn't allow me to go away to college. I wasn't
allowed to read the newspaper until I was a sophomore in college
because so many of our acquaintances were getting murdered; William
Desmond Taylor, the Fatty Arbuckle scandal all over the front pages. She
thought it was pretty disgusting and she didn't want me to read about it.

I was nineteen when I graduated from college. I handed father a cum
laude and I thought that would make him happy. Mother told me the next
day that she was going to leave him. I went into shock, so did my sister.
We had not been brought up to know about people who got divorced or
were disaster cases. It happened, God knows, but we didn't talk about it.

God gave me the drive to overcome the power of my mother. It took
years to break loose. My sister escaped by running off and getting married
when she was twenty, but I was older by a couple of years. I finally fell in
love with a boy that she disapproved of. She disapproved of every boy
that she felt was paying attention to me. She didn't mind my pining but
she didn't like my being the recipient of amour. She put her whole life
against this one. I nearly died of it. In the course of it I moved out of her

house. I took a flat in New York City. You could in those days. I first went to the Ansonia Hotel, which in those days was really disreputable. It was shocking because things went on that couldn't be explained. I got a suite for twenty dollars a week. Can you believe that? It had no sunlight. It was simply hideous, with dark-red plush furniture and very dirty, but it was mine and I used to go in there after a day's rehearsal and shut the door and think, "This is mine, mine, and nobody is going to ask me a question." I just fell on the bed and was grateful.

It was very rough going out into the world. It needn't have happened that badly if I had had any professionalism. I should have made demands of myself I didn't make. I would present work that wasn't ready, that wasn't thought through. My work wasn't good enough, my technique wasn't sound enough, my hair would fall down, my stockings were wrinkled. It just wasn't professional. It wasn't even neat. I didn't have a classic body. I had a long torso and shortish legs. They are pretty legs, but very short. What I did have was a real acting ability and inventive, creative thought. I couldn't fit into the mold so I made my own, that's all.

At that time, the commercial theater was geared to a totally different kind of entertainment and show. They didn't have many dance concerts. Isadora Duncan had left, cursing America. She was in Europe. Ruth St. Denis had her own company with Ted Shawn and they were in a world of their own. They had to make their own theater, their own school, their own everything. I felt they were not quite first-class. Now when I see all the pictures of her, I respect her more than I did then, and him less. But it was to me not interesting, or exciting like the Russian ballet. I had seen the Diaghilev, you see.

There basically was no ballet around except at movie houses. They did prologues to the big moving pictures and that was pretty commercial work. "Roxy" Rotherfel gave me a chance to do something and it was immediately a hit. Then I did another one because the ballet master was on vacation in Europe. But when he got back and found that a new girl had made a hit and Rotherfel told him I wanted to do some more, he just kept delaying and saying "Next month, next month," and it never transpired.

That was probably why I didn't get ahead. I had to do certain kinds of dances because nothing else was accepted. My point of view was not accepted because they hadn't seen it and they didn't want it. They wanted someone who could tap, or sing a song quite prettily; they just wanted nice little soubrette stars. Well, I'm a sticker. I very seldom say "The hell with it." What made it worthwhile was when I stepped in front of an audience and heard their laughter. I did studies of ballet girls fainting and getting exhausted and there were screams of laughter. I didn't know I was a comedienne. I thought I was a serious dancer. My mother used to say, "Oh Agnes, this is so sad, this is tragic, I can't look."

Dancing didn't give me any freedom because Mother moved right in with me in New York. She supervised all my costumes. I designed them, but she saw that they got made. She tried supervising my music, even though she didn't know a thing about music. That made me pretty mad.

She wanted to be present at every one of my business interviews. I couldn't have any kind of a business talk without Mother being right there. It was a hassle. Other people didn't like it. She was like all those theatrical mothers except she wasn't smart, not that way. My mother delayed me because I was kept always smothered up in a comforter with adulation, being cherished and petted and pitied.

I was starving when I signed up to do the choreography for Richard Rodgers's *Oklahoma!* in 1943. The Theatre Guild said, "Sign this, fifteen hundred dollars, no royalties, or don't sign it." The producer, Lawrence Langner, had seen many of my concerts but he also knew I had to have work, so he squeezed me. They all do. I think it is disgraceful.

When *Oklahoma!* opened I went out west to get engaged to a soldier, Walter Prude, the man I married. When I came back two weeks later I was having lunch with a reporter from the *New York Times* and he said, "Miss de Mille, I don't think you know what kind of success *Oklahoma!* is." I said, "No, I've never had a success before, so what kind is it?" He said, "The biggest success of the twentieth century," and I said, "Oh!" Well, that made me think a little and then I went back to Lawrence Langner, who was one of the heads of the Theatre Guild, and I said, "Lawrence I understand you're doing very well, and are paying off all your debts, so I'm going to ask you to give me a raise." After the opening in Boston, Richard Rodgers had arranged for me to get fifty dollars a week. Now you could have lived off that in New York City at that time; it was hard but you could, but you couldn't pay off debts.

I said, "I have ten years of debts and I married a soldier, a second lieutenant, and he has no money and he's in the army for the duration, and I'd like to have a little bit more because I'd like to save for his return. Also, Oscar Hammerstein tells me I mustn't take just any job, but I must choose very carefully now. So this would make it possible. Would you make it seventy-five dollars a week instead of fifty?" Lawrence said, "No, I can't do that because I couldn't face the backers." They made more money at that time than had ever been made in the theater. They bought a building on West Fifty-third Street that was later acquired by the Museum of Modern Art. It had a big marble staircase, and they used to give enormous parties there. They were trying to spend their money so they didn't have to pay such gigantic income taxes. They knew how to spend it, but they wouldn't pay their workers more.

People in the theater take advantage of everybody they can. Now for the first time in thirty-seven years I'm getting royalties on *Oklahoma!* for the revival on Broadway. Recognition is coming in a way now. It's extraordinary. In fact, my name's up in lights on Broadway and people want me for all sorts of things. They are going to do a lot more revivals than *Oklahoma!* I did eighteen shows on Broadway and about ten or twelve of those are bang-up ones.

I didn't set out to try to change the world of dance. I had to do it because nobody cared a damn about dancing and I got fed up with people's ignorance and indifference; particularly the American men scorned it. Well, my father did, so the pattern was set.

What moves me to do what I can do is that I am essentially a storyteller. I've tried everything in dancing . . . I've done classical work, I've done romantic, pantomime, abstract, I've done everything. What I'm good at, what is easy for me, what is my natural language, my idiom of speech, is to make a point telling a story. Now that doesn't mean that the stage can't be universal. Charlie Chaplin was a universal. But he was very particular, and very detailed. I think he is a good example of what I'm talking about. So is Mark Twain. Their stories are about special people and special circumstances, but they are immortal and we have taken them as symbols. They make us laugh today as they made us laugh in the beginning.

I have a knack for musical comedy theater. I have a very good sense of where a song will lend itself to a dance. In *Oklahoma!* there is a song "Many a New Day" and the dance is just girls having fun, and girls being bitchy, or being cute and twirling around in front of the mirror. It had nothing really to do with the song, except for the mood. Oscar Hammerstein loved the dance. He was astonished and said, "I had no idea anyone could do something like this to that song." I tried to do a dance that complements the song, not illustrates it, because if the song is any good, it's enough. The dance is an addition. The knack is to fit in the dance so it doesn't come as an unwelcome interruption, which it can be.

In the musical comedy theater there are so many elements: the book, lyrics, spectacle, and they all have to be jostled into place and arranged. They are all fighting for air, for time, for stage space, for attention. Sometimes you have to adapt your work, remodel it, so that it is unrecognizable. It has to be done on the minute. That's when you have to be a hack. Sometimes it turns out pretty well, but it's like plumbing, it's like being a carpenter; you'd better be good.

The great dances were done quietly by myself in the first two weeks of a show when the pressure was not on. My regular work was done by getting veterans and paying them myself. They came into the studio and let me try things out on them. I could only work a couple of hours a day at most with them and then I'd think and think and work by myself, then go back the next day with some more ideas. That would go on for two weeks.

Now that was against union ruling. It was called prerehearsal choreography. You weren't supposed to try anything out or prepare anything before the regular choreography started because the kids would then be due union wages. It is a burden and expense the management will not take. You can only work with them for five weeks and then they go on performance salary. I didn't pay them what the union requires. I paid them a very decent wage for two hours of their bodies, but not a performing salary. I have been up in front of the Board of Censors seven times for this.

These restrictions destroy the quality of the work. Nobody can work under these circumstances in the theater, and nobody does. Everybody cheats. Michael Bennett did a very revolutionary thing in *Chorus Line* by putting the dancers on salary. It was low but I think it was for six months. Then he gave them a share of the show. They're very rich now. He did the same thing in *Ballroom.* That was not a success so they're not rich; they lost. That's a pity. They took the chance and the union said O.K. That's an innovative thing. Even though this helps the quality of dance, the union doesn't care about quality. All unions are backward. Jerome Robbins and I kept saying, if you have better dancing, then you have more dancing and therefore you have more jobs.

I think there are more good men choreographers than women now, but the great creative figures, the revolutionary figures, have been women. That's true in every country and that's extraordinary. I don't really know, but I think one of the reasons is that men haven't really respected dance as an art. If men have that kind of creative brain, they go into science.

I never had a young married life. My husband went into the army right away. While he was in the army I was in England. I came back six months pregnant and he was in the hospital, with gallstones.

My son was a sick child. He was born with an impaired intestine and he was mortally ill. By the grace of God, a surgeon invented an operation that saved his life. His was the twenty-third operation of its kind in medical history. The first four and a half years of his life we didn't have a nursery, we had a clinic. It was terrible. I had a trained nurse living with us. He was more sick than well, fragile and very small. When he was four years old he weighed only twenty pounds. He lost two or three years' growth, so his pictures in school show gangling ten-year-olds, and then little Prude down there. And of course it was very hard for him because he couldn't play with the boys, couldn't hold his own in their rough games. He couldn't really hold his own with the girls either. He always got the fat girls.

It was difficult. I spent a lot of time in children's hospitals and I spent a great deal of time just plain nursing in the nursery. I would be up all night, spelling the trained nurse, take the night watch, and then go in for an all-day rehearsal. Every contract I had was written with the clause "if the baby's health permits." Sometimes I lost out, but I was so powerful in those days that people just used to wait for me.

When I couldn't dance anymore, I started writing. I had a husband and child and that was the time to do it. The writing wasn't easy, but it was private, so I could make all my mistakes without public mockery. I've had a great deal of pleasure out of writing. I don't give myself deadlines. Every contract I've signed with the publishers has been with the understanding that I could set my own pace. I would get it done when I could. I never sit steaming over a typewriter because I don't type, but I don't steam over a pen or a pencil either. I let it simmer, accumulate, and then when I'm feeling ready, I take a pencil and a piece of paper. I used to do it in restaurants, just take a piece of paper out and write like mad for half an hour, forty minutes. Then I'd have something I could chew on and correct, edit and fix in place. That's the way all my nine books were done.

I had a stroke in 1975 which left my right side paralyzed. My illness has enriched my life, in a peculiar way, very much. In a strange, dreadful way, it has. It's awful that it takes this, but it did. My husband and I have both reached another plateau. Our relationship is quite different. I was always working. I had spent so much time with the child and the child was so ill, and my husband was so distressed by a sick child. I just realized that he loves me very much because he does. He brings my dinner to me every night. The maid cooks it but he serves it to me at my bedside. I can't take a bath without somebody helping me. If she isn't here, he is. He does things he wouldn't ordinarily have to do for anybody, let alone a woman. If he takes me walking I have to be on his arm, because the pavements of New York are as uneven as a rocky mountain path, and as hazardous. I can't feel, you see. I have no feeling in the right side of my body. If I put a foot out and it strikes something, I don't know what it's struck. You don't realize that your body is getting radar signals all the time. Now when I walk down the street, my head is low because I have to see the pavement, I have to see where I'm going. So I take his arm and that makes me steady. He cares, period. In the hospital, it was very surprising, revelatory, it was remarkable, he didn't know he felt so deeply. He didn't know he could give this kind of loving dedication to another human being. It had never been demanded of him.

I'm quietly contented now. It's happiness that I didn't know before. My last book, *Where the Wings Grow,* has a different mood than my other books because I wrote it in the hospital with my left hand. The pages would fall on the floor and I had to leave them there. I was dying and remembering the happy days. I had to be beaten to dust in order to find out what I wanted from life. I know a little now. I had been hectic and didn't feel I had done what I wanted to do, I didn't feel I had been represented in what I wanted to be represented in. Well, I was dying and I realized I had done the very best I could. If I couldn't do better, I wasn't designed to do better and I wasn't worthy to do better.

I don't feel worthy of having done first-class dances. Martha Graham has real creativity. Real creativity is very rare. There are very few people in the world who are truly creative. I wanted to be one of them. I had to examine why. That's the new book. I'm still thinking that one through. It's vanity, of course. I'm a manipulator. I think Beethoven is a real creator, I think Aaron Copland is a manipulator. He takes what has been done before, rearranges it and is like a first-class goldsmith. I'm a goldsmith first class.

I haven't done but one choreographic work since I've been ill. What I've lost is the energy. It takes great passion and great energy to do anything creative, especially in the theater. You have to care so much that you can't sleep, you can't eat, you can't talk to people. It's just got to be right. You can't do it without that passion.

# Margaret Mead

Margaret Mead (born Philadelphia, Pennsylvania, 1901, died 1978) was an anthropologist whose innovative research methods helped cultural anthropology come of age as a science. She played a major role in expanding the anthropological data base by drawing on the findings of other scientific disciplines, particularly psychology and its techniques, to broaden our understanding of individual and social life in our own and other cultures. Through her field work with seven preliterate peoples she contributed to new thinking about ways in which people cope with change as individuals and as societies. She published hundreds of articles and twenty-three books, many of which have become classics, including Coming of Age in Samoa (1928), Sex and Temperament in Three Primitive Societies (1935) and Male and Female (1949). She held the post of curator at the American Museum of Natural History for more than fifty years and was an adjunct professor of anthropology at Columbia University.

# Margaret Kuhn

*Margaret Kuhn (born 1905, Buffalo, New York) founded the Gray Panthers in 1970, a national political organization with 150 affiliates, based on her philosophy that young and old should work together in the continuing struggle for human liberation to eradicate discrimination against the elderly. She advocates a public policy that promotes a positive attitude toward aging and a need for fundamental social change to provide such services as part-time employment after retirement, more humane health care and shared intergenerational housing.*

WHEN I WAS FORCED to retire from my job with the Presbyterian Church at the age of sixty-five, I was given notice that I was going to be terminated on my birthday. It was a shock because my birthday was in August and I expected to stay on until the end of that year, 1970, which was the policy. I had been commuting from Philadelphia to New York. My mother was still living and my brother was still living. I took care of them. They were my responsibility. My father had died three or four years earlier. He left what he thought was enough to take care of them, a secure future, but it turned out not to be the case. His long illness and my mother's illness and my brother who was never a well person—he was in and out of mental hospitals, lots of problems—made me recognize how expensive sickness was. So I was glad I had a good job, very glad that I was able to swing it. I needed to work.

Just before I retired my mother died. My brother was still living with me here. The prospect of coming home, living and ending my life just here, depressed me beyond description. I knew I wasn't going to have it. What I was going to do in my old age was not clear but I knew that I didn't want to just vegetate and I knew I would if I stayed at home. My brother was very demanding, very self-centered, very emotionally tied to me. I couldn't face going down. Many people do, many people do.

So after they gave me notice, six of us got together. We were all thinking about what we were going to do with the rest of our lives. We were all women and all of us had been friends and loved each other and we were being separated when we were retiring. One was going to Cleveland, two of us were coming here to Philadelphia. We got together and we said, "There's work that we must do, what is it?" So we decided we were all going to use our efforts to end the war in Vietnam. We sent a message to the retired people that we knew among us, which was a large number, and we built our whole Gray Panther movement on the network principle, on people we knew.

Our first intention was not to become bogged down in what I call old folks issues, or the special interests of old people—never. You have to have transcendent issues in the country. And so this has been our stance.

**103**

We're not a gray power lobby. It's very hard for people to understand
that. We're intergenerational and we have centered on issues that affect
people of all ages. Our analysis is very radical: racism, sexism, ageism and
economic imperialism are all of a piece. They're all oppressive, they're all
alienating and they all have to be stopped, eradicated, and there has to be
a grand strategy, a convergence. We're looking for a convergence, where it
all comes together. We found it a couple of years ago on university
campuses over the investment of university funds in South Africa. You
find it in the environmental issues today. I've been deeply committed to
the ending of nuclear power. Gray Panthers have marched in all the
demonstrations and made major speeches. I've been the only old person
who has spoken out. I say this is essential. I'm concerned about the
future. As long as we have those power plants, as long as we have nuclear
weaponry and an endangered environment, there is no future.

Most groups only focus on one issue. This is one of the reasons why
the Gray Panthers is focusing on coalitions. It's unique. We've drawn
from the Black Panthers; some of that has its place, but it is pretty
separatist: "Black is beautiful, black is separate, whitey get off our backs."
What we've taken from them is the political base and the philosophy that
social change must be systemic and societal. It can't affect just one small
segment. There has to be a radical critique of the whole society. It is
definitely based on a class analysis, and nowhere do you see it more
clearly indicated than in the issue of age. It depends on one's social class
as to how one approaches age. The rich are never deemed old, never.
They still retain their power, they still have income, they still can do what
they want to do. They're not neglected by their families.

There's a difference between men and women in old age too. Men are
not the survivors, women are the survivors and we don't know why
precisely. There are different opinions about that. It's probably genetic,
hormonal to some degree, and partly because women in a sense have
been protected from some of the terrible jobs and the stresses of those
jobs that have sickened men and caused their early death—in steel and
coal, in certain manufacturing, chemicals, deadly stuff. We're just
beginning to catch up with that, the hazards of the workplace.

Social change is continuous. Change is occurring in small ways, some
forward, some backward. Our Gray Panther model of change is to
develop small models that show the future, that test the future. One
example is intergenerational housing. It's not yet codified anywhere. In
fact, it's illegal in lots of places. There's no public money for it. Our
Housing Task Force has made a very substantial study out in the Bay
Area in California and we're about to introduce some legislation in the
State of California and in the Congress that will begin to raise the
question of age-segregated housing. We're going to have a Presbyterian
Church meeting here at the house where we're going to talk about the
church's policy with regard to age-segregated housing. Every
denomination—Jews, Catholics and all the Protestants—have built, and
continue to build, age-segregated housing. Some of it is done with partly
public money. They have long waiting lists because old people have no

other options. The Gray Panthers say we're redefining the family on the basis of choice and on the basis of common interest, not necessarily on the basis of kinship or age group.

After we get the models in place, the next thing is publicizing them. We've been very successful in reaching the media. We've got a good press. We have speakers' bureaus. We're fanning out, letting the message be heard, creating hope and excitement, getting a positive response to some new ideas. And people are hungry for new ideas. This is the existential moment. Sure, there's a profound cynicism among people now, but there's also a willingness to listen. Part of it is that we're saying something new. We're saying something people can relate to. We have a realistic approach, and we're moving beyond the dreary recitative of problems. We're affirming the positive values without being Pollyannas. We're saying, "Look, it's a great time to be alive." And that we, the old and the young, have much in common.

In some ways I have always been a rebel. It probably began in my early adolescence, standing up to my father. He was a very stern and disciplined kind of man and he had extraordinary hopes and expectations for his children, my brother and me. He was the head of the house in the old Germanic fashion and it took a lot of doing to stand up to him, but I learned I had to do it in order to survive. In the end, I think my father appreciated it and could understand it because to some degree I was like him. I've always been hard-driving, I worked all my life very hard. Nothing has come without a lot of work. My father was like that too. He thought we must excel—and we must do what he said.

My mother was a very gracious, beautiful person. She had moments of rebellion too. Their marriage was not without storms. She had ways of managing to deal with my father without being overtly on her own, so to speak. Her older sister was a suffragette and a very ardent and dedicated leader in the women's movement at the turn of the century in western New York. She became widowed when her husband was killed in a train wreck. He was terribly burned and injured. He was an engineer on one of the fastest trains out of the old New York Central Railroad. The railroad never paid my aunt a cent, not even funeral expenses. She was left with an eighteen-month-old daughter and no income. So she came home to my grandmother's to live and this and her own anxiety, I think, radicalized her. She recognized that there were many things wrong, that women were cruelly used and exploited and that they had no rights.

My mother was torn all her life. She was ambivalent about a lot of this. She had some ideas of her own. Both my parents were from Buffalo. She and my father had been married twelve years before I was born. She wanted to have children. My father wasn't too keen about it. When she did become pregnant, they were living in Memphis, Tennessee, and she came up north to be delivered in my grandmother's house because she didn't want me to be born in the South. My mother was very resentful of some of the racial practices that she saw, and Southerners' attitude.

I'd expected to teach when I graduated from college in 1926. I was twenty years old. I was going to teach English and French. I had a double major in sociology and English, and a French minor. I got a job as a practice teacher at a local junior high school. It was an eraser fight that settled matters. You know, small things often have a large impact. There wasn't much difference in age between the students and me. Most of the kids in the school were bigger than I was.

The first time I had the class on my own, I was teaching a class in grammar, parsing sentences, which can be very dull, terrible. So I introduced the idea of a relay race, having the people in the first row put the sentence on the board, the people in the second row underscore the subject, the third the predicate and then the modifiers, down the line. I thought it was a good idea and they liked it and it worked very well until the end, when there was a slight altercation about who finished first. Pandemonium broke out, it reigned, and no matter what I did, it was out of hand entirely and the kids started hitting each other with erasers, which was really beyond the pale. I yelled and tried to calm it down. Nothing happened except it got worse. So I picked up an eraser and threw it at the biggest kid, just as the teacher came in. You can imagine, can't you picture it? I was white with chalk dust, just letting them have it. That was the end of my teaching career, quite literally.

So my father said, "Why don't you take a year to look around and see what you'd really like to do?" I did some volunteer work at the YWCA, then a friend of my mother's, who was on the board of the YWCA, got me a committee appointment. I served on the board of the Committee of Management of the central branch, Cleveland. That was really a turning point in my life. I just knew that this was what I really wanted to do. The young women I was working with were young, very poorly paid, very poorly prepared to work. Many of them had not finished high school and they came from very poor families and they did marginal work. They worked in bargain basements and as file clerks in big offices or in the factory. There were no unions and no protection for the women and a good salary was ten dollars a week for six days of work. It seems unbelievable. No vacations, and a long day. Finally they made Saturdays half days and then, oh, it wasn't until I was working here in Germantown that there was a five-day week. It was a six-day week for everybody.

I went around to the stores and factories in Cleveland, or talked to the women at lunch, about the programs the YWCA offered. We had what we called a supper club and they would come and have a very modest meal, which they helped prepare themselves. Then we talked about all kinds of things—etiquette, their lives, their problems, their work, what was happening in Cleveland politics—really simple adult education, which was the YWCA's approach. We had occasional dances, too.

Then I left the YWCA. I worked first for the Unitarian churches. I had a national job in Boston with the Unitarian Women's Organization, and then I got a job with the United Presbyterian Church in the field of social action. The social action group I worked with again shaped my thinking in many ways. They were people who were ecumenical in spirit and very

concerned about a proper philosophical, theological, ethical base for
what they did.

In the church, there has always been a controversy between profit and
the view of profit and what was a faithful response to God's action in the
world. One of my father's most interesting friends was a man who came
to clean up the pollution in Cleveland. This was in 1920. He was hired to
do a smoke abatement campaign, to get scrubbers in the smokestacks. The
city of Cleveland was a thriving lake port city, with a huge dock and a
huge shipping service for passengers and for freight, for the iron ore
carried down to the steel mills and the steel-processing plants in
Cleveland. It was very, very prosperous and very, very polluted.

This man tried to get the business people to mend their ways. It had to
be voluntary compliance. There was no city ordinance in those days.
Sherwin Williams, the paint company, had their home office there, a big
plant. The lead products and residues that they produced were pumped
into the river, which emptied into the lake. The irony of it was that all
those men who ran the plants, and this man too, sat with my father on the
governing body of the Old Stone Church in Cleveland, a very big old
church right on the public square. Yet their daily lives were quite
separate from that church connection. My father used to say they wore
two hats, the hat that they wore to church on Sunday and the hat that
they wore when they went to business.

I saw that two-world mentality very clearly when I worked for the
United Presbyterian Church. The church made profit a virtue. In the 1920s
came the social gospel which Walter Rauschenbusch and other church
leaders affirmed. They said that this two-world view of the world was
contrary to the teachings of the Gospel.

At that time there were enormous numbers of people going to church
school. In the fifties, the Presbyterians built enormous educational plants
and there were sometimes three and four sessions of church school every
Sunday morning. One of my jobs was to get a social-responsibility point
of view into the curriculum, into the teaching materials of the church.
While I worked for the Presbyterian Office of Church and Society, which
was part of the Board of Christian Education, the church sold millions
and millions of dollars' worth of Sunday school materials. They made a
profit, $10 million, even though it was a nonprofit organization.

I was quite well known, and in some instances infamous, for what I
did in the Presbyterian Church. I went to the General Assembly every
year, worked with standing committees, and I would recommend the
social action policy of the church. At this time we came within just a
couple of votes in the General Assembly of an absolute pacifist stand
against war. Very close. We also supported organized labor, and this was
a big fight because a lot of Presbyterians are rich and powerful.

I was infamous too for a stand that I took on a program that was the
forerunner of Medicare. In 1955, a good ten years before Medicare, I did a
study of the cost of illness in old age and suggested that there ought to be
some coverage of that under an expanded Social Security system. The

staff concurred and we issued a study document which was supposed to be read by the General Assembly delegates, and recommended for study in the churches. It was leaked to the press before the General Assembly met in May 1955. There was a UPI release and also a release in the *New York Times,* and the American Medical Association picked it up. My name was mud, really, oh, oh! Every one of the nine hundred voting delegates at the General Assembly got telegrams, some got as many as a dozen, from doctors in their states asking them to vote against this resolution. And the resolution was only to study the problem. It was referred to a standing committee that I chaired. There were fifteen of us on that committee, seven clergy and seven lay people and me. We locked ourselves in a small room for fifteen hours. We left only to go to the bathroom and we recessed only to have food sent in while we debated this. It was not approved, but enough educating had been done so that the next year it was approved for study. But I had all kinds of hate mail, awful mail, and I was, you know, a controversial person.

In my case, there's been a continuity and a kind of progression and I've been able to do in my old age things that I wanted to do earlier but was restricted from doing. You see, I didn't do anything in my jobs with the YWCA or in the Unitarian Church or in the Presbyterian Church that was not mandated by the overall policy. The national board determined the policy. I could influence it but I did not determine it. Now, with the Gray Panthers, it is sheer joy! We're making policy! We're determining policy! And we've had a great deal of influence.

I get away with saying a lot of outrageous things partly because of the way I say them. I don't come on like a heavy. I've learned to speak simply, use simple language. If you put it in a clear direct way and if you couch it in some humor, with a light touch, people accept it. I say, I'm not here to convince everybody. I'm simply pointing out the way it looks to me after having lived seventy-five years and seeing these and these and these changes. And people are willing to listen to me.

The media have been unhelpful because the tendency is to build the whole Gray Panthers around me. I resist that and resent it. We're building a movement, it's more than me. I've been the spokesperson. Every movement needs a charismatic person. I've been studying movements and many movements die with the charismatic leader unless they've been able to build a base that transcends that.

Now this organization can exist without my leadership and my presence. We had our biannual meeting in 1979 and there were four hundred people there from thirty states, from sixty-five network groups, and I said very little. I made the opening speech and did a workshop, and on the floor I said practically nothing. I didn't have to. And people were not deferring to me, "What does Maggie think?" I was sitting quietly, which was great. There are new voices and new vigorous leadership.

I believe that age does count. We are the wise ones. We have seen much and we point that out. I think that in itself has some validity. There's an historical perspective that Americans lack. We do without any historical base. It's part of the frontier mentality in America. My grandfather was a carpenter in western New York and he had contempt for the farmers that worked out their land and moved on. They didn't do anything to preserve it, to cultivate it, to protect it.

That's what agribusiness is doing today, pushing the land. We're losing millions of acres of cropland every year, around the world, by intensive cultivation, by pushing cash crops, by refusing to rotate crops, by overchemicalization of the land. We are taking ourselves that much closer to hunger. Hunger, for you and me. We thought there would always be more land.

That was the rationalization of those people back in Cleveland, like Sherwin Williams, who were polluting the lake and the river: Look at that lake, a great inland sea. What harm would a little lead do here and there? And we can't afford to clean it up  We can't afford to put scrubbers in. And yet today Cleveland is a dying city.

The Gray Panthers are providing, in some small measure, an historical perspective. We've got work to do, homework to do, a lot of cerebral activity. A lot of people don't like that. My detractors say I'm an egghead. I say I make no apologies for having a head. You ought to be glad there are people alive today who use their heads. I make no apology for saying we have to analyze this, we have to know what we're talking about. And not just a few people, but everybody who's in the action has to know why we're here and what we expect to do.

You've got to trust the people. People have a right to learn. People on the streets have to know. And it has to go beyond that one little narrow group in one neighborhood. You have to have a metropolitan strategy. Some people have to be thinking in big-picture terms. That's what the Gray Panthers are trying to do.

From a personal point of view, I can test some theories that have been percolating in my head for a long time, and some guidelines that I try to live by, and some hopes and dreams that I have for the future. Yes, I think of myself as a crusader. I think it's an accumulated matter of a long life, a life involved in social change, seeking social justice.

The Gray Panthers recognize that we have a hard job. We're not denying that. We're sobered by the responsibility. In the words of one of our Gray Panthers from Boston who's ninety, "We're on a long, long pilgrimage, a march that has discipline, but it's a lark." When we are at a meeting or convention, we always take time out from our heated debate and our resolving to do our panther growl. You stand up and get a good firm stance of your body; you swing your arms back and forth, to limber them up. Then you reach out with both arms and open your eyes as wide as you can, wide, and stick out your tongue as far as it will go and then you growl, "Grrrrrrrr!"

# Dorothy Height

Dorothy Height (born 1912, Richmond, Virginia) is a civil rights leader who worked with Martin Luther King, Roy Wilkins, Whitney Young and A. Philip Randolph in the civil rights movement of the sixties. As a member of the National Board of the YWCA for thirty-three years, she was dedicated to making that organization one of the earliest practitioners of integration long before it was mandated by the Supreme Court. In 1965 she helped develop and was made director of the Center for Racial Justice. She is now president of the National Council of Negro Women, an umbrella organization with an outreach of 4 million members, a position she has held since 1957.

# Rosemary Ruether

*Rosemary Ruether (born 1936, Washington, D.C.) is a Roman Catholic historian and lay theologian who has been a harsh critic of historical theology as it has been used against oppressed and powerless groups. Her writings on liberation theology, advocating a humanist, nonsexist church, have had a wide impact in the Catholic community and have made her equally influential with theologians of other denominations. She is a professor at the Garrett Evangelical Theological Seminary at Northwestern University in Chicago. Her books include* Liberation Theology: Human Hope Confronts Christian History and American Power *(1972) and* New Woman New Earth: Sexist Ideologies and Human Liberation *(1975).*

WHEN I STARTED COLLEGE, Scripps College in Claremont, California, I was fairly innocent of the idea of theology. I wanted to be an art major. My college had a humanities program which integrated the history of Western civilization in a very creative way. The entire faculty lectured across all the disciplines in the same historical period. If we were doing fifth-century-B.C. Athens, the literature professor would be lecturing on Greek drama, the philosophy professor would be teaching Plato and Aristotle, the history professor would be having us read Thucydides and the art professor would be doing something else in the period. In that way we marched gracefully through Western civilization from the Tigris and the Euphrates to modern Europe. That program was very important for me. It still shapes my methodology. I always come at things in terms of the history of ideas and their total cultural, historical context. In a certain sense I never really got out of freshman humanities.

The first year of humanities integrated the development of the Hebrews into the context of the ancient world and then the Christian Church into the context of the Greco-Roman world. This was so fascinating to me that I kept working on it right through graduate school, trying to understand how Christianity developed in the context of the ancient world, and how it integrated the philosophical traditions, in fact, practically all the religious ideas that were floating around at that time.

It was the questions raised by the professors themselves that got me interested. My professors were people who really didn't like Christianity very much. They were classical humanists and they liked the ancient gods. One of them was a brilliant Viennese Jew who was one of the great scholars in Neo-Platonism; another really loved the Homeric gods. It was interesting to play off the issue of the rise of Christianity with people who deplored Christianity as barbarism. For example, with regard to the fourth century, when Christianity was winning, my professors' sympathies were with the classical humanists, who were losing. When I was a sophomore in college I was quite taken with their point of view. Then, increasingly, as I studied all this, I began to decide there was a lot more to the biblical tradition. Then ultimately, I realized that if anything remained of that great synthesis between classical humanism and Christianity, it was because the church itself had synthesized it. In fact, by the fourth century the church had become the synthesizer. And so I wrote my Ph.D. thesis on Saint Gregory Nazianzen, who integrates the classical, rhetorical and philosophical traditions with Christian theology.

So I would say I got into the question of the development of Christian origins from a side that is fairly unique. I think most people tend to come at it the other way. If you went to college thinking you were going to study theology, you would take Old and New Testament and then gradually you might open up, whereas I began with the non-Christian environment and then focused on the Christian development. That was how I got started. It was very fascinating. It was pretty academic, but I don't mean it wasn't personal. I was truly asking all kinds of questions about what Christianity means, through a search of its origins.

But the other side of that was, as I came out of all this training in the early sixties, two very large social revolutions were suddenly happening. On the one hand, there was the Second Vatican Council, which from the point of view of the Catholic milieu, suddenly opened the policies of the church to all kinds of questions, and on the other hand, there were the civil rights and peace movements. So I began writing in order to integrate the historical and critical perspective into the questions of church practices, on the one hand, and the questions of social renewal on the other.

The first job I got was at Immaculate Heart College, a private Catholic women's college. This was in 1965–66. The college was in the midst of all kinds of renewal, and radical Catholics like Sister Mary Corita and Father Daniel Berrigan were there. They were engaged in an increasingly destructive conflict with the cardinal. It was very much a countercultural Catholic milieu. The school wanted me to teach Western civilization to nuns who came back to college to get their B.A.'s.

The next year there were some rumblings. By that time, I had written some articles on birth control. In 1962 I wrote an article in a book sponsored by Archbishop Roberts called *Contraception and Holiness*, which included a lot of criticism of the traditional Catholic birth control policy. It was circulated at the Vatican Council and the issue broke open in the Catholic lay press in 1966.

There were some small forces among the alumnae of Immaculate Heart who complained about my teaching there. The Immaculate Heart Sisters circumvented this complaint by hiring me through the order so that I taught their novices. I taught them the history of theological thought, classical and Renaissance, Neo-Platonism, all kinds of esoteric stuff. Then the next year my husband got a job at the American University in Washington, D.C., so I left.

I cast around for something to do. I was interested in continuing to work in civil rights and the black community as I had done in Mississippi during the summer of 1965. The chaplains in the Claremont colleges (Scripps and Immaculate Heart among them) were all engaged in leading people into civil rights and peace marches, so they organized the group that went down to Mississippi. After I'd come back from Mississippi I'd done some work in Watts, which had burned up while we were away. I was interested in contributing that kind of commitment, so I got a job at Howard University at the School of Religion, which was made up of blacks of all Christian hues but was probably predominantly Baptist. I taught at Howard for ten years. Then I was offered the position I have now at Garrett Theological Seminary in Evanston, Illinois.

You might say that I kept putting together questions of how Christianity developed with questions of modern social and church renewal. When you're talking about civil rights, you start looking at black theology and the peace movement and feminism. I just sailed along with all of them, integrating them theologically. For example, you say, Well, feminism, now let me see, what was going on with the church fathers? Then you study the church fathers and you discover that they're male chauvinist pigs and that they are extremely pathological on the subject of sex and then you begin to say, Hmmm, so that's where it all started.

Basically, I see in the biblical tradition a dialectic between two different perspectives. One perspective tends to make religion and God "the sacred canopy of existing reality." God is modeled after the king and the patriarchs, and the law that comes from God is simply a sacred reflection of the patriarchal society, a religious sanctification of the existing social order. There's a certain amount of that in the Old Testament, particularly in the legal structure. Then you have a whole other perspective on God which comes from a people who recognize themselves to be an oppressed people, buffeted between the great empires, sent into exile, originating in slavery, whose very origin as a people is one of being liberated from the great empire of the pharaoh. "I am the God who led you out of slavery in Egypt."

That kind of perspective deepens as Israel ceases to be able to make it as a viable nation and falls under the sway of the Greek and the Roman empires. It sets the God of Israel in conflict with the powers of the world. That perspective breaks apart the perspective of the "sacred canopy" because it means that the true God is a God who is in conflict with the existing powers and kingdoms, who takes the side of the oppressed.

Now that perspective gets read out on two different levels. It gets read out in terms of God taking the side of the oppressed nation against the great empires, but also in terms of God taking the side of the oppressed classes within Israel. "I am the God who vindicates the widow and the orphan against the rich landlords. . . ." It's that kind of perspective that I would call the prophetic perspective. It really subverts or critiques any kind of sacralizing of the social hierarchies, and suggests that the whole process of God acting in history is a process of overthrowing social hierarchies and leading humanity into some new era. This is the messianic vision: The kingdom of peace and justice, the lion will lie down with the lamb and nobody will have war anymore . . .

I see the New Testament as carrying on this idea in two ways. First of all, probably even more sharply than in the Old Testament, the drama of the Gospels is that the messianic is in continual confrontation with the religious authorities not of some other religion, but of its own religion. Christianity has sometimes obscured this by turning the religious authorities into Jews up against Christians. But Jesus was not a Christian. The religious authorities that he confronts are the religious authorities of his own religion. A lot of what he says only comes into focus when you realize that. Instead of saying, Woe to you scribes and pharisees, hypocrites, you say, Woe to you clerics and theologians, hypocrites; you bind heavy burdens on people's shoulders. What it means in its original context is a critique of clerical power. Jesus' death comes about not only from confronting political authorities but also religious authorities.

Another side to the prophetic perspective, which isn't as strongly preserved but is still there in the synoptic tradition, is the sense of righting social wrongs: The mighty shall be put down from their thrones, and the poor shall be lifted up, the hungry filled with good things . . . Or the kind of message Jesus preaches in the synagogue of Nazareth: I have come to liberate the captives, to set at liberty those who are oppressed . . . You have that kind of language. And even the Lord's Prayer is essentially a prayer of this world. Jesus prays for God's kingdom come, as God's will be done on earth. So you have the social and the religious message.

That's the kind of biblical tradition that I think is hot stuff. Although it's not explicitly applied to women, it's applied to parallel kinds of conflicts. I would see it as the key to all kinds of critical and transforming dissent when you apply it to race, or sex, or class. I guess the reason why I found Christianity to be more exciting than classical humanism is that the Bible had those ideas in it and Homer didn't. You don't have that sense of God as being on the side of the poor and oppressed except in the biblical tradition. I'd say that I probably already had that sense of social justice and then was delighted to discover those ideas in the Bible.

I don't know where my sense of social justice comes from except that my mother gave us all strong egos. I think I was brought up with a sense of my own rights and integrity and the attitude that nobody better step on me. But also, that if you didn't want people to step on you, you shouldn't let anybody step on other people. I attribute this to my mother's personality, not explicitly but just because of the kind of person she was. She was a person with a very confident ego herself but also spontaneously sympathetic to many other kinds of people. I think part of that came from her growing up in Mexico. She spoke Spanish fluently. She always had great sympathy for the poor Mexicans in San Diego. They'd come to clean her house and end up being her friends for the rest of her life. She even hid an occasional wetback. She wasn't particularly radical but there was a special element in her personality that communicated a feeling of freedom and sympathy for others.

My mother was a Catholic of English and Austrian background. She gave us a particular background which seemed perfectly normal to us, obviously, but I think it was perhaps not normal American immigrant Catholicism. It was a Catholicism which was personally appropriated, pretty intellectual and not at all impressed by what clerical authorities had to say. It was expressed as, "Well, the priest says we should do thus and so, but he's just an Irish peasant." It was almost a kind of European aristocratic attitude toward the clergy.

When I was a child in Washington we always went to the Jesuit parish, so we heard people whom my mother thought of as better educated. We lived in Georgetown and around the corner from us was a very nice Carmelite home for the aged, which had great big apple orchards, right in the middle of all the Georgetown town houses. My mother was on the board. The nuns were very beautiful people, very dedicated, sort of happy people too, gay spirits. I remember they once asked me to teach them to ride a bicycle. My mother very often went to daily Mass and she'd go over there, so here again was this somewhat special milieu, an elite. The Catholicism I was exposed to was affected by the idea that Catholicism has deep and profound truths expressed with great symbolism, great art, that it leaves you room for your fullest development. That was the message, that if people tried to put narrow dogmas on it, it was just because they really didn't understand; they had a low level of culture.

There was a conflict between my parents about religion but they were Victorian gentleman and gentlewoman and hid their conflict. My father was an Anglican and thought that church was something one ought to do twice a year, on Christmas and at Easter. I think he always had Anglican suspicions of the Church of Rome. The kind of path my parents had worked out was based on the old way that Catholics were married. He had, in effect, relinquished our religious upbringing to my mother anyway, so they didn't compete for us at all.

My mother was born in 1895 and my father in 1888; he was forty when they got married, she was thirty-three. My mother went to college in 1913 and so belonged to that early feminist generation. This, like the religion, was communicated to me implicitly. A lot of these things were not evident to me until I got more of an historical perspective on what those kinds of women were like.

My father was away in the war for much of the time when we were little. When he came back in 1947, he went off to be one of the directing engineers of the reconstruction in Greece. We went over to join him and he died in 1948. I was twelve years old. So for me he was a Virginian gentleman, a ghostly figure on the edge of my life.

My mother and my two sisters and I became a kind of women's community that made it together. We went back to Washington. Before she married she had worked as a secretary, so she polished up those skills and went back to work as a private personal secretary. My mother hated Washington, the big old house and trying to cope with Eastern city life.

As soon as she could she carried us all back to California, to San Diego where she'd grown up. That's where I really saw her kind of women's community, because there were all the people she had gone to high school with and who'd gone on to college and then come back west to become the leaders in the La Jolla and San Diego community. Those women were very much her kind of feminists. Some of her old friends came and offered her a house and then she worked as an accountant in a women's dress shop. She worked, not for our total maintenance, but to add to it.

I was implicitly a feminist because my mother taught me that I could do anything I wanted to. I proceeded with the assumption that I didn't have to take a back seat to anybody. I never heard about the idea that women ought to be anything less until later, and I was kind of surprised.

When I look back in my history I find myself spontaneously responding to all the movements, without even asking why. It was just natural. When I started responding to the civil rights movement in the early sixties, I also began to think about it in terms of women. I was concerned with looking at the issues of race and sexism and class and their connections to the whole social system. If you start looking at race and class and sex, eventually you discover that the way you integrate them into social theory is Marxism.

Marxism is basically the tradition of the critique of the class structure. You discover that in junior humanities when you read Marx. If you work in Mississippi in 1965 and then go to work in Watts, you discover that there are class distinctions in this country. My humanities professors were Europeans, and so I think we learned a bit of Marx the way you do when you study modern European thought. They presented it in a way that immediately made sense. As a tool for analysis, it became more useful as I really began to look at the social structure of American society in the context of the civil rights movement, and then to look at the roots of our American power in international economic power.

I think the way one addresses that idea in a Christian-Marxist dialogue is to really see that the prophetic messianic tradition is the religious counterpart and the religious roots of what Marxism is for the secular world. Marxism is a scientific economic theory. The Bible has rhetorical and symbolical ways of saying the same thing. When the Bible says, The mighty shall be put down from their thrones and the poor filled with good things, you're suggesting class struggle, a social revolution. Luke in the Beatitudes makes that even starker: Blessed are the poor. They shall inherit the earth. Woe to the rich, they shall be sent unto you. I'm not sure I even want to push class struggle as far as Luke pushes it. He takes it almost to the point of a negation of the rich. Whereas I guess I have this notion that we have to remove the rich from their unjust riches so that we can be reconciled in some future community. You have that kind of social confrontation and that vision of the new world of justice in the Bible. Marxism is really a secular version of that same thing. In both cases you also have the tradition of critique of religion. Marx says religion is "the heart of a heartless world, the sigh of the oppressed people, the opiate of the people." The Bible criticizes religion whenever religion is used to sanctify injustice.

The women's issue is pretty important to me now. I'm interested in it primarily in terms of the patriarchal religious symbol system. I want to draw out the possibilities for critiquing it within biblical language. The reason why that happens to be very important is that the Bible is still the chief tool for beating women over the head. You can confront this much more powerfully if you use the Bible's own language. There's both a truth and a practical element in this approach. The truth of this approach is that the critique of patriarchy is in the Bible. The practical element is that you can confront patriarchal Christianity or Judaism powerfully with biblical language.

I'm not personally interested in being ordained because I think I have another vocation and that's to be a theologian and a teacher, which I regard as a distinct vocation from pastoral ministry. I enjoy preaching, but only occasionally. I also don't think that preaching ought to be confused with being ordained. I think we need less clericalism and more of a general sense of the empowerment of the people. So I prefer to be a theologian, a lay theologian. Also, being a cleric in the Catholic Church, there's always some kind of control over you and I certainly would never step into any system that any bishops could control. If there were a different kind of system, maybe that wouldn't be a problem. But in terms of a Catholic framework I would never put myself in any kind of situation where they could control me, either as a priest or teacher in a Catholic college. Even the best of those people are still constrained and intimidated.

I could probably get ordained as a Methodist minister and I'm happy to help along my Methodist friends in whatever way I can, but I still have this sense of a primary responsibility for Catholics because of my experience as a child and because those roots continue to be meaningful.

Certainly my training was as an autonomous intellectual, concerned with the history of ideas, the history of Christianity, not only in all of its various traditions but also the Christian tradition within still larger contexts. But on the other hand, I think there's a certain kind of Catholic identity I feel that I would almost call a kind of ethnicity in the sense that these are my people, not in the sense that I am limited to some particular period of papal thinking, but that I need to help Catholics liberate themselves.

That's a kind of warm and happy feeling because I don't do that alone. My growth has been paralleled by the growth of a community that is of the same mind. I do what I do in concert with the whole community of like-minded Catholics. To repudiate the Catholic Church would not be to repudiate some abstract idea. It would really be repudiating my friends or my people. I need an historical community. That's the base of my identity, and it also happens to be a collection of the best people I know and the most exciting community I know. They like what I'm saying. They call on me to say that to them. They need me.

# Justine Wise Polier

*Justine Wise Polier (born 1903, Portland, Oregon) set legal precedents during her thirty-seven years as a New York Family Court judge in advocating the rights of children, especially children of minority groups and the underprivileged. She supported the first program that gave juvenile delinquents the right to a choice of lawyer, almost a decade before a similar Supreme Court decision in 1967. She was a pioneer in making mental health services available to family courts, providing not just help for the children and their parents but guidance for the judges themselves.*

I DON'T THINK OF MYSELF as a crusader, just a hard-working old dray horse. I would think crusaders are much more sure of their positions. Unfortunately, if you've learned to look at both sides of things, life gets more complicated.

I was working as assistant corporation counsel in New York City in 1935 when Mayor La Guardia called me one day and asked how I'd like to be a judge. I said I hadn't thought about that. He said he'd like to appoint me to what was then the Domestic Relations Court. This meant work with children and families. I said I thought I'd be more interested in the Magistrate's Court, where injunctions against trade unions were being issued in wholesale fashion. He said, "Well, take a look." I did, and the first case I heard was one in which a man and woman had been living together and had several children but weren't married. A judge announced that he would give them two weeks to get married or he would take the children away. That was my initiation.

I went back to La Guardia and said I knew I wanted to sit on that court for a few years and then do a report. I stayed there for thirty-seven years because I was challenged and fascinated, horrified at times, hopeful at other times. As case after case came up, I saw the vast chasms between our rhetoric of freedom, equality and charity and what we were doing to, or not doing for, poor people, especially children.

This perception wasn't something that emerged all at once. When I went on the court, there was complete racial segregation and almost a complete exclusion of nonwhite children from private social services in New York, certainly from any of the residential services. Nonwhite children were placed in a very few segregated and inferior institutions; they weren't even considered for adoption and were rarely considered for foster home care. It was assumed there were no good Negro foster homes and, of course, it was assumed you couldn't put a nonwhite child in a white home. There was also a pervasive atmosphere of discrimination within the court itself in religious terms that reflected existing law. A probation officer had to be of the same religion as the child's parent. Similarly, by tradition, a Negro probation officer could only take care of a Negro family, although white probation officers could supervise Negro families.

Over the years, what hit me most was the way in which so-called well-intentioned people in sectarian groups felt they had the right to bestow their charity, their goodwill, their efforts on those whom they chose to help, without any regard to those whom they excluded. It was reminiscent of the old orphan asylum days when poor children had to sing little poems of praise to their benefactors. One of the most troubling aspects of the ongoing discrimination was the extent to which, both by law and by judicial temperament, discrimination which destroyed children was sanctioned, approved and reinforced by the state, and that no one, or very few people, were ready to stand up and challenge it.

Over the years, then, the ongoing challenge was how to change the laws, how to challenge practices in the courts and how to find a more creative way of meeting social problems in one's daily decisions. There was never a day when the facts were the same, the cases were the same or the problems were the same. Court became the place where you saw the problems of the city coming before you one by one, sometimes tragically, sometimes humorously, always making you question where to move, how to move, where to go. Occasionally some successes followed years of effort as when the legislature changed the laws so that a child's adoption would not be entirely limited by the parents' religion, but had to take into consideration the best interests of the child.

Looking back, I can see the succession of fashions and fads that have dominated child welfare and the juvenile justice system. In my lifetime, I have seen and welcomed the assault on the congregate institutions, the movement toward foster home care, the substitute home, the attack on foster care as leaving children in limbo too long, and the movement from exclusion of nonwhite children to the broadening of adoption services.

A new set of reforms for juvenile justice has been proposed recently, in large part growing out of Watergate. At the moment, many reformers feel the state is not to be trusted and that one should limit public intervention wherever possible. Certainly, in times past and today in many areas, the state has overreached and continues to do so. This has rightly led to new concerns for due process. Poor people are subjected to investigation by Welfare and have their lives scrutinized and computerized in ways that the middle- and upper-class people never experience. In the present mood of disillusionment about government, distrust and cynicism have also led to such a sense of failure that a very strange alliance has developed between idealistic young reformers and people whose real interest is in cutting budgets for services. This is a very dangerous trend at the moment, which grows out of a sense of impotence and despair rather than hope and determination.

One example is the sound and strong drive for the
deinstitutionalization of both children and adults from the back wards of
state hospitals and other institutions. Unhappily, this reform is not
matched by equal concern for what happens to people after they are
removed. One sees people dumped in a city without any services; not only
the tragic "bag women" but children are discharged without treatment.
They become turnstile children, going in and out of state hospitals.

In similar fashion. in the juvenile justice field proposals for reform are
based on the statement, We've done so badly, let's go back to "Let the
punishment fit the crime." This is a prevailing doctrine which results in
once more separating out those children we think we can help, and whom
we want to help, from those "bad" children for whom the answer heard is
"Lock them up and throw the key away." This position is very attractive
to people who want to save taxes, to people who don't like troublesome
youths, to people who are fearful of them and to people who don't have
the will to use what we know to really help troubled and troubling young
people. It holds a very easy political appeal for many reasons. There is no
slogan a politician likes better than "Get tough on crime." Who the people
are who are troubled and how they're living is of no or little concern.

This reminds me of the history of battles about child abuse. First we
didn't believe that there was such a thing. Then we began to recognize it,
then some people began to say that the abusing parents were pathetic,
lonely people, psychopaths of one kind or another. Then there were some
who urged that we look more carefully and recognize that the problems
of the individual parent also reflect the problems that society has imposed
on that parent. They insisted that one could not separate the individual
pathology from social pathology.

There are always going to be problems between human beings. What I
hope is that we will turn toward greater recognition that while we don't
want a return to the dowager duchess of yesterday, with Thanksgiving or
Christmas baskets, we also won't accept an impersonal, "cheap" handling
of troubling human beings as "the answer." All of us know that's not
enough in our own lives, and we ought to reject it as part of our social
policy as well.

My rather sheltered life and idealistic home did not prepare me for
either the degree of racial discrimination or religious separatism, or for
the battles and hostility between religious groups that I saw in the courts.
My father, Rabbi Stephen Wise, was one of the signators of the call for
the creation of the NAACP in 1909. My mother and father were involved
in many social problems and battles for social justice, whether it was for
blacks or Jews or Armenians; our home was a place where people came
from everywhere without any feeling of looking up or looking down.
People concerned with similar problems always gathered. My parents
were among the first progressive parents who thought their children
should always be at the dinner table, to be heard as well as seen.

I don't know what expectations my parents had for me. My education was fairly conventional until I went to work in a textile mill in Passaic, New Jersey, when I finished college. Those were the days of the battles for the right to organize, and the conditions of workers were abominable. I'd studied economics and social problems in college, and I wanted to understand them more closely. It was a very important year in my life.

I saw how the workers were treated and how their children were treated. I was very much troubled by the extent that women worked on the night shift while their husbands slept, and then they went home and had to take care of their households and their children in the daytime while their husbands went to work. It was at that time that the mills would send women down to Trenton to testify that they loved night work. The bosses always chose the plumpest women they could find.

I think my parents were worried, but they were wonderful about it. They were very understanding and very supportive even when I caused plenty of trouble. I was working in Passaic, trying to learn what happened to families and children under the spy system of those days, until I was blacklisted.

My father said that he knew my intentions were good, but he questioned what skills I had to do anything about them. I then decided that in view of what had happened to me in Passaic, it would be a good idea to get some legal background and know what my rights and the rights of other people were, so I enrolled at Yale Law School. I must say that at that time (1925) there was no difficulty. I didn't have to take aptitude tests. There were only two good law schools in the country that accepted women in those days, Yale and the University of Chicago.

By the end of my second year, the great textile strike had broken out in Passaic where I had worked, so I commuted between Yale Law School and Passaic, to the horror of some of the reputable people at Yale.

I married one of my teachers, Lee Tulin, at the end of my junior year at law school when I was twenty-four. He encouraged me in my studies and work in every way. I had one son by my first marriage. My husband, who taught at Yale and Columbia Law schools, was stricken with leukemia and died when my son was four. I married again four years later and now have three children. My second husband, Shad Polier, was marvelously understanding and supportive of my work. I think the only time I really had a terrible time was when he was in the Air Corps and I had the three kids, and our maid left for the factory. I'd try to get up at five or six to do the laundry and get the children off to school, and then go to work at court, then come home, prepare dinner and put the children to bed. One day, when my husband called from the air base, I said, "You don't mind if I sell the house and place the children for adoption, do you?" He said, "Have you lost your mind?" I said, "No," and told him what had happened. We managed. There was a great deal of understanding and working together when he returned to civilian life. He was an outstanding constitutional lawyer and very active in the NAACP Education Defense Fund, then he became active in the American Jewish Congress, and he drafted a lot of the social legislation for child welfare in New York State. We were always working together on all sorts of issues, in addition to our life with our children.

I said once to my husband, what I think is true, that if I was a good judge, it was because I felt I might have committed every crime or offense charged against the children brought before me. That I had not was largely a matter of luck, privilege and always feeling loved.

One of the tragedies today is that so many of our children grow up thinking they are looked down upon, that their parents are looked down upon and that there's very little hope for themselves. The self-image of a child who feels his parents are not anything, and that nothing good is going to happen to him, is probably the most destructive ethos to which any child can be exposed.

Many problems in a family can be sensed by watching in the courtroom the way a child looks at his parents, or is afraid to look, the way a parent reaches out with eyes to that child in sadness, in anger or in fury, how far apart they stand or how closely they huddle together—all are clues to a relationship about which one has much to learn. It is not as simple as people like to believe. There's so much torture and sadness and a sense of failure behind the things that are reported. Lectures to children do little good. There is little value in saying to a parent, "He's your child, it's your job, he's your responsibility."

When a child is charged with delinquency, the parent will generally stand up in court to defend the child. When a parent comes into court and says, "I can't do anything with my child," that's quite different. Usually there is a very long history, a slowly attenuated relationship resulting from all sorts of problems in the family, in the school, in the street. Often a parent would file a "status" petition saying that her child stayed out late and that he did not go to school. Later one learned that the parent knew he was stealing from home to maintain his drug habit, and that she was terrified. She wanted to say the least bad thing she could to have somebody do something. Usually she had tried to get help elsewhere without success. There is an exaggerated caricature of such parents as eager to rid themselves of their children. The pain and anguish of parents not knowing what to do, and their fear for the future of their children, are too often not seen or understood. This is one of the reasons I feel differently than people who say, "Oh, these children are incorrigible and their parents just want to get rid of them." I rarely found that. They would feel hopeless, they would feel there was nothing more they could do. They feared that a child would die of an overdose, that a daughter would become pregnant and a prostitute, that a son would rob a bank. And there was a sense of helplessness, a gradual straining of the parent-child relationship until it was worn so thin that they couldn't even look at each other or talk to each other. This was the tragedy for both child and parent.

We demand of poor people in this country more than we demand of

**125**

ourselves. We're not a poor country. Yet there is no country among the developed Western nations that doesn't provide a family allowance as a matter of right when a child is born, except the United States. We talk about the importance of the family, the moral values of the family, but we're not willing to provide the underpinnings to which every child is entitled. There will still be problems, but we must provide a healthy base through which families have the means to do a better job for children. We're much more willing to give money to the aged, the blind, the disabled. Children get the lowest amounts of money support in this country. We have over 7 million children on Aid to Families with Dependent Children, most of them living below the poverty line. A state like Mississippi gives sixteen dollars a month for support of a child for all purposes. No minimum standards are required by the federal government, though it contributes to each state program.

I get weary of being told we're a child-centered, family-centered society. I don't think we really are. It is hard to know how well families functioned in the past. But such families now have plenty of problems as our mores and institutions undergo ever faster changes. There is no crystal ball to tell exactly where the changes will take the family, while some follow old mores and others adapt to modified mores or embrace new ones. Still, one thing is clear: many human beings and their children are going to need care, love, basic economic support and also greater respect from the larger community.

Where I come to after all these years of watching and trying to do some things that would be useful is the ongoing hope that somehow Americans will find a way to combine the knowledge that is available with an awareness of the absolute necessity for personal immediacy in the lives of children. There has been an understandable reaching out to new, abstract ideas, new reforms, new ways of doing things, some of which have been extremely useful. Some gains have been made: the move away from congregate institutions, from vast state hospitals, from incarceration in large state training schools. These have been gains. My concern is that for a time we have lost a sense of personal responsibility and sensitivity to people, and our faith that we can do more for people who need help if we care. In other words, I don't believe we can have justice without caring, or caring without justice. These are inseparable aspects of life and work for children as they are for adults.

Thinking about my own feelings about these things takes me back to one of my first recollections as a child. I don't think I was more than eight or nine. My parents had invited a group of New Yorkers to dinner to meet one of the first distinguished black painters in America, H.O. Tanner. He had come back from self-exile in Paris. We lived in a brownstone house. There was a living room and a dining room and a foyer between, typical of the old brownstones. I was standing with my father in the foyer when a very distinguished-looking, white-haired man turned to my father and said, "Rabbi Wise, you cannot expect me to sit down with a colored man for dinner." My father responded politely, "Oh, I'm so sorry. May I take you downstairs and help you get your coat." I remember holding onto his hand and walking down the stairs, my father reaching for the coat, helping the gentleman on with it and saying "Good night." I whispered, "Who was that?" and my father answered, "He is a Christian minister." Nothing more was said. Somehow this strange flashback reminds me of values: the strength, the courtesy and the absolute unyielding on matters of principle that I have come to value very very much and that have continued as most important and most beautiful in life.

# Elizabeth Duncan Koontz

*Elizabeth Duncan Koontz (born 1919, Salisbury, North Carolina) is an educator and civil rights activist who worked to change school administration policy, improve working conditions for teachers and establish the rights of students. In 1968 she became the first black woman to head the million-member National Education Association. President Nixon appointed her director of the Women's Bureau of the Department of Labor, a position she held until 1973.*

WHEN I WAS A THIRD-GRADER my mother, who was a teacher, and my father, who was the principal of the school, had a concern for adults in the community who were illiterate. My mother taught those adults at home, evenings. Sometimes she would check on something being cooked or whatever, and she would leave me to listen to these adults' lessons as they read. I was a good reader, and I was able then to correct them in their reading. I was seven. That was my beginning interest, I suppose, in teaching, but it was also something else. A healthy respect for the fact that a lot of people had not had the chance to go to school.

I lived in the South and the schools were segregated as was the society. Education was held out as something very important and there was also a kind of family understanding that those of us who were fortunate enough to get an education were obligated to use it on behalf of other people. Growing up with that, there was constantly a feeling of sharing whatever there was. I remember my father used to bring home the groceries on Saturdays, the day he usually shopped. He would bring them to the house and my mother would put things away. She would divide up flour and sugar and eggs and butter, even baking powder, in these little bags and put them in another kind of bag, fold it up, tell me to take it down to Mrs. So-and-so's, and her words were, "Keep your mouth shut." That meant I was not to tell anybody—not my father nor my brothers and sisters. I didn't know that all of my brothers and sisters had gone through this as kids until after my mother died and we were sitting around the dining room table talking about things out of our childhood that we remembered most. When someone mentioned the secret errands everybody turned to him and said, "You, too?"

We were a large family. We didn't have a lot of money. My mother had always expected to teach. She had done so shortly after she finished the normal school at Livingstone College where she met my father. The family were educators; my father taught math and Greek at the college, three of my brothers are in education.

Among the students they taught, my mother and brothers always used to identify the young people who were bright and deserved a college education but couldn't afford it and those became our sort of extended family. We gave them board and lodging and sometimes help with tuition.

We had some pride and a lot of pushing from parents to "become something," take advantage of an education. Having always thought of being a teacher, I had some other ideas, too. That was my first idea, but I also wanted to be a women's and children's doctor. I also wanted to be a chiropodist. All of this had to do with things, bodies, what made things work; people's feet were fascinating to me. I can't tell you whether or not it was due to seeing so many black people whose feet were in bad condition because they couldn't afford the right kind of shoes, or their work demanded they be on their feet, or their poverty prevented their care—I can't tell you. I do know that my interest in women's and children's medicine came in part from hearing adults talk about women who needed medical care and who couldn't afford it.

Now medicine was sort of out of the question for a black child, especially a girl child whose father had died when she was nine years old and whose older brothers and sisters were helping to raise the younger ones on a teacher's salary. So I sort of put that aside. But the main reason I put it aside was that I had to drop chemistry in high school when my eyes began reacting to the fumes. Had I been able to continue with chemistry, I also would have gone into medicine, by some means. I believe my older brothers and sisters would have sacrificed; but having to drop chemistry sort of just shook my curiosity about it out of my mind. In a measure, I came back to wanting to be a teacher. I'm not so sure my desire to be a teacher wasn't just as strong.

It was my work with professional educational organizations beginning with the Organization of Classroom Teachers that formed the foundation of a lot of experiences I've since had. My goal was more or less to change the system. These organizations provided the means to do that. My first objective was to change the lot of beginning teachers. They didn't know what was expected of them and ofttimes became disenchanted with teaching because nobody was helping them. I wanted to make administrators realize that teachers needed time to learn, to adjust, and that they also needed some hand-holding for a while, until they could get the routine. We called it the buddy system.

I held state office and then national office in that organization and finally became the president of the National Education Association (NEA) in 1968. At NEA I started the Center for Human Relations. It was one of my major goals and it is still alive today. It has been the center that has tackled desegregation of schools, civil rights for all kids, bilingual education and thorny problems that have arisen in a pluralistic society in which some people have not been represented. Our work took on different forms at different intervals.

With the recognition that there are large numbers of children in this country who do not speak English as a first language, NEA went on record to raise people's consciousness about children's rights. At that time, the NEA had to consider exclusion of a Texas organization for allowing a systemwide policy to exist which punished Spanish-speaking children for speaking Spanish in the classroom. We said that if the association allowed that policy to exist, then legally, morally and ethically we ought to lift their charter. I was president at that time. They finally took the action required to change the law. But that kind of situation existed.

The treatment of Indian children who had attended reservation schools but were not attending public schools also became an issue as to whether or not there would be recognition of their culture. I visited classrooms on reservations and in public school systems where there was no indication that Indian children had made any contribution in terms of physical objects in the classroom. There would be all kinds of pictures and gadgets, but they were all symbols of Anglo culture. We had to change that kind of discrimination.

I was president for a one-year term. In the middle of my term, President Nixon invited me to be director of the Women's Bureau of the Labor Department. That was a tough, agonizing decision to make. It was Secretary of Labor George Schultz who convinced me that it was a place where I could do some good. I had known him when he was at the University of Chicago and he had done some writing about the economic status of women. When I talked with him he made me feel that I could make a contribution and that my being black, having a name that was well known at that time and being from the South, as well as being a Democrat, were all important assets, but the main thing was that he expected me to do something in that position. So I accepted.

At the Women's Bureau I had some notions as to how certain things such as having a baby were used against women in the work force. If you were a female teacher your job was not guaranteed after pregnancy. You had to take your chances. The bureau itself had worked to secure protective labor laws for the protection of women workers. That's what women in the union had wanted. But something had happened to those protective laws over the years and they were not enforced in as many states as people thought. A closer examination revealed that they had been extended to men in many instances or they had been considered unnecessary or they had been used to hold women back, so, in effect, the laws did not exist. So we changed the position of the bureau and persuaded the Labor Department to give its support to the ERA. I like to think that if I'd stayed on we would have gotten national ratification.

The main work of the bureau was to break out a lot of the Department of Labor's information about the labor force statistics, specifically about *women* in the labor force. We were responsible for breaking it out in the form that you get it today. Women are classified by age, type of job, salary and so forth. The Women's Bureau is not always given credit because the statistics are published under the name of the Labor Department.

The bureau had a project that was funded by the Ford Foundation. The aim of it was to improve the skills of the household worker. Well, when I went there I couldn't buy that because they were assuming that if you improved the skills of the workers they'd get paid more, but there was no guarantee that they would. So I changed the direction of our support from solely improving the skill of the household worker to fighting for an increase in pay for the job. Household work was not subject to the minimum wage, which meant women couldn't get any other kinds of training or education, so it was at that time that I set another goal for the Women's Bureau—the minimum wage for household employees. You have to remember, it was the women in women's organizations who used hired household help and they hired at a low rate because a higher rate was not within their household budgets. This allowed them to exploit other women, so we had to expose that, and we got the minimum wage.

We had some good results come out of it. One product was the Heart Project in Philadelphia. A woman there, Mrs. Uvelia Bowen, took women forty-four to fifty-four years of age who were working in household employment and trained them over a period of twelve weeks so that they not only knew how to do a better job, but they also knew how to do it more efficiently, with less wear and tear on their own bodies, with dignity; they deserved the money that they made. They were making seven and eight dollars a day at first and were subject to many indignities. After training they made from twenty-two to twenty-five dollars a day, going to work with a great deal of pride, under specified arrangements with their employers that they would have a place to change their clothes and to wash up afterward, and they worked by contract in terms of what was expected of them. Now Uvelia Bowen has applied for funds to develop the training in other parts of the country.

As head of the Women's Bureau, I recognized that I was a Democrat in a Republican administration. Maybe people did not expect me to do very much, but I was very proud of my accomplishments and hoped that my work would continue after I left. Women's groups then started strengthening their own organizations and found the bureau was too slow in what it could do. They continued to use some of our statistical data, but I think there was a little bit of an effort on the part of the administration to clip the bureau's wings. Nobody could do very much clipping when I was there because they didn't know quite how to stop me. We weren't going beyond our mandate. We weren't actually doing all these things ourselves, we just caused them to be done.

I have always been more prone to speak out on delicate issues than a lot of people I know, and to feel that I could do something about them. People have asked me, "Why do you knock yourself out with that?" And I say, "Well, there's an awful lot of satisfaction in knowing you had a part in bringing about change." I'm aware that a lot of the insight I have has come from a variety of experiences and a lot of other people haven't had that chance; not just education because it doesn't come through education alone. How do you know that a prostitute would give up that job if she had a chance to get training for a job that would pay her and take care of her child at the same time? You'd know by talking to prostitutes. I used to talk to them around hotels. But how many people would feel comfortable doing that? That's where my experience comes in.

I always said that maybe my exuberance comes from the fact that, even as a teacher, I never had any money, not even any salary. So I had to be ingenious and creative. And I had to use people's talents as I was able to find them. That's why I make the statement that, to some extent, there were values and learning and skills that came out of segregation that I have found useful. When you've been able to make things happen without the means, then you don't stop when you don't have all the means. I think you're able to strategize and look at what you can do out of your own efforts and you start from there.

I'm proud of the kids I taught who everybody said were mentally retarded. I proved they were not, and they've gone on and grown into adults and are doing things. I'm proud of the union women we called together with sack lunches in the basement of the Department of Labor to talk about their common responsibilities as women, who formed the CLUW (the Coalition of Labor Union Women), and all the support they gave me in the bureau. I had tremendous support. I attribute that to my being willing to take a stand. I never backed away from what I believe in and I've been vocal on many issues. I feel comfortable taking the risk.

Having gotten fired from my first teaching job might have had something to do with all of this. I'd always lived under segregation, knowing that as a teacher I could be fired in a system that did not afford tenure or any protection. They could dismiss you at the end of the day without even a reason. After I was fired for being willing to open up and complain, I was never afraid of being fired for speaking out. I always had the confidence that I could do something else to survive.

I started once to give up teaching. I had a principal who was timid or scared. It was the time of the 1954 Supreme Court *Brown* decision that made segregation in the schools illegal. He felt that we would be placing our jobs in jeopardy if we were too outspoken about children and schools. I told him he was far too late because I'd already started preparing my students for what this kind of new freedom and responsibility would mean. He went around the school warning everybody that I was a troublemaker who would get us all into trouble and make us lose our jobs. I decided I couldn't work in that kind of milieu, under that kind of man's leadership. My brother urged me to analyze what made the principal insecure, what he had, what he did not have, what he could not do if he lost that job. In effect, he taught me not to take ownership of that man's insecurity by giving up my profession. That was a good lesson because I haven't allowed people to place their fears and insecurities on me, and it's probably the reason I can deal with people who have such opposite points of view.

It's difficult to put into words, but when you put it all together it keeps coming back to the same thing—that little scene in the kitchen, the family all together, helping each other and others. There have always been a lot of people around me who were very close, both those who could give to me and to whom I could give. To give of ourselves is about the only thing we can count on in this world.

The only way to strengthen a racial group, or any other kind, is to share the knowledge and the talent and see that others are able to achieve. That was my goal in teaching and that has been my major concern over time. I suppose that's what really ties everything together.

# Constance Baker Motley

Constance Baker Motley (born 1921, New Haven, Connecticut) is a judge who began her career as a lawyer with the NAACP Legal Defense Fund and, over a period of twenty years, argued cases that were crucial in the Fund's historic legal strategy to desegregate public schools. These cases paved the way for the landmark 1954 Supreme Court decision, Brown v. Board of Education, that legally desegregated schools in this country. In 1966 she was appointed to the federal bench in New York and became the first black woman to become a federal judge. She was also the first black woman elected to the New York State Senate, in 1964, and the only woman borough president of Manhattan, in 1965.

**T**HE REASON I CHOSE TO GO into law was because of my interest in civil rights, a very early interest which developed when I was in high school. The fact that I was a black, a woman and a member of a large, relatively poor family was also at the base of this great ambition.

I remember very clearly the year 1938 when the Supreme Court rendered its decision, the first in this century, directly affecting the equal protection rights of millions of black Americans. It was the *Lloyd Gaines* case which arose in Missouri. It involved a black man who sought admission to the University of Missouri Law School. As with all Southern and most border states, Missouri's policy was segregation in public education, the cornerstone of the segregated way of life.

In 1896, in the now infamous *Plessy* v. *Ferguson* case, the Supreme Court had affirmed that Louisiana had the power, notwithstanding the equal protection clause of the Fourteenth Amendment to the federal Constitution, to provide separate but equal railroad accommodations for blacks traveling within the state. As a result of that decision, the doctrine of separate but equal received legal sanction and racial segregation became the dominant pattern of American life.

Missouri had one state-supported law school—only whites could attend. Missouri offered Gaines what was then called an out-of-state scholarship. Such a scholarship would have permitted Gaines to go to any law school outside the state of Missouri which would accept him. Missouri would have paid the difference between what it would have cost Gaines to go to the University of Missouri and, say, Columbia or NYU. The out-of-state scholarship program was a plan that developed around the South in the early thirties to meet the federal Constitutional requirement of providing equal education for blacks, particularly at the graduate and professional school level. The Southern states had not been financially able to duplicate graduate education for blacks such as had been provided for whites. Moreover, there was a paucity of black students at that juncture in our history seeking graduate and professional education, largely because of the separate and unequal elementary and high school training they had received in segregated school systems.

The Supreme Court ruled in the *Gaines* case that the state could not meet its obligation under the equal protection clause to provide blacks with equal educational opportunities within the state by sending blacks out of the state. The result of the court's ruling was to require the state to provide equal protection for blacks within the borders of the state. The ruling thus cast on the Southern states the burden of providing a separate school within the state for blacks or of admitting blacks to the white graduate and professional schools.

When that decision was rendered in 1938, I was in my junior year of high school in New Haven, Connecticut. It seemed then as significant a decision as the Supreme Court's *Brown* decision in 1954 in terms of the national interest which it captured, particularly in the black community. I remember that black New Haveners met at the community center for blacks. One of the two black lawyers in town, George W. Crawford, who

**136**

graduated from Yale Law School many years before, about 1901, explained the meaning of the decision. He emphasized its limitations. He noted that the decision was not as great as it seemed to laymen because, contrary to what everyone thought, Missouri was not compelled to admit Gaines to its white law school. It could build a separate one for him within the state. Crawford pointed out that the decision was therefore still within the separate-but-equal context.

It was my good fortune that my parents settled in New Haven. There was relatively little overt discrimination there and race relations at that time were not as damaging to the psyche as they were in the deep South. Some restaurants denied service to blacks but it was before I was old enough to go to them. That's not to say I wasn't aware of discrimination, because we heard and read about it all the time. But race discrimination was not a crushing experience of my childhood.

My parents, each of whom had completed eight years of schooling, came from the island of Nevis, a British possession in the West Indies. They grew up in a society which reflected the culture of Great Britain. They spoke with a British accent, and when my mother was growing up she was playing *Rule Britannia* and *God Save the Queen* on the piano. They were third-generation Anglicans.

In the British West Indies many blacks had been freed from slavery prior to its official ending in 1837, twenty-eight years before slaves were freed here. Moreover, after slavery, blacks in the West Indies became the dominant group, particularly after the sugarcane business went downhill in that part of the world; plantation owners and white overseers left the islands and went back to England. The islands became black and black-controlled. Blacks in Nevis were thus unaccustomed to segregation as experienced in the South and even in some Northern cities.

Significantly, the English slave system had provided for each of the slaves to have an acre of land, even before they were freed, to grow their own food. England also provided the former slaves with training for jobs as laborers and other more skilled jobs. Education through the eighth grade was mandatory. Thus the middle-class concepts of home ownership and education, and their realization, was a part of my parents' background.

My parents chose to settle in New Haven because my mother's older brother, who landed in Boston in 1905, was able to get a job in New Haven. He became a pillar of the West Indian community when he got a job as a steward at one of the Yale clubs. In those days, you could come to the country if you knew a property owner who could guarantee you wouldn't become a pauper. My uncle's job and home ownership enabled him to aid at least one hundred other Nevisians to settle in the area. My father, whose trade was that of a cobbler, came in 1906. My mother married my father after she came here in 1907 at the age of eighteen.

If you go to New Haven now, you will see the descendants of these early immigrant Nevisians, all relatively successful middle-class people. They have homes, jobs, cars, their children go to college and beyond, an indication of the kind of progress blacks have made in this country.

When I came out of high school in 1939, a mere ten years after the Great Depression, not many black women were even considering law as a profession; they had no role models. Most black women were still scrubbing floors. I, fortunately, had known two male lawyers in New Haven who were black.

My parents did not encourage me to go into any profession because they did not think that was possible. Their aspirations for me were much lower, especially since I was a female, but they clearly understood the importance of education. In New Haven I had access to what were, by today's standards, good public grammar and high schools.

I also had early exposure to educated people, many of whom were considering professions. My family and I met many white professionals in the normal course of a day. We always lived near Yale University. Everybody we knew worked at Yale in one of the fraternity houses or dining rooms as a steward, a cook, a dishwasher or waiter. So I knew from my earliest years what it meant to be able to go to college.

However, I suffered the limitations that affect all poor people. I did not have much opportunity for travel; we did not have many books at home, but we had a good public library. I discovered books in high school and read everything I could. I graduated with honors.

About a year and a half after I graduated, I spoke at a meeting, as president of the New Haven Youth Council, at the Dixwell Community House. The subject I was addressing at the meeting concerned the low participation level on the part of blacks at this community center, which had been built for them largely as the result of the generosity of a Yale graduate and highly successful white businessman, Clarence Blakeslee. I said it was because "Negroes" were not sitting on the Board of Directors, setting policy. Projects were designed for us, not by or with us.

Mr. Blakeslee heard me speak. The next day, he asked to see me. He offered to pay for my education, as far as I wanted to go. It was like a fairy tale. I have met very few other people of my generation who experienced such utter good fortune.

While I was attending Columbia Law School, in October 1945, the NAACP Legal Defense and Educational Fund needed a law clerk at their national office in New York City. I got the job. The opportunity to clerk for Thurgood Marshall, who was then the chief counsel and is now a Supreme Court Justice, was another most fortunate event in my life as it relates to my legal career. But for that fortuitous event, I do not think I would have gotten very far as a lawyer. Women simply were not hired in those days. I might have ended up getting some low-level job in a federal or state agency. But to end up as a lawyer who has had the opportunity to try cases in eleven federal courts around the country, to argue many appeals in federal appellate courts, to argue ten cases in the United States Supreme Court is the kind of opportunity in the legal field I would not have had if I had not been with the NAACP.

After the *Gaines* case World War II broke out and the United States entered the war in 1941. Civil rights activity declined as blacks and whites focused on patriotism and the war effort. The NAACP, the parent organization of the Legal Defense Fund, concentrated on helping blacks obtain employment in defense industries and on segregation in the armed forces. Black servicemen overseas joined the NAACP in record numbers, much to the organization's surprise. They complained about segregation in the armed forces and mistreatment, particularly with respect to courts-martial, which often meted out long sentences disproportionate to those given white servicemen for similar offenses. When I began as a clerk in 1945, the staff and I worked on hundreds of courts-martial cases. When I finished law school in 1946, the NAACP decided that because the treatment of blacks had received a great deal of publicity during the war, they would pick up on the progress that had been made and continue the drive to get segregation in the society wiped out. The militance displayed by black servicemen spread to civilian life.

Those in charge of the legal program of the NAACP, Thurgood Marshall and others, decided to direct their resources toward the elimination of segregation in education. They felt it was the heart of the segregated system. The segregated school was the prime symbol of segregation in the South. They began their legal efforts at the vulnerable graduate and professional school level where "separate but equal" facilities had never been provided for blacks.

The first case I worked on was a case which involved Heman Marion Sweat, a black man who wanted to study law at the University of Texas and who was denied admission in 1946. Two years later, a black woman, Ada Lois Sipuel, wanted to go to law school at the University of Oklahoma. These two cases reached the Supreme Court about the same time, but *Sipuel* got there first. It was the first such case since *Gaines* to be heard by the Supreme Court. In the *Sipuel* case, the Supreme Court took a step further on the road to desegregation. The justices said, in effect: We held in the *Gaines* case that the state had to provide equal protection within its borders; we now hold that the state must provide that equal protection *at the same time* that it provides it for all other citizens.

The decision made it more difficult for the state to escape admitting Ada Lois Sipuel to the only existing law school in Oklahoma, which was for whites. In short, the Southern states had not heeded the Supreme Court's decision in *Gaines*. Initially there was resistance in Oklahoma. They tried hastily to set up a law school, then they abandoned that and let her in. Ada Lois Sipuel is now a practicing lawyer in that state.

The *Sweat* case, on the other hand, resulted in the first decision by the Supreme Court directing the admission of a black student to a previously all-white educational institution. The *Sweat* case took four years to go through the state court because of the elaborate court system in Texas, so it did not reach the Supreme Court until 1950. By that time, the University of Texas had set up a law school for Sweat in the basement of a building. They had gotten a few books for him, assigned four professors from the University of Texas law faculty, and claimed equality with the University of Texas Law School. Manifestly it was not. As the Supreme Court said, to Sweat, the state could not provide a separate legal education in a separate institution because one of the main ingredients of a legal education is an opportunity to discuss legal problems with classmates and future fellow members of the bar.

Another case which also reached the Supreme Court in 1950 involved G. W. McLaurin, a black graduate student, who wanted to get a master's degree at the University of Oklahoma. Oklahoma decided to admit McLaurin to the graduate school of education. However, he was required to sit in an anteroom adjoining the regular classroom and at a separate table in the library and cafeteria. The Supreme Court ruled that once the state admits a black student, it cannot segregate him within the institution.

As a result of these three catalytic decisions, there was much hope and momentum generated in the country among blacks. There was soon a demand for an attack on segregation at the elementary school level.

In 1954, the Supreme Court had before it the *Brown* case and four others from different parts of the country involving the elementary schools. It ruled that segregation in public education was unconstitutional. The decision legally ended the separate-but-equal doctrine in education, but its effect on other areas was soon apparent. Then in 1955, the Supreme Court rendered its "all deliberate speed" opinion regarding implementation of *Brown*. As we now know, this later decision retarded rather than speeded the end of segregation. The court abandoned that decision in the 1960s. The Legal Defense Fund continued to handle college-level cases, I got involved in the well-publicized University of Mississippi case brought on behalf of James Meredith, whose admission to the undergraduate school had to be secured with the use of federal troops in 1961.

Generally it was regarded as a new experience to see a black woman trying or arguing a case in court in the early fifties and sixties. I was probably the first black woman to argue a case in the United States Supreme Court when I argued a case there in 1961 involving the right to counsel in a capital case.

I remember when I first went to Mississippi in 1949 to participate in a trial involving the equalization of "Negro" teachers' salaries in Jackson. It was the first trial in which I actually participated. There were no black lawyers appearing in the courts in Mississippi in those days. There was one black lawyer, whose name was Moon. He didn't appear in court. If he got a case he would give it to a friend of his, a white lawyer, who would go to court if it was required. I imagine that during Reconstruction, when blacks controlled the state government in Mississippi, there must have been several black lawyers appearing in the courts, but certainly none had appeared as trial counsel in any case, as far as I know, since then.

When I went down to Jackson with a colleague, Robert Carter (now a federal judge), we were the first black lawyers that anybody had ever seen try a case in Mississippi in this century. When the people in Jackson heard there were going to be Negro lawyers and that one of them was a woman, that brought out a crowd. In a state courtroom blacks would have had to sit in the balcony, but in the federal court there could be no segregation. I remember that the doors to the courtroom were kept open during the trial so that local whites could parade by all day and see the "Negra" lawyers from New York, as they called us, because blacks had taken all the seats.

I have clippings from the Mississippi newspapers of the day that describe what I was wearing. They refused to address me as "Mrs. Motley" because black women were not addressed as "Mrs." in Mississippi. The first day, one Jackson newspaper called me Mrs. Motley, but it was promptly eliminated the next day because someone had protested. From then on, they called me the Motley woman.

There was massive resistance in some Southern states to accepting the end of segregation. They just did not accept the Supreme Court's decision. After *Brown* in 1954, we engaged in a case-by-case struggle to get the school systems desegregated. The *Brown* decision did not end de facto segregation, but it represented the end of an era in American society, the end of segregation decreed by law.

As far as black Americans were concerned, this meant that they were now first-class citizens. It also meant that there could be no legal basis for denying blacks access to any public institution, any publicly supported institution or any publicly aided institution. We then entered the era of desegregation which we are still in. It began with a kind of tokenism and has proceeded to affirmative action, the process by which all Americans are seeking to remedy the effects of a century of discrimination.

Civil rights is now a major chapter in our constitutional law book. When I attended Columbia Law, civil rights merited only a footnote in the annals of American jurisprudence. Women's rights were also unheard-of in the law schools. There will be a woman on the Supreme Court someday, just as there is now a black man on the high court, not because there are no better qualified white males but because the Supreme Court is this nation's prime symbol of American justice.

What we Legal Defense Fund lawyers did certainly helped expand the role and the significance of the courts. After the *Brown* case, it was clear that the law could be effectively used as an instrument of major social change. As a by-product, we also developed a way in which minorities could successfully deal with the majority. We now have the Women's Rights Movement, the Poverty Rights Movement, the Consumer Rights Movement, the Environmentalists and other minorities such as the Asians, Puerto Ricans and Mexican Americans, who have similarly pooled their resources and have hired lawyers to go to court to secure their rights. All these groups can look at black Americans and see the success they achieved by resorting to legal action.

This pattern, having been developed, is not going to be abandoned, because it has been successful. And I think that the courts in our society will be compelled to continue this role of trying to protect the rights of minorities in the way they have in the past. We are now a society of litigators and change is everywhere.

# Eleanor Holmes Norton

*Eleanor Holmes Norton (born 1933, Washington, D.C.) is a lawyer and advocate of civil rights who has been instrumental in effecting real gains for minorities and women. As head of the New York City Commission on Human Rights from 1970–77, she created new techniques to speed up the process of redress for violations of human rights. When she was named head of the U.S. Equal Employment Opportunity Commission (1977–81), she used these techniques to eliminate a backlog of seventy thousand discrimination cases.*

**W**HEN I WAS SWORN IN as chair of the Equal Employment Opportunity Commission in 1977, President Carter didn't say, "I know Eleanor Norton is going to go in there and before we know it the EEOC is going to be in shape." He said—I'll never forget what he said—"If anybody can straighten out the EEOC, Eleanor can."

All right. When someone asks me, did I have any doubts I could change the EEOC, all I can say is that I was expected to. I had done something of the kind at the New York City Human Rights Commission and I had the confidence I could. If you go into as tough a situation as I did then you already have a healthy respect for the beast. You don't go up to a lion and say, "Look, I've dealt with lions before, " and then you see the lion coming at you. You go in there, you realize he has sharp teeth, that not everybody who's gone in before has been a fool. In fact, those who preceded me at EEOC had been quite able lawyers. I had a healthy respect for what I was taking on.

I really think people are products of their times. I came to consciousness as the civil rights movement was born, from a family that had a high social conscience. Nothing mandated my becoming a civil rights lawyer because of that. There was a convergence of my own family background and consciousness, my own skills and talent, and the cresting of issues that were getting their first public reconsideration in one hundred years, just as I became a young adult.

At home there were always discussions of politics and of social problems that helped form my values, you know, the way you learn to say thank you and please. It's the same process really. I grew up in Washington, D.C., and went to legally segregated schools. But because of the special nature of my upbringing it was not a cultural shock for me to leave the segregated schools and go to Antioch College. I graduated in 1955 from Dunbar High School, which was a very unusual school. Until shortly before the 1954 Supreme Court decision on the *Brown* case that ended school segregation, Dunbar High School was the only college preparatory high school in Washington, D.C., for blacks. Many of the black luminaries one thinks of historically went to this same high school—

**143**

Ralph Bunche, Senator Edward Brooke, Judge William Hastie, the first
black to become a federal judge.

In this city, which is middle-class, there was government work. Black
people were not necessarily middle-class, but their aspirations were.
Perhaps a greater percentage of them had these aspirations because
government work provided a mostly layoff-proof way of earning a living.
That combination meant that there was a special black culture,
achievement-oriented, even with the peculiar disadvantages of complete
segregation. The only thing that wasn't segregated in Washington when I
was a child were the buses. You could ride anywhere on a bus, but if you
had a charge account at Hecht's Department Store you still couldn't use
the bathroom there. So this was a real Southern city.

I was rather science-oriented when I went to college and it wasn't
until my second year that I decided I wanted to be a lawyer. I genuinely
wanted to advocate, particularly the civil rights cause. I believed that my
own analytical abilities fit in with the law because it was a highly
analytical profession. Martin Luther King emerged in 1957 and here I was
in college. It fit in with my sense of a useful way to spend one's life.

There was little civil rights consciousness among black people at that
time. I could not understand why black people were abiding this
treatment. As a young person who had felt segregation but not inferiority,
it was almost embarrassing to me that there was not a civil rights
movement. I couldn't understand why there weren't people in the streets
saying, "How can you deny people the right to vote?" I couldn't
understand why there wasn't some kind of revolutionary act. Certainly
not a bloody act—I didn't particularly see that as the way to go about it—
but something that would cause black people to demand that this end.

So I was traveling a path that had not been trod before, at least not
recently, and you had to figure these things out for yourself. Of course
historically it had been trod, and there were models to follow. There'd
been great women leaders in civil rights, like Mary McLeod Bethune. In a
school like Antioch there were hardly any blacks so there weren't any
models in that way. I remember in '57 coming to Washington for a prayer
pilgrimage which was one of the first Washington rallies featuring Martin
Luther King. Mostly southern black church people had come up on buses.
And we had come from Antioch, most of us white.

It was not until February 1960 when the sit-ins started in the South,
with the dramatic effect of people daring to challenge segregation at risks
to their lives, that there was a challenge that caught on. Martin Luther
King's bus boycott had been most important in the late fifties. That
strategy was slowly spreading but, you see, it would have spread much
more slowly without the students because you need the gumption and the
sense of winner-take-all that students have. Martin's way to go was to
organize people in their churches and so forth and he was doing it
brilliantly, but the reason the sit-ins created a mass movement almost
overnight is the dramatic effect of these young people being willing to sit
down, unarmed, and say, "I'm not moving until you arrest me or give me a

cup of coffee." You can't imagine what a revolutionary act that was. And they did it all over the South in places where they had no idea what the consequences would be. Today when revolutionary acts consist of bloodshed and other irrational acts, dramatic nonviolent techniques perhaps do not seem revolutionary, but they had an effect that certainly was unparalleled in this country.

I think growing up in Washington, going to Dunbar High School, my mother and father, being the first child of the first of three daughters—there are a lot of reasons why all these things would converge in me. I wasn't some orphan out there who had to make herself from scratch. It is true that the world was run by white males and nobody expected little black girls to do anything, but that's not saying very much. A lot of people have become successful where nobody expected their kind of people to do that. I think the influences in a volatile, dynamic society like ours are there to be picked out. The question is whether or not all the elements somehow converge. The pieces really form a kind of strange mosaic.

I chose to go to Yale Law School with malice of forethought for three reasons: because you could pursue a master's and law degree at the same time, because since the 1930s it had an approach to the law that placed some considerable reliance on social aspects and because it did not limit scholarship aid the way Harvard did. That second reason was quite important. Yale was full of socially conscious people. Also, it should be noted, it was full of very conservative people. Quite amazingly, in 1960 there were a lot of people still arguing the validity of the '54 decision. For them this was still a most controversial decision, the way abortion is today. So there were tugs both ways.

But Yale was a good place to be if you believed in civil rights. You got a fine legal education and yet you were with like souls, though not very many blacks and very few women. Women were irrelevant. This was about civil rights. The women didn't even know they should be feminists. The civil rights movement was at its zenith then; the feminist movement hadn't begun. But there would not have been a feminist movement in this country if it hadn't been for the civil rights movement. Most of its strands go back to civil rights—its techniques, its philosophy, its sense of the place of woman. The women's movement is the first to acknowledge this debt. One of the reasons why I was such an early feminist, I think, is that the connection to equality and its universality had been made to me through my experience as a black person, so to me the women's issue followed as night follows day.

I was involved with the civil rights movement in Mississippi while I was in law school. I spent the summer of '63 there. My family thought it was very dangerous. But they never said no, it never created such consternation that they stopped me, but my mother was upset and both my parents thought it best not to be involved. Most parents thought that. The FBI took the position that they could not protect civil rights workers, that there was no federal basis for it—which everybody knows is ridiculous now. We use the same statutes to protect people now that were passed during Reconstruction. But it was not a time when people could have confidence that everything was going to go all right.

The Student Nonviolent Coordinating Committee (SNCC) had a strategy. They believed that if you opened Mississippi, if you showed that a movement could thrive in Mississippi, then it would quickly spread into other states and the rest of the country would fall, because we believed that Mississippi was the hard nut. We believed it was the key to the whole thing. We opened Mississippi but the rest of the country had still to fall.

The civil rights movement had all kinds of strategies for how you plotted going from town to town, city to city. Nobody just did things. Every part of the movement had its special role. For militant students the place to be at that time was SNCC. CORE focused on voter registration in certain places in the South. The NAACP was mostly for middle-class people who were somewhat older, although I was president of the NAACP chapter at Antioch. NAACP was not where the action-oriented strategies came from.

Where I went in Mississippi in 1963—the delta area of Mississippi— there was no movement. It was still perilous territory. The day I arrived, Medgar Evers took me around Jackson that whole day. Medgar Evers had just broken open Jackson, sitting in, very bloody sit-ins there, people not fighting back. They were hit and bruised and cut. Medgar tried to convince me to stay in Jackson, and I said I had promised Bob Moses I would go to Greenwood to run what the next summer became the freedom schools. The freedom schools were really about teaching local blacks about civics, about how the Constitution protected citizens.

That night Medgar took me to the bus station in Jackson and I rode two hours and I must have gotten to Greenwood at about eleven at night. Anyway, when I got there, I never felt I was a stranger coming in. In their wonderfully hospitable way, the people told me that Bob Moses was in New York and Lawrence Guyot was in charge there and they had a place for me to stay. The people with whom I stayed were wonderful to me. They rose every morning very early to pick in the fields, so before I went to bed they showed me what to do when I got up, including, for the first time in my life, how to heat water and how to put it in a washtub. That's how you washed up. They treated me as if they'd known me all my life.

I was sitting in that tub that first morning when a child from our center came to tell me that Medgar Evers had been assassinated. When I got to the center they said, "We believe you are the oldest person here. Guyot has been arrested having gone to get Miss Fannie Lou Hamer out of jail, and would you go there and get them both out of jail."

There had not been people killed up to that time, and if I was not afraid it wasn't because I was brave but because we hadn't seen anybody die. We didn't know the danger. It was a band of the young and the foolish if ever there was one. But I believe I was afraid when I found out Guyot was in jail.

Mrs. Fannie Lou Hamer was coming back from a Martin Luther King training session at the Southern Christian Leadership Conference in South Carolina, and she used the bathroom in the bus station in Winona, Mississippi, pursuant to the interstate commerce laws, but she was arrested. Winona was only about twelve miles from Greenwood. SNCC sent somebody over to get her and they put him in jail too, and then Guyot, who was in charge, was sent over to get both out and they put him in jail as well. That night Guyot and the other fellow had been given over to the White Citizens Council and they'd been beaten. And I was the next one to go to get our people out.

But I was not Joan of Arc running off to save the world. The police chief in Greenwood was known to be an unusually civil man, a racist and a segregationist, but he didn't abide violence and lived in peace with the civil rights movement in Greenwood. I decided on this strategy: I said I wanted to come down and see him. I said to him, "I would like you to call the police chief in Winona and tell him that I'm coming." I told him my name was Eleanor Holmes and I was a second-year law student at Yale, one of the few times I brought an establishment name into it. "Everybody knows I'm here and I made all kinds of phone calls and I'm not here helpless. You don't want violence here but the fact is, what they're doing to those people over there is going to cause some trouble. They have got a right to get out of jail with bail set and I'm going over there and I don't mean to be put in jail. The way to bring a whole lot of problems down on this part of the country is to have me getting jailed."

I went over to Winona. They let me see Guyot. He'd been beat so bad he had nothing on; he had to put his pants on before I came in. Mrs. Hamer had been beaten too. She was then in her forties and limped from having had polio as a child. She was already becoming something of the grand matriarch of the movement. She had been beaten by other prisoners. When I came in, things had already gone their course so we were able to get them out.

At that time I was scared. I did not know what it would mean but there was no way in which I could not have gone. The strategy of going to the Greenwood police chief first may seem smart, but remember now, I was training to be a lawyer and I should have been able to think of things like that. The police chief did, in fact, call.

The next year, in 1964, I helped write the legal brief for the Mississippi Freedom Democratic Party which challenged the state's all-white delegation to the Democratic National Convention in Washington. We really felt we were taking part in something momentous because the Democratic Party, like all other political parties in the United States, had virtually excluded blacks from participation in the conventions and the party network. It certainly had not reached out to them even though it had gotten their votes. In point of fact, the challenge to the Mississippi delegation gave birth to what we now take for granted, that both parties will do affirmative action in order to get minorities and women represented at the convention and in party affairs.

After I graduated from law school I clerked for Judge Leon Higgenbotham, and then I got married and got a job with the ACLU and worked there for five years before I became commissioner of human rights for New York City. I always assumed I'd have a career and a husband and children too. I was aided by the fact that I didn't get married when I was in college the way so many of my peers did. That was very important because when I did, I was a developed woman. I knew who I was and where I was going. Nobody who wanted a housewife to stay home would have married me. My husband knew up front what kind of person I was. My husband had been in the navy and was going into his last year at Columbia Law School. Thus my marriage wasn't bothered by confusion over the change in role that many women go through, these bright women who have been housewives who become interested in developing themselves late, and then their husbands feel that somehow the rules of the game have changed and they haven't been given notice.

I always assumed we'd have children. We waited five years to have them. If your scenario includes them, then they are part of what you build into what you have to do. I figured that you didn't need any time off before they were born and you'd need a month afterward, and that's what I did with each of my two children. I was seven months pregnant when I was appointed to the New York City Commision in 1970, and that was before EEOC's pregnancy disability guidelines.

I was lucky because I had a mother-in-law who took care of my children from the time they were infants. I brought my children to her house because I realized that the best mother in the world was not me but my mother-in-law and she was willing to take care of them. Many, many women do not have that available to them. Had it not been available, I would have had to find a very good nanny for my children, and that becomes very expensive. Most women would not have been able to do that either because they do not make the kind of salary that I made.

I was a First Amendment expert at the ACLU and thus had the opportunity to work on a number of famous civil rights, First Amendment cases. I helped write the brief in the Julian Bond case, but I also represented George Wallace. I represented the first soldier arrested for First Amendment activities in the Vietnam war, but I also represented the American Nazi Party. We at the ACLU more or less embraced the Hugo Black theory of the First Amendment. You can't yell "Fire!" in a crowded building but you can say almost anything you want to. Basically, the best way to make a First Amendment point is by representing somebody you don't agree with, especially if you are trying to educate the public about the importance of the First Amendment. I'm sure people sneered about the ACLU's First Amendment cases, but the notion of a black person representing somebody like George Wallace might well make the First Amendment point in a way that representing a black man like Julian Bond, whom I love, does not.

George Wallace had asked to use a public facility in New York City, Shea Stadium, during the 1968 presidential campaign, and was refused.

Well, anybody can use a public facility. It's taxpayer-owned, and that was as clear as the nose on my face. A colleague said, "Eleanor, you want to represent George Wallace?" I said, "I'd love to." He said, "You're joking. You don't really mean it." I said, "But I want to do it." I just thought it was the greatest opportunity in the world to dramatize the importance of the First Amendment.

When I walked into court, Wallace had a local counsel from Queens, as I recall, but he also had some of his young staff there. I was impressed by the fact that they were clearly Southern, Princeton-, Yale-educated types, not George Wallace, man-on-the-street types. They had no idea who the ACLU was sending. To their credit, when I walked in there, no one batted an eye. "I'm Eleanor Norton. I'm here to argue the Constitutional part of your case . . ." "Very glad to have you, Mrs. Norton." And we went about our business. The case was easy. The law was clear. It never had to go above a local New York City court. We won.

After I represented people like George Wallace, blacks, instead of thinking that was a terrible thing to do, when I spoke at churches, unions or black fraternal groups, would delight in introducing me as "the sister who George Wallace needed to get his freedom." It was during the time that some of the most provocative speech in the country was being exercised by black people. It was during the time of Rap Brown and Stokely Carmichael. Black people had enough sense to know that if the powers that be shut George Wallace up, they were going to get to Brown and Carmichael.

In a real sense, speech is the only weapon that black people have consistently had. It's never been wholesalely denied. There was a black press even during slavery. To be sure, you couldn't say anything you wanted to your white masters. There was lots of persecution of blacks in the South but there was always a black voice, there was always black dissent. Frederick Douglass was, after all, first and foremost a journalist. His voice, his eloquence, is remembered by the printed word.

So I also think there is an appreciation for free speech in the black community that there may not be in communities which have not been so disproportionately dependent upon it. Just in the same way there's a respect for the courts, because black people have seen that the political institutions were highly unresponsive and repressive. The courts, although far from perfect, at least had a mandate to judge on the rule of law, and ultimately it is the court that opened the way for everything else with the 1954 *Brown* decision, which led the way to the laws that Congress ultimately enacted. The courts were the only institution in American society not totally closed to blacks. I was most aware of this when I chose law.

No one would doubt that very substantial progress has been made. Millions of black people today are registered to vote. Interstate commerce is completely desegregated. Public accommodations are desegregated. But if you're among the early inhabitants of this country along with the original Anglo-Saxon Protestants, as blacks are, and you're where black people are today, you can't talk about progress, not in a country where time and place have usually meant automatic mobility. Basically, success in this country is a generational phenomenon. Those who've been here longest are the best off. More recent ethnic groups, such as Poles and Italians, who came later than the Germans or the Irish, will be a little less well off. Well, blacks know that. They know that they have all these Anglo-Saxon names like Eleanor Holmes Norton because they can trace their lineage back to some slave master in the eighteenth century. They also know that people who've been in this country for one generation are middle-class. In that context, progress is not the word for what blacks have achieved.

However, if you measure it against where blacks were in 1950 when 51 percent of black people lived below the poverty line, then of course there's been progress. Today only one third live below the poverty line. Perhaps—I don't know for sure—8 percent of white Americans live below the poverty line, and you see, that must be the measure. Judged by that measure, blacks are disadvantaged in this country. The great thing about this country was that it didn't take very much to become middle-class. There had to be something pressing down on people not to achieve.

I'm one of the people from the civil rights movement who perhaps has been most fortunate, both in terms of the civil rights movement and the feminist movement, because I have been able to participate in institutionalizing the goals of our movements in the place where it counts—government. I have been a part of the advocacy and have literally been in a position, both at the New York City Commission and then at the EEOC, to execute what I was advocating, and that's a particularly marvelous role to have been able to take.

I came to the New York City Commission as a lawyer with the lawyer's mentality and soon became interested in whether or not government institutions were capable of taking what was clear progress in the law and transforming the legal principles into equality gains for minorities and women. Thus I became interested in running an institution and making it work. The NYC Commission provided me with absolute freedom to develop the systems that we put in place at the EEOC, that were allowing us to get rid of the backlog of discrimination cases so the EEOC could run on a current basis. It's always hard to find out how much real gain flows from any single institution, but anyone looking at these institutions today can see remedies for people coming out of them that would have been impossible only a few years ago.

The key to it is management. Management is about trying to be very analytical about process. Now you've got to want to do that. Part of being analytical about the process, I hasten to add, is being analytical about how you deal with people. When I came to EEOC, the employees were ready for a change. There had not been a chair in the agency for over a year. The agency had been crucified in the press for its processes and so the employees wanted somebody to take charge.

The first day I was there I said, "I want to speak to the staff." "All of them?" "Yes." Apparently the headquarters staff had not ever been spoken to all at one time. "There's no place big enough," I was told. "Now if bad comes to worse, I'm going to speak to them outdoors." Well, they came back and said, "Would you like to speak at three in the cafeteria?"

When I spoke to them I was very clear that I thought I couldn't do it by myself, that I had a lot of ideas and they were going to be carried out with unseemly haste, that it had to be done that way. There was a governmentwide civil rights reorganization study going on, and either we would get new functions or we might lose some. We later administered three statutes instead of one as a result of that. I also made it clear that I knew I had to do it with them. At the same time I tried to be very determined that there was no stopping me.

I came there in June 1977 and by September 1977 we were putting in place three model offices to test all these systems out. We had to move that quickly, given the position the agency was in, the grave criticism it had incurred for a number of years and these exalted expectations of me because I had something of a reputation from running the NYC Commission. It bothered me having to live up to people's abstract expectations. Congress and the president were impressed by how those model offices were doing. As a result of the new processes there, I got a huge increase in my budget, a 30 percent increase, unheard-of in the federal agencies. When you consider what was changed in this agency, which is everything, from top to bottom, you see that the agency was able to absorb it at least partially because everybody got something out of it, including the employees. This agency increased its staff by 50 percent since I was there, and everybody had a chance to try for promotions.

Did I have doubts? If I simply said I had no doubts I could do it, I wouldn't be conveying at all the complexity of why I knew I could proceed to do this. I've left out one piece of the mosaic—my grandmother. She lived in the house right in back of us. My grandmother thought I was the smartest child that was ever created. She never said to me, "You are the smartest child in the world," but I knew she thought it because the way she related to me made it clear that she expected great things of me. So in point of fact I believed I should get 100 on every spelling test and that I should be able to answer every question. The reason that's important is clearly that, in addition to my own parents, there was this matriarchal figure who considered me the center of the universe and that helped to build self-confidence and the sense of ego that drives a person forward. If you said to me, Did I ever have any doubt that I could get the EEOC running effectively? all I could say was that my grandmother expected me to. It's the last piece of the mosaic.

# Ruth Bader Ginsburg

*Ruth Bader Ginsburg (born 1933, Brooklyn, New York) is a judge who, during her career as a lawyer, briefed and argued several precedent-setting cases before the Supreme Court on sex-biased discrimination. These cases have done for women's rights what the historic NAACP Legal Defense Fund legal strategy did for civil rights in the 1950s. A former professor at Columbia University Law School and founding director of the American Civil Liberties Union's Women's Rights Project, she is now a circuit judge for the U.S. Court of Appeals for the District of Columbia Circuit.*

I WAS TEACHING LAW at Rutgers University in the late sixties when sex discrimination complaints began trickling into the New Jersey affiliate of the American Civil Liberties Union. Those complaints were referred to me because, well, sex discrimination was regarded as a woman's job. At the same time my students wanted to put on a Law Day program about sex discrimination and the law, a subject I had not studied in a disciplined way at the time (1968–69). I repaired to the library and spent the better part of a month reading every article written and every published federal case in the area since the nation's start. That was not an awesome task by any means. There was so little, it was amazing how little. In all that time there wasn't as much as is produced in one year nowadays.

In the process, my own consciousness was awakened. I began to wonder, How have people been putting up with such arbitrary distinctions? How have I been putting up with them? I can't claim I suddenly saw a bright light one morning. It was a gradual process. Both the ACLU and my students prodded me to take an active part in the effort to eliminate senseless gender lines in the law. Once I became involved, I found the legal work fascinating and had high hopes for significant change in the next decade.

The turning-point Supreme Court decision came in November 1971 in *Reed v. Reed.* I was a principal author of the brief, but did not argue the case. *Reed* was a unanimous decision overturning a law that preferred men over women for appointments as administrators of decedents' estates. It was the first time the Supreme Court ever overturned a law in response to a woman's complaint of unfair sex-based discrimination. The ACLU was heartened and, to build on the *Reed* victory, its board voted to establish a Women's Rights Project.

The project's goal was to get decision-makers to understand what sex stereotyping is and how the notion that men are this way (frogs, snails, puppy dogs' tails) and women are that way (sugar, spice, everything nice) ends up hurting both sexes. Our idea was to try to find the right cases,

**153**

bring them before the most sympathetic tribunals, and help develop Constitutional law in the gender classification area step by step. It didn't work out exactly as planned, but on the whole I think it worked out well.

A major problem was the impossibility of organizing a step-by-step litigation campaign immune from disturbance by others bringing up weak cases in the wrong order and at the wrong time. The ACLU doesn't control the civil rights litigation world, or even a small part of it. In the old days, when school desegregation law was in its infancy, Thurgood Marshall, then chief lawyer for the NAACP Legal Defense Fund, was able to manage the development of the litigation, building block by building block. The NAACP was then the only show in town. If you wanted representation in a school segregation case, you went to them. That's no longer true of black civil rights cases, and it has never been true for women's rights cases. Since the women's rights litigation started, there were always lawyers somewhere who would take sex discrimination cases without thinking how they fit into a larger pattern. The courts needed to be educated. That requires patience; it may mean holding back a case until the way has been paved for it.

A good example of this education process is *Duren* v. *Missouri,* a case the Supreme Court decided in 1979. *Duren* involved automatic exemption of every woman from jury service. The court held the exemption unconstitutional. If *Duren* had been brought to the Supreme Court in 1972, the year after *Reed* v. *Reed,* it would have been a loser. Steps had to be taken in between.

One of these in-between steps was *Weinberger* v. *Wiesenfeld,* a case decided by the Supreme Court in 1975. The case involved a woman, Paula Wiesenfeld, who happened to be the principal wage earner in her family. She died in childbirth. Her husband, Stephen, wanted to take care of the baby and not work full-time until his son reached school age. If Stephen had been a widowed mother, then unquestionably he would have gotten Social Security benefits. Because he was a widowed father, the law provided no benefits for him. Yet Paula had paid the same Social Security tax as a man pays. The justices were able to see clearly in that case what sex stereotyping is.

*Wiesenfeld* set the stage for harder cases. One such case was *Califano* v. *Goldfarb,* decided by the Supreme Court in 1977. The issue was survivor's benefits for an elderly gentleman whose wage-earning wife had died. Mr. Goldfarb wanted to collect Social Security benefits under his wife's account because he was not independently covered by Social Security. His case was less sympathetic than Stephen Wiesenfeld's, because there was no child in the picture. But once you explained that the woman worker should get the same protection for her family as the male worker gets for his family, the courts could see the point. The *Wiesenfeld* and *Goldfarb* cases were brought by widowers, but the discrimination started with the women workers. In effect, Paula Wiesenfeld and Hannah Goldfarb were not getting paid what a man would be paid. They were not getting the same fringe benefits for their families. The Social Security Act, as passed in the 1930s, ranked women as dependents. The law protected a woman as an appendage of a man but did not give her a full count when she was self-standing. If she was working, she was treated as a pin-money earner, not as a real breadwinner.

The very same preconception is reflected in the notion that women do not have to pay alimony. If the Supreme Court had gotten the alimony case *Orr* v. *Orr* in the early 1970s, the justices never would have understood it. By 1979 they did.

There are still some loose ends, confusion and untidiness in sex discrimination law. The Equal Rights Amendment would help get us past the confusion, but the amendment is encountering a hard time. One reason is a lack of understanding, all the scare stories about what the ERA would do.

Any human rights guarantee that is phrased in grand, general terms is vulnerable to a scare campaign. That is what's happening to the Equal Rights Amendment. The Equal Rights Amendment is not comparable to the amendment that says eighteen-year-olds can vote. That amendment plainly means eighteen and not seventeen. Because the ERA reads, Equality under the law shall not be denied or abridged by the United States or by any state on account of sex, people can distort its meaning. They can say, well, the ERA means you can't have single-sex bathrooms, they can say all manner of similarly outlandish things. In its generality, the ERA resembles the Bill of Rights guarantees of freedom of speech and religion. Think of the fear tactics that could be employed if the freedom of speech and religion provisions were before the public today. As to free speech, well, what about crying fire in a crowded theater when there is no flame? Freedom of religion? Does that mean we have to allow far-out sects to handle poisonous snakes at religious ceremonies, endangering children as well as adults in attendance?

Without the ERA, the controversy will drag on as case by case is reviewed, ideally by legislators, but if they default, then by judges. It will take a long time, but I am confident the equality advocates will emerge as the winners.

We believe in racial equality, we believe in free speech. We have recorded those beliefs in the Constitution, our fundamental instrument of government. We are advancing toward the belief that men and women should be seen as equal before the law. We should record that basic principle in the Constitution. We should do that in preference to reading the principle into Constitutional provisions drafted in the eighteenth and nineteenth centuries.

We know the Founding Fathers in the eighteenth century did not think men and women were or should be equal before the law. During the nineteenth century, after the Civil War, there were still tremendous differences in the law's treatment of men and women. It was accepted that men should vote and women shouldn't vote. It's hard to read into provisions written over a century ago our modern concept that men and women should have equal opportunities, so far as government action is concerned. Yet the Supreme Court Justices have been doing just that. They have done so because our Constitution is meant to survive through the ages; there must be some adaptation to changing times and conditions.

But it would be so much cleaner if the Constitution were amended to state the sex equality principle expressly. A case by case approach could achieve the same end, but not as solidly or securely. The same issue would have to be fought out again and again and again, in the several states and up court ladders. It is a tedious, wearing process. I would much prefer that the society register its commitment to the equality of men and women before the law up front, that we say where every nation can see it, right in our Constitution, Government shall not deny people equal rights on account of their sex.

When I graduated from law school in 1959, it was not possible to move legislators or judges toward recognition of a sex-equality principle. The idea was unfamiliar and therefore unacceptable. I did not go into law with the purpose of becoming an advocate of equal rights.

I became a lawyer for personal, selfish reasons. I thought I could do a lawyer's job better than any other. I have no talent in the arts but I do write fairly well and analyze problems clearly. At Cornell, where I was an undergraduate, I was influenced particularly by a government professor, Professor Robert Cushman. I studied with him and worked as his research assistant. That was in the mid-1950s, an interesting time, the heyday of McCarthyism. Cushman was a defender of our deep-seated national values—freedom of thought, speech and press. He wasn't outspoken about it. He was a very gentle man. His own credentials were impeccable. But he could not tolerate threats to our American way, whether they came from the left or from the right. The McCarthy era was a time when courageous lawyers were using their legal training in support of the right to think and speak freely. That a lawyer could do something that was personally satisfying and at the same time work to preserve the values that have made this country great was an exciting prospect for me.

I didn't have difficulty being accepted at Harvard Law School, nor was I treated as a person of lesser worth by my peers and teachers. In fact, my experience in law school may have been deceptive in that it didn't prepare me for the job market as it then was.

I started law school in 1956, one of nine women in an entering class of over five hundred. We wondered why there were only nine, and asked a faculty member—he was a good friend, his wife was a lawyer. "Is it discrimination?" we inquired. "Certainly not," he said. "From the large gray middle of the applicant pile we try to take people who have something unusual, something different about them. If you are a bull fiddle player, for example, you would get a plus, and if you're a woman you would get a plus." If that suggested there was no discrimination in admission, it also suggested that women in the law were strange, unusual.

The small number of women in law school in the 1950s was largely a result of self-selection—women knew that opportunities to make a living as lawyers were limited for them. So many places were closed to women in those days. The most prestigious clerkships with judges were not open to women. Some of our most distinguished jurists simply refused to interview a female. No U.S. attorney's office would hire a woman as a prosecutor. U.S. attorneys were beginning to hire women for civil litigation, but not for criminal cases. That seemed to me ironic. The excuse was women are too soft, they can't handle hardened criminal types. But if you looked at the other side of the street to see who was defending indigent defendants, it was Legal Aid. Legal Aid was full of women. The relationship between the defendant and the defense lawyer is much closer than that between the prosecutor and the accused. So it wasn't women's inability to deal with hardened criminals. Women did just that in Legal Aid, where lawyers tend to be paid less than they are in other legal jobs.

Why were there so few women in law school a generation ago? It was the sense that, well, I can go through three years of law school and then what? Who will hire me and how will I support myself?

I was aware of the limited opportunities to some extent when I entered law school. I was already married and had a child and the response of my own family at the time was, Now she can do whatever she wants because she's got her man so she will never starve. It was the tail end of the Korean War and my husband went into the service after his first year of law school. I was with him in the military for two years. Our daughter was born during that time.

It wasn't as hard to go to law school, being married and with a child, as people think. I thought it would be an overwhelming burden and when I became pregnant I began to think I would never earn a law degree. Early on, my father-in-law said to me that if I decided not to go to law school because of this baby, that would be fine. No one would think the less of me for making that decision. But if I really wanted to be a lawyer, having a baby wouldn't stand in my way. I realized he was absolutely right and I think he gave me sound advice for most things in life. If you want to do something badly enough you find a way, somehow you manage.

In Cambridge, we found a New England grandmother type to be a baby-sitter for my daughter. She came in the morning when I left for class and stayed till four P.M. My husband and I have always shared the household chores, and he has always outrun me in the kitchen. He's a super chef and I'm, at best, a low pass as a cook.

My husband is my biggest supporter. That was certainly true my first year in law school. Like all first-year law students, I had concerns about how I was doing in relation to all those brilliant people. My husband told his classmates and mine, "My wife is going to be on the *Law Review*." Colleagues told me later they thought he lacked judgment, saying such a thing about a woman who didn't look particularly impressive. But that's the way he was, in law school and in most stages of our life after that.

The women in law school were more conspicuous than the men. If you were a male law student you could blend into the crowd, and if you weren't so well prepared you could hide from the professor's view on a back bench. But if you were one of two women in a section, you felt (and this was not paranoia) that you were in plain view, not only in the eye of the instructor but also in full vision of your classmates. You were on your guard in a way that women law students today are not when there are over a hundred in each class. It wasn't harassment as much as it was fun and games: Let's call on the woman for comic relief. Most of the professors didn't do that, but some of them did, and they did it pointedly.

There were other petty annoyances. At that time Harvard kept one room in the Lamont Library closed to women. It was symbolic of the old days, but it happened to be the old periodical room and I had to check a reference in an old periodical for the *Law Review*. I went over there rather late at night. The man at the door barred my way. I said, "Well, I'll stand at the door and you bring me the magazine and I'll check the reference." He wouldn't do it. I had to call back to the *Law Review* and say, "You have to send a man for this job." It was a trivial thing, as were other encounters of a similar kind at law school. There was no outrageous discrimination but an accumulation of small instances.

I transferred to Columbia Law School at the end of my second year. I graduated in 1959, tied for first in my class. I signed up for all the law firm interviews I could get, but no one offered me a job. I think a combination of factors contributed to this. In the fifties, the traditional law firms were just beginning to turn around on hiring Jews. In the forties it was very difficult for a Jew to be hired in one of the well-established law firms. They had just gotten over that form of discrimination. But to be a woman, a Jew and a mother to boot, that combination was a bit much. Probably motherhood was the major impediment. The fear was I would not be able to devote my full mind and time to a law job.

I ended up clerking for a distinguished federal district court judge, a man I deeply admire, whose friendship I cherish to this day. Another very dear friend, then a teacher of mine, told me years later that he had spent quite some time persuading the judge to hire me, assuring him that I wouldn't be calling or running home constantly to attend to my then-four-year-old child. At the time my reaction was to prove that motherhood posed no problem at all. I worked probably harder than any other law clerk in the building, stayed late whenever it was necessary, sometimes when it wasn't necessary, came in Saturdays, and brought work home.

After the clerkship, and based on a high recommendation from the judge, I got a number of law firm invitations.

But instead I came to Columbia and worked on the International Procedure Project for the next two years. I did that for a few reasons, some clear to me then, others probably locked in my subconscious. One reason was the opportunity to write a book. The idea that I would have something of my own between hard covers was tremendously appealing. Another attractive feature was going off to a foreign land I knew nothing about and being wholly on my own. The book was about the Swedish judicial system. I was tutored in Swedish for several months, then went abroad for two separate stays, the first, four months, and the second, two months. For the first stay, I departed alone. My daughter, who was turning seven, joined me a few weeks later at the close of first grade and my husband joined us for his vacation. The next year I waited until my child finished the school year and we traveled to Sweden together. The University of Lund, where I did much of my work, had a fine day-care center for children of students and faculty, just an excellent place. That kind of all-day center was just about unknown in the United States then.

After the Columbia project, I started teaching at Rutgers. A teacher of procedure at Rutgers was leaving to become dean of the Howard Law School. He was a black man. Not only did Rutgers have a black man on the faculty, it also had a woman, and she had smoothed the path for me by the excellence of her performance. That was in 1963. It was extraordinary for a law school then to have even one woman as a full-time teacher.

Women did not begin to appear in law school in numbers until the late 1960s. The law schools were concerned that with the heightened Vietnam War draft calls, a considerable number of men might not show up. They began to accept more women and to make it known that women were genuinely welcome at law school. The big change came in 1970 when enrollment by women took off. Across the country, women are now over one fourth of all law students, and the percentage is higher at some schools. Cardozo Law School in New York, which is part of Yeshiva University, has close to 50 percent women; NYU, close to 40 percent; Columbia, about a third.

I found I liked teaching. I liked the sense of being my own boss. I had the good fortune not only to teach one of the subjects I wanted to teach but also to write about what interested me. That was different from a law firm where the notion of the hired gun is true to this extent: You have a client, he or she has a problem, and you work on that problem. There's a tremendous luxury in being a law teacher in that you can spend most of your time doing whatever interests you.

In teaching it's very hard to be a devil's advocate. Sometimes if I think that the students will have a knee-jerk reaction one way I will deliberately present the other side as strongly as I can, without saying where I stand personally, then have the students defend their views.

But I don't pretend to be neutral on issues when I am not. I like the students to understand that most of us have a perspective, most thinking people do, but that it's important to disclose one's biases. I'm not trying to brainwash people, but I'm not going to present myself as neutral. I don't think my students have any doubt where I stand on the Bill of Rights.

I'm still involved in the ACLU's Women's Rights Project, now as a kind of grandmother. We have filed a friend-of-the-court brief with the Supreme Court for a case that's going to be decided this term. This case involves a workers' compensation law that provides benefits to a spouse when a man dies on the job, but not when a woman suffers a fatal industrial accident. The same principle is at stake as the one involved in 1973, 1974, 1975 and 1977 cases. It's exciting to be able to use your professional tools to advance a cause you believe in.

**159**

# Gloria Steinem

*Gloria Steinem (born 1934, Toledo, Ohio) has worked for more than a decade for the equal rights of women, as a writer and lecturer, and as editor and co-founder of Ms. magazine. Her name has become synonymous with the women's liberation movement and she has been one of its most rational and effective spokeswomen. She convened the National Women's Political Caucus, helped found the Coalition of Labor Union Women and is a member of the National Advisory Board of the National Organization for Women.*

IN THE LAST TEN YEARS I think the women's movement has gone through a couple of stages. One was the middle-sixties stage, which was very important though not yet feminist. It seemed to me more reformist than feminist because it was women, well-educated women in the suburbs, saying they had a right to be in the job force and the system as it exists. I support that, but I was already working at that point. It seemed to me that what they were saying is that they wanted to be where I was, and I was already getting screwed so I supported their right too but it didn't hit me as something that spoke to all women.

It wasn't until the late sixties, early seventies, that real feminist statements began to be made. It wasn't just some women who were in trouble but all women. Radical feminists began to talk about patriarchy and about sexual caste and women as a group. That set off all kinds of recognition in my head, as in millions of other women's heads, because I think many of us, especially those of us who were in the civil rights movement and the old left, had identified with all other "out" groups, all other powerless groups, without understanding why we felt such a strong sense of identification. Women were not "serious" enough to be an out group ourselves.

I think that this understanding is what has made this last decade so mind-blowing and exciting and angering, because we have realized we are living in a sexual caste system and it's unjust, as is the racial caste system. We've begun to question and challenge and discard all of those arguments that say biology is destiny and that we were meant to be supportive, secondary creatures. So if you can generalize, which is awfully hard to do, I guess this decade has been about consciousness-raising and building a majority movement and getting majority support for the kind of basic issues of justice for women, whether it's reproductive freedom or equal pay or equal parenthood.

Also in this decade we're accumulating a few important tools and symbolic victories, legal victories and particular kinds of legislation and so on, as well as the examples of individual women who've served to

**161**

raise all our hopes because now we can say, Ah, yes, a woman can do that. But we haven't really yet begun to initiate institutional change. So we have a long way to go. Well, the last wave of feminism lasted a hundred and fifty years, more or less. We're only ten years into this one.

The feminist movement is the only major movement in the country that's really moving. Much more is happening around the country than in New York. The problem with New York, for me, is that it's more rhetorical here than real. People talk revolution but it's harder to organize. In Cleveland, there's a women's center for all the local women's groups. One group is a job placement group at the executive level. Another group does part-time placements. There's a displaced worker group, a battered women's group, a rape group, a newspaper, theater groups, rock groups, poetry readings—a whole range of activities going on. The problem for women today is communication and information, trying to stop leaving notes in hollow trees and whatever it is we do. It's very hard to communicate with each other.

I think part of the reason why the women's movement isn't as visible today is that it used to be so small that it was one story in the newspaper. You would read about these women libbers doing such and such. Now it's become a part of many stories. If you see a story about unemployment, you're likely for the first time to see the statistics broken down for women—black women, white women, different groups of women. You don't see that enough but you're beginning to see it. Or if you see a story about the presidential election, you may also see stories about the women's issues. The candidates are rated on the women's issues. They never were ten years ago. Those issues are now part of party platforms. Many social policy issues weren't ever diagnosed as being women's issues; welfare, for instance. It started out as a mothers' allowance—it's women and kids, that's who it is—but until this decade it was never perceived as a women's issue. It was a racial issue, perhaps. It wasn't diagnosed that way and consequently you could never do anything about it because unless you got rid of the sex discrimination in job training programs and got child care, you could never do anything about welfare because women and kids were the ones on welfare. And yet nobody ever looked at it that way. So it's part of every story.

I see it with our readership. As the women's movement gets bigger it gets younger, but people go out on the campus and say, Where is it? It's there, even if you don't see it. We had a campus issue of *Ms.* We asked questions like, "What's the big political issue on campus?" We'd hear, "Divestiture, get rid of the stock that's in South Africa." "How has this manifested itself?" we'd ask, and be told there was one four-hour demonstration all year long. That's because they've been trained like all the rest of us to see what's male as political and see what's female as cultural. In other words, women themselves don't take themselves seriously enough to know that they're the biggest issue on campus. They've got an antirape network, a women's center. Women's faculty members are involved; it's the only issue involving lawsuits. There are sexual harassment suits, tenure actions. The women who are the nonprofessional workers on campus, who work in the cafeteria, they organize with the students and faculty, it's a revolution. Nobody ever crossed those lines before. But if you go on the campus and ask women what's the big political issue—it can't be us, we're not political. So it's our own definition sometimes.

We've gotten where we are today, I think, mainly through individual women telling the truth. I mean, the consciousness-raising group is still the cell of the women's movement. That means that one woman dared to say that she thought it was unfair that she had to both have a job and take care of the kids while her husband only had a job, and she said this unsayable thing that all of *Ladies' Home Journal* was devoted to keep her from saying. And then ten other women said, "Oh, you feel like that? I thought only I felt like that." And we began to realize that was political, there was a reason why that was true. Or one of us, or a few of us, spoke out about having an abortion and what it meant to have to get an abortion and risk your life. As more and more people spoke out, we began to realize that one out of three or four adult women has had an abortion, so we began to see the politics behind that, that we're the means of reproduction and that patriarchy was the basic reason for our being in the trouble we were in the first place.

The problem is that the ideas are there but not the structure. For instance, you've got the hope that parenting can be equal and certainly you've got lots of women who are not having children until that's true. They're on kind of an unconscious baby strike. If we have to have two jobs while men have one, well forget it. But we don't have the structural change to make it happen. We don't have parental leave instead of maternity leave. We don't have shorter work days or work weeks for parents of young children, men and women. So I think we're in a very uncomfortable period now because we've got lots of hopes and aspirations and changed ideas of what our lives could be, but not the structural change that would make it possible for most people.

The way to bring about structural change is to look to the groups that have the greatest bargaining power. What are these? Unions. So unions, especially teachers' unions, are beginning to bargain for parental leave. Then it gets to be a demand on employers, then it starts to spread. That's the way. It's not fast. Obviously structural change is much slower than consciousness-raising, so we're in for a really long haul. We've probably gotten as much as we're going to get by working through the political parties, in my opinion. I think we're going to have to be able to turn out our own vote, regardless of party, on specific issues, women and men who care, say, about reproductive freedom, who say, "Wait a minute, reproductive freedom is like freedom of speech. I'm not going to vote for somebody who doesn't support this, and whether I'm a Republican or a Democrat is immaterial because neither party supports it." So on the electoral level, it's true that there's going to have to be much more orchestration of women together as individuals.

The first wave of feminism in the nineteenth century had a big advantage, which was that women identified with each other on the basis of their condition. So you had shop girls and prostitutes working together with Mrs. Rich Person without being self-conscious at all because they came together on the basis of their condition. In the intervening years, Marx came along and did two things, one bad and one good. One was that his theory divided up women falsely, by class, so that by Marxist theory, the wife of a middle-class person is herself middle-class, or the wife of a rich capitalist is herself a capitalist—which is bullshit, she's not. She has no power. She can be traded in on a younger model. That's been unhelpful because it's kept us from making connections.

However, what has been helpful is that Marxist theory got into the culture enough to say, It's environment, not nature, not biology. So I think we now understand that it's the individual difference that matters, and the gender is just one little part of that unique person that is each one of us, male or female, and that there's less difference between men and women as groups than there is between you and me, that sex and race are just one element of a thousand elements that make up each individual.

What we're really talking about is populist revolution—overthrowing or humanizing, you can pick your verb depending how patient you are, a sexual caste system that's also dependent on race. So it means you actually have to deal with the restrictions on white women and the exploitation of black women at the same time. The sex and race caste systems are very intertwined and the revolutions have always come together, whether it was the suffragist and abolitionist movements or whether it's the feminist and civil rights movements. They must come together because one can't succeed without the other. We're trained to focus on the differences between us because there's so much fear of our getting together. You can see that especially by looking at the first wave of feminism. It's too bad we didn't learn from history when there was a majority coalition of all women and black men. They both had the status of legal chattel in one degree or another and everybody had common cause. The white liberal men divided this coalition very consciously by giving the vote to black men first. And it was another fifty years before women of any race got the vote.

There's a constant effort to divide us, but the truth is that the women's movement, for all of the problems we have on race and class, is the most integrated social movement this country's ever seen. The environmental movement isn't, the antiwar movement isn't, the black movement wasn't enough, by itself. There weren't enough white people who saw their self-interest in it and there were many more men than women, for obvious reasons, who were working in it.

I'm not trying to downplay the problem of division, because we need to work on it constantly, but we also have to be conscious of the effort of employers who try to get us to fight over 5 percent of the pie while they have 95 percent. I mean, nobody walks into the Republican Party and says, "This is a white middle-class group," but they would walk into a women's movement meeting which has a third black and Hispanic women, and it's maybe the only meeting in this town that represents the town, and they'll say, "It's mostly white, middle-class . . ." It's a way of downgrading it, of saying these people are silly, not serious, not united.

The populist movements in this country had a very clear ideology, whether they were antitax or whatever. I think populist just means an ideology that arises out of shared individual experience, rather than an ideology that is written by one person, with a lot of words that end in -*tion,* that is imposed. I used to say feminism is a revolution, not a reform, which is certainly true. Then I realized that the reason I was saying it was because my male colleagues on the left took *revolution* seriously, as a word. I was trying to make them see that feminism was serious.

All the years I spent trying to make my experience fit into Marxism weren't nearly as constructive and changeful as just seeing my own experience and seeing that that was feminism. There's value in all of these things and we have to look at them all, but you can't build a house from the top, you can't build a revolution from the top.

What my male colleagues meant by revolution was taking over the army and the radio stations. I mean, that's nothing. That's very small potatoes. What we mean by revolution is changing much more than that, not just on the top. It means changing the way we think, the way we relate to each other, what we think divides us or doesn't divide us, what we think our power relationships are in our daily life.

I think the fact that I've become a symbol for the women's movement is somewhat accidental. A woman member of Congress, for example, might be identified as a member of Congress; it doesn't mean she's any less of a feminist but she's identified by her nearest male analog. Well, I don't have a male analog so the press has to identify me with the movement. I suppose I could be referred to as a journalist, but because *Ms.* is part of a movement and not just a typical magazine, I'm more likely to be identified with the movement. There's no other slot to put me in.

I've been attacked viciously on a personal level for my ideas. It makes you want to go home and cry and never do anything ever again. The attacks are sort of inevitable. It's hard to be opposed by men and/or women who feel women are inferior. That's hard. They do a lot of things to you. They're always attacking you sexually or saying you're abnormal as a woman, that's the most prevalent kind of attack, 98 percent. But I think what's harder for all of us to take is attacks by other women who appear to believe the same things we do. It's a tiny percentage of the attacks but it's much more painful. It isn't as if women had a choice. We're all damaged people in some way. If you're a woman who hasn't been able to do what you want and need to do as a human being, and you see some other woman who is apparently more successful, then you want to say, "How dare she, she's just another woman like me." It's self-hatred. It's something that happens in the black movement. It happens in every group that's been told systematically that it's inferior. Ultimately, you believe it. You believe that your group is inferior, then it makes you angry

at the other members of it and it makes you devalue them. There's no
solution for it, I don't think, except to make a world in which women can
be whole people. I only speak about it because it hurts the most.

I do get burned out from time to time. In the beginning I thought, Well,
this is something I'll do for a couple of years. It's so reasonable. Certainly
if we just say what's wrong, people will put things right. So I didn't pace
myself. I just went flat out, lecturing, organizing. I felt that this was a flat-
out effort for a few years and then I would stop doing it and do something
else. Since then I've realized that it's something that will take a lifetime.
It's not just a year or two, it's our whole lives. So that helps you to pace
yourself. You realize you can't be flat-out active all the time, that you
need time to think and read. You've got to be active in cycles.

It's always hard to see yourself, so I'm not sure that I know what my
role has been in the women's movement. You get up every day and do the
best you can. But I think because I'm a writer by trade and because I'm an
in-between person from a generational point of view (when the
movement started I was neither the mother nor the daughter), I see my
role as a bridge between generations, between ideas and action, trying to
state things in a new way so that it frees our brains of the old ways of
thinking and leads to action.

In later years, if I'm remembered at all it will be for inventing a phrase
like "reproductive freedom" because before that we talked about
"population control," which meant that someone else was going to make
the decision, not us. It meant minority groups were understandably
fearful that they were going to be controlled more than others. It wasn't a
feminist phrase because it implied control elsewhere instead of by us as
individuals. So "reproductive freedom" as a phrase includes the freedom
to have children or not to have children, both. So it made it possible for
us to make a coalition. I think the revolutionary role of a writer is to make
language that makes coalition possible, language that makes us see things
in a new way.

I'm not sure, frankly, what direction the feminist movement will take
in the future or what my role will be in it, because a lot of it is running as
fast as you can to stay in the same place. Money is a constant problem.
It's very hard, but I hope that I will be lecturing, organizing and traveling
less and writing more, because I think I could contribute more that way.
It's much more efficient. You can travel six months and not reach as many
people as you can if you just write one thing. But you have to have the
solitude and concentration to sit down and write something, not to
mention the discipline to say no to a bail fund benefit or things like that
where you feel you can't not go. But I would prefer to be writing.

The kind of writing I'd like to do has to do with both theory and
reporting. These two things have to be hooked up. I think that's what
feminism has to contribute to the world at large; that you can't just write
theory out of no reality, that you have to start as we started, in
consciousness-raising groups and say, Here's the real situation and here's

the theoretical conclusions that the real situation leads to. The separation
between experience and theory is part of the whole split between the
intellectual and emotional that's such a problem. I mean, it just doesn't
exist. It's part of the male/female split in our culture that has caused us to
cut off qualities in ourselves. It's not that there aren't two sides to some
things. I'm sure there are, but there aren't two sides to everything. There
are eleven, or a hundred and fourteen or one, and it's a gross distortion of
reality to say there are two sides or to say there has to be a winner or a
loser. Reality is much more diverse and interesting than that, and all the
splits of intellect and emotion and body and mind should be mended. Feminism is the belief that women are full human beings. It's simple justice.

# Billie Jean King

*Billie Jean King (born 1943, Long Beach, California) world tennis champion and winner of a record twenty Wimbledon matches, fought for women's right to perform in sports. She was the driving force behind the creation in 1971 of the first professional tennis circuit for women, the Virginia Slims Circuit. This breakthrough led to an examination of management policy in other sports, opening up professional and amateur opportunities, and establishing larger purses for women. In 1971 she was the first woman athlete in any sport to win more than a hundred thousand dollars in one season.*

As a child I wanted to be the best tennis player in the world. My first love was music but I found out that I didn't have much talent. I realized very early in my life that I was better coordinated than most children. I enjoyed sports and always did well in them. That's one thing my parents understood, especially my father. He's a baseball scout for the Milwaukee Brewers now. He knew that I loved to run—he used to time me from one tree to another—and he knew I loved to hit a baseball and throw a ball, but he also knew that there were very few sports available to girls. He suggested either golf, swimming or tennis.

We couldn't afford golf. I took swimming lessons at the YWCA and practically drowned. Swimming didn't fit me at all. I like to dance and prance and jump up in the air. So I said, "What's tennis?" My father didn't know much about tennis. Nobody in the family plays tennis to this day, but he knew enough about it to know that running and hitting a ball were part of the game.

I was eleven when I took up tennis at the public parks in Long Beach, California. The first day I hit the tennis ball I knew I'd found what I loved doing. There was something special about hitting the ball, the way it felt. There wasn't a doubt in my mind.

My mother took me home in the car and I remember telling her that I would be the number-one tennis player in the world and she said, "That's fine, dear." She and my father thought, This will last two weeks and then we'll be on to something else, which is pretty normal at that age. But ever since that moment, tennis has been my medium of self-expression.

From the beginning I was very aware of being a girl in sport, even at home. My brother Randy is a relief pitcher for the San Francisco Giants. He's five years younger than I am but when we were growing up, he always got to do more because he's a boy, even though I was more responsible. My parents told me that if they had only enough money to send one of us to college, they would send Randy because someday he would be a breadwinner. That ticked me off a little. They said, "That's the way life is." They always thought that if Randy really liked baseball and he had a high enough skill level, he'd have a career doing something he loved to do, but they didn't think in those terms about my playing tennis.

Even so, they were terrific. My parents did everything to get tennis shoes on my feet and get me to a tennis tournament. My mother was very shy at the time but she became an Avon lady, she sold Tupperware, she did anything because she didn't have any experience. My father took on another job and they had three jobs between them so that Randy and I could have what we wanted. They never slighted me at all in those terms, but in their perceptions, in their own frame of reference, I was different. They've changed now, but you can see that the way the world perceives what your sport is worth, or the value of what a girl is doing versus the value of what a boy is doing, is totally different.

It was the same at school. As long as you were involved with boys and cheerleading, basically these were the two things. The kids thought I was nuts, going to tennis tournaments every weekend. "Why don't you come to our slumber party? You're going to play tennis? Oh, what's that?"

It's hard to explain that to people today because Andrea Jaeger and Tracy Austin, who are both still in high school, are famous in their schools. Their friends celebrate and put up banners for them when they win a tournament. Their teachers let them out of school for weeks, not just days.

Right after the time I started playing tennis, I realized that the sport of playing tennis was not right. At that age it was difficult to articulate, but tennis wasn't available to everyone, number one; it was too stodgy, number two. See, in basketball, baseball and football, all the team sports, hooten' and hollerin' were all right, but in tennis you had to wear all white and you could never speak your mind; you had to be a lady or gentleman at all times, whatever that means.

My parents had always taught us that if you don't like something, you should stop complaining and do something about it. That very simple instruction paid off later.

When I was starting out in tennis, Wimbledon was *it*. There were no other opportunities for women tennis players. I played in ten tournaments in 1966 and had to look hard to find even ten. Now we worry about which weeks we're going to take off because there's a tournament for us to play in every single week of the year.

My husband, Larry, played a big part in helping me change the structure of tennis. I was going to college then and Larry and I had been dating for a while. He said to me, "Why are you in school? You don't go to class, you run to the library in the morning to look at the sports page to see where all your friends are playing. Do you really want to be here?" I didn't, except for him. I wanted to be playing tennis. Together we started dreaming about how we would like to make tennis a more popular sport.

Then in 1968 tennis became open, which meant that amateurs and professionals could compete together for the first time. Open tennis was great because it got rid of the hypocrisy, but it meant less money for the women players because men controlled the game. They were the promoters, the administrators, and they didn't want to share any of the prize money. So they started cutting out all the events for women. The justification was that women don't draw as large an audience as men.

That year Rosie Casals, Françoise Durr, Ann Jones and I joined the National Tennis League, which had six members, all men—Rod Laver, Pancho Gonzales, Ken Rosewall, Roy Emerson, Andres Gimeno and Fred Stolle. For two years, the ten of us went all over the world to these out-of-the-way places playing one-night stands. I was never so tired in my life. The traveling was a killer. The only way we could get to some of these places was to drive five or six hours. We'd play our guts out for a hundred people, get a few hours' sleep and then drive to the next place. The men were terrific, true pros, and the one saving feature was we were able to laugh at ourselves.

While we were on the road, in cars, trains, planes, hotel rooms, the four of us women had a chance to communicate with one other. We discussed our philosophy of tennis and talked about where we'd like to see tennis go. One of the dreams we had was to form a women's tennis association. We decided, Let's do something.

So we started holding meetings in the locker rooms at tournaments. The other women players thought we were nuts, but we kept saying to them, "You aren't going to have anyplace to play next year because the men who promote tournaments aren't going to stage any women's events except for a few major ones. We should have our own circuit." They said, "Oh, no, the men will take care of us." We couldn't convince anybody. You know how human nature is. People always wait until a crisis, then they react and start waking up a little.

It went on like that until 1970. Jack Kramer was having a tournament and the prize money had an eleven-to-one ratio. That's all the women were worth, according to Jack—one-eleventh of what the men got. We asked Gladys Heldman, at that time publisher of *World Tennis* magazine, to ask him if we could get more prize money. He said, "No way." So Gladys said, "I'll tell you what. We'll just get our own tournament organized. I'll talk to Joe Cullman of the Philip Morris Company. He's a friend of mine." Gladys got Virginia Slims to put up seven thousand dollars and we played our first Virginia Slims tournament in Houston on September 23, 1970. That's how women's tennis got started. Everyone thinks we broke away from the men, but it was because we didn't have any choice. All we did, we did to survive.

When the USTA heard about the Virginia Slims circuit, they saw the handwriting on the wall and created their own circuit. They got Evonne Goolagong, Chris Evert, Margaret Court and Virginia Wade, all the players who wouldn't go with us. The only reason the USTA organized the circuit was because they didn't want to lose control.

Larry and I flew to Florida to try to convince Chris Evert and her father, coach Jimmy Evert, to join our circuit. Even then Chris and I got along great. We said, "We're hurting women's tennis by being divided. Please come with us because we're really the future." Chris said, "It's unfair to the USTA. I don't want to rock the boat." Her father agreed. I said to her, "Chris, I'll talk to you ten years from now and you'll think differently. You don't understand what you're doing. The only reason any of us are getting any money is because Gladys and Joe were willing to take a risk. Do you think USTA would have started a circuit unless they were forced to?" "I don't know," she said.

It was tough on us, but you can't force people. All you can do is try to persuade them. You can be persuasive if you explain to people that it is in their self-interest to do something.

Eventually, in 1973, the USTA gave up and the Virginia Slims circuit became the one and only women's circuit. It was then that we got Margaret, Chris, Evonne and Virginia. To this day everybody thinks that they supported us and we were all in it together. Due to all the women pulling together, we finally formed the Women's Tennis Association during Wimbledon of 1973.

I think we worked so hard for a women's circuit because we wanted to be appreciated and to have our sport appreciated. We wanted to create a system that could perpetuate itself so we could play every night of the week, compete and make a living and we as athletes would be appreciated and our sport accepted.

People think tennis is beyond them. When you talk to taxi drivers, blue-collar workers, they're really nice but they've never come to a tennis match in their whole lives. They watch on televison sometimes. Sure, people know my name, they come up to me and want my autograph, but they've never come and paid money to see me or any of the other players play tennis. Tennis is really a small-time sport and that bothers me.

See, I want tennis to be a huge spectator sport. There should be more opportunities at every level. The way to do that is to bring back team tennis, have tennis teams in each city like the other professional sports have. In 1978, the last year of team tennis, there were ten teams, one in most of the major cities. Four million people that year saw men's and women's professional tennis combined, which is really minute. But of those four million people, one million of them had seen team tennis.

Team tennis provides a base of watching. Children in the community can get involved. They can be ball girls and ball boys. When they're growing up they can dream about making their tennis team, just like they dream about making their basketball or football team.

In tournament tennis, you don't belong to the community. You can't go to small cities because they can't support a tournament. You only have two or three stars. The tournament doesn't really care about the other twenty-nine players. They only contribute 8 percent of the total gate. The top three players are everyone else's meal ticket, whether the players want to admit that or not. In team tennis, you have at least one star, male and female on each of the ten teams. That provides more tension and provides a better living for more players. Each star on each team would bring in tickets instead of only two or three people in the game.

In the back of my mind, deep down, I've always wanted to change sports. That's the reason I started the Women's Sports Foundation and *womenSports* magazine. I enjoy creating new opportunities.

I would like to see sports treated like any other field of endeavor. A person should be able to go to school on a scholarship and still be able to participate and receive money in his skilled area. Colleges are supposed to help young people prepare for careers. If a student on a music scholarship cut a record, the college would think that was great. Do you think they'd keep her from taking the money she made on the record? But take a woman tennis player going to college on a scholarship and playing for her school tennis team. If the Avon tournament is in town that week and she's good enough to get into the tournament, and she wins, she should be able to take the prize money and still go back to school and play for her team.

Right at the moment, a person in that position at eighteen years of age has to make a choice. Girls come up to me all the time and ask me, "Should I go to college or try and make it in the pros?" They shouldn't have to make that choice. Only in sports do you have to make that choice. It's the only field I know of, for both men and women, where there's that discrimination. No one has really thought much about this and it's so simple really.

What I'd like to see is the amateur athletic associations, the National Collegiate Athletic Association, the International Olympic Committee and the Amateur Athletic Union make sport honest by not making a distinction between amateurs and professionals, but making it depend on skill level like any other job. That would really clean up sports.

When schools recruit athletes, that's supposed to be against the rules. Well, we live in a free-enterprise system. If a college wants to recruit a good athlete, they're going to find ways, incentives to offer him so he'll go there. If a college wants to pay someone thirty thousand dollars or give his parents a house and it helps that person get his career going in sports, what's wrong with it?

A scholarship is a contract. You can label it anything you want, but what they're saying is, I will pay you to come to my school and in return you will play on the tennis team and maintain a certain grade-point average.

I hope that someday the athletic associations will make those changes because those organizations are so powerful that if they don't make the changes, I don't know if sports ever will be changed. That's going to be my theme if I stay involved. It would probably take the rest of my life.

I do something because I want to do it, not because I feel a sense of responsibility. Sacrifice is doing something you don't want to do. Yes, I get tired, cross, lose my temper, get ticked off and sometimes I don't feel appreciated, but as I told the women players when we started with Gladys and Joe, "If you think that we're going to be appreciated ten years from now, I got news for you. You should get joy and gratification out of it now. You know that you've done it. If that isn't enough for you, don't bother."

Working to change things gives me the most long-term happiness.

Performing is very temporary. To me, winning is doing what I want, what makes me happy, doing the best I can at this given moment in my life. That's all I can ask of myself. If each person does the best with what he has, that's winning. He's fulfilling his own potential.

The thing I like about tennis is that you're using your mind and body as one. There's a lot of work in bringing them together, a lot more than people realize. Tennis is not something you can buy. You can't buy a great backhand or a great forehand, or a great serve. You have to learn your craft. Tennis can be very boring at times—the practicing, it's so repetitious—but tennis is more fun than most things because the ball never comes over the net twice the same way.

Perfection is something you never reach although you keep trying. Always. It's being in perfect balance. If you're planning a topspin backhand, that's exactly what you produce. That doesn't happen very often. Even if you hit it almost perfectly, you think, Maybe I could have hit it just a little closer to the line, a little bit harder or softer. You just keep extending yourself. It's fun to see if you can do it.

Injuries take their toll. Players who have injuries generally have a much more erratic career because they're playing when they shouldn't be playing and they have a lot of pain. I've had three operations on my knees and one on my foot. Rehabilitation from an operation is very difficult. It's much more debilitating, mentally and physically, than working toward any Wimbledon title. Those are the most revealing times in a person's life. It takes spirit, willpower, character—all the things people say sports are supposed to do for you.

The pain level is so excruciating you don't know whether you have the courage to persevere. When you get out of bed in the morning you can't even bend your leg. You appreciate walking, going to the bathroom, being able to get into a taxi without being in total pain. You can't go to a movie, you have to stick your leg straight out, just these little things. That's really very basic everyday life. Sometimes I say, It's too tough, I can't do it. Then I think about giving in to it and I get going again because other people have it so much tougher than I.

Now if it ever gets to the point where I no longer have fun playing tennis, let me out. But that's for me to decide, not the world. I've already retired once, in 1975. It's very frightening. Even when I was eleven years old, watching the older players, I'd say to myself, You little thing, that's going to be you someday. I'm going to have to own up to the fact that I can't run as fast, my eyes aren't quite as sharp, all the things that performers, especially athletes or dancers, have to deal with.

People who love their work keep going back for more. The public doesn't understand that. They keep asking, "Well, why do you keep playing? You have enough money, you've won everything you ever wanted to. Now why do you want to go out there and beat your head against a wall?" Well, because I *like* it. It's in my blood, it's a part of me.

Each generation makes its statement and leaves something for the others. Every time I walk onto the center court at Wimbledon, I think of all those people who came before me—Suzanne Lenglen, Alice Marble, Helen Wills Moody, Althea Gibson, Maureen Connolly—all those players left me something. I wouldn't play the way I play without them. And all I can do is leave the next generation something—my personality, my style of play, my titles.

The kids in tennis today are younger and they are more readily accepted. I didn't play full-time tennis until I was twenty-one. Today at fifteen you're a professional. Tracy Austin is seventeen and she's already made over a million dollars just in prize money and over another million in advertisements. Her frame of reference is totally different. These kids have much higher expectations than we did, which I love about them. It's their system now and whether they'll keep it or not, who knows? That's up to them.

My sport can perpetuate itself because we created a system and the system is healthy. We did make an impact. It's trickled down to the grass roots level and it's been accepted. Children at seven, eight, nine years of age are motivated. We got them excited. They could see there was a vehicle of opportunity for them.

You have to think about solutions all the time. Very few people have vision. They can't perceive the future, or the consequences of an action, a change. They can't visualize, they can't imagine. Imagination is probably the most powerful thing we have and yet how few people ever use it. That is why dance and music are so wonderful. How to shape time and space—imagination!

Take the Bobby Riggs match, for instance. To beat a fifty-nine-year-old guy was no thrill for me. The thrill was exposing a lot of new people to tennis. But the most important thing about the match was that women liked themselves better that day.

In Philadelphia a few weeks later, I walked into the offices of the *Bulletin* to meet the editor, and all the secretaries stood up and clapped. They just went berserk. The editor said, "You have no idea what you did. The day after you played Bobby Riggs, all of these women asked for a raise."

People don't change overnight. It doesn't matter what the law says. You can have a civil rights act, you can make abortion legal, but you still have to deal with what people feel and think. And that's what it's all about. You slowly have to persuade people and hope they are reasonable enough to see things in a logical objective way.

I don't think about the past too much, only if it's going to help me today. The danger of thinking about the past all the time is that you live in the past. A lot of athletes do that. They remember when they were number one. That's all they talk about to their friends. How boring. You don't want to hear about somebody who was champion in 1958. They don't live in 1958, they live in 1981. I get burned out a lot, sure. I take a rest and then get charged up again. I want to shape the todays and tomorrows.

# Addie Wyatt

*Addie Wyatt (born 1924, Brookhaven, Mississippi) is a labor leader and one of the few women in the labor movement to wield power. Since the age of twenty she has dedicated herself to improving working conditions for women and all workers, and to the concept of equal pay for equal work. She is vice president of the United Food and Commercial Workers International Union and the director of its Civil Rights and Women's Affairs Department. In 1974 she helped found the Coalition of Labor Union Women (CLUW), the only trade union women's organization of its kind in the country.*

**W**HEN I WAS TWENTY years old, I applied for a job as a typist at one of the meat-packing plants in the city of Chicago. I had to go to work for the same reasons most women have to go to work, because I needed the money. All of my life I've had to stand up for myself. I was the second of eight children in my family, the oldest daughter, and from the time I was three years old I had the responsibility, like many older black children, to hip and to lap all the younger children, and to sort of fight for them and protect them and look out after their best interests.

I could type sixty to seventy words a minute and I thought that was sufficient for me to qualify for a typing job. It was the only marketable skill I had at the time. I was hired for the typing job, but I was sent to the canning department to pack stew in cans for the U.S. Army. I would tell the workers on the line that within a short time I would be assigned to work in the office. I didn't understand why they sniggered about it, but they knew that I'd never get that job.

I began to inquire about the wages and conditions of the workers on the line. In the early forties, in most places, if you got hired as a white typist you might have earned something like $19 a week. If you were hired as a black typist of a fair complexion you might have earned about $12 a week, and if you were black like me—dark—and got hired at all, you might have earned somewhere around $8 a week. We were just coming out of the Depression. Working in the plant on the stew line I was making 62 cents an hour, which came to at least $24.80 a week. That was more money than I had ever seen at one time in my life. I thought that the job with the most prestige would have paid more money than the job that required the laboring skills, but I found out that prestige didn't always beget money. I stayed in the plant.

I discovered that I received better wages and working conditions working in the plant because the workers in the plant were organized. After a while, I was assigned a job to place caps on the cans, which I thought was a better job than packing stew in the cans. I liked that job, but after I'd been working there for several weeks, a young white woman was hired and given that job, and I was sent back to the stew line. I protested.

In most black families such as mine, there was always the hope, the prayers, the encouragement and the inspiration for the children that they would grow up to be something, and most importantly, that they would believe in themselves and believe that they could be whatever they wanted to be.

So when a young black woman who was the union steward in my department at that time took up my grievance and told me how I could really deal with management, I was determined to follow it through to the end. When I found myself sitting with the union on one side of that big table and the people who ran the packing house sitting on the other, I felt power. I got my job back and I knew why—the union was behind me. I joined the United Packinghouse Workers Union in 1942.

As a black woman I feel the pain of both racial and sexual discrimination, and both are very evil. It is hard to say which hurts the most. You're just in pain and you'd like to see the shackles of both sexism and racism removed. The lives of many women are very lonely and if you happen to be a worker and rearing a family, it can be a very depressing, lonely, frustrating experience with no one to share it with.

I was in my early twenties when I raised two of my own children and five brothers and sisters. Like most women, I didn't have an easy job. It isn't an easy responsibility to be a homemaker and jobholder outside the home. Ofttimes I'd have to work very long and tiring hours, and the responsibility of holding a job and then trying to make a home were very frustrating and difficult. It was especially critical when the children were small and we didn't have child-care services available. Every morning was a child-care crisis, wondering what would happen to the smaller children while the other children went to school. Ofttimes I had to leave them with neighbors and friends. When I worked in the plant, I very seldom had a rest period or lunch hour because I used that time to phone the children, trying to comfort them so that they'd get the feeling that I was somewhere near rather than afar.

You don't always know the damage that you've done to your children or to yourself. You don't always know. Sometimes when you look back over it you think you might have done some things differently, but you don't know how things would have come out even if you had. So you just conclude that you did the best that you could with what you had and you don't regret it.

There were other women in the plant going through the same things, and I guess all of us at some time felt very lonely because we always feel that "nobody knows the trouble *we* see." You feel that your experience and your problems are unique, but that's why the union became so important for us.

My first union meeting—that is a picture I could never forget. I walked into that room and there were white workers, black workers, Spanish-speaking workers, young and old, male and female, all talking together about their problems and mapping out strategy to resolve those problems. Some of the leaders began to explain that this was union policy, this was its procedure, workers meeting and sharing together. They were using slogans such as "Black and White, Unite and Fight." Well, I had never really seen that picture before and I had never encountered that experience anywhere else. I learned that I was part of a labor community and that community had banded together for the purpose of improving our lives through collective bargaining, political and social action. These were goals that I had set before me too. These were objectives I had dreamed of for a long time. The union helped to clarify those goals and those objectives and to learn how I could best achieve them through unity with other workers. One of the most prized pictures that I have of myself was taken in 1951 when ten thousand or more workers were rallying together in the stockyards of Chicago, on a cold day, ten degrees below zero, carrying signs saying, "Negro and White, United and Fight," "We want a wage increase," "Let the packers pay, we want a decrease in our taxes." But then there's another little sign which I'm holding. I'm stuck down between my brothers, trying to keep warm. It reads, "Equal Pay For Women."

My union had a women's committee and we talked together about our experiences. We shared our techniques, our strategies for overcoming some of our problems. This was always comforting.

After I had been working at the meat-packing plant for several years, I became pregnant and needed to take a leave of absence. Well, at that time most women who took leaves of absence wouldn't have a job to return to. But in this instance our union had a provision in its contract whereby I could take a year's leave of absence and return to my same job, with my seniority and other benefits intact. This was very important to me, being a young woman, and being black.

When you look at some of the goals that unions have achieved, I think you have to conclude that the only way we were able to achieve these seemingly impossible tasks is that there is much more unity among trade unionists than most people realize. When I became active in the United Packinghouse Workers Union, I began to tell my story, how I was discriminated against at the front office and was refused a job as a typist and ended up in the plant. The union banded together, took on the major packing companies, the Armour, the Swift, the Wilson and the Cudahys, and succeeded in breaking down discrimination in the front office, not only in Chicago but in their plants, north and south.

At the same time our union was fighting to eliminate a wage differential of at least 14 cents an hour between the earnings of women and men, even when men and women were doing identical jobs. There was also a wage differential that existed between workers in the North and workers in the South. In the South, one of the companies had two pay lines—white and black. When it was raining, the white workers had a canopy over their heads and the water would run off onto the black workers who stood in the next line.

The union took the position that we had to have an enforceable antidiscrimination clause in all our contracts, and that was before the Civil Rights Act of 1962, and by the 1950s, all our major contracts had completely eliminated the wage differential and the geographical wage discrimination, and this was before the Equal Pay Act of 1963.

But for one union to succeed and move ahead, you have to have coalitions. The merger of the AFL and CIO brought together unions all over the country to deal with programs and strategies for the entire organized labor movement. Union leaders now get together and determine what the concerns of their members are and how we can best accomplish the goals we've set before us. We have lobbyists in the Congress, in the state legislatures, trying to move our nation in the right direction and endeavoring to protect the interest of working people.

Working people ought to be able to enjoy some of the fruits of their labor. They ought not to have to spend all of their lives living on prespent income to the extent that there is nothing they can have beyond just the everyday grind and just the bare necessities of life. That is why the union bargains for vacations and holidays. There was a time when you would negotiate contracts and if you talked about vacations, the employers would say, "Who's going to pay a worker while he's off doing nothing?" And now some workers have up to five weeks a year vacation time. Some even have sabbatical leaves. More of them have better wages so that they can purchase some of the enjoyable goods and services.

In 1973, several trade union women who had been active in the labor movement for a number of years got together and decided it was time that trade union women began speaking for themselves, time that we took our rightful place in the labor movement and in our society, and that nobody could really speak for us except ourselves. We had been told that women would not respond, that they were not interested and that you couldn't get union women together. We didn't believe that because we had been together and we knew other women wanted to experience this sharing.

We sent out a call for union women in different parts of the country, and the response was overwhelming. We held regional meetings where women came and talked about their concerns and strongly supported the idea of a coalition. At our first founding conference, held in Chicago in 1974, we were expecting some 1,500 women to attend, but more than 3,200 women came to that conference. Most of the women came on their own, at their own expense.

As a result of that meeting we founded the Coalition of Labor Union Women (CLUW), of which I am vice president. We've had several conventions since then, and we have local chapters throughout the country. Our four major goals are: (1) to strengthen the role and participation of women within their unions and within the trade union movement as a whole; (2) to seek affirmative action in the workplace and to obtain equal rights for women in hiring, promotion, classification and pay; (3) to encourage union women to play an active role in the legislative and political processes of their unions and the nation and (4) to organize the millions of unorganized women workers.

Unions offer some fantastic opportunities in which workers can participate not only in their union organization but in many other areas of our society. We've learned great skills as we participate in union meetings and conferences and conventions, and we use those same skills to help build our world, our churches, our communities, our government, wherever we are. CLUW is organized so that we can develop and pass on these skills to women and to establish very important networks so that union sisters and working women, wherever they are, can find a listening ear, a reaching hand; to find satisfaction in their lives, in their work, in their home, in their community lives and in their political lives. This is all very, very important.

When I think about what I've contributed to the organized labor movement and what I have received in return, I can only conclude that it has been a profitable venture. I've contributed so little and received so much. I think this is basically true for most workers. I'd be the first to say that the unions have not really achieved all that I thought they ought to achieve. This is understandable . . . though you have to define who and what the union is. We're the union. It is an imperfect institution because it is made up and led by people like us, who are imperfect but seeking to perfect ourselves and seeking to perfect our movement. Imperfect as it is, it's the best that we have as working people, therefore it's up to us to strengthen it and to make it as effective and as responsive as possible to our needs.

We've got more work to do to completely bridge the gap between the promise of equality and the fulfillment of that promise because it's the only way to win for ourselves the fuller and better life we all seek. I'm a part of that movement and I hope to remain a part of it.

# Bella Abzug

Bella Abzug (born 1920, Bronx, New York) is a lawyer and politician who has been an outspoken crusader for peace and human rights, a leader in the political struggle for equal rights and opportunities for women and an advocate of responsive and open government. She was United States representative from New York from 1971 until 1977, the first representative to run with a strong feminist plank. She founded the National Women's Political Caucus, Women's Strike for Peace and the New Democratic Coalition.

**W**HEN I FIRST RAN for Congress, people said to me, "How long have you been a feminist?" And I said, "I suppose from the day I was born." I was born in 1920, the year that women got the vote. I come from a home of immigrants and like many other immigrants, my parents came to this country because they were either persecuted religiously or they needed economic opportunity or had no political freedom. So my parents raised us to feel for the right of all people and imbued in us a deep sense of social justice.

I grew up during the Depression and my life was very much affected by it. No matter what the hardships, my parents believed deeply in America and in their lives and the lives of their children. As children we believed we had to influence our own lives, not only by making something of ourselves, but also by making sure that society would make for us and do for us as a result of our influencing and affecting it. So for all these reasons, I have been a socially conscious human being from the day I can remember.

I can remember my first political struggle. As a kid I was a very active Zionist and I used to go on the subways of New York City and collect money for the Jewish National Fund and make little speeches when the train stopped at the station, to explain to people why there should be a homeland or a state for the Jewish people.

It was hard. A lot of things were not available to us. We had a modest life, a humble life, and also there was a difference between what boys got and what girls got. I didn't accept that. I wanted to ride a bike. But my folks thought I should not have a bike, it wasn't safe for girls, and so I used to ride other people's bikes. I wanted to play all the games that I wanted to play—checkers in the streets of New York—and I did. I went to Hebrew school. Fewer young girls went than boys.

My folks were very good to me. My father died when I was thirteen. My mother was fantastic. She always backed me up and thought everything I did was great, and that's probably responsible for much of my confidence and sense of self. When she came to this country she was very young. She was studying and doing well in elementary school. She wanted to be a teacher, but her father took her out of school and she became a bookkeeper in his store. When my father died, she always felt that had she had a profession as a teacher, she would have been much better off financially. So she was very strong for educating my sister and myself. We went to public schools and then we went to Hunter College, which had no tuition. We would never have been able to go to college if we couldn't get a free education. Then I wanted to go to law school and my mother was very supportive.

I decided I was going to be a lawyer when I was eleven years old. I can't tell you that I had a role model of a woman lawyer because I really didn't. There were some, a few, but I didn't really know who they were. I made up my mind that you could fight for social justice more effectively as a lawyer and so I became a lawyer.

Since there were only a few women lawyers, I knew that it was going to be very rough. I applied to Harvard Law School because I heard it was the best law school. Harvard wrote back and said they didn't accept women. I was outraged. I always tell this story because it's so cute about my mother. I turned to my mother and I said, "Can you believe this?" I always say "I turned to my mother," because in those days there was no women's movement so you always turned to your mother. Now I always say, my two daughters have the best of both worlds. They're able to turn to me and the women's movement at the same time. But anyway, I turned to my mother and said, "This is an outrage." (I always had a decent sense of outrage.) My mother said, "What do you want to go to Harvard for? It's far away. You haven't got the carfare anyhow. Go to Columbia. It's near home. They'll probably give you a scholarship and it only costs five cents on the subway." And I did that. I got a scholarship and it only cost five cents on the subway. I always say that's when I became an advocate of low-cost public mass transportation.

But I became a lawyer too. I was interested in the labor field. I graduated from law school at the top of my class and I was on *Law Review,* which meant that I was supposed to have my pick of the top law jobs on the market, but when I went for a job, law firms asked me questions like could I type and they offered me salaries that were lower than the salaries of the clients they represented. It was dreadful. And in the court, it was more dreadful. Judges behaved outrageously toward women. Lawyers and clients were similarly disposed. The labor field was full of male union leaders. My firm sent me to a big labor board hearing and everybody figured I was some secretary. After the negotiations were over they came up and told me what they'd been saying behind my back. When they got to know me they realized I was a hardheaded and competent person but it was a struggle all the way. I practiced law every day from the day I got out of law school until the day I ran for public office.

When I first came on the political scene, many people thought I just stepped out of the kitchen right into Congress. They thought I just decided to run for Congress and won by a fluke or something. I didn't. I had a long history before I came to Congress. I was an activist, active as a lawyer and as a citizen in the civil liberties, civil rights, peace and women's movements. Politics was my extracurricular work.

I worked in a lot of campaigns and I did a lot of issue building and tried to pressure candidates to take positions on issues I was committed to. Then when they did, I would help mobilize large numbers of people and support for them. I helped in the campaigns of a lot of politicians who promised change, yet I saw little change.

I was very fed up with the war in Vietnam, very anguished. We were making some progress but it wasn't going anywhere. There was the invasion of Cambodia. Here we were working . . . my mother used to say, "I can't understand it. You work every day and night for peace and we still have war." She had such confidence in me that she figured if I was working at it, it should have been ended. But that's it, we were working day and night and day and night and it was getting worse. The movement was getting bigger, but our representatives were not doing enough in Congress.

I never expected to run for Congress. It was not part of my game plan or anything like that. My decision came from years of frustration and disappointment and will, I guess. Finally one of the politicians I had helped to elect said to me, "Well, you always criticize. Why don't you do it yourself?" I said, "You know, you've got a point there. I think I'll do it."

I ran for Congress as a representative from New York City in 1970. Everyone was startled by my platform. I said, "I'm going to Congress because I think Congress needs women. There's no diversity there, and I'm going to fight for women's rights." My campaign slogan was "This woman's place is in the House—the House of Representatives." That's where that slogan came from, from my campaign. Well, Congress, the media, they all went bananas. That was a shock. Nobody had ever run on a women's rights plank in their platform. Other women in Congress were for women's programs but they didn't run on them. I was the first organized feminist to run for political office, and although my platform dealt with such issues as the needs of the cities and ending the war in Vietnam, women's issues were prominently emphasized.

So when I went to Congress in 1971, I fought for equal rights for women, yes, but I fought to end the war in Vietnam and for my city to get its share of the tax dollar and for open government and against the seniority system. I've been fighting that male seniority system all my life. I was also the first to call for the impeachment of Mr. Nixon. I didn't worry about taking risks. I believed in things and went to Congress to change the things I believed in, even though it was difficult until these views became more popular.

I'm not a believer in utopia. I think change will take place, but not without tremendous conflict. Women cannot secure their economic or political needs under our present priorities. There's no room for us in the system as presently organized. This is one of the critical problems. There wasn't any plan for us and there's still no plan for women in this country.

Most government policies were developed when women had different lives and families had different lives than they do now. If you have a huge military budget and a synthetic fuel program, you can't provide the services that women require, even equal pay for equal work. There's no room for that in the budget. The money has gone into other things. That's why President Carter fired me in 1979 as head of the Women's Commission, because our committee said to him, "You can't cut the little that women have in the budget. The majority of women in this country are suffering. They are the majority of the poor, the majority of the unemployed, the majority of the old; they can hardly survive in this period of economic crisis." Carter's answer was that economic policies were not women's issues.

Culturally and sociologically, the women's movement has made an enormous impact. Men and women accept the equality of women as an ideal. We're on the threshold of enormous change but we've made little progress economically or politically, and until we do, we're going to be nowhere.

This country unfortunately is a fragile democracy. Our sovereign control is wrested from us if the people withdraw from participation, and many have withdrawn at this point. The women's movement is out there but it has to get mobilized on a political and economic level. It has to get very stubborn and say, "All right, we gave you a chance. We've begged, we've pleaded, we've prayed for our rights. We've supported men for office who made promises and then broke them. We now have to make up our minds not to do that anymore." Women have to promote their own interests. We must develop our own independent political power to show our clout. We must be able to develop a women's political machine that can deliver a vote or withhold one when it counts.

The American women's movement is no longer one organization or one ideology or one life-style. It's affected every home, every life. Women should not feel guilty about being wives and mothers. If they love it, that's what they should be doing, that's where they should stay. I'm all for it. One of the first bills I introduced in Congress was Social Security for homemakers. I knew there would always be women who were going to stay in their homes. They should get some protection for their old age. Everybody said, "Oh, she's crazy again." It was a nonsubject when I introduced it, but now Congress is talking about it seriously.

If women work, either because they must earn a living or because they want to, then they should be able to do that too. That's what it's all about, the right of choice. I want everybody to have the right to do what they want to.

My private life is a conventional one. I have a conventional nuclear family, I'm married thirty-six years, I have two daughters, I'm a monogamous type, stuff like that. But it is unconventional in other respects. I was married when I was in law school and I had my kids and I continued working.

Everybody in politics has to make sacrifices, but first of all, I didn't run for office until I was fifty. My kids were grown, my older daughter was twenty, my younger was seventeen, they were in school. My husband was alone a lot. That was a little hard, but it's hard, I think, for every political family. I hated living in Washington alone. There was no one to talk to.

I have been a working mother all my life. That has never changed. I wanted everything. I wanted to be a wife, a mother, a lawyer, an active citizen. And all the things I wanted to do, I became. I never intended to become a politician but I became one and I want to be one.

Recently I've been traveling around the country. I've been in most every state and people listen if someone leads them toward the truth. But they need the leadership. I tell them that this is their country, it belongs to them, it's their institutions, their taxes, and they have to participate and exercise their sovereign rights to find the vehicles of pressure and to influence the course of this country. No change ever took place in this country without pressure from grass roots movements, nothing; whether it's ending the war in Vietnam, or sexual discrimination, it always comes from outside of government institutions.

It isn't enough for individual groups to organize only around their own needs. They must also coalesce with others who share the same ideas or have similar needs. Women's issues are not separate from the interests of everyone in this country. You cannot eliminate sexism unless you also eliminate racism, poverty and institutional violence at home and abroad— all go together. The women's movement is therefore a humanist movement.

I think women are the most dynamic, moving force today. They have enormous needs, they have a majority, and they can't make it in society as it's now moving. They therefore have to be a force for changing priorities. It's absolutely critical. They will come to see that, little by little. They are beginning to see that now.

When I go around the country talking like this to people, I get a terrific response. I feel a responsibility to speak out and organize and activate because I believe every individual can make some difference. I believe I can make a little difference in the atmosphere needed for change. I've seen that through pressure and education, people came to understand and they have changed, and have changed government policy.

Over the years I've become very sensitive to an audience and a mood and I sense if I'm reaching them. I watch them carefully and I see what they're interested in and what they're reacting to. It's like playing different chords. I always try to get my message across, but in different ways, with reason, with emotion, with humor—it depends. That's something that people who lecture develop. With me, much is instinctive, but a great deal is also from experience. Don't forget, I've been making speeches since I was a little kid. To do the work of a member of Congress or to be a public figure takes skill. You also should know what you're doing, it helps to be smart, to be knowledgeable, to be a hard worker and to be determined. You have to get up every morning as I did when I was in the Congress, for example, and say, "What am I going to do today or otherwise they're going to do it to me?"

It's very hard to get yourself to do that every day. It's like being a Spartan. I believe that what keeps me going is my idealism, my belief that this country belongs to the people and that no power structure should block our rights. I don't do things for my own satisfaction alone. I want to see change in my lifetime, yes, but I want to see my daughters have a chance to flower without having to battle every inch of the way.

It hurts to be attacked the way I've been for taking forward positions or speaking more strongly than some. To give some leadership, you have to take positions on the issues that are ahead of the moment. You feel

pain and you feel rejected, but you go on because you believe you're right.
People tell me that my caring comes through. I hope so. You have to have
a lot of ego and believe in yourself too, in what you think and what you
are.

You see, it is important to point out that although the women in this
book may appear to have had easy success, actually these are women
who have conducted some kind of struggle around their lives. And most
women are conducting a struggle of one kind or another, whether it's a
homemaker who wants some value and dignity for her work, or whether
it's a widow embarking on a new career, or a working woman pursuing a
career, seeking equal pay, or a student pioneering in a field formerly
closed to women or a poor woman seeking to survive and so many
seeking control and choice over their bodies and their lives. The only
difference is that the women in the book are women who conduct their
struggle on more visible and public levels. But everybody is engaged in a
struggle today; everybody is examining the human condition, women in
particular. That's why there's so much potential strength in this
movement, because it touches so many places.

What I try to do is make women feel that there isn't anything they
can't do if they want to. And when I speak to them or meet with them, I
try to give them that feeling, that this is their right. Whatever they want to
do, they have a right to be and a right to expect support from institutions
which affect their lives. I also try to awaken young people. This is their
future. They're going to be in charge in the year 2000. I tell them that they
are the major force for change in this country and that they can change
their own lives and the lives of others by acting on that together with
other people. When I've finished, I like to think they believe it.

# Shirley Hufstedler

*Shirley Hufstedler (born 1925, Denver, Colorado), one of the most distinguished jurists in the country, was the only woman on a federal appellate bench from 1968 to 1979. She set a standard in her knowledge and application of the law and was recognized for her liberal decisions; she has been considered the most likely female candidate for the Supreme Court. In 1979, President Carter appointed her secretary of the federal government's newly created Department of Education.*

I CAN'T PINPOINT THE TIME when I decided I was going to have a career, but from the time I was a very young child I knew that I was going to be an independent person. And I also knew that I was going to marry and to have a family. My mother taught school before she married. She was not someone who was totally enchanted with the role of a housewife. And while she never said so in so many words, one absorbs attitudes all along. Nonetheless, she insisted I learn the household arts, and I did. That knowledge has always been useful.

Both my mother and father expected me to excel intellectually and to use all the talents that I had. Neither of them ever made a speech to this effect. The ideas were dripped over my head from the time I was an infant, and I received occasional encouragement from some schoolteachers along the way and from other people who were older and outside my family.

When I grew up, the term "role model" had not been invented. But even if it had, it would have been very hard to meet a career woman. Women who achieved outside their own homes were rare. To be sure, I was aware that there were some women in the world who "did things." I admired Mrs. Eleanor Roosevelt and Amelia Earhart, but I never expected to meet either one of them. When I was growing up, almost all women and girls responded en masse to the prevailing social dictate: The place of women was in the home. And they dutifully obeyed.

Apart from my immediate family, my ideas were formed primarily from independent study. I discovered libraries and museums when I was a small child. Books opened my mind to ideas, to the knowledge of history, and turned my attention to people, times and places all over the globe. Museums are wonderful teachers. I could wander around and think about the fascinating array of all the things there, all the creatures of the earth and all the people, both living and dead. I began studying the piano as a young child. I dreamed of a life as a concert pianist. I did not abandon that idea until, after many years of work, I realized that I lacked one essential ingredient for success: real musical talent. But music became a lasting part of my life.

When I was fourteen years old, I had my first paying job as a salesgirl. All kinds of jobs followed. I did door-to-door canvassing for statistical companies, I was a proofreader for a newspaper and a business manager for my college newspaper. I worked in a mortuary. As a nonprofessional teacher, I taught music, shorthand, English and typing. All of that time, I was searching for a career in which I could grow and in which I could succeed.

Although my family did not have specific career plans for me, they did for my brother, Kenneth. He was expected to follow in my father's footsteps as a naval officer and to enter my father's construction business. He did both. In contrast, I was supposed to find something marvelous to do and go do it without any specific direction—not surprising at the time. The more visible "feminine occupations" were nursing, schoolteaching and housewifery. Although each of those occupations has merit, my family knew that I was not attracted to them. My family also knew it was futile to try to force me in directions that I did not want to go.

I did not choose my career until after I had graduated from the University of New Mexico with a Bachelor of Business Administration. Following graduation, I worked as an executive secretary for Paulette Goddard and Burgess Meredith, at the same time continuing to explore avenues for graduate work. I found out that many of the interesting career possibilities were effectively closed to me.

I considered medical school, but scratched that idea rather quickly. My undergraduate background did not adequately prepare me for entry and I didn't have enough money to repeat undergraduate training. I was interested in the foreign service. I explored that possibility carefully, and I abandoned the notion when I found out what happened to women in the foreign service—nothing.

I was still determined to become a professional woman. I had had some undergraduate courses in law. I enjoyed them and I did well in them. After discussing my interest in the law with the few people I knew who had experience in the law, I decided I would go to law school.

From the little I was able to glean about law practice, I believed that the law would give me more choices for career development than any other available route. I had only a hazy idea about what lawyers actually did. There were no lawyers in my family. The only lawyer I knew was the family lawyer—a comfortable, pleasant man. To me, practicing lawyers were an amalgam of Darrow, Dickens and Daumier. Despite my galloping ignorance, I was convinced that at the end of three years at law school, I would emerge with a profession and with much greater freedom to control my own life.

My plan was to select an excellent law school, obtain admission and perform well, but first I had to find a school that would accept me. Many law schools did not admit women then. I chose Stanford Law School. I was admitted and I was a good student. I was selected for the first issue of the *Stanford Law Review,* and in my third year, I became article and book review editor for the *Review.* Although I did not know it at the time, my work on the *Law Review* was a turning point in my life.

One of my classmates with whom I worked closely on the *Review* was Seth Hufstedler. He was first in our class, president of the student body and a man of extraordinary depth and talent. I admired and respected him, and before we graduated, he became first in my heart as well. We married shortly after our graduation from law school. Our classmates on the *Review* and the professors who advised the first *Review* members became my close personal friends for life. In professional terms, the meticulous legal analysis and critical writing skills learned during the two years of *Law Review* work strengthened my professional competence.

The class of 1949 has no counterpart today. Law was a masculine profession then. The few women who went to law school were generally considered to be peculiar—or worse. When I entered Stanford in 1946, the overwhelming majority of my classmates were returning World War II veterans. In the freshman class of some 279 students, five of us were women. Three of the women decided they did not like law school, and left after the first year. One other woman and I graduated in the class of 1949. Of all the law school graduates admitted to practice in California in January 1950, seven of us were women.

After graduation, I went job hunting. It was a tough job market for both men and women. I not only wanted to practice law, I wanted to become a trial lawyer. The idea that a female would aspire to become a trial lawyer was thought to be not only peculiar, but downright bizarre.

I was offered a clerkship with the California Supreme Court in San Francisco. In the meantime, Seth and I had married. He wanted to practice law in Los Angeles. I hesitated in helpless indecision for about a half second before I turned down the clerkship and joined him in Los Angeles. I found a job as a researcher, but it very quickly became evident that I was going to have to make my own market as a lawyer because there were so few opportunities for women to enter litigation.

I volunteered at the Legal Aid Society to gain experience. I had a deep set of convictions about the need to use law not only as a tool for civil rights and justice but also as an instrument of social accommodation and change. The law was the glue that held society together under pressure. I saw that the law could do that. I also learned the limitations of the law in dealing with human beings and their very real problems.

My experiences in growing up in several states and attending many schools under different circumstances gave me personal insight into the reality of injustice. I saw firsthand how one set of human beings treated another set of human beings. I found out there were all kinds of discrimination against children. I saw what happened to youngsters who were gifted and Hispanic or Indian and how the treatment of the larger society affected their lives. I found out that, in many respects, the good kids didn't always win. All kinds of roadblocks had been placed in the path of many youngsters I knew. I saw talented youngsters being squashed. It was obvious that there was injustice.

Although I had a quite lonely life as a child and, as did many people who grew up in the Depression, knew what it was like not to have any money, I never thought of myself as some kind of victim. I saw myself as a person who could help others and as a person who could do something significant to fight the injustices I knew about. At the same time I recognized that if I were going to be doing anything effective, I was going to have to do an outstanding job in the areas of the greatest intellectual challenges in the law and be recognized for it. It took a good deal of time and a great deal of effort to be able to accomplish both.

Law practice was not what I expected it to be. Life is full of surprises and law practice was too. It wasn't the sort of era, perhaps it never is, in which a person could decide upon a very specific blueprint and have the world fit into it. Trying to write history in advance does not work. One must appreciate and seize the opportunities and, in many respects, make the opportunities for one's self. As one branches out, continues to learn, consolidates experiences and takes new directions, personal growth and development will follow. That is what I did.

I developed my own practice. I undertook to become a lawyer who would specialize in complex civil litigation, primarily as a person to be retained by other lawyers to do this work. That kind of practice specialty hones the talent for dealing with extremely complicated issues. It builds a reputation for quality among other lawyers. It requires a certain expansion of the mind in exploring nonlegal materials.

To become successful as a litigator in complex litigation, it is necessary to be able to analyze nonlegal details and facts in many settings. One must not only learn "the law," one has to learn how businesses are put together, how industries work, the details of technology involved in the litigation and how people in any litigation setting think, react and behave. For instance, to prepare to cross-examine an expert witness on any subject, the lawyer who is to cross-examine the expert must learn the area about which the testimony will be given as meticulously as the expert himself or herself. The litigation lawyer must be able to master not only the law but also the subject matter in which the litigation arises.

As I was developing my own practice, I was also associated with the firm that later became Beardsley, Hufstedler and Kemble, my husband's firm. To practice both in and outside a law firm, as I did, was not uncommon many years ago, although it is unusual today. At the same time, I was also a housewife and mother to our son Steven, born in 1953. Steven graduated from medical school in 1980, and he is interning now.

Perhaps everyone who becomes a litigation specialist thinks about being a judge someday. At first the idea was rather an amorphous one. I knew that I would have to learn my craft as a lawyer before I could consider the bench. I also had to have the feeling of confidence that I could do the job and do it very well. By the time I had worked as a litigation specialist for a decade, I believed that I was ready for the bench. Fortunately, Governor Edmund G. Brown thought so too. In 1961, Governor Brown appointed me judge of the Los Angeles County Superior Court. At that time, I was the only woman in a court of 120 judges.

In my five years on that court, I served two years in general trial departments, two years in highly specialized law departments and one as appointee to the Appellate Department. In 1966, Governor Brown appointed me to the California Court of Appeals, and after two years on that court, President Johnson appointed me circuit judge, United States Court of Appeals for the Ninth Circuit. During my eleven years of service on that court, I was the sole woman in the United States serving as a federal appellate judge. The late Judge Florence Allen, who was appointed by President Roosevelt in 1934, was the only other woman to have a seat on a federal appellate court before I was named. I left the bench in 1979 when President Carter named me the first secretary of education.

People have different opinions about what it takes to be a good judge, or jurist. But I believe that most lawyers would agree on several points. A good jurist must have the intellectual capacity to deal with difficult issues. When I was young, I placed intellectual capacity higher on the list of judicial virtues than I came to do later. It is not that intellectual strength is not important, but, especially for a trial judge, temperament, courtesy and humanity may be even more important than crystalline brilliance. Next, I believe that every good jurist must have the faculty of judgment. Judgment means the ability to decide, to decide promptly and to decide rationally. But the concept involves much more than that. Judgment includes the ability to understand what things motivate people, the kinds of options that make sense for people in the circumstances and environment in which they live and in which they will live. Every capable jurist always has to know that he or she should try to avoid doing anything that cannot be undone if the decision is wrong. In human affairs when there is a choice, lesser rather than greater intervention is usually the wise course.

I am not saying that a fine jurist has to be a candidate for sainthood. The kind of person for which one searches for the bench is an individual who has a spacious mind: a person who has a quality of experience, a basic understanding of the law, an appreciation of the limitations and the possibilities of the law, a sense of discipline about adhering to the law whether the judge personally likes it or does not. A fine jurist has to be willing to work very hard. He or she must deal with the persons before them honestly, without fudging the facts and with courage to do what is right under the law no matter how generally unpopular the decision may be.

Both men and women have these qualities. Many women,

nevertheless, have some distinct advantages. Because boys and girls in our society are differently socialized from the time they are very little, it is difficult for many men to use the intuition and the compassion with which they were born. Women, more than men, are likely to listen to what is not said, to observe and to appreciate the nuances of behavior. That talent has been both inbred and taught, because women for so many centuries have been dependent on the will and the whims of others. Dependents must always be wary and observant because misinterpretation of the intent and motives of the dominant persons can have grievous effect on them.

It takes a very very strong man in our society to be compassionate. There are individual circumstances in which a man can be compassionate. You can take care of your aged and crippled mother and that's all right, but it isn't so all right to show that supportiveness and concern in other structures because men and boys have for a long time had to believe that that isn't their function or role. That's one of the pities of sex stereotyping. I'm not saying it's innate in the human being.

The world has changed in the most extraordinary way in the last forty years. Our society is much more complicated. We are affected dramatically and immediately by events that happen in the remotest corners of our globe. We have all kinds of power groups forming for particular causes. Whole industries have grown where seeds were not even planted a few years ago. For instance, thirty years ago industry did not need to worry about protecting its software; the computer industry did not exist. The whole information society did not exist. The potential for multiplying information and telecommunications systems did not exist.

The electronics industry has been built. Conglomerates have been created. We have become concerned about the environment. Different minority groups that had been left out of the social equation have now come forward, bringing to the surface problems that were always there, for which there had been no representation. In short, there are multiple factors which have made these issues more complex and there has been a feeling that government has not been as responsive as it might have been. In terms of growth, larger structures are much more impersonal and much more difficult to deal with.

I empathize with those who yearn for a simpler world—for some bygone golden age of domestic and international tranquility. Perhaps for a few people at some time in history there was such an age. But for the mass of humanity it is an age that never was. We are an immensely rich and powerful country, and we have enjoyed for more than thirty years unprecedented growth and prosperity. However, even in the boom years, millions of Americans were never invited to the banquet table. Women, children, old people and minorities have just demands. Violence, bigotry and hatred are always simmering, even when they are not conspicuously erupting. It is not remarkable that the human capacity for evil has not vanished during an era of prosperity. What is perhaps remarkable is the resiliency of our people in responding to stress. Despite all of our buffeting by national and international events, by great turbulence caused by convulsive technological and social changes, we are still a generous people, a patriotic people and a religious people. Although we chafe at the restraints of both law and government, we believe in both. No matter how short we may fall in reaching our ideals of freedom and justice for all—we cherish those ideals.

# Nancy Hanks

*Nancy Hanks (born 1927, Miami, Florida) is responsible for organizing substantial government aid to the arts. As chairman of the National Endowment for the Arts from 1969 to 1977, she worked with Congress to significantly increase the endowment's budget and develop a successful program to match government support with state, municipal and private monies. These efforts made theater, music, dance and the visual arts available to a public outside urban centers throughout America that had never before had an opportunity to enjoy them.*

**M**Y ARTISTIC APPRECIATION WAS very limited when I was growing up. I was raised in Miami Beach, Florida, and at that time we did not have a museum, nor an orchestra. My own university, Duke University in North Carolina, provided very few artistic opportunities at the time I graduated in 1949.

When I moved to Washington in 1951 for my first job with the federal government, my eyes were opened. The museums in Washington were great then. Arena Stage was starting that year, the Old Gaiety Theater had road shows and the National Symphony struggled to play. It was a new world for me. From that time on, I took every opportunity I could. I went to concerts all the time, and the theater and the museums.

My first job was as receptionist at the Office for Defense Mobilization, a civilian agency set up to run the Korean War. It was more than slightly different from the kind of work I had thought of taking when I went to Washington. Actually I wanted to do research or something that would call upon the very fine education in economics and political science I'd received at Duke University. But I was offered the ODM job and something told me to take it. Smartest thing I ever did. Everybody came to that receptionist's office to find out where to go, so in order to be able to direct people to all the right agencies, I had to learn the entire defense establishment.

Later I worked for the President's Advisory Committee on Government Organization with Milton Eisenhower, Arthur Flemming and Nelson Rockefeller. My primary work was typing, but all the time I was learning about the domestic government agencies. So in three quick years I basically had a firsthand course in how the federal government operates, which you could never get out of any textbook. You cannot overestimate the importance of knowing how things work. If you know how something works and you're comfortable in the situation, even though you're going into a different area like the arts, you can make it work for you, not against you.

I never thought about what I was doing. It just seemed natural. I'm not a long-range planner. I believe in planning for everybody else but not for me. I've always been surrounded by people, including my family, who encouraged me. My mother was the daughter of a medical doctor. She and my dad married before they graduated from college. My father was a lawyer and my mother worked for a while but she basically was a housewife, a very independent one. Both of my parents were always very supportive of anything that I wanted to do.

Then I was extremely fortunate with the people with whom I worked. Basically, I never received anything but encouragement, all my life. I never was in a job where there were barriers. My first advice to anyone is to learn how to do anything you do very well. I couldn't type very well when I went to Washington, and the first thing I learned to do was to type up a storm and I still type very well. It is an invaluable tool. I'm never in a situation, when push comes to shove, that I can't type and get something from my head into somebody else's head. I have typed documents, some when I was chairman of the National Endowment for the Arts, that went all the way to the president of the United States. On several occasions the White House called me at home in the evening and requested some information by seven the next morning. Well, now, how could I find somebody sound asleep at home to go down to the office, type something and deliver it on time? I was lucky to be able to type myself.

Next thing I did was learn how to take shorthand, speed-writing. I am not very good but I can keep up and I can put my thoughts down and I can usually read them afterward without having too laborious a time. So many people are worried they will become stuck in a clerical position because they have skills. Nonsense. In my mind, if you type or take shorthand well, you have an even greater chance to participate and learn.

When I moved to New York in 1956, that was another advanced world and it gave me even more cultural opportunities. However, I still was not known by many people, certainly my early associates, as having much involvement in the arts. My interest was strictly a personal appreciation.

In New York I assisted in studies that were being carried out by Nelson Rockefeller and then later by his brother Laurance, on a variety of issues—defense, international economics, education and Christian ethics. Governor Rockefeller was a real believer in bringing people with different experiences together to focus on one subject. While he was in the government he brought together economists, sociologists, historians and military experts to discuss matters of military or international or psychological concern. Frequently it was the first time that a military person had ever talked to a sociologist or an economist. They found they had a lot to discuss. After Mr. Rockefeller left government, he decided that if this process worked so well in government on highly classified issues, why wouldn't it work in broad areas of public policy? This was the concept that initiated the Rockefeller studies. They were known as the Rockefeller Panel Reports and they resulted in the book called *Prospect for America*. Henry Kissinger was the staff director. I was the executive secretary/coordinator.

One of the important things I learned from those studies that helped me all my life is that if you develop good information and if the people who discuss the problem are knowledgeable about their subjects, then you have good results. You do not have to settle for watered-down compromises.

When we finished those panel reports, I had an opportunity to be involved in a study that Laurance Rockefeller was chairing on outdoor recreation. I learned a great deal about the development of our natural resources around the country, about the demand of people on our natural resources, and about the very great difficulty we have in preserving our natural resources so that people can enjoy them. I learned a lot about leisure time. This was a fascinating subject to me—the use of the outdoors and the use of space within the city. All this knowledge also turned out to be extremely useful as the flow of time went along.

Then Mr. John D. Rockefeller III asked me if I could organize a study on economics and public policy in the performing arts. He thought if his brothers could study international economics and defense and outdoor recreation, we could organize a study on the performing arts. He became interested in this subject because when he started to develop Lincoln Center in New York, he realized that there was really very little dialogue about public policy and the performing arts.

What we found out was that it was incomparably more difficult to study the performing arts than it was to do the other studies, because there were no basic sources of information. There was no collection of data. There were no experts. It took us a year and a half to find two economists who knew anything about the arts, and one was a sculptor.

As a result of not having any experts readily available, we had to do several things. First of all, the staff and I had to become experts in the arts. Furthermore, we had to depend on the most diverse set of opportunities that came our way. For example, we were probably the only people in the United States who were very grateful for the *New York Times* strike. The day after the strike began we got on the telephone. We quickly involved many writers from the *Times* who were able to handle disparate information and not worry, as academics do, about having a depth of knowledge in the field. As history would prove, we chose well and we finally published *The Performing Arts: Problems and Prospects*.

As a result of that study, it became clear to me that my own personal history was not the least bit unique; that the key problems of the arts in the United States were economic and geographical. There were just very limited opportunities for people in many parts of the country to enjoy the arts. Tickets cost a lot, and audiences tended to be highly educated and affluent. Enjoying the arts as much as I did personally, it did not seem right that they were not available to everyone.

Given the other work that I'd done, particularly in outdoor recreation, it seemed to me the economic and geographic factors could be overcome. We've handled geographic problems before in the country, we've handled economic problems before, so it didn't seem to me it would be too difficult to handle those in connection with the arts. I became fascinated with the subject.

I never for a moment, and never since, have doubted the ability of the arts and the vastness of our resources to meet public demand. There were all those people who said if you spread the arts around the country, you will lower the quality. I've never been able to find any mathematical philosophy that would prove that to be true, let alone artistic philosophy. The more you have people involved in the arts and the more respect the arts have, the more good people you're going to have and the more talent you will uncover.

Now of course, there's always the possibility that funding sources, be they individuals or governments or corporations, can support second-rate work. But if your philosophy is to put your dollars behind first-rate work and quality—which fortunately is still very true in this country—then the good is encouraged and the second-rate does not overtake.

I became very interested in the state arts council movement and the community art movement as a result of my work with the performing arts. Eventually I was asked to be president of an organization that's now the American Council for the Arts. I came to know people and see arts all over the country. A lot more was going on than people thought, especially if they lived in New York. People were becoming interested in their cities and if they're interested in their cities, they must be interested in the arts. You can't just be interested in efficient sewers.

The Museum of Modern Art asked me to interview some of the top museum professionals in the country, so just by happenstance I had a real opportunity to learn about museums in some depth, the way I had learned about performing arts. After that I had an opportunity to serve on the Belmont Report committee, the first national study of museums. It basically covered the same areas as our performing arts study did.

So when I look back, I had an absolutely tremendous lifelong education. My learning about the development of natural resources, and the importance of nurturing and preserving them and making them available to people, made me understand the importance and problems of nurturing our cultural resources and preserving them and making them available to more people. Both are absolutely fragile and God-given resources. If you tamper with them or do not handle them professionally, you can destroy forests and mountains, or painters and paintings. I realized that it was a direct parallel and that there were many parallels not only between what we needed to do but also how we needed to think.

I was asked several times, after Roger Stevens left in 1969, to take the chairmanship of the National Endowment for the Arts. I wasn't too keen on doing so. I had some ideas about other people who I thought could do the job better than I could. My strongest feeling was that it should be a man, because the arts then were too often viewed as the responsibility of women, and I thought it would be better if a man were chairman. People in government would take the agency more seriously. When you think back to 1969, there were very few women at high levels in government at that time. There still are very few.

I'm not one of those who lays out a career or a work pattern, but a whole part of my life was directed toward enabling me, at that particular time, to become chairman and to see the endowment progress as it did. In addition to my experience in the arts I'd had quite a few years working for government, so I knew the Congress very well and how it worked, I knew how the executive worked and how the Office of Management and Budget worked.

In going to the National Endowment for the Arts I knew where I was at. I had no illusions that I had any artistic judgment whatsoever, so one thing I felt most strongly about was keeping artistic decisions in the hands of professionals. The other thing I brought to the job is that my whole life had been directed toward working on a cooperative basis with people, and trying to interpret people's ideals and their dreams and make them work.

I had tremendous support from the whole artistic community of people around the country, and a superior staff already in place. It was very small, only thirty people, but they were absolutely terrific people and knew what they were about. We were able to build that staff up to two hundred over the eight years I was there. Monies went from $7 million to something like $115 million. People wondered if we could spend that money. I never had any questions about the money being spent well because we had panels of experts who knew what was going on all over the country and they knew the arts and they knew what was needed. All I had to do was be a pretty good sponge.

First of all, when you're talking about the arts, you're not talking about money of any meaningful amount. What in the world is $100 million in the federal budget? And $7 million wouldn't even buy postage stamps for most departments. So we started from almost a zero budget.

In 1969 when I became chairman, everybody was talking about the financial crisis in the arts—trustees resigning from boards, gloom and doom, how the arts couldn't survive, etc. Well, the first thing I did was to agree with all my associates never to use the word *crisis*. In my first media interview in San Clemente, the press asked me what I was going to do about the financial crisis in the arts. I said, "Nothing, because there isn't any crisis." Well, you could say I was just hopeful.

When I'd been at the endowment three weeks, the staff and I started visiting around on Capitol Hill. I had friends in Congress whom I'd known more than fifteen years. Very quickly, I realized nobody knew what the National Endowment for the Arts was. Well, why would they? It was tiny. Between me and Michael Straight, who was deputy chairman, we saw several hundred members of Congress. The only way for people to know what you're doing is to tell them.

We liked the whole experience because it gave us an opportunity to find out what was on the congressmen's minds. We'd go into offices and say, "Hello, Congressman or Senator, we've been talking to the people in Spokane and one of their primary interests is the support of the Spokane Symphony, and they want to develop their museum." Or, "Kansas City has one of the great museums in the entire country." In other words, we knew what was going on in practically every city in the country. Why wouldn't any congressman want to know what was going on at home? Of course they'd want to know and to be proud.

As we made our visits to these gentlemen and ladies (not very many ladies), we also wanted to communicate to them the depth of our belief and the depth of President Nixon's belief that the agency should be a nonpartisan, a bipartisan effort. In the early years, the program had been almost totally Democrat in its support, except for the leadership of Senator Javits of New York. We were able to get Gerald Ford, among others, to back us and support what we were trying to do. From that time on we had quite good relations with the members of Congress on both sides of the aisle. I had tremendous respect for them and I'm very grateful for their counsel. Of course, we might not have always gotten everything we wanted, but we always got a hearing and you can't ask for anything more than that.

I believe that we were not totally successful, but during our stint at the endowment we were able to see a tremendous change in attitude toward the arts. Our greatest pride and joy was not the federal support we mustered for the arts but what was going on in the country in private support. The most remarkable change in the decade of the seventies was private support, what happened with corporate support and surely what happened in the states and municipal governments. Federal arts dollars were being used to encourage other people to become involved.

I've always believed in the value of using government money to encourage private money and encourage private initiative. That's its strength. Too often the federal government comes in and because it's big and everybody says, "We'll let Washington do it," it takes over and people pull their money out. The corporations and private donors say, "Well, the feds are in there, let them do that." You see that in many social fields.

In the arts we felt just the opposite. We felt that federal monies should be used to encourage other sources of money, and the philosophy worked. That was part of the original legislation setting up the National Endowment. It's one of the best pieces of legislation that I've ever seen. It's brilliantly written. It recognizes the arts, it recognizes their fragility, it instructs the Arts Endowment to stay out of everything that has to do with the interior workings of an arts organization.

The difference between the Arts Endowment and the WPA, instituted by Roosevelt in the 1930s, is that the WPA basically said, "Artists are people and artists have to eat, therefore . . ." The endowment legislation does not address problems of economic and social needs at all. The policy is to encourage the arts, to make them more available to more people. Sometimes in testimony, members of the artistic professions have said to

Congress: "We have economic problems and unemployment conditions." I've heard one Congressman after another answer, "This isn't an economic welfare bill or social welfare legislation, it's a bill to encourage the arts." It's a different way of looking at a program. It really is. And to me, that is the strength of government involvement in the arts in this country.

The other key to the government arts structure is its dependence on strong private initiative. There are people all over the country who are working hard as volunteers and as patrons. Most American arts institutions have been built by volunteers, and that's private, not government.

While I was at the Arts Endowment, I traveled extensively and I learned that people had great pride in where they lived and wanted to improve the environment in their own hometowns. With this attitude, it was just natural for the arts to develop. At the endowment, we were basically, I guess you'd say, a catalyst.

My own personal interest today has moved from the arts specifically to the use of urban space and the revitalization of our cities. With the energy problem, it's clear that mobility will cut down and a good many people are going to have to be involved in our urban centers. If we're going to refocus life in our urban centers, then how are people going to lead wonderful lives in the city unless they have the arts? We're going to have to put more money into the arts.

# Ada Louise Huxtable

*Ada Louise Huxtable (born 1921, New York City) is an architecture critic known throughout the world who has raised public and professional awareness of the "built" environment by focusing on the quality of the urban environment and its effect on the way we live and work. Her column for the New York Times was the first on architecture criticism in the country. Her books, informed by exhaustive research into social, economic and political issues, include* Classical New York *(1964),* Will They Ever Finish Bruckner Boulevard? *(1970), and* Kicked a Building Lately? *(1976).*

LOOK AT OUR CITIES. You wouldn't recognize many of our cities today if you had seen them twenty-five years ago. They're not the same cities, they're not enduring. In addition to the natural processes of change, new landmark buildings have been created and there has been a great deal of destruction for urban renewal. The Singer Building is gone, one of the most distinguished skyscrapers in New York before World War I. Unfortunately, I think we're going to be seeing more of this sort of destruction.

There are common threads running through all the work I do. I'm trying to see that architecture and its relationship to the environment is properly appreciated and understood. When buildings are understood in terms of their aesthetic or urban value, then they become of pragmatic value; they become of economic value, of social value, of political value.

A lot of buildings have been saved. I think the Quincy Market, the Faneuil Hall Market in Boston, is a good example. It was touch and go what would happen with those buildings. Those buildings were important to me. I wrote about them in *Progressive Architecture* many years ago. They were the result of exemplary urban planning of the 1820s. They were absolutely topflight vernacular architecture of the Greek Revival period. When urban renewal came to Boston they were also important to I. M. Pei, who did the master plan and said they should be included, but there was no plan for them, no understanding yet of *how* they could be included. If certain kinds of developers had been listened to, they would have been demolished for office buildings in the downtown development. It's a long, complicated history, but eventually they were recycled in a very farsighted plan for commercial development which is not just a commercial development but also a very lively socioeconomic center of the city.

What I'm trying to do with criticism is not a simple, one-track thing. I am very concerned with my own feelings about the subjects I write about. I am concerned with the quality of the cities we're building, with how they serve people and how they contribute to the arts that are involved in building them. My first consideration is to meet a set of standards that is terribly important to me. My next consideration is to share those standards with people who should be concerned and who should care, or who are concerned and do care. As for criticism, analyzing and discussing how these various subjects or buildings or actions fit into those standards is apt to engender a sense of pleasure or a sense of outrage, all of which comes through in the writing.

You start by saying, "This building is good and this is why. This is worth caring about." That basic understanding and appreciation is what criticism must carry above all. Then, what you do about it is next. I am trying to inform people about what the issues are and how to deal with them, and they're very complicated issues. They include highly technical areas like zoning. They also include issues that are hard to get a handle on, like aesthetics, which people are always trying to understand and set standards for. I'm educating people. If you want to do it effectively, you must have credibility and you must also have reliability. Therefore you must know yourself, you must analyze the issues in terms of all the options. Politics, economics, they all come into it. You've going to give a very lopsided kind of education if you don't try and lay out everything that's involved in an issue that's going to affect its ultimate resolution. It's rough, it's a lot of work, but it's terribly interesting and it has results.

My worry about other criticism—and there's more of it coming along in this field—is that I'll sometimes read a piece, find it's well written and well reasoned, but then I'll go back to the sources and find it isn't a fair piece at all because an awful lot of the essential elements have been ignored or left out, either deliberately or through oversight, so that the conclusion is not valid. Your conclusion has got to be valid. Of course, you're going to have a point of view. There's no such thing as criticism without opinion, but it's got to be valid in the sense of being based on full information and full consideration of all the factors involved.

For me, becoming a critic was a straight-line path in a very funny way because there was no prescribed way to get there so I simply invented my own way. It was not in a conscious, "I'm going to follow this path," sense; I just knew what I loved, what interested me, and I didn't know where it was going to lead. It was art and architectural history. It was the experience of cities. I've always been a tremendous city walker long before I knew what the buildings were I was looking at, and I enjoyed them as a very young person.

I know I was visual from a very early age. I grew up in New York. I lived in one of the oldest apartment houses in New York, the St. Urban at Eighty-ninth Street and Central Park West. That was a time when you were much freer in New York than you are now. As a child, although I was carefully watched and protected, as soon as I was able to, I was allowed to walk down to the Museum of Natural History at Seventy-seventh Street. I adored it. I think museums are places of discovery for children who are at all sensitive.

Then when I was a little older I was allowed to go across town through the park to the Metropolitan Museum of Art. I did all these things myself. I fell in love with the Egyptian collection. I thought I wanted to be an Egyptologist, and that kind of thing. And I fell in love with little limp leather-bound books that I saw in some department store. I picked them up, I liked the leather, the gold imprint on them, and I think they were fifty cents each, one dollar each, something like that. They were Emerson and Thoreau, so I read Emerson and Thoreau. One thing leads to another. Your whole sense of identity develops if you have that kind of curious mind. Maybe it comes from an appreciation for quality.

What I got at home was a sense of the authentic, a sense of quality. My mother was and is a woman of extraordinary taste, but it was never anything that was forced upon me. It was never anything that we even discussed. You're really not too aware of this unless they become matters of attention, but I did grow up with real things, not with fake things. That's one very good way of finding out that real things have enduring pleasure and fake things go flat.

My sense of the city, the buildings, we were concerned about none of that at home. We would have been if my father had lived because even at a very young age he was guiding. I was an only child. He died when I was eleven. He was a doctor and he was a playwright. He had a play produced on Broadway when he was quite young, before he went into medical school. He had also won some kind of art scholarship. He had a very wide range of interests. When I was writing poetry at the age of seven, he had me writing it in those little marbleized notebooks and he was teaching me iambic pentameter and how to scan at a very young age. I didn't really know what was going on and I wasn't sure whether I liked being severely criticized at that age. On the other hand, he had a strong parental interest in what I was doing. My mother was not interested in those things so that when he died they went out of my life.

My mother is very much a Victorian. She's now ninety-three, and she came from Boston. She is a bright woman and a tasteful woman. Her philosophy of life was that women were background. It didn't mean that they didn't have minds and didn't achieve what they wanted to do, but the idea of a career woman was nothing her generation would have thought of at all. I know her feeling about me was that I seemed to be developing interests that were not anything that she had cared about but she approved of my having those interests and therefore I was encouraged, but it was not a matter of being pushed or of having things laid out for me or standards set to reach. It was just if that was the way I wanted to go, fine. I really set my own education. She wouldn't have cared if I'd gone to college or if I'd preferred not to. When I did want to go to college and there wasn't any money, I went to Hunter on a Regents scholarship and I did all my graduate work on fellowships.

While I was in college, I entered an interior decorating contest at Bloomingdale's with a friend. There was a hundred-dollar prize. That was a lot of money for us. She did the drawings and I wrote the captions and we tossed a coin to decide whose name would go on it and my name came up. We won the hundred dollars, and when I graduated from college and couldn't find a job I wrote to the president of Bloomingdale's saying I'd just won their interior decorating contest and I'd like a job in his store. He was nice enough to interview me himself.

They had a marvelous furniture buyer then who was very modern-design conscious. They were sponsoring the Museum of Modern Art design competition furniture and Bloomingdale's was setting up to sell that furniture. People like Eero Saarinen and Charles Eames had won the prizes and produced the designs, and Bloomingdale's thought it would be dandy to put someone of my background into the display and sales of that Museum of Modern Art furniture, so that was how I worked in Bloomingdale's. That was how I got a job when jobs were very hard to get, and that was where I met the man who eventually became my husband. Many young architects and designers came in to see the display. Many bought. My husband was an industrial designer. He was furnishing his bachelor apartment and I came along with the furniture.

I married right after graduation. Although I had a partial economic responsibility for my mother, there was no pressure on me to earn a living. Believe me, my husband and I lived in one and a half rooms and there was nothing to spare, but you're as rich as you think you are. I felt I had options at that point, and I then had the leisure to pursue my interests.

If you do love certain things you tend to look for knowledge, you look for information, you want to know more about them. I think it's a matter of (1) liking something and (2) being curious about it and then (3) finding a way to put it all together.

My way of putting my interests together was not so much making a conscious package but going to graduate school at the Institute of Fine Arts, taking all of the art and architectural history I could and confounding the professors with my papers, because instead of writing about Baroque churches, I was writing about the first public housing in New York. I wanted to write about the things I could see. I didn't want to write about something in Rome if I couldn't go to Rome and see it firsthand. At that time, thirty years ago, there was no such thing as modern architectural history at the institute. It just stopped dead with a survey course of the nineteenth and twentieth century. The whole teaching of art and architecture has gone far beyond that now.

My first architectural job was assistant curator of architecture and design at the Museum of Modern Art. It was an incredible first job. I was so lucky; Philip Johnson hired me after contacting the Institute of Fine Arts and reading my graduate school papers. We did the Miës van der Rohe show at the museum in 1947 and I wrote all of the captions and worked with the photographic enlargements. Philip Johnson did the layout and the design with Miës, but I followed through and helped Philip in a routine mechanical way with the book that was published at the same time. I also did a lot of small shows completely on my own and found it absolutely fascinating, but felt I wanted to do more in a broader way. I left the job at the museum after I'd been there three years. I had learned a great deal, but I had a great deal more to learn. I really didn't ever want another institutional full-time job.

I applied for a Fulbright to Italy and got it. I traveled all around the country studying "stile liberty" and Art Nouveau and then looked at the perfectly fascinating early twentieth-century architecture right up through the period of Fascism and early Modernism. I thought I was just satisfying my own interests and curiosity. I brought back large photograph files of pictures nobody else had and nobody cared about, and then I find—this proves it's good to live a while, things come around and get doubly fascinating—that the young intellectual architects in this country are now having a field day with work by Giuseppe Terragni of the late twenties and early thirties in and around Como, which I thought only I knew about! It's a very interesting style, pure, formal rationalism within the modern movement, something of very great interest to the younger architects now. So no knowledge is ever wasted, no pursuit, no research is ever wasted.

I started writing criticism for *Art News* magazine and *Progressive Architecture* when I got back from Italy. I discovered that was my interest and I guess my bent. I could only make about five thousand dollars a year free-lancing but I was doing exactly what I wanted to do, studying, doing research, writing, working on scholarly subjects. I did a series of articles in which I simply investigated buildings which interested me because they were indicative of new things in design or structural engineering or an attitude toward the city, and it tied in perfectly with the magazine because they called the series "Progressive Architecture in America." Then I got a Guggenheim grant and worked on that project for a couple of years. I liked moving where my interests led me without being tied down to real deadlines and editorial responsibilities.

You know, everything in life is a trade-off—what you're getting for what you're giving up. When I became a critic for the *New York Times* I gave up my freedom. I gave up the freedom to pursue whatever interests fascinated me at the moment because something else was more newsworthy or more valuable or more critical to the public at large. I gave up the leisure of scholarly research for crisis fact-finding. What I have gained is a magnificent platform from which to work, a fascinating involvement with all the issues of the day. I think that's a pretty good trade-off, although at times I miss terribly being able to follow through on personal projects, books I'd like to write. I'm very torn because I believe this is a very important phase in the history and development of the art of architecture.

On the other hand, I can use my column to make the public aware of the question of aesthetics. I'm not sure those are my most popular pieces of criticism. If I write something about an Aldo Rossi show, only a small handful of people know who Aldo Rossi is and what he's doing, but I have the news peg of two exhibitions at once so I can try to explain what the aesthetic issues are that make people put on two shows at this moment, which is quite different from deploring the refacing of a fine old building on lower Broadway as part of the development of new office space down there.

A sense of values about what architecture is really ties those two questions together. Aesthetics are important but that's only part of it. I'd say it's a question of quality. Quality of environment, quality of life in terms of how environment or architecture affects how we live and work, quality of life in the sense of aesthetic pleasure as well as utilitarian response. Beauty has been shunted very much in the background by the problems we have today; there should be beauty in life. But I hate to even say that because it becomes so shallow and so superficial when people take beauty up for its own sake, but it is part of a whole that enriches life.

Newspaper work is demanding. I never had children. I don't know if I would have been up to it. It takes a strong woman to be a journalist and have a family. It's done; I assume it's being done well; I hope so. But I think women are terribly conflicted, they're not going to resolve this in a hurry, and it takes a very strong belief in what you're doing to make the trade-offs seem worthwhile.

There's no equality. The woman works twice as hard as the man. What the young woman doesn't realize is that she's taking on something now that she's never given the man credit for before, which is the intense responsibility of worry for other people, for the economic resources that keep the family going. Now women have done that too, and they still have the prime responsibility for the family in spite of all the sharing. I am not very sympathetic to women who take on careers as a self-fulfilling luxury.

I have a very supportive husband. He always has been. He is terribly interested in the issues I bring home from the office. He has no desire or capacity to learn the things that young women think men should know how to do today, which proves to me that it's attitude that's important because then you don't have conflicts. The relationship between two people is composed of more than "Are you fulfilling this obligation?" I go to professional dinners. He does not. Some nights I'm not home. There is no sense of "A meal is supposed to be here and you're supposed to provide it." He can't cook, but if I thought it was important to come home once in a while to a meal, he'd prepare it. He is sympathetic and understanding and knows that I'm working hard and making a contribution too. He has a mature sense of values, which again is what I think it comes down to: What is important?

All judgment, I think in almost anything, even in your own personal life, grows out of being able to measure one thing against another. You measure your own judgments, you measure your own values against things that have happened to you. And you measure the value of an art against things that have happened in that art in the past. Every creative act draws on the past whether it pretends to or not. It draws on what it knows. There's no such thing, really, as a creative act in a vacuum.

Someone claiming to be uninfluenced by history and the past is being influenced by popular culture. It's coming out of whatever is around.

The knowledge of history of architecture is essential for any architectural critic, because, as Philip Johnson says, you cannot not know history. You have no basis for qualitative judgment unless you have some idea of what the standards and constraints were in other ages and what was produced as a result.

Of course I have personal tastes, whether I'm a critic or not. I think I'm entitled to them. I am also terribly aware that whatever my personal taste is must come out of a very careful and considered analysis of other aspects of taste. In other words, I have to justify my taste to myself and my public, all the time. That's an essential part of the critical process, it's not a visible part. If I think Miës is great and other people think he's not great, that Miës is a bore—less is not more—I have to have very, very solid reasons for thinking he's great. That is how my taste is justified. There's no such thing as a critic without taste. Judgment is another word for it, a partial word for it. With judgment must go preference, a considered and qualified and careful preference that you have the right to express because you have given it so much careful study.

If I seem less passionate now in my criticism, it's because things are moving, things have happened; I've had an effect with my writing. While there are just as many battles to be fought, it's in a different climate. If what I write doesn't always seem quite as outraged or quite as desperate as fifteen years ago, it's because we're fighting these battles on better ground. It's nothing I've done alone, but it would be false humility to say that I haven't had something to do with it. I'm not a one-man band at all. I wouldn't feel that I have achieved anything if I was still a "voice in the wilderness"—not at all. There's a great deal more writing on the subject, and there's also a great deal more awareness of the subject. There are a lot of good examples to follow. Now there's a lot of recycling of old buildings that demonstrate how to deal with the past. It wouldn't have happened if it hadn't been economically feasible, but it also wouldn't have happened if someone hadn't learned to appreciate the values that these buildings represent.

I don't keep score. Occasionally, when I've been asked, I've tried to add up some of the more obvious results, but I think the chief thing is not the specific defeats or victories—and there are a lot of them—but the change in atmosphere, the change in consciousness of the environment, of the built world.

# Diana Vreeland

*Diana Vreeland (born in Paris, France) has been an arbiter of style in America since the 1930s, setting trends in both fashion and magazine layout as fashion editor of Harper's Bazaar from 1937 to 1962, and then as editor of Vogue until 1971. Today, as special consultant to the Costume Institute of the Metropolitan Museum, she continues to influence fashion and the public, drawing vast audiences to her exhibits of fashion of the past, which illustrate the evolution of style, costume as history and garment design as art.*

**I** THINK STYLE IS A totally natural thing. One has standards and through concentration maintains them, that's all it is. It's a normal rhythm which covers everything. There's nothing difficult about anything that is innate. Style is a wonderful thing to have because it maintains you thoroughly— the way you behave, the literature you read, your life with friends, with children and with your family. Style is always growing and changing, always finding new outlets and interests, of course, particularly through work. I can't imagine anything more onerous than not having a regular standard, a rhythm, a behavior and a work.

Money has nothing to do with style at all, but naturally it helps every situation. You need money to eat and sleep and look properly, to have a good life. Of course, people have grown up from under a stone and have come up with plenty of style. We're all born to have it, we just need to get on to our own thing.

Fashion is not the same thing as style. Fashion is everywhere, on the daily air, and it's always moving. People can pick up fashion in boutiques, or seeing something on the street, etc., but that doesn't mean they have style. They can be very, very badly dressed, very badly put together, and have no authority because perhaps they have no authority within themselves.

I was born and brought up in Paris, remember that. You can say, "What difference does it make?" It makes all the difference. People who are born in Paris are a little different. I do believe that. It is a fact that people there are most interested in those sorts of things. Then once you have that standard, you must maintain it.

Before I went to work for *Harper's Bazaar* in 1937, I had been leading a wonderful life in Europe. That meant traveling, seeing beautiful places, having marvelous summers, studying and reading a great deal of the time. I lived in London, a wonderful town to read and concentrate in. I read Russian, English, French and German literature, the classics—always in translation. My intense reading was natural. Everybody young reads and reads. I would have even read the telephone book for hours at a time. It's the concentration, it grabs you.

My education was rather spotty because my parents were very careless. They always forgot when it was fall and time for little girls to go to school, but then when they remembered they sent us. For years I was in ballet schools. I never went with the idea of becoming a professional. At a certain point I couldn't really go to a regular school because I didn't know anything, and ballet school was the only school my parents could keep me in. I was perfectly happy in a ballet class on a barre. I think that it's the only way to bring up a girl, you see, because it gives her a feeling, a rhythm. Through dancing you interpret the music, and you feel the wonderful, natural things of the earth. It's the discipline, doing everything absolutely perfectly, meeting the standards because, by God, with a ballet master like Fokine, if you didn't you were in trouble.

Before I went to work, my life was a life of leisure. I'd no responsibilities except my house, my family and my friends. I could never have lived that kind of life in New York. I think it's something in the climate that makes one want to get out and about. To me, people live in New York to work, not to dream or to have a leisurely, imaginative life. There's too much interference, and there are too few people who can join you in leisure. There's great imagination here, but it's of another kind.

In Italy, there's a natural rhythm and it starts in the beauty of the people. When a stone rolls loose in Italy, it arrives at exactly the right place. It's an ancient land and it's grown very naturally in its own soil and things have evolved.

When I left the magazines I didn't miss them. When I left *Vogue* I had a holiday of three months. I had a wonderful time . . . I was in Spain, Italy, London and Paris. It was all very gala and attractive. When I came back, the Metropolitan Museum of Art asked me if I'd like to work in their Costume Institute. They hired me to do whatever I felt should be done. I decided to do a show on Balenciaga.

You know, people like to look at pleasurable things, but I think so few people believe in pleasure. That everything should be attractive, for me, this is essential to every day. That's all I've been concerned with. I think the gondola . . . and the horse . . . are the two most beautiful things in the world. The Islamic saying, "Thy name is horse, born of the south wind, you will be one of the five wonders of the world, forever and ever." I've got it all crooked but it's to that effect and it's very beguiling. I'm mad about horses and the world of animals because they, of course, have style and beauty. Seeing animals and people together is something many of us miss today.

I say to evoke the imagination of the public is a wonderful thing if you can manage it.

Through the whole world there's always been the spirit of ornamentation, and providing something for the onlooker, and we mustn't forget it. People have always loved to look at fairy princesses, queens, beautiful objects, buildings and gardens. Looking at beauty is a natural part of life. Beauty has nothing to do with possession. If possession and beauty must go together, then we are lost souls, a beautiful flower is not there to be possessed, it's there to be beheld. You're not going to take a beautiful painting off a museum wall. It's there for your pleasure.

Here I always have doubts about what I do. When I start a show, I'm very timid and nervous for weeks and months. It takes a great deal out of me. It's not easy to give the number of people who come each day to see a show the pleasure that I hope these shows do. It's hard work. You start with an idea and you believe in it and then it grows around you. As you see things starting to grow, you gain confidence. Some days are big days. You jump. You get a whole excitable, marvelous, wonderful, wonderful, it-doesn't-balance, what-the-hell-are-we-going-to-do feeling. Then you know. It all comes gradually and then entirely. Then it somehow ends up that people like it and I'm very happy, and very proud and very, very pleased, because that's the job. You feel it's the best that could be done with the available material. Somebody else might be able to do a much better job, but I'm only talking about what I've accomplished. I hope I'm giving people pleasure, something to look at, to think about, something that fills their imagination or evokes a few thoughts.

# Julia Child

*Julia Child (born 1912, Pasadena, California) launched the epicurean cooking craze of the 1960s and 1970s. The two volumes of* Mastering the Art of French Cooking, *Volume I written with Simone Beck and Louisette Bertholle (1961) and Volume II written with Mme. Beck (1970), are the most thorough teaching books on French cooking technique in the English language. Her popular television series* The French Chef *"took the fear out of haute cuisine" and made French cooking an accepted part of our culture.*

I WAS THIRTY-TWO WHEN I started cooking; up until then, I just ate. I think it kind of crawled up on me. My mother didn't cook because I grew up in an era when most all middle-income people had maids. So she never learned, and I never really learned at all. But my grandmother was a great cook. She grew up in the farming country of Illinois—she made doughnuts and cakes and wonderful chicken, as I remember. We always had good food at her house, and at our house too—plain good American food. But we never discussed it; it was expected to be good.

After college I worked in public relations and advertising, and then my mother got very sick so I went home and helped take care of her. After she died, the war came along, and I eventually went to work for the Office of Strategic Services (OSS), first in Washington, and then in the China-Burma-India theater, and that's where I met my future husband, Paul. We were married after the war, and that's when I started to cook. Paul remained in the government service, and we were sent to France. He spoke beautiful French, and had lived there with his family in the 1920s. He knew about food and wines, and his mother was a wonderful cook, from all reports.

It was great fun living in France. We got to Paris in 1949 and spent five years there, then we had two years in Marseilles. I had to go to school to learn French; I went to Berlitz every day for two hours, and then we made some French friends almost immediately. So one learned by being thrown into it.

I was hysterical about everything in France. I thought it was so wonderful, and it took me several years at least to calm down and not be so pro-French. After one taste of French food, after our very first meal in France, at Rouen, on the way from Le Havre to Paris in our old blue Buick that we had brought over with us on the boat—after that first unforgettable lunch, I was hooked. I'd never eaten like that before, I didn't know such food existed. The wonderful attention paid to each detail of the meal was incredible to me. I'd never really drunk good wine before, and knew nothing at all about it. It was simply a whole new life experience.

But you don't spring into good cooking naked. You have to have some training. You have to learn how to eat. It's like looking at a painting: If you don't have any kind of background, you don't really know what you're looking at. The French have training from their families, they grow up with an appreciation of food, that it is an art, that it is worth considering carefully and looking at. I had to learn, and both cooking and taste developed simultaneously for me.

In those days the Cordon Bleu cooking school had some wonderful chefs of the old school, and I decided to enroll. Why not? There was only my husband and my pussycat to look out for, and as soon as I got our living arrangements settled and a little French at my command, I started in. I was able to take the serious course that was designed for people going into the business—which meant that I entered a class of former GIs, who were studying under the GI Bill of Rights. (This was in 1950, and the war was barely over.) They very kindly didn't object to my joining them, nor did their fine old chef, Max Bugnard, in his seventies and trained in the fine old ways. We started in at seven A.M., cooked until eleven, then I rushed home to cook lunch for Paul—our embassy followed the French hours, which meant a two-hour lunch period when everyone came home to eat with the family and then I rushed back in the afternoon for the demonstrations. That's how I got started, and I never looked back.

I stayed at the Cordon Bleu for as long as I thought useful, which was six months or so—until they began repeating fancy dishes like *poulet en chaud-froid* several times. After one or two hassles with that you *have* it. It was expensive, too, and we were living on a very strict budget. Just when I felt I'd spent enough of my money there, I met my future colleague, Simone Beck. She was mad about cooking, too, and was delighted to find a kindred spirit, because way back then not many middle-class people had even the slightest interest in it. She asked me to join a French ladies' gastronomical club, and that, for me, was a sort of postgraduate course. It meant talking and spending time cooking and eating entirely with French people, and that made a tremendous difference to me because I got their attitudes and points of view about good food, menus, gastronomy and so forth. And Simca, who was just a few years older than I, had been cooking since her childhood. I learned an awful lot from her.

I was planning to go into this cooking thing very seriously and take a long time studying and learning, but then I was suddenly thrown into it for keeps. After I had met Simca, I also met her friend and colleague, Louisette Bertholle, also a member of the gastronomy club, Le Cercle des Gourmettes. She and Simca were working on a cookbook for the United States, which had been going on for some time. One day the three of us had invited some American friends of mine for lunch. They wanted cooking lessons but said they didn't want to go to the Cordon Bleu because they didn't speak French, and so why didn't we teach them? I thought, My heavens, I wasn't nearly ready for that. But Simca, who is always ready for anything and was far more experienced than either Louisette or I, said, "Well, why not?" And we started our cooking school, L'Ecole des Trois Gourmandes, just about the next day.

Of course, we learned an awful lot by doing, and we often were able to get our two fine chefs, Bugnard and Claude Thilmont, a *patissier,* from the Cordon Bleu. They loved coming to us, they enjoyed showing off to our ohs and ahs, our pupils loved it, and we literally had free lessons every time from them, of course. We all had a very good time, never took more than eight students but preferred six, and it was a completely participation class. We cooked an entire meal, then invited guests to participate—often husbands, and always Paul. But guests had to pay 350 francs for the meal with wine. That was only one dollar then, and certainly one of the best and cheapest meals in Paris. It was lots of fun for us then, but loads of work, and sometimes we didn't make expenses at all. You know how people are, they wouldn't show up and there we'd be with all that food. We never did figure that one out.

We kept up the school together for about a year and a half, and during that time the American collaborator working on the book with Simca and Louisette faded out of the picture—I don't remember why. But I was delighted, because I really wanted to get in on the act. I had found that most of the cookbooks I read didn't give enough detail, and I thought we could really do something to explain French cooking to America. So we started in, and it took us nine years to write the first draft of that cookbook. Of course we were learning while doing, and were being very thorough indeed. Our first submission, nine hundred pages on French sauces and French poultry, was roundly rejected. It went into the most infinite detail on every aspect; it was really an academic treatise which was, as our first editor pointed out, utterly unpublishable. She suggested we write a regular cookbook.

By that time Paul and I had moved from Paris to Marseilles, to Bonn in Germany, and back to Washington, D.C. Simca had come to America on her first visit, and was here for the rejection. I was crushed, but she, as always undaunted, was all for going on and giving them a regular cookbook. That took another two or three years, and by the time that was finished, we had been posted to Norway. It was still a long and detailed book, because it was a teaching book, and had come out of our experiences with our school. Simca and Louisette kept on with the school in Paris, and I gave lessons wherever I happened to be. Louisette, who has now published three books of her own, did not then take a large part in the final version for personal reasons, and it was Simca and I who batted chapters and recipes back and forth, she in French and I in English. But that new version was also rejected by our Boston publisher as being just too complicated and special for them. Luckily our Cambridge friend, Avis DeVoto, who had introduced us to the first publisher, had another up her sleeve, the house of Knopf. She sent the manuscript to them and some of their people, who were cooks, liked it. And that's how we finally got published, and I have been with the same editor ever since.

By the time the book was in galleys, my Paul had resigned from the diplomatic service and we had moved to Cambridge, Massachusetts. The book, *Mastering the Art of French Cooking,* came out in the fall of 1961. Simca came over again to this country, and we invented our own publicity tour. At that point, as far as I know, nobody ever did anything of that kind. But Simca, always full of vim and vigor, said, "Well, we'll just go to Detroit and Chicago and California, and get hold of all our friends and give demonstrations." That's what we did, and I'm sure it helped us a lot because we were unknown, and had to get a start somewhere.

Then Simca went back to France and we came back to Boston and I was giving cooking lessons. I found the best way to do it and not keep losing money was to invite likely customers for lunch at our house, and then tell them that I'd love to give them cooking lessons, but in their own kitchens. Much better, said I; then they'd be using their own stove and own equipment, and could get their own friends to be cooking along with them. That meant, also, that they bought the food and wine, and they had to do the washing up. I arrived an hour before class, got the preparations ready, then we cooked and laughed and lunched, and I got my fee and left them with the dishes. It worked out very well for all concerned.

At the same time our local educational television station had a book review program, and a friend of ours suggested that perhaps we could get our book on the show. The man who did it was a very literary type; the idea of a cookbook didn't appeal to him at all, but he agreed. Well, you can't talk for half an hour about cooking, so I brought my own little hot plate and made an omelette on the air, and beat up some egg whites in my big copper bowl. Afterwards quite a number of people wrote in and said to the station that it would be nice to have a cooking program. The station asked us if we were interested, and although we had hardly ever seen television at that point (having lived abroad for so long), we said, "Sure, why not?" We did three pilot shows which were aired locally in the summer of 1960, and there was indeed interest in cooking. The station asked us about doing thirteen more shows, and we again said, "Why not?" Then other stations wanted it, Pittsburgh, San Francisco, Chicago, New York. And that's how the *French Chef* series got started, little by little.

In those early days, 1963, the J.F. Kennedys were in the White House. There was a lot of talk about Mrs. Kennedy's fine French chef, René Verdon, and the wonderful French food at the White House. More Americans, too, were beginning to go abroad and to appreciate the finer things of life, and it was a pretty flush period in the economy, as I remember. Suddenly there was a great deal of interest in French cuisine, much more than there had ever been before. I was in the middle of it, happening to be the right woman at the right time. Very lucky for me.

I think you have to decide who your audience is. If you don't pick your audience, you're lost because you're not really talking to anybody. My audience is people who like to cook, who want to really learn how to do it. I don't pay any attention to other people because they wouldn't look at such a program anyway. I'm a teacher. I like it. I want people to be able to do things that will turn out properly. Of course, I am interested in people who want to learn, and my books are written for people who really want to cook, and to cook the right way. If you are going to make French bread, for instance, you want to make the best possible bread—or, at least, I think you should want that. It should have the best possible texture and taste, and if it doesn't, why bother doing it?

I had assumed it would be impossible to make French bread at home with American flour—I just assumed that, without ever having tried it. No French people ever make bread at all at home—unthinkable. But while we were writing Volume II of *Mastering,* our editor suggested we try French bread because there were so many people who wanted to make their own. That interested my husband, Paul, so we started experimenting on it in Cambridge. We tried sourdough, and all the American recipes we could find for French bread—there were none in French cookbooks, of course— but it never turned out to be quite like the best French bread in France. However, I knew of a professional baker in Paris, Raymond Calvel, who taught at a school for bakers, and I wrote to Simca asking if she couldn't look him up. So she arranged it, and the next time Paul and I were in Paris we spent a fascinating day with him. Because Simca and I had spent so much time on yeast and doughs, we knew immediately what he was talking about and what he was doing, and we gradually saw what we had been doing wrong—which was just about everything. Our dough had been too stiff, it hadn't risen nearly enough, it wasn't formed correctly, and we needed a hot baking surface for our oven, as well as steam.

As soon as we arrived back at our little house in Provence, we started in anew. Paul, who is a practical Yankee and very good with his hands, got us a big sheet of asbestos cement (we later changed to quarry tiles) for our hot baking surface in the oven. Then he used a pan of water in the bottom of the oven into which he plunged a red-hot firebrick when the time came; it made a perfect burst of steam for those essential first five minutes of baking. We worked on the forming techniques and the rising— Paul taking photographs for our illustrator to follow when the recipe was ready for the book. Finally, I think we managed to make about as good a facsimile of professional French bread as one can make in a home oven. It took us two or three years to perfect, and I think it is one of the best things we have done. Now our system is used by many home cooks as the normal way.

It took us fifteen years to develop a technique for making French puff pastry. Ordinary American flour, the all-purpose type, just does not work properly. Simca and I tried many a system and formula, and it would rise nicely, but it was just not the tender flaky wonder that it should have been. The real breakthrough came when I was filming *White House Red Carpet* during the Johnson administration—how the White House entertains. They had a fine French pastry chef there in the kitchen, Ferdinand Louvat, who had made some perfectly splendid and tremendous *vol-au-vents* for the banquet's first course; those cases were cylinders about twelve inches across and five inches high, tenderly flaky and buttery, just first-class in every way. I asked him what flour he used, expecting some special chef's mixture. Oh no, he said, he used unbleached all-purpose white flour and plain bleached cake flour, one part cake flour to every four of all-purpose. We had tried cake flour, Simca and I, way back in the 1950s, but it hadn't worked out—we'd not experimented enough with proportions, and we never pursued it. It was one of those instances when you think you've tried everything but you haven't tried hard enough. But that experience with the White House pastry chef put us on the right track, and puff pastry appeared in all its glory in our Volume II.

Provided you have fine ingredients, I think that cooking is mostly a matter of technique. And it's the technique that I am interested in trying to show, because if you master that you can do whatever you want. Although there is much decrying of classical cooking nowadays, and of Escoffier and so on and so forth, I do think most of the talk is from people who are not real students of cooking. The classical training teaches you what to do with food and how to do it. If you don't have that background, you really have nothing solid to depend on. Of course, you have to develop your taste for food, but that comes from experience—from eating, discussing, studying, experimenting—from taking food seriously.

With a solid classical background, you are ready for improvisation. That is what is happening in France, now, with their so-called *nouvelle cuisine*. The chefs and society have released French cooking from the straightjacket of classical dishes, and it has now become accepted—even demanded—that the chefs improvise and create. Unfortunately, because that is the present mode, you do get cooks who have little taste and training who produce dishes that are quite inedible and utterly strange; they do it because they feel they must be new and different. But judging from our last trip to France, I believe things are settling down and much of the silliness is no longer acceptable. At least I hope so! As a friend said to me the other day, "No wonder the old-fashioned French cuisine was so popular—it was so damned good to eat!"

To be a good cook you have to have a love of the good, a love of hand work, and a love of creating. Some people like to paint pictures, or do gardening, or build a boat in the basement. Other people get a tremendous pleasure out of the kitchen, because cooking is just as creative and imaginative an activity as drawing, or wood carving, or music. And cooking draws upon your every talent—science, mathematics, energy, history, experience—and the more experience you have the less likely are your experiments to end in drivel and disaster. The more you know, the more you can create. There's no end to imagination in the kitchen.

# Sylvia Porter

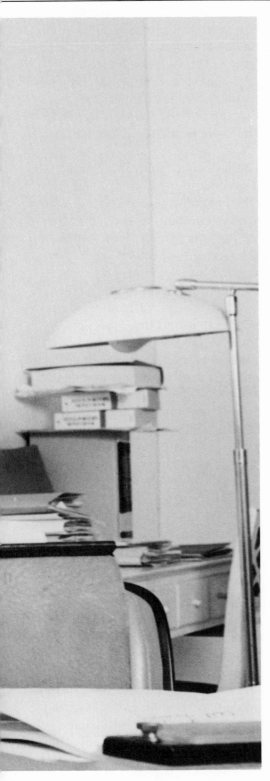

Sylvia Porter (born 1913, Patchogue, Long Island, New York) is a financial writer who was a pioneer in reporting on finance for the general public as opposed to the financial elite. She was the first woman hired on the financial desk of a newspaper. Through her best-selling books and her daily syndicated column, which reaches an estimated 40 million readers, she has been instrumental in eradicating "economic illiteracy" and educating a consumer public. She is the author of Sylvia Porter's Tax Book published annually since 1960 and Sylvia Porter's New Money Book for the 80's.

I've DEDICATED MY LIFE TO fighting what I call economic illiteracy, to breaking down the barriers against women and to fighting for the freedom to choose your own role. If you want to choose a role as a housewife, to devote your life to bringing up a beautiful next generation with as much love, caring and time as you can give, that's your choice. God be with you. If you want to devote your life partially to working on the open marketplace, then again, bless you. Accept that role as an equal, paycheck for paycheck, achievement for achievement and recognition for recognition. If you want to try to combine the two by having a family as well, that's tougher to achieve but worth it. I've done it and I've had a ball.

Let's talk for the moment about consumer economics. That's what touches the real day-to-day lives of real people. In my column, I educate people on how to get a mortgage, what the best mortgage is for them, how to get the best rates, how to compare rates, what "points" are, what the usury laws are, what closing charges are; how do you go about getting an installment loan, what is a finance charge, an interest rate, how do you save on food, how do you buy a refrigerator, etc.

For instance, do you save money with a freezer or don't you? The answer is, you don't, unless you live on a farm, keep it fully stocked and load up on the specials. When's the best time to buy things? Air conditioners in January? Yes. Bathing suits? After the fourth of July. Christmas presents? Anytime but. Costume jewelry? January, when it's on sale after Christmas. There are three major clearance periods during the year, one after Christmas, one at Easter and one after July 4. Excellent times to buy furs: in August; appliances, in January; ski equipment, in March. This is *consumer* economics. These are facts.

That's a jungle out there. Giant labor unions, giant corporations, global oil companies . . . Both industry and the consumer are recoiling against regulation. Deregulation is the only solution. The American consumer suffers.

At the same time, with inflation running at a rate which should never have been permitted to happen, the need for the consumer to know how to handle his or her own money, and how to take on his or her own responsibilities, is greater than ever. I think that American consumers have finally gotten around to realizing that we have to do it ourselves. "Washington" isn't going to do it for us. The Great White Father isn't there. "God was here but He left early," to quote Irving Shaw. Wall Street has been a disaster area for years. It's about time it turned around—which is what I'm betting on.

I like to think I've contributed in some way to the increasing willingness of the American public to take on the responsibilities of the economy. That's what we have to do now. The American public can decide to take action, as when the price of coffee went out of sight and consumers cut down on the consumption of coffee and suddenly a lot of coffee appeared on the market. I was in Cartagena, Colombia, one of the three largest coffee producers in the world, at the time the price was going up, at a meeting of the Inter-American Press Association of which I am the only member in my category—Syndicated Columnists. I got hold of the president of the Colombia Coffee Association by wangling my way into a lunch with him and one of the hostesses of the conference. I do not speak Spanish, damn it. I'm so provincial. He spoke beautiful English.

I asked him about coffee, which was about four to five dollars a pound in the United States. I said, "People are cutting down on coffee. Are you aware of it?" He said, "That's the one fear I have above all others. If you, the greatest coffee drinkers in the world (which the U.S. is) cut down only one half cup a day, you will destroy the coffee grower of Colombia." I said, "You're breaking my heart. Why don't you release some of the coffee you're holding and hoarding here?" "Oh," he said, "we're not doing that." I said, "Well, then who is? You've got coffee here."

Then he admitted that a lot of the speculators were doing the hoarding on the wharfs, both in the United States and Colombia. So I came back home and wrote a series of three columns and I ended the third one by saying, "You want to know how we can beat those speculators? Don't buy coffee." ... People were already doing it on their own. The point is *we* pushed that coffee back on the market.

I'm trying to be a teacher, to teach economics, to help give consumers a break, a chance to win, to avoid being booby-trapped. I've done a lot of studying, I study every day, so I have strong feelings, great convictions, about economic policy and I write about that too. I cover the waterfront. I never get tired or run out of ideas. I love being alive. And far be it for me to rust out. I'll wear out. I glimpse results in what I've done. I feel I've contributed in some part. Whether it's small, medium or large, is for others to judge.

When I was growing up I wanted to be a poet and I wanted to be a writer. That's all I ever wanted to be, but I majored in economics in college because of my family. My father, who was a physician, had died and left my mother with a trunkful of IOUs. What else does a good family doctor leave except a trunkful of IOUs? He couldn't send you away from his door because you didn't have the money. He'd treat you and say, "All right, you owe me." So they never paid up. Then when he died, they all brought my mother sacks of potatoes. Anyway, she promptly lost what little money we had in the Depression and the stock market and then she went to work. She insisted that my brother study medicine as my father had planned to have him do, and she insisted that I have a career.

I remember that from the time I was in the cradle she told me I would have the career that early marriage had denied her. She was an early suffragette, a liberated woman, but my father was a typical ... you know, father figure. He was a typical male chauvinist. Women were just not the equals of men. So if it hadn't been for my mother, I'm sure I never would have gotten my education. My brother went to Columbia, University of Pennsylvania and Johns Hopkins and I went to Hunter College in New

York. It was then a very, very hard college to get into. Because it was free, you had to have a minimum of B+ for four years to get in.

When I graduated from college, I studied at night for my master's degree in economics. I had tried writing a novel and it was a typical eighteen-year-old-girl's novel. I found out that my ear for dialogue was not as good as I'd hoped it would be and I realized that I'd never really be a novelist. So I said, "Well, my first great frustration."

I was pounding the streets looking for a job, and working at anything I could get. I went to the Associated Press. I went to all the morning, afternoon and evening papers and they all laughed. A woman? A girl? They closed the door on my face. One afternoon, after I finished whatever job I had then, I went back to the *New York Evening Post* because they were an afternoon newspaper, they worked late. The managing editor was rip-roaring drunk, absolutely rip-roaring. He saw my face and he said, "You know, I think I'll give you a chance. It will be awfully funny. I'll try you out at space rates. Start tomorrow."

I used every friend, every source, every contact I had in New York City. I was ruthless in my pursuit of good stuff. I sent in so much copy that was original and fact-packed that they printed it and finally they found that paying me space rates, it was ten cents a line or something, was more expensive than hiring me, so they hired me. That was the first wall broken down right then and there against women in the financial world. There had never been a woman on the financial desk of a big city newspaper before.

The first time I was sent out on a story I had to phone it in. I had written it out in longhand, but when I got on the phone I suddenly became speechless. I lost my voice, I froze. One of the very nice reporters who later became a good friend, he was on the *Times,* saw what was happening, took pity on me and said to the man on the desk, "Sylvia got too frightened to talk. Here's her story, I'll read it to you." And he read it for me. I'll never forget that.

The economics writing that was done then was all done by men and most of it was completely incomprehensible. It was all written in what I call bafflegab. Everybody tried to be more complex than everyone else. The *Wall Street Journal* was written for the elite who could read it, the *New York Times* financial page was laughable, it was so difficult, the *Journal of Commerce* was a popular paper . . . they were all very bad. Then came this little breath of fresh air—me—saying, "Let's write this so people can understand it." It's a funny thing to realize that this was a brand new idea.

Had I been conscious of what I was doing, I would have been terrified. But I was utterly unaware that I was doing anything unusual, that this was breaking ground that had never been broken before. I was utterly unaware that I was moving into uncharted fields, that I was combining a writer's instinct, to write, with economics in an attempt to reach people. It seemed to be a natural thing to do instead of trying to write for my peers, who would only appreciate it if it was gobbledegook.

People who read my columns in the newspapers didn't know I was a woman until 1943, because I wrote under my initials. I had to. When there were appointments to be kept, the financial editor would send a man in my place and I'd remain behind. Finally I came out and started to show up. Oh, breaking down those walls, those were very high walls, against women. They were higher than the walls in medicine. Women had broken into medicine long before. Women had broken into law and the university, but they hadn't broken into the world of finance, particularly the world of writing about finance. The only person I could be compared to was that unbelievable, greedy scarecrow, Hetty Green. But Hetty Green was a money-maker. I wasn't a money-maker. I was writing about it.

I was teaching. I call what I do teaching. My daughter, who would like to know when Mama's going to slow down—she should know I'm not going to—would love to see me walk into a university and do it face to face because I love to teach. I say, "What's wrong with doing it so that I can reach 40 million people instead of a couple of hundred?" She'd say, "Because it's fun to listen to you in person."

Now the barriers against women in my field are all breaking down. I think there must be hundreds, if not thousands, of women in it now. Do you know, one of the greatest kicks I got was years ago when I saw an ad from AP in *Editor and Publisher* for a woman financial columnist. I was alone in my office uptown and I just sat there and grinned, just as I'm grinning now. You could have painted me on a pumpkin. "A woman?" remembered I in the back of my head, "Never!"

# Muriel Siebert

Muriel Siebert (born 1932, Cleveland, Ohio) is superintendent of banks for the State of New York, where she supervises the management of $400 billion in the nation's largest state banking department. She is the first woman to hold that position and to attain power in the financial world. She opened her own brokerage company, Muriel Siebert and Co., in 1967 when she became the first woman member of the New York Stock Exchange.

**W**HEN A FRIEND SUGGESTED to me that I buy a seat on the New York Stock Exchange I said, "Don't be ridiculous." He said, "There's no law against it." Then it became a challenge and a game. It took me about six months until I got up the guts to do it. I kept going over it in my mind: "Gee, I want to do it, no, I don't want to do it." . . . I was "hocking" myself. Four hundred and forty-five thousand dollars is a lot of money for something that isn't tangible. I also didn't know how many of my customers would still continue to do business with me. I was earning my living on the commissions I got from institutions based on the research I did for them, and it would mean I would have to go from an existing brokerage firm, although a small firm, to being on my own. I would still clear through a major firm so there was no risk for my customers, but until you take a step like that you don't know how people will react. You just don't know.

I applied for a loan to buy a seat and I was turned down even though the loan had been completely collateralized, yes ma'am, by one of the major banks in this city, the bank that I had had an account with for a long time, and had borrowed from to buy securities, and knew me. They loaned me my deposit but they would not loan me the purchase price. I later got a loan from another bank. I found out later there was a bet going around that the bank would never have to make the loan because the Stock Exchange was not going to sell me the seat.

You know, whenever you break a tradition that's 187 years old, not everybody's going to love you. People who had volunteered to sponsor me, when the time came, ran out the door. On the other hand, some of the toughest people turned out to be my best friends. My two sponsors were both upstairs members. I could not get anybody from the floor to sponsor me, and some of those people had promised me. That was pretty tough. That's hard to take.

When I finally got my seat, everyone said that the reason there had never been a woman on the floor of the Stock Exchange before was because no lady could stand the language (so I learned the language) and because there was no ladies room on the floor—which is a lie. There is a ladies room, it's been there since the war days. I received three portable johns that weekend from friends—I said I never had so many people concerned about my toilet habits before in my life.

I spent twenty days down there on the floor of the exchange as a trainee, with my little square badge, and test by test, I qualified to do any piece of work I wanted to do on the floor of the New York Stock Exchange.

My family lived in Cleveland, Ohio. I was going to college there, but instead of going to class I was playing bridge. I guess I'm a lousy student if I have to do certain things I don't like to do. Things I like to do, I do very well. I probably didn't have the discipline then to force myself to stay in school. I dropped out.

At the same time, my father had cancer and his illness was a long, protracted one. He was sick about three years. He'd been used as a guinea pig in a series of three operations. They had taken tubes from his kidney and bladder and put them into his rectum. His illness was a terrible thing to watch.

I'd been to New York once on a vacation. I had visited on the balcony of the Stock Exchange. It seemed very, very exciting. They used to give tourists their names in ticker tape as souvenirs. It said, "Welcome to the New York Stock Exchange," with your name and date on it. Well, I took that home and, strangely enough, I saved it. I have that tape at home in my den now, framed. I told myself then that if I ever came back to New York, I'd like to work on Wall Street.

You have no idea what New York is to people who aren't from New York. There's a fascination, it beckons. I thought I'd go, stay a few months and come home. I was prepared to work there for a few months to support myself, just to see New York.

I have a feeling for accounting and for numbers. I used to cut classes in college and get A's in accounting. I think you're born with different talents. Then you capitalize on them, you define them. Why can some people pick up a pencil and draw? Sure it can be taught, but the great artists didn't have to be taught. In my case, I was very good with numbers.

So I first applied for a job at Merrill Lynch, the stockbrokers. They asked, "College degree?" I said, "No." So they said, "No job." The next day I applied to Bache and when they asked, "College degree?" I said "Yes." It was an instant degree. If I hadn't been lucky enough to be hired, I would have been a bookkeeper somewhere or an accountant. Luck plays a part that they didn't check.

Every time you sign an application to become a partner of a firm, they put a detective firm on you, but it never came out. That was luck. Otherwise I would not have been able to become a partner and I might have lost the opportunity to make the kind of money I did, which enabled me to buy a seat on the Stock Exchange.

The Stock Exchange checks very thoroughly on people. I put down the right information when I bought my seat on the exchange because I realized that was an historic application, and you are dealing with people's money and trust. The exchange wrote the college and I guess some clerk at the college said I had attended the school for four years, which I really hadn't done, and they took it as a degree.

This world is the only world I know. To me it's represented a constant challenge. I've seen things I've wanted to do and I've done them. In some cases being a woman was an obstacle, but it probably gave me more incentives than I would have had if I'd been a man. It's possible, because when I wasn't being paid as much as a man, I changed jobs, found a firm who'd pay me as much. When I went down on the scale I changed again. I always found a new job before I left the old one. Once I didn't do that and

I'll never make the same mistake twice. You can be sought after, but if you quit first, before you get the job, you're not as valuable. I've given that advice out to people. Employers feel much better if they are the aggressive ones and take you out of a job. I think anybody who is successful takes risks. I think you have to analyze and study the situation.

I was a partner for two different small brokerage firms for three years each. I found I was doing a lot of business, concentrating on only a few stocks in aviation and transportation. I developed a reputation for knowing these stocks very well, and I knew the management of these companies. I'd go to see the management four or five times a year and I might talk to them once a week. When you're with a small firm and you've done the research on Beech Aircraft and written a report, and an institution goes and buys 200,000 shares and you handle the order, you're going to get the credit. If you are with a big firm, let's say you are working for Merrill Lynch, or E. F. Hutton, the credit is going to go partly to the salesman who's covering the account, partly to the man on the trading desk, maybe you'll get a cut of a piece of the research pie, but you're not going to get that credit directly, which is why I decided to work for small firms.

I think one of my strengths is that I'm very sensitive to people. It enabled me to be successful on Wall Street because when I was doing research I was depending on my relationships with my clients and with the companies I was following. My clients were the biggest institutions in the country, and they had faith in me. When I went into business for myself, I did three financings the first two years that came from larger Wall Street firms. That means that I raised $30 million for Seaboard World Airlines, jointly with two other companies. I wasn't even incorporated then. You just don't get those kinds of ratings, but Seaboard World Airlines was a company I'd followed, they had faith in me, and I found a way to do their financing and brought in two larger firms. When companies have that kind of faith, they're buying your ability but they also trust you as a person.

When I started my own business, I also decided to change policy and give discounts to individuals instead of just corporations. The commission structure was changing then so that instead of having a fixed commission base, commissions became negotiable on everything. So I realized there was a market. I saw the way the rates were developing, and I saw that they were staying the same for the individuals but that they had come down sharply for the institutions. The individuals were paying ten times per share basis what the institutions were paying. For example, I was doing business with one hundred shares of stock at ten cents a share for the banks on hundred-share lots. We'd go down six or seven cents a share for the institutions, but the individuals were paying fifty cents or sixty cents a share. So I just felt that individuals weren't being treated fairly. If the larger firms had lowered the rates for the individuals then I never would have gone into that business, but they didn't.

So when I realized that this was a trend that was not going to change, I decided that everybody would pay the same for the same size order in the firm. This meant giving the individuals a shot at lower commissions. I thought it would be profitable. You don't know when you take a step like that. I was not loved when I did that, by the Wall Street firms, but I did it. They wouldn't have minded if I had done it without the advertising, but I was running some very powerful ads and it worked out. We got an enormous response. Then a lot of companies followed suit. There are a lot of people in this business now, maybe ten or fifteen members of the Stock Exchange are doing it.

I'd say a woman does have to work harder, put more passion and commitment into what she does, than a man in this business. I don't know if it's going to be that way ten years from now. I think women are coming out of some of the graduate schools and being given at least an even opportunity. In some cases, because the institutions are playing "catch-up," women are being given an advantage. I think ten years from now they'll just be treated equally. It won't be a game to them, it will be work. I think for a lot of us, during the years that I made it, it was a game, but a serious game.

I'm the first woman superintendent of banks in New York State and I was the first woman member on the New York Stock Exchange. As such, I've filled two of the highest financial jobs in the country that any woman's ever had. Sometime down the road when there have been maybe five or six women superintendents, will the next one work as hard? That's what I mean by a game. It's work but it's also a challenge to dig in and do something well.

I don't think it would have been possible to have had the career I have and been married. Maybe in today's environment it would be because people accept it. I see it in the younger people. People did not accept it twenty years ago. It was very rare. If women worked, it was as schoolteachers. I have to do an awful lot of traveling, calling on the companies and my clients. Twenty years ago a lot of people would not have accepted that.

I was growing pretty fast in my career and, when I look at the various people that I dated seriously over the years, they haven't kept up with me. I mean I've changed terribly as I've grown; because I was succeeding pretty fast, I grew and changed as a person. So I might have had a couple of divorces behind me, too. I would say that most of the women that I know who have been successful do have a divorce or two behind them, because you end up growing sometimes so much faster than your husband. If you're lucky, you're married to someone who's also changing, and changing in the same direction. I don't regret that marriage wasn't possible in my time. You can't have everything.

I don't think ahead. I don't know what I want to do next, whenever I do it. I don't know what other possibilities there are. I wasn't looking for the superintendent job, it came along. There was no guarantee I'd do a good job. I think I've squeaked through. You don't have guarantees in this world. You've got to take chances.

# Sarah Caldwell

*Sarah Caldwell (born 1924, Maryville, Missouri) is the conductor, artistic director and founder of the Opera Company of Boston. She has gone beyond the conventions of classic operatic staging to present opera as a vital theatrical experience. Her productions include American premieres of difficult and little-known operas, such as Tippett's* The Ice Break, *Schoenberg's* Moses and Aaron, *Berlioz's* The Trojans, *Rameau's* Hippolyte et Aricie *and Nono's* Intolleranza. *She is the only woman who has conducted at the Metropolitan Opera in New York and one of the few to guest-conduct regularly with major orchestras.*

$I$N THE LAST TEN YEARS opera has become far more popular in this country than I think anyone realizes. There's a statistic I'm very fond of: more people attended operatic performances last year than attended baseball games. I think that opera should be performed both for the highly cultivated opera fan, the very knowledgeable opera buff and at the same time for an intelligent human being who comes into the opera for the first time and does not know the piece. We should be trying to communicate this experience to a broader, wider range of people, and that is beginning to happen.

My concept of opera is of a total musical and theatrical experience, in which the theatrical elements and the musical elements are very carefully combined so that they enhance one another. When all the various aspects of the performance do meld together, when the performance of singing actors is marvelous, when the staging has been planned so that it fits the musical forms, when the music underlines the dramatic tensions—you have something that is beyond any one of the components of this terribly exciting thing called opera.

Opera is very definitely a collaborative art form and no one should go into opera who is temperamentally unsuited to collaboration. I think that first of all you must have an exceedingly strong ego and you must have a lot of pride, and because you have this kind of pride, you take pride in your ability to work with other similar people. That's really the fun of this profession.

I didn't start out wanting to be a conductor. I began to play the violin when I was four years old. In my family I was surrounded by musicians and it was a very natural thing to do. We went to the theater and to concerts a great deal when I was a child. My mother was a musician and she was a very fine pianist. The Depression came, which made it very difficult for careers, and she had to work teaching to help support her family. She taught choral music in the public schools of Kansas City, and was a choral conductor, so it never occurred to me that it was a strange thing for a woman to want to be a conductor.

I was very fortunate. I graduated from high school quite young and when I went to college, my stepfather, who was a university professor, said to me that I could have all the musical training I wanted but that life offered many interesting opportunities and why didn't I study something besides music. I majored in psychology. I thoroughly enjoyed what I was doing, and I think that this has been very important to me in my life—that I didn't just study music.

When I came to Boston to study violin, I attended some opera classes at the New England Conservatory which were taught by Boris Goldovsky, who's a brilliant, brilliant teacher and very important in the development of American opera. Some of the work being done in those classes was tremendously exciting; the theatrical and musical elements really came together. I was enormously attracted to it, and I went to Goldovsky and said that although I had been preparing myself to be a violinist, and I certainly wanted to be a violinist, that I wanted very much to do what he did, and I'd like to study with him. He very kindly took me as a student and said something to me then that really made it all possible. He said that there was nothing to be afraid of. The fact that I didn't know anything about opera, at that point I hadn't studied conducting and I really knew very little about the technical aspects of the theater, didn't matter. He said that everything was learnable.

Since I was studying here in Boston, I decided it was here that I wanted to live my life in opera, to be a conductor or stage director. At a certain moment in time I had an opportunity to start an opera company here, and it just seemed a natural thing to do.

We have a very interesting audience base of highly educated people in Boston. We have a large number of university professors, students, doctors, research scientists, engineers and so forth. This means, it seems, that in Boston we're free to perform a number of unusual pieces, pieces no one ever heard of, and have a sellout. Some of my colleagues in other cities are nervous about performing these pieces. *Carmen, Bohème,* everyone feels safe in performing but last year we did the American premiere of *The Ice Break,* by Sir Michael Tippett, and we had sold-out houses and people clamoring to get tickets. We've done such operas as Schoenberg's *Moses and Aaron,* Berlioz's *The Trojans,* Glinka's *Russlan and Ludmilla,* pieces one doesn't hear anywhere else really.

I suspect I'm a controversial figure in this world. In addition to putting on new operas, we have done a number of our productions in rather strange places, not ideally suited or equipped for opera. The theater we performed *The Flying Dutchman* in, last night, is not an opera house. It's a stage 30 feet deep, and normally a good opera house has a stage of 150 feet. The limitations of the stage forced us into a very unconventional presentation, in which the Dutchman's ship actually framed the proscenium and its bowsprit went up into the second balcony. I think this design added an element of excitement which was perhaps unique to this production as productions of *The Flying Dutchman* go. But it was legitimate because I feel we were trying, aesthetically and intellectually, not to do something that would create an impression just for its own sake but rather to find a way to express this work in this theater. In a different theater, in different circumstances, the ideas would come in a different way.

If I am controversial, it is also because I believe that to give a really exciting operatic performance, the stage director and the conductor must work very closely together. I do not believe that it is possible for an operatic director to be good regardless of his skills in the theater unless he's a very, very sensitive musician. I'd go further and say trained musician. I would go still further and say this is true without exception. And I don't think that it is possible for a conductor, regardless of how fine a musician he is, to be a good opera conductor unless he is as fascinated by and as knowledgeable of the theatrical elements of opera as he is of the musical ones. Now those are controversial ideas. When I perform both of these functions as I did last night, that's when one gets the best results.

When we begin a new opera, first of all we approach it from the point of view of content. Fortunately we have a remarkably rich heritage of operas to choose from, in many styles from many countries. I think what makes a work great, a work which will endure throughout the ages, is its subject matter. It must be about something which touches the human experience and which will continue to touch the human experience. There have been many operas inspired by the importance of human freedom and the great variety of human relationships and human suffering and human problems that are common to everyone and to every age.

We try to approach every work that we do, whether it's a new work or an old work, as if we were viewing it for the first time. And we try to find out what meaning we see and hear in the piece. Then we study its background. We try to determine how it came into being, what it was meant to express, what political and personal ideas were behind it, what made the composer choose the subject, what made the librettist write the work. Was it—and it usually was—the product of a particular moment in time? That is, did it express the particular problems of a particular era, a particular country? And how did it affect its audience? What impact did its composer and librettist hope it would have? We also try to determine how it was produced, what the scenery looked like, what the costumes looked like, what the theatrical conventions were.

The core of this process, the heart of it, is to try to keep the piece itself continually in mind. As a director I feel the most important point of view I have is that of the audience who has never seen or heard this work and comes and sits down in the seat and receives a series of visual and musical impressions which are going to add up to something. Some of them will give him information, some of them will have an emotional effect on him, and hopefully illuminate and do justice to the work.

There is no doubt that the quality of a great human voice is very thrilling, and certainly unless one has great voices the opera does not come to life, does not really take off. On the other hand, it is possible for a singer to have an extraordinarily beautiful instrument and not sing very expressively, which means that instrument is completely wasted. It is only if the singer can express human emotions with that instrument and color the instrument and make the instrument serve all the musical and human functions that are at its command, that all of this works.

The job of a singing actor is extraordinarily complicated. We expect our singers to be remarkably versatile, to be able to sing a great variety of musical styles, to be able to express thoughts and feelings in a number of languages, to act as skillfully as any actor in theater. Then, in addition to that, they are often called upon to dance or duel or climb masts, to do all kinds of things that would be expected in the theater. They are supposed to do all of these together, to make them mesh, to blend them until it's very difficult to separate the various elements. This requires an enormous amount of time and patience and energy and devotion and experimentation. We have great respect for instrumentalists and we very rightly respect the members of a fine string quartet, but just think: All these people have to do is sit quietly with the music in front of them and concentrate on music-making. When a singer has gotten to that point, he has just barely begun to fight. He has to memorize the music and he has to make it function for him as an actor. It's really a very, very remarkable human achievement.

Our most successful performances come when the singer takes a really active role from the moment of conception. Some of the best productions that I've done with Beverly Sills over the years have been those in which we even discussed the scenic design of the shows. We've discussed the way these models would work and the way they would affect her.

I think that the qualities we connect with the superstar, that is, the impact and magnetism of the personality, the brilliance of the singing, the brilliance of the acting, are essential to any operatic performance. The measurement of this in terms of, let's say, press treatment is irrelevant. The young lady who sang Senta in last night's production of Richard Wagner's *The Flying Dutchman* is a Czechoslovakian soprano, Elizabeth Payer. No one has ever heard of her in Boston, and yet I think she made a tremendous impact on the audience.

We sometimes joke and say that by the time people become known as famous, important singers they can no longer do it. The truth of the matter is, oddly enough, the singer's life is somewhat limited. The longevity of the human voice is questionable. Also, by the time singers are in superb physical condition and have developed their voices to their full potential, they are not children anymore. How long your career lasts depends on what you look like, how long you can sing and act and play parts of seventeen-year-olds.

The Opera Company of Boston is really a group that is assembled anew for each production. There are certain people who are in almost every production, which I suppose means that they are regular members of the company, but the problem of opera in this country, and in Boston, is that there's not enough money to give any kind of permanence and financial stability to the large number of people required to make up an opera company. Even at the Metropolitan Opera, where they are in session over a longer period, the chorus may be a permanent feature, the orchestra is more or less permanent, but directors, conductors, singers, designers, go in and out very often. I wish that we could find a way to create a situation in Boston that would enable us to engage people and make it worth their while financially to rehearse for a much longer period of time. We can only do that if we can offer many more performances.

I became successful, if you can say I am successful, by virtue of the remarkable experience I've had in the Opera Company of Boston. I had fine training, but to learn the craft of conducting, the art of conducting, whatever you want to call it, you just have to have the chance to work with an orchestra, to learn rehearsal techniques, to understand the best way to help to make performers do their best; there's just an unending series of problems that one must learn how to face, and I was able to do it here. When I began to be invited to conduct in other places, I had done so much conducting that I really felt I knew what I was doing. And that's why I'm very fortunate. I was able to learn it before too much attention was focused on it.

Success is important only to the extent that it puts one in a position to do more things one likes to do. In this very peculiar kind of profession you can't have it continually. Of course, you don't like to fail. The production that we did of *The Flying Dutchman,* I feel, worked. Some people may hate it. Some people, I hope, will find it very exciting. Success, if you define it as universal approval, is not important to me. I don't think it exists, but success in terms of the approval of people whom one respects (and it's a batting average) is important.

There are so many wonderful pieces I'd love to produce, I'll never in my lifetime, no one in a lifetime could, tackle all of them, or even begin to scratch the surface. It takes too much time. For example, we did *Louise* by Charpentier. I went with the designers and spent some time in Paris and we were able to dig up the archives of Charpentier and to walk the streets he had walked until we found a number of very beautiful period photographs of the time, and in his archives we found a number of papers that I don't think musicians have really looked at since his death. They gave us a fascinating viewpoint, and we were able to re-create the atmosphere of Paris at that time and of this work in our production. We just immersed ourselves in it until we felt that we knew what it was about, and then we could produce it. That's the way I like to do it.

With every opera production I do, I enter a new world. It's a kind of time machine. I've become interested in areas I wouldn't have been interested in before. One comes in touch with real people who really lived, who really sat in a particular kind of chair and wore particular kinds of clothes and had a particular set of problems, and it's interesting to learn about all those things. It's like being in another world for a little while and that's interesting, that's fun. That's really being alive. Maybe it is an escape, but I've never thought of it in quite those terms. It's a little bit like an adventure, exploring new worlds. You don't know what's going to come around the corner.

# Alberta Hunter

*Alberta Hunter (born 1895, Memphis, Tennessee) is a blues singer and composer who has written for and performed with the greats of jazz. In America, she has performed in bordellos, in jazz clubs and nightclubs, in vaudeville and on Broadway, but it was in Europe that she established her reputation. After a twenty-year hiatus from public life she returned at the age of eighty-two to perform again, singing songs inspiring brotherhood and love. Her career spanning seventy years is a prime example of fortitude, endurance and unwavering spirit.*

NOTHING GOOD EVER COMES TOO LATE. It's good, I'm very happy about the recognition I'm getting now, but I mean I'm the same person I was years and years ago. Nobody paid me any attention, but now that I am made and going pretty good, everybody seems to want me. That's what makes me furious, you see.

Many times I've walked to offices, different agents' offices, and they'd be sitting right in their offices and the secretary, she'd pretend to be calling one, and if she did call him, he'd say, "Tell her I'm not here." They didn't recognize me. Now some of those same agents have been down to The Cookery to hear me sing and want me to work. They want somebody else to build you up. They don't want the responsibility themselves.

Barney Josephson of The Cookery has built me up now, in his later years. Barney gave me the opportunity. God and my voice built me up.

I've always been independent. That's what I wanted and what I needed. For me, show business was just a matter of working. I wanted to stay up, and I wanted to be big, I wanted to become a star, of course, but I never thought, Well, I'll just make a niche for myself and forget everybody else. I thought the field was open, big enough for everybody. So you make your niche, I'll make mine.

When I was a little kid, growing up in Memphis, there were little kid concerts and things. I used to hear the schoolteachers say to one another or to somebody about me, "She can sing, she's got a good voice." That's the only way I knew. I just had plenty of nerve and I was going to try it. What I heard the teachers say slipped my mind, I forgot all about that, but I'd just go start singing whether I could or not.

My mother had a friend who had a daughter. This daughter was in Chicago. I knew that her name was Ellen Winston but she had changed her name to Helen Winston. She used to write home to her mother and tell her that the girls in Chicago were making ten dollars a week singing in the nightclubs. I heard her mother telling my mother about this and I heard her say this was in Chicago. I just decided, well, I'm going to get some of that ten dollars they got there in Chicago.

One day my mother sent me to the store to buy a loaf of bread and I went inside and got the bread and then I saw my schoolteacher, and my schoolteacher says, "I'm going to Chicago." I said, "I wish I could go." She said, "I have a child's pass. You can go if your mother says so." So I ran and hid between some houses and I came back and told her my mother said it was all right. I went down to the station and got on a train and went to Chicago. I hadn't been near my mother to tell her, but you see, children in those days would spend nights with their chums and things and my mother thought I was with one of my chums.

My being a child I didn't know, I thought you'd go to Chicago and you could walk there and find whoever you were looking for, not realizing that Chicago was a big city. So when we got to Chicago I got on the streetcar with my schoolteacher and her husband and I got off the streetcar, where? Why I got off at that particular spot, I don't know. I got off at that spot all alone and where I got off, the streetcar's going this way and I'm facing this way, and I walked right into the building, the Burlington building. I shall never forget it because I can see it right now with my mind's eye. I walked into that building and there was a lady washing, and I said to this lady, "Do you know a girl by the name of Ellen Winston?" and she said, "No, I don't, but there's a girl that lives here by the name of Helen Winston." God's hand, baby. I said, "Will you let me stay here until she comes?" And she started questioning me then, saying, "Who are you, what are you doing here?" And when this girl came, it was my mother's friend's daughter. God's hand.

All my life, God's hand has guided me to where I am right now, what I'm doing, my success, all of that. So this girl says when she sees me, "Pig, what in the world are you doing here in Chicago?" They called me Pig when I was small because I used to get so dirty. "What is Miss Laura going to think?" That was my mother. I said, "She thinks I'm over to Irma's house." That was my little chum in Memphis. She said, "Are you hungry?" I said, "No." That's the first thing the lady asked me, too. I said, "No, ma'am, I'm not hungry." So she said, "What in the world will I do? Well, sit down. I'll take you out to where I work." She was the second cook in this boardinghouse and she took me out to the boardinghouse and she asked the lady could she give me a little something to do, some work to do. She said, "She's nothing but a child, what could she do? Just let her peel potatoes." They let me peel potatoes.

In the meantime, while everybody was asleep at night, having heard about these girls singing in the places, I sneaked around and found where the places were. I would go out at night while everybody was asleep and go into the places, but they'd kick me out because I was too young. I remember so well this fella named Roy. He was the manager of the place, Dago Frank's. He put me out every time I'd go, but I kept going back. I've always been very determined. So every time he put me out, I'd go back again. So the last time he went to put me out, Bruce, this fellow named Bruce, he was a pianist, a crippled fellow, I can see him so well, said, "Oh, Roy, give her a chance. You can see she's nothing but a child."

So he let me come in and sing. I had learned two songs. "All Night

Long" and the other one was "Where the River Shannon Flows." Those two songs I had learned on a player piano that was downstairs in this building where my friend was staying. I'd go there, not realizing nothing about range of voice or anything like that, and I was singing in a high soprano. God, I think about it some time and I get so tickled. The last time I went, he let me stay, so I stayed a year and ten months.

You see, it was a brothel and it was where all the white pimps and the girls hung out, but classy, though. I was too young at eleven or twelve to realize what it was, but I knew the girls used to bring the fellows in and they'd sit there and drink and then finally they'd go upstairs. That didn't faze me. The police was going to close them up, but before the police got a chance to close them up, Roy closed the place, Dago Frank's. That was at Archer and State streets in Chicago.

Then I went to another little place called Hugh Hoskins, that's at Thirty-second and State. By that time I was beginning to get kind of seasoned. I stayed there, oh, a long time. That's where the Negro men were confidence men and their girls were pickpockets, but classy, all this was class. They used to, all of them, even down to Dago Frank's, they gave me money and the girls'd go out and buy me little dresses to make me look nice. I was still staying where the woman who was washing let me stay, and I had room and board at the boardinghouse so I could stay either place. I sang at Hoskins all that time, and I started getting famous then and the people started coming to hear me. That's where, not knowing what I was doing, I composed "Downhearted Blues," my first song that sold millions of copies, Bessie Smith's first hit, the song that made Bessie Smith famous.

I stayed there such a long time I was getting more popular and more popular and then I went to a place called The Panama, that was at Thirty-fifth and State. We had five girls upstairs and a pianist and five girls downstairs and a pianist. The girls were Bricktop and Florence Mills, they were downstairs. I was upstairs where the swingers were. And the people would pass on by Bricktop and them, the classy singers, and come on up and hear some swing, you know. Al Jolson and Sophie Tucker and Ray Samuels and big white artists from downtown would come upstairs to hear me sing, sing the blues. And each one of us five girls had our own style. The place was packed all the time with famous people from downtown come in to enjoy the Negro entertainment.

Then I went from that place to the Dreamland. That's where I became very famous. That's where I sang with Joe Oliver, King Oliver's band with Lil Harding, who later married Louis Armstrong. Mr. Bottoms, the boss, heard about this famous young man who could play trumpet, so he went down to New Orleans and brought Louis Armstrong up, to work with Joe Oliver as second trumpet. So there's where I got very famous.

Around that time I met a fellow in Cincinnati and married him. He was, oh, he was fine. He finally became the only Negro on the executive board of the CIO. I had brought my mother up from Memphis by then and I was living with her before I got married, and then when I got married

we both lived there. He'd get up in the morning and I'd get up and he'd go
out on the street and I'd go downtown or something. I'd come back and
I'd go to bed and he'd go to bed, but he'd be in his room and I'd be in my
mother's. I slept in my mother's room. I've always been old-fashioned,
always. So many things I see girls do now, you'd be surprised how it
embarrasses me. I see a lot of girls getting undressed before each other.
You couldn't pay me to do that, get undressed in front of anybody. I'm
still old-fashioned. I'm an old woman living in a modern age.

A lot of the fellows, they used to tell my husband, "Why do you want
to work when your wife is making a lot of money and she sings?" I didn't
say anything because I knew what they were trying to make him do and I
wasn't fixing to give anybody one fifteen cents, not a penny. So every time
I was supposed to be going home at night after work, I'd go down to the
pier and get my passport and everything ready. So before he heard
anything, I was in London. He went on back to his mother in Cincinnati.
There was no man that was going to depend on me. We were good friends
until he died. Whenever he came to town, he'd come to see me.

Well, I started traveling then. I made my first record, on Paramount.
"Downhearted Blues" was my first and it went over so big. Then people
started asking for me. I'd go out of Dreamland for a few weeks or a month
or so and come back, like I'm doing now at the club. Then I went to
Europe on a holiday, like a vacation, and I went to Paris first and from
Paris I went to Monte Carlo and while I was in Monte Carlo, Noble Sissle,
Eubie Blake's partner, he knew I had been trying to get into England. You
couldn't get into England without having a labor permit first if you were
an artist. He said, "If you want to get into England here's your chance. If
you want to go and do a benefit for the flood-sufferers of England at the
London Pavilion, you mention the lord mayor's name when you get to the
border. But you have to pay your own expenses." I didn't mind that. I
said, "I'm on my way." So I went to London, and I went directly from the
station to the London Pavilion Theater and I did a benefit in London.
Josephine Baker was on the bill too, marvelous. Mr. Hammerstein and Mr.
Ziegfeld and Jerome Kern were there. They were looking for somebody to
play Queenie opposite Paul Robeson in *Showboat*. They heard me.

The next morning I got a call to come down to the Drury Lane Theater,
that is the theater of London, and I sang for them. They didn't say
anything to me then, but the following morning I get a call to come down
and sign for the part. Then after I did all right in *Showboat* I did
vaudeville, they called it variety in England, did variety all over the
English provinces and then Cairo, and Turkey and Greece, Iran.

Well, after that I came back to America to see my mother, and I
worked at the Sunset with Earl Hines and the group. I worked a lot of
places in America and then I went back to Europe again. When Josephine
Baker went to the Folies Bergères, I followed her into the Casino du Paris.
I got a lot of recognition then. And I made records for His Master's Voice
(RCA). I was at the Dorchester when the Duke of Windsor used to come.
Peggy Joyce and Gloria Swanson and Michael Farmer, most of the big-

timers, used to come in and hear me at Chez Florence's. Things like that, and I became bigger and bigger and bigger.

The first show I opened on Broadway was a show called *How Come?* Sophie Tucker and all of them came to see me. I was recognized then, but it died down, you see, because they wouldn't keep pushing us Negroes or letting us Negroes go. We had to struggle hard. Very few Negro girls and boys had a chance to hit the big time, 'cause they were pushing the white girls and boys. The Negroes didn't get the chance. It wasn't that we didn't have the same ability. If there was a white girl that was a star and if a colored girl was clever, if she was a little stronger than this white star thought she should be, she'd have her moved off the program altogether, or put in a spot where she'd have to open the show and warm it up for her. Don't think we haven't had a hard time, baby. Some of the clubs were just as bad. The only thing to do was have the willpower, the strength of character, be ladies and gentlemen at all times, when you're working, get it down so nobody could beat you doing it.

When I'd see the other girls on big time years ago and I wasn't on it, I always said to myself, One of these times I'll be there. And I knew I was being held back. For instance, if somebody would call and ask for you, this agent would tell them that you're not available but they can get so and so. So that's killing you in order to push the other person forward. I've been pushed back that way. But I never became discouraged. I used to get kind of angry, but I used to say to myself, There's time, I'll get it. I always figured that I would make it, because I knew that if you got that determination, nothing and nobody can hold you down.

I've always known how to take care of myself, honey, 'cause there were plenty of stones, potholes you could fall into in those days if you didn't have a mind of your own and weren't strong. But I had a mind of my own and I've always been strong. Places I've worked, people have tried to get me to do things that I knew were wrong . . . I was always taught by my mother and grandmother to do what is right and "do what we're telling you. We're telling you to be a good girl." Everytime somebody tried to tell me to do something wrong, no, no, not me. They didn't say "chicken" then, "Don't be a chicken." They'd say, "Come on, be a good sport." I'd say, "You do what you want to do, I don't want to do it." No one could persuade me to do anything I didn't want to do.

That's been an obstacle sometimes in my career. A lot of times I could have gone with one of those kinds of fellows and do things that I knew weren't exactly right to get hired. Why, I think it knocked me out of several things, but in the long run it made me wonderful. It helped me. Because I don't care how much some girls think it's helping them, in the long run it's hurting them because a man who can have you can go out and tell somebody else, "Go get her"—not me. If you believed in something and you knew that what you was thinking was right, hold out for it. I did. I didn't have any agent. I was doing this all on my own. I could have had several agents if I ever had wanted them physically and otherwise. But it didn't mean a thing. A lot of them asked me, "Are you lonesome?" For what? My name is very clean, you can ask anybody about it. I've got good health, two beautiful homes, one on Roosevelt Island and one on Riverside Drive, radio, television, telephone and a bank book.

It was fortunate that I had a chance to go to the London Palladium. I was at the Palladium six weeks and that was history. You see, when we first went to Europe, it was really something to go to Europe. Josephine Baker, Bricktop, Mabel Mercer, Jimmy Daniels, Garland Wilson, Harry Watkins . . . the Kentucky Four, Eddie Coleman and that group. We paved the way for some of those that are going now. Jazz has always been more readily accepted in Europe than it is here, even today. The people in Europe can tell you every instrumentalist, what his name is and everything. So-and-so plays trumpet, so-and-so plays sax. They know them by name, every one of our musicians.

I gave up singing for a while when my mother died. My mother and I were very close. Always, all my life, I've looked after my mother. The first job I had, when they let me peel potatoes, I sent my mother my first two dollars that week when I got paid, I sent it to my mother. that's the reason I know that God's been good to me. I didn't scream and cry when my mother died because my conscience was clear. I knew that I had done my best. My mother didn't have to work or anything like that, she just stayed right at home and I looked after her. I didn't want her to have to get out and try to work, so I took it on myself, to do it.

When I first left Chicago and made the first bit of money, I bought a co-op, put my mother in it, 133 West 138th Street, directly in front of Abyssinia Baptist Church. I traveled all over everywhere, everywhere, everywhere, and she was right at home, didn't have a thing to do. I don't think I'm boasting, but I was making my change, and the money I was making I'd send it to her. She wrote me a letter, I hope I still have that letter, she told me to stop sending her money. Isn't that cute? Sure, besides paying the expenses and everything, when I came back to New York, she had every bit of it. I said, "Why didn't you spend it and enjoy yourself?" She's very conservative, like I am. And she always stayed home. She had two friends and they always came to her house, she didn't go to theirs. I lived right with her always. I looked after her, you see, until she died, and when she died, where was I? I'm sitting there by her bedside.

Maybe being at the hospital while my mother was dying and sitting by her bedside all that time and seeing how she needed to be helped and everything like that, I figured that maybe I could help in my way. Before that, I couldn't even stand to go to a hospital, to even visit, because I couldn't stand the thought of looking at sick people and being around sick people. Then when my mother died, I said, "Well, I'm going to see if I can do something for humanity."

So I went to school and took up nursing. I went to school at the Harlem YWCA on 137th Street and I was too old then to be accepted, but a woman, Phyllis Utz, the director there, she accepted my application and I started to school that next day, the Harlem School of Nursing, and I

stayed there and graduated and I affiliated at the Harlem Hospital and
Goldwater Hospital on Welfare Island, they call it Roosevelt Island now. I
liked Goldwater so I stayed there for twenty years. I was never late one
day, twenty years. You young people learn what time means. Twenty
years I was there.

I was the happiest person in the world when I was helping my
patients. I never complained a minute about overtime or anything like
that. It never crossed my mind. If my patient was sick and I had to stay
longer than my time, I would gladly stay. Sometimes I could see my
patients passing, going, see 'em going and I'd stand there and try to soothe
them, maybe rub their heads or fluff their pillows or something, to let
them go peacefully. It gave me a lot of pleasure, but I used to hate to see
them go and not be able to do anything for them, only try to make them as
comfortable as possible.

I never sang at all during that time. They didn't want to hear no
singing, baby, those patients wanted to get well. It never crossed my mind
to even hum a song while I was nursing. Never. Sometimes the ones that
couldn't see, or couldn't talk, when they'd hear my voice, you could see
them pull out a hand or something, or look up to let me know they were
looking. They knew me. It's a wonderful feeling. And, after my days off,
the nurses would say, "I'm glad you're here. Stevie sure was acting the
fool yesterday, he's crazy, acting terrible 'cause you're not here." Yeah, I
was good to them.

I was hurt, so badly hurt, when they told me that I was past the
mandatory retirement age, and I had to leave. That hurt me because I
thought after I have given everything I have, that I can give, to try to be a
good nurse and to serve sick people to the best of my ability, to think that
I'm being retired. Sixty-five was the mandatory age. They let me stay five
years longer, but you see every time they asked me how old I was, I told
them twenty-one-plus. So I was really eighty-two when they retired me.
They didn't know it.

I think music has a tendency to give you more feeling toward
humanity. There's a certain touch. I mean, if you go to touch a patient,
there's something in a note of song that will make you hold that patient
tenderly, I think. Yeah. Music gives you heart, soul, music gives you soul,
real soul. Jazz is a medicine. It's like a spiritualism medicine, and all
music is derived from jazz and spirituals, all of it, including some of the
operas, the songs in the big shows and things that other people got credit
for, derived from spirituals and jazz. So jazz is 100 percent American
music. Personally, it means to do unto others as I wish to be done to at all
times. It's my music, I love it. I can touch a person. I can touch different
people that never paid any attention to me before through my jazz. Yeah,
touching. It's a language. Jazz has a language all its own. Naturally it's an
expression of love.

My satisfaction in music comes from telling a story that needs to be
told. And I'm trying to get that story across and I seem to be, not just me,

we all seem to be getting that story across, through our music. A lot of people who wouldn't have accepted me originally will accept me now because of my music. My music has spoken a language to them. Sometimes when I'm standing up and singing a song, I've seen people, maybe in a conversation, they be busy talking or something, and something that I've said, or the way I've said, it has attracted their attention to the extent that they stopped talking and listen, because I was telling them a story that needed to be told. I think they wanted to hear it. The story is love. A lot of people need it and want it badly but they haven't had it. They're beginning to get it now. Some of them have wanted it for years and years and it just didn't come across to them, it didn't strike them, but now it's beginning to strike them and they're beginning to listen. There's a message somewhere and they're listening to that message. It's a great pleasure to be able to spread love and to be a participant in it, to be one of the messengers. I came to bring a message and I'm trying to deliver that message. I'm waiting for you to accept it.

Jazz and blues are becoming very big in America again. I think I've had quite a bit to do with it, just the little time I've been back. I know a lot of the old-timers are trying to get back into show business because of me. I don't know if I'm so great or not, but I think they want to come back in because they figure I'm old and if I can come back . . . but they don't realize you got to have a story to tell, too.

After I retired from nursing I went to Bobby Short's party, the famous entertainer. At Bobby Short's party was Charlie Bourgeois who is associated with the Newport Jazz Festival. He was there. And I kept seeing this man watch me, looking at me, and I said to myself, "What is this?" So he finally said to me, "Why don't you come back into show business?" I said, "I'm not interested." He said, "Why?" First of all, in my mind I was thinking I was too old. Who's gonna accept me at my age? So he said, "You call Barney Josephson." I said, "If Barney Josephson wants me, let him call me."

So he, I suppose, sneaked and called Barney and Barney called me the next morning. I told him I wasn't interested. He said, "Well, come down and talk to me anyway." I went down and talked with him and after having talked with him about three minutes, not longer than three minutes, I was certain I wanted to go back into show business, especially if I only worked for that man because he had such an honest appearance, such an honest face. You could see his countenance was so open; you could see he was a good man, a man with a heart. So I went to work for Barney, October 10, 1977, and I stayed there three years.

I have a good story. I'm eighty-five years old, first of all. Then I have a story to tell, what helped me to get where I am and to stay where I am. There are plenty of people eighty-five years old and what are they doing? Plenty of people have voices that could run rings around my voice, but it's my style and no need of trying to copy it, because I'm going to change it every time I get ready.

I was doing a lot of the same things then that I'm doing now, but I'm just doing them in a different way. I'm more seasoned and I have my own individual way of doing something. Maybe it's like Barney says. Barney says songs that he used to hate he loves to hear me sing. I'd say I'm going to sing so-and-so and he'd say, "Oh, I hate that song," but when I'd sing it, he'd say, "How did you do that?" I have my own way of doing a song. Not only my style, but a lot of people forget diction is very important when you're singing a song. People want to know what you're saying. And if a song has a lyric and a story, tell the story, don't just hang onto the music because there's some notes there. I'm not boasting, but my diction was always supposed to be very good.

A lot of times a song will come to me on the impulse of the moment. I write my words down right quick before I forget them 'cause if it goes away from my mind, I don't remember. Sometimes the music comes first, sometimes the words. The melody will come to me and I'll hum it to myself until I get it in my mind, and then I'll hum it to my pianist, to Gerald Cook, and he'll put the notes down so I can send it in for copyright. I don't know one note from the other, baby, but you hit the wrong note and I'll tell you you hit the wrong one. I know music. When I hear it, I know what I hear. Just lucky.

I'm working now on a song. A lot of kids get away from home, you know, and they forget all about their parents. They get away and they get with new company. They forget the people that carried them across. I'm trying now to bring some of those things back today to children, to remember their parents. Maybe their parents were not in a position to give them everything they wanted. Most parents gave them what they could. And another thing, a lot of them that get away from home, they become discouraged, and they're embarrassed because maybe they feel they haven't lived up to their parents' expectations and they're ashamed to write home or to call.

So I tell 'em, "Write and call." There's always a welcome waiting for you at home, always. So write home, call. Somebody else who knows you want to call home might let you use their phone. So call. You don't have to write a long letter, just a few lines on a postcard or any kind of piece of paper, so long as there's a stamp on it. "There's a welcome always awaiting you at home, sweet home."

I sang it at the club a few times. Barney was sitting out there and one young man says, "I'm going right downstairs now and call my mother." He said he hadn't written to her for fifteen years.

Sure, I've got something to do, a mission, and eventually I'll do it. I want to try and think of something different that nobody else has thought of that will be beneficial to others. Eventually something will come to me that nobody else has thought of. It will be to help humanity. I want all my things built on that strain, to help humanity. It won't be nothing frivolous, foolish. It's going to be something that's going to be a help. I can give of myself and still have something left. You can always give of yourself and still have something left, because after you've let something out, God's going to push something else into you, help you to do something else, so there's always something you can do.

# Mary Steichen Calderone

*Mary Steichen Calderone (born 1904, New York City) is a medical doctor and public health educator who in 1964 cofounded SIECUS, the Sex Information and Education Council of the United States, which established the inclusion of information on human sexuality as a part of medical and public health practice. Her prior work as medical director of the Planned Parenthood Federation of America resulted in the acceptance of responsible family planning as a health practice by the American Public Health Association in 1959 and the American Medical Association in 1964.*

**M**ANY WOMEN HAVE SIMILAR ENDOWMENTS, or different endowments of similar caliber, yet have not accomplished. Why? What prevented them? In this book you are really looking at a biased population. For every one woman you have included, there may be a hundred women out there equally endowed, but things have happened to them from birth on that play or prey upon the natural endowments.

I never grew up with any sense of limitation on what I might want to be. Nobody ever said, "Women can't do this," or "Women never do that." And if, as a teenager, I hadn't gone to live with Dr. and Mrs. Leopold Stieglitz, would I have become a doctor? See, there are a lot of watershed places. Would I have been where I am now if the job at Planned Parenthood hadn't been offered to me when, at fifty, I was finally ready to go seriously to work for the first time in my life? This is a big question in my mind. All that was luck, plain, damned fool luck—the right person for the right job at the right moment.

Given my capabilities and training, would I have succeeded in *anything* I tried? I doubt that very much because I don't think I could ever have been passionate about such fields as tuberculosis or cancer. I need total, passionate involvement, and a sense of meaning in whatever I do—and I surely found it.

In my twenties, I had my first two children in a messy period with my marriage soon followed by divorce in the 1920s. I was casting around then for something to do to earn our livings, and took some aptitude tests which indicated I should go into one of the sciences, probably medicine. Fortunately I had completed a premedical course at Vassar, so I decided to become a nutritionist.

It was just luck that on my way out to the University of Rochester to begin work toward a Ph.D. I stopped by to see dear friends, the psychiatrist Dr. Florence Clothier and her husband Dr. George Wislocki, then dean of the Harvard Medical School. They both jumped on me: "The woods are full of lady nutritionists. You don't want to be a nutritionist. Get an M.D., it will take only one more year; after that the choices of what you could go into are enormously multiplied."

So naively, when I got to Rochester just two days before school opened, I went to see the dean. I said, "Dr. Whipple, I've changed my mind. I'd like to go to medical school." "Well now"—he looked over his glasses at me—"why do you want to go to medical school?" We had a long discussion and finally he said, "All right, why don't we give it a try?" That was it. Years later I found out he disliked women in medical school because so many dropped out of medicine for marriage and children. But it was a policy of that school, as it was at Johns Hopkins at that time, to take 10 percent women students, so in a class of forty-five there were four of us. I graduated thirteenth in the class, and have blessed that man ever since for his generosity.

I had no idea what kind of doctor I was going to be, and that was another piece of luck. I had applied for and gotten an internship in pediatrics. I was still interested in nutrition because, though I had lost my eight-year-old daughter, I still had a child of my own, and in those days child nutrition was a big subject. But the trouble was, I did *not* want to spend several years in hospital residencies, because I wanted to be with my daughter during the rest of her growing years. I'd had to be away from her the last two years of medical school anyway. (That's Linda, she is now a therapist qualified in transactional analysis.) We were together on vacations, but she had lived those two years with a dear friend of ours near New York. Obviously as a preadolescent it had been difficult for her, and she has had to deal with that separation on her own, in her own history.

One of my professors suggested I try public health. I said, "What is that?" The University of Rochester Medical School had no public health department at all in those days. The professor sent me to two public health colleagues in the New York City Health Department, and after my internship I was awarded a fellowship from the City of New York to study public health, two hundred dollars a month for two years—a lot of money in those days. We could live on it. The first year I did field work—and met my second husband. The second year I went to the School of Public Health at Columbia and got married. So now there I was, age thirty-seven, with an M.D. and a master's in public health, just the right credentials for what I was eventually going to do, again sheer luck.

I had worked only a few months for the American Public Health association when I got pregnant. My husband had never had children. He asked me before we married if I would give him children, and I said yes because I adore little babies. With miscarriages in between, I eventually had two more, one when I was thirty-nine and the other when I was forty-two. I enjoyed hugely staying at home with them until the youngest was six and in school. Dr. Whipple was right! However, I did do some part-time health work in the public schools in Great Neck, Long Island. But I looked upon that as playing around and I was just getting to the point of wanting to sink my teeth into something real, I didn't know what, when one day someone telephoned. "How would you like to be medical director of the Planned Parenthood Federation of America?" I was interviewed, they hired me, and I started in September of 1953 in my fiftieth year. I didn't realize until some time later that I had been offered the job because no really qualified male physician would even consider it.

It's hard to realize now, but in 1953 birth control was more of a propaganda than a medical movement. The medical profession generally distrusted PPFA because they disliked Margaret Sanger. She had tended to make enemies of the medical profession. Doctors subscribed to birth control in theory but in practice only prescribed it for their private patients, and very few really knew how to fit a diaphragm. Birth control, as I remember, had never once been mentioned during my medical training—just forty years ago.

I knew about birth control because by then I had been to see the great Hannah Stone as a patient. She and her husband Abraham Stone were pioneers in the family planning and marriage and sex counseling movements. She fitted me with a diaphragm, of course. If I had had the bad luck to live in Podunk instead of New York, I couldn't have gotten birth control. Also, I could pay for it, but millions of women had no access at all to family planning services. No medical health facility in the country administered birth control services. Their husbands could use condoms or withdraw—what else could they do? That's about all there was in 1953, twenty-eight years ago. In the following ten years, the new method came in and changed everything, and by that time Planned Parenthood was ready for them.

With the PPFA medical advisory committee, I began developing PPFA as a sound, medically based organization. And things changed radically when a fascinating product called Emko Foam came on the market. A man in St. Louis, Joe Sunnen, was a fanatic on population control, and birth control for women. He had made packs of money out of a little spark plug measurer or something, and he wanted to use the money for this. So the medical committee decided we'd test the foam, an aerosol— among the first products to be packaged in this way. But instead of testing the new method on a hundred women or a thousand, I suggested, "Let's test it out in a number of our strongest Planned Parenthood centers around the country."

So I picked out eight or ten of our medically strongest centers and set up the Cooperative Testing Program. I met with their medical directors and we developed uniform methods for dispensing the product and for collecting and reporting the data. No testing as extensive as that had ever been done before. It was really very well organized compared to what had been, because by then we had working with us on the medical committee Christopher Tietze, a wonderful statistician.

We were more or less in the middle of this when the Pill came along with the chance to test it also. The whole thing snowballed and eventually we ended up testing the IUD and all other methods.

All in all I believe I had some real influence on the family planning movement at a time when the public health approach was critically needed. In 1956 I wrote the American Public Health Association suggesting that it might be the moment for them to take a public stand on birth control. Three years later, the APHA came out with a positive policy on family planning. This was epoch-making. But it wasn't until 1964 that the American Medical Association came out with its policy—think of how recent that was, we tend to take it for granted now. The AMA official statement said, "Family planning is not only responsible parenthood, it is responsible medical practice."

Then I left Planned Parenthood. It was time for me to go anyway, because I figured I would not get any further in it. I was replaced by *two* male physicians. Today the medical department in PPFA is ably headed by a woman physician who has the title of vice president and medical director.

For some time I had been very concerned that the family planning movement was dealing primarily with numbers of births, population problems and techniques of birth control rather than with human beings with human problems. Many people were writing to me with sex problems because they had nowhere else to turn to. I wanted to deal with the relationships that made family planning necessary.

There has always been a drive in me to understand life and its processes. My work at PPFA was focused on the reproductive area, but very early in the PPFA phase I was already thinking about its relationship to sexuality. I remember waking up one morning and having this insight: My goodness, people never have sexual intercourse in order to have babies, people have intercourse in order to have *pleasure*. You love each other, so what is wrong with pleasure? How can we deny it so fiendishly when it's universal? Every baby experiences sex in the cradle. How can it be wrong? And I kept coming back to that. I was thinking to myself, There *has* to be a way of legitimizing sex, not just by the marriage ceremony, but legitimizing the *being* of sex. Just the fact that it exists should be enough to legitimize it, but for centuries the hair shirt thing is what people have been doing. Deny and suffer and that means you are pure and good, the old puritan Christian attitude.

I'm not a scholar, I haven't read profoundly at all, and yet I've had over and over again the experience of having something here in my head, and then later reading research somewhere and thinking, My gosh, I guess my insight was right! But then research wasn't accorded the right to say sex was a natural, normal thing, though so many people had felt it. Now, with this series of insights, I wanted to change the whole society—a modest goal!—and I knew I couldn't do it alone.

By early 1960 I was fairly well known. I had been invited to speak at the National Council of Churches' North American Conference on

Church and Family, in Wisconsin. All topics relating to sex were discussed at this conference—masturbation, homosexuality, premarital and extramarital sex, all the difficult areas—by some of the top social scientists and sex researchers in the field. I had been invited to talk about family planning. I remember saying to myself, Why do I need to talk about family planning? Everyone here is already convinced. So I said, "What I'd like to talk about is sex education, and the role of the churches in sex education. The schools won't do it and the parents don't know how, so the churches must." This got a very good reception.

In the three years following, many of us who had been there would run into each other at various conferences, and we'd sit around and talk, and we kept saying, "What *are* we going to do about this sex mess?" Finally at one meeting in 1963 a number of us had a dinner to discuss the situation again. This time I brought with me a piece of yellow paper on which I had outlined a voluntary health organization, following the model of PPFA: a board of directors, a staff under the direction of the board and affiliates.

It was to be an organization designed specifically "to establish human sexuality as a health entity." That turned out to be a magic phrase. We were saying, Sex is a part of total health. It doesn't belong to the church, it doesn't belong to the law, it belongs to *you*, the person, and it's part of your total health and your total personality structure. We called our organization the Sex Information and Education Council of the United States (SIECUS). We were chartered in 1964 as a nonprofit, educational health organization.

It took us three or four years to sell the word *sexuality*. Everybody hollered, "What *does* that mean?" The word wasn't in use at all then, it was confused with the word *sensuality*. But today everybody seems to know what it means and how it should be used. The media, professional organizations and universities picked it up, and everybody now uses it. We made *sexuality* mean what we intended it to mean—the whole person *as* male or female, whatever his or her age.

I have always been analytical, so I keep coming back to the same question, why is something that is universal to everybody considered bad or nonexistent? There is a unique piece of research that illustrates this: Nancy Blackman of Rhode Island University recently researched four- and five-year-old children—Anglo-Americans, Afro-Americans and a settlement of Cape Verdeans in a state down South. She found that, almost without exception, the area between the knees and the umbilicus was perceived by them as "not me," a totally silent, nonexistent area.

Two weeks before I saw this research, I had written something for the SIECUS *Report* that again was one of my six-in-the-morning insights: Very young children know they are experiencing powerful sexual feelings every day, as I remember well. I experienced sex powerfully as a child, because I don't remember *not* having orgasms. I masturbated and my mother tried to stop me. It was all very punitive and destructive for me.

Now, everything else children experience, parents acknowledge by commenting on it. They acknowledge their children's pleasure in ice cream, or in swimming, or in ballet or reading. But this one pleasure is either acknowledged by punishment, which produces fear and guilt, or it's never acknowledged at all, which to the child means that it is considered not to exist. But the child *knows very well that it does exist.* So it's like punishing him because he's lefthanded, and the child finds himself condemned to a kind of existential nightmare.

That's what parents, with the very best of motives, are still doing to their children about sex. You carry your parents around with you to the day you die; you internalize a parent figure who may not be exactly like your parents but who is probably based on them, who says you should or you shouldn't. I had carried my mother around with me, then "buried" her because she had been so damaging to me—hostile about this thing that was so much a part of me. She's been dead for many years, but not long ago I was finally able to bring her to life again and to deal with her openly.

It happened because I finally opened myself up to my own feelings. One day in 1978 I woke up feeling low and sad, hearing my mother's voice singing, "My Old Kentucky Home," and she was crying. I'm musical and a lot of music goes through my mind all the time, and as I woke up I was singing it in my mind, and I wanted to cry too. I dressed and started out with my hat and coat on, and then thought, "I want to call Linda," and I did, with the excuse of telling her some little business thing. But Linda said immediately, "What's the matter, Mother? I hear something in your voice." And I burst into tears and told her I'd been hearing my mother's voice singing and crying. Linda said, "Sing the song to me now." So I did, as well as I could, but I couldn't finish it because I was crying (as I feel like doing as I tell this), and because what came out very, very clearly, was that I could finally deal with all this now.

My mother's singing went back to the time when she was a young wife and a mother and we were living in a little village in France. I could see her there at the piano in our tiny *salon.* Here was this young woman transported from Springfield, Missouri, to Paris by her husband, my father Edward Steichen, the photographer. He was a tremendous man, passionate, marvelous, gifted and a great womanizer, as she must have known by then. I was under ten at that time. Now here I was in my seventies, and I could finally say, "Mother, I understand why you were so hostile to me," because I was very much like my father, who adored me. She simply lumped us together. She couldn't handle us or the situation she was in, homesick in a strange land.

That was an incredible therapeutic experience, because it relieved me of a terrible incubus I'd been carrying around all those seventy-three years. Here was my daughter, skillful and trained as she was, leading me through all of these steps over the telephone from Chicago. She said, "Now forgive your mother, can you do that?" And I was able to say it aloud. She said, "Now tell your mother what you want from her." And I was able to tell my mother, "I want love from you, Mother." "Now tell your mother what you wish you could give her," said Linda. I was able to verbalize all of it and work through it, and an extraordinary feeling of peace with myself as well as with my mother has been with me ever since.

At the beginning of World War I our family came back to the United States as refugees. I was ten, my sister Kate was six. France was the only home we had ever had, poor as my father was, so eventually my mother and sister returned and went through the war years there. My father was in the war. He joined as a second lieutenant and came out a lieutenant colonel because he developed aerial map photography. He described to me how he was flown very low over the German trenches, clicking his camera. Then the staff would develop and print the photographs, and he would spend the next twenty-four hours on his knees on the floor putting the prints together. People forget that about him. When he came out of the army he lived with friends too, who must have suffered because my father was the world's messiest person. I was too, until marriage and children taught me I had to organize myself.

I lived in New York with a friend of my father's, Dr. Leopold Stieglitz, and his family, and went to the Brearley School. There was a very strong feeling at the Stieglitzes' for people who were *not* family. I think Jewish people are like that, their loyalties are fierce, as are those of other ethnic groups I have known. I remember the dinner parties there at Aunt Lizzie and Uncle Lee's. It was always the same people, their relatives *and* a couple of good friends—and me. It was really very wonderful, but it doesn't take the place of mother and father. I was lonely, I had to visit around in the summer because I didn't have a permanent home and family. Sometimes I stayed with my Aunt Charlotte and Uncle Billy in Connecticut on their farm. She was my mother's sister and, after my father, the strongest influence in my life. She taught me to love hard work, no matter what it was.

I was very romantic in the 1920s when I married for the first time—one man in the world for me and all that. After my first marriage failed, I led a totally celibate life all through medical school until I met my second husband, the first man who really interested me—that's the truth—for ten years. It seems that I have to be turned on by the *person* before I can be turned on *sexually*.

When I helped to form SIECUS I was sixty, and without being aware of it, I began to recover the sexuality I had experienced as a child because by then I was giving myself permission. I began then to be myself. I have grown up myself along with the human sexuality movement which is now all over the world.

Sometimes I get terribly discouraged because human sexuality, though by now established as a professional field, is a difficult and hazardous one. SIECUS—and I—have been and are being attacked cruelly; 1968 to 1970 was the worst, but now it's beginning again with the Moral Majority. Such clearly fabricated falsehoods very definitely get to me. I went down to the lowest point I ever got to in my life when I was saying to myself,

These things have to be true. How could people say these things if they
were not? And if so, then I am a bad person. Then a wonderful thing
happened.

In 1969 I had an appointment for a meeting with some clergy friends.
They wanted to discuss what the churches could do to counteract the
wave of attacks from extremist right groups, which was affecting not only
SIECUS but church programs in their local communities.

I remember vividly that I had to climb the mezzanine stairs in the old
Pennsylvania Hotel. I felt that each foot had ten pounds of lead on it. I
didn't think I was going to make it to the top. Now I realize medically that
I was in a true depression. I walked in and saw the loving faces of friends.
I said, "You know, I just can't function. I don't know what to do." They
said, "Don't worry, Mary, go home and rest and we'll think of something."
I walked out of there thinking, Well, I've let them down. I haven't helped
them produce something that might be useful to them in their dilemma.

About three months later, out came a little bulletin from the
Committee on Family Life of the United Methodist Church. It gave the
names of every one of the thirteen attacking organizations and their
methods of operation, including the fabrication of pornographic materials
for children in order to "prove" that *that*'s what SIECUS and sex
education wanted to do. The bulletin went on to give an explanation of
what SIECUS is, and what schools and families could do together for sex
education. That's what those friends did when they saw that I was
absolutely helpless to help them.

In the end I became aware that I was not the person described in the
attacks. I knew who and what I was, and those lovely people and anyone
else who took the trouble to find out knew who I was. Today, in the face
of the renewed attacks, I can say the same thing.

Through all my career I've worked very slowly, taking small but
strongly professional steps. I tried never to say something that I couldn't
back or that's not based on research. I know who my authorities are and
never claim to be one myself. I always say, "I'm not a therapist, a
psychiatrist, a sociologist, I'm not competent to answer that question. But
such-and-such research shows . . ." I've done everything I've done with as
much honesty and integrity as I could manage—and I really like that in
myself. It makes me feel I've lived up to myself, to the best in me, which is
what has been expected of me by the people who went before me—my
father, my teachers, the people who have loved me.

My father never followed any star but his own. Neither did Dr.
Stieglitz or his brother Alfred Stieglitz, the great photographer, or his wife
Georgia O'Keeffe. They knew they were good. I know I'm good.

In Brazil last year I spoke at a conference of teachers. I usually open
by saying, "We are each one of us unique sexual persons. No one else in
the world has had, or can ever have, the same exact combination of
heredity, prebirth experience and learning and experience after birth, so
value yourself as a unique sexual person, and learn to be that person in

the best way possible for you and those who love you. That's what I'm here to talk about." After the talk, when I walked in to lunch, those Brazilian teachers swarmed around, men and women reaching out to me—they were embracing me, holding me in their arms, thanking me for what I was teaching. It was the most remarkable experience I ever had. One woman put a little note in my hand. It said in Portuguese, "Thank you for existing. You make us proud to be women and to be human."

People speak to me often, everywhere, on the street, in airports, and thank me. I'm always amazed, and happy—not proud, but happy because I've been able to do something. I feel that I do have a gift to bring them—the gift of honoring their own sexuality. The poet Milton said it: "And that one talent which is death to hide . . ." Talent is something you *have* to share. If it's something like what I try to do, it isn't looked upon as art, yet I think it is. It has somehow to do with the art of being fully alive, of being human. I am living it . . . a special passion. Each one of us can live it.

# Elisabeth Kübler-Ross

*Elisabeth Kübler-Ross (born 1926, Zurich, Switzerland) is a psychiatrist and pioneer thinker who challenged the taboo surrounding death. As a professor at the University of Chicago Medical School, she began interviewing terminally ill patients in 1966 and discovered that dying people go through five stages: denial, anger, bargaining, depression and acceptance. She reported her insights in her book* On Death and Dying *in 1969, and she has toured the world, lecturing and giving workshops on the care of the dying. Her work has opened up a new field of health care.*

**W**HEN I STARTED WORKING WITH dying patients, my original fantasy was just to bring a bit more humanity into medicine, make doctors and nurses aware that although we cannot help those people medically, there are a lot of things we can do for them. We can't just drop them like hot potatoes if they don't gratify our need for them to get well. Hope for dying patients only at the beginning is associated with cure, treatment and prolongation of life. I talk about accepting that there is no hope.

Many have accepted that they have a terminal illness and that they're finite, and the hope of cure is replaced by a totally different quality of hope which is very beautiful; when you hear that kind of expression of hope, then you know they've reached a state of genuine acceptance of death, not resignation, but acceptance. Many of my patients, when they were able to do that, used this freed-up energy to get into remission and get home again. I'm sure they lived much longer because of that and whatever time they had, they used to live a very different quality of life. My patients live until they die, they don't just exist, or vegetate.

I started teaching seminars in death and dying at the University of Chicago Medical School. In those classes, I had standing room only. I got the favorite-teacher award at the medical school for five consecutive years. I knew the students loved my style of teaching, but the system, the school, the faculty, had really no use for this kind of approach. As far as they were concerned, it wasn't scientific enough. It was just totally alien to them. Why should you focus time and energy on dying when we try for years to become famous and known for our excellent cancer care?

Then, I can't say fortunately or unfortunately, I guess it just has to be that way, *Life* magazine came and did an article about me and published nine large pages in the magazine and that changed my whole life. It was a new beginning of a totally new life. My seminars became famous.

After that I got invitations from, first the United States and Canada, then from all over the world. In the last twelve years I've traveled about a quarter of a million miles a year, just in the United States alone. I always have about fifteen hundred people on the waiting list. Every town I go to for lectures—which I do about four times a week—I stay in a motel and then I see patients until about two in the morning, and I make house calls.

I love to work with dying children. They're just so beautiful. Nobody knows what pearls they are. They have all the wisdom in the world. They know that they are dying. They know how and when they are dying. They teach you all about life if you can hear, if you can listen to them. They use an incredible symbolic language to convey to you how much they know. If people would only understand their symbolic language.

One of my girls, I took her home to die, but she couldn't die. She was just lying there week after week after week. And the father couldn't communicate with her. He was a very nonverbal man. The mother was very verbal and a practicing Catholic. Every family member was at a different stage and used his own coping mechanism. That's the time when you have to help always the ones who limp behind because they're going to hurt the most and they're going to have the most unfinished business. We try to help them finish the unfinished business *before* somebody dies, otherwise they have all the grief work afterward.

Grief is the most God-given gift to get in touch with your losses. You shed your tears, and then stand up and start again like a child who falls and hurts his knees, cries for fifteen seconds and then jumps up and plays ball again. That's a natural thing. My work is preventive psychiatry, it's to finish as much as possible before death, like we bring flowers to our patients before they die so we don't have to pile them up on the casket afterward. If I love somebody I tell them "I love you" now, so I can skip the schmaltzy eulogies afterward.

One day I asked the father of this twelve-year-old girl if he would give me permission to talk to the other children, six, ten and eleven years old. He said, "They don't know about it." I said, "Come, your child's arms and legs are like pieces of chalk, and her belly is like she's nine months pregnant and she's lying there slowly dying in the living room. How can a six-, ten- and eleven-year-old not know?" I said, "All I want is for you to give your permission for me to sit with them without grownups and I'll ask them to draw me a picture." We used the Susan Bach method. She's a Jungian analyst from London who worked in Zurich in my hospital there with children who had brain tumors. She saw that children who had brain tumors, little children, show in their pictures that they know they are going to die and they share their concepts of life and death and unfinished business in their pictures.

I use this technique daily. In a few minutes I can evaluate the whole family and know who needs the most help and who's O.K. and who's in pain. You don't need hours and hours of psychiatric evaluation, which is just talking and just touches the surface. This is all preconscious material. It's the same material that you would get if you had ten consecutive dreams, but I can get it at a morgue, at a wake, in a church, in a school, in a motel, in a shack in Alaska in an Eskimo family, with Aborigines in Australia; it costs nothing, it takes five minutes, it transcends language, it's human. All human beings are the same anyway.

So the father finally gave me permission and I went there at three-thirty when school was out so that the father wouldn't be back, you know, and have second thoughts and give in to his own anxiety. The children were absolutely gorgeous. I locked the dining room with a key so no grownup could interfere and I said, "Let's have a competition. We're going to draw a picture and we have ten minutes." I limit the time so they don't start thinking, so it's as genuine and authentic and spontaneous as possible. In every picture these children revealed they knew that their sister was dying. I just said, "Use any color and draw a picture."

Anyway, the six-year-old was just gorgeous. His picture was so clear. I talked with him about it in the presence of the others. I said to him, "What your picture is telling is that your sister is dying." He said, "Yes." I said, "Well, if she's going to die tomorrow, is there anything you haven't done because this is your last chance to say or do anything you want to do, so that you don't have to worry about it afterwards when it's too late. That's what grownups do, but you don't have to do that." That challenged him. He said, "Yeah, I guess I'm supposed to tell her I love her." I said, "God, you're already a phoney-baloney at six years old." Children shouldn't be that contaminated. I said, "I've never seen a six-year-old who goes to a twelve-year-old and says, 'I love you.' There must have been a lot of things that she did that drove you up the wall, that she was unfair, you know, negative stuff." I said, "You can only really love her when you get rid of all the negative stuff, all the fights that you had, and when you get rid of that, then you love her so much that you don't need to say it, because she'll know it anyway and you'll know it."

He was fidgeting around at the table and I said, "Come on, you're the youngest"—and the younger, the more honest they are—"get it out, what bugs you?" And he said, "Well, I really would like to tell her to get it over with already. I would like her to drop dead already." And I said, "Yes, naturally," as carefully as I could. And I said, "Why does it bug you that it takes so long?" He said, "I can't slam the doors ever, I can't bring my friends home and I can't watch television anymore, and it's sickening how long it takes." You know, very natural, honest answers for a six-year-old.

I'm sitting there putting fuel on the fire and encouraging him to talk. The ten- and eleven-year-olds just sat there and stared at him. I said, "I wonder if you're honest enough and have the courage to share that with your sister." He said, "One ought not to do that." I said, "Who says? Do you think it's better to swallow this down and then after she dies you have all these guilt trips and later on need counseling, or is it better to share it with your sister now and then you can love each other or forgive each other, whatever is necessary? And then you'll really feel super-duper. You will still miss her." They will have grief, you understand, but not grief *work*. He said, "Oh, I would love to be able to do that."

So you have to visualize . . . we go out into this living room where she lies there. And the six-year-old sits next to her and I'm behind him, then the ten-year-old is behind me and the eleven-year-old behind her, then the mother came in and at the very end, the father behind her. And the arrangement was very symbolically beautiful. They came in the right chronological order in the courage they had to do that. Then the six-year-old starts procrastinating a little and I gave him a little nudge in the pants with my foot. Then he blurted it out and said to her, "You know, sometimes it takes so long, sometimes I pray to get it over with."

He was just ready to explain and something very beautiful happened with that symbolic language. His sister lifted her arms up with her last strength and fell over his shoulders, and hanging on to him she started to sob and sob and cry, not painful crying but tremendous relief. It was just like floodgates opening. In her sobbing she kept repeating, "Thank God, thank God, thank God. I prayed for the last three days for God to take me already because it really is getting too much now. And every time I finish my prayer, Mom comes in and stands in the doorway and said she spent the whole night sitting up, praying to God to keep me." And she said, "If you help me, then together we can outdo Mom."

Children take everything very concretely. And he was the proudest man in the world, he was just beaming and they were holding onto each other, crying and laughing. It was one of the most moving moments of house calls, and I've made lots of them. The other siblings naturally were envious that they weren't the ones who had the courage to do that.

About three days later I went back to see not just how she was doing, but how the six-year-old was doing, if he had any second thoughts about it. He was in super shape, he was high. But the girl couldn't die and so I asked the mother, I said, "If you don't mind, I'm just going to ask her straightforward, not in symbolic language, why she can't die, if that's O.K. with you. And I want you to come in and see how I'm doing that so you're never worried that I'm hurting anybody." She had great faith in me.

So I walked into the living room and I looked at her and I said, "You just can't die, can you?" She said, "No." I said, "Why?" She said, "Because I can't get to heaven." I said, "Who told you that?" She said she was always taught for twelve years that nobody gets to heaven unless you have loved God more than anybody else in the whole world. Then she lifted her arms up and whispered in my ear as if she would try to prevent God from hearing her. She whispered very quietly, "You understand that I love my mommy and daddy better than anybody in the whole world."

That made me very sad that children have to apologize for that. What you then have to do is to set aside your own anger at the people who teach this kind of punitive approach. I said, "We're not going to get into an argument about who is right and who is wrong because each one believes what they need to believe. I can only work with you and talk with you the way I always have. You and I always talked about school, and the biggest dream of your life was to be a schoolteacher. The only time I ever saw you devastated was in September when the school buses rolled up and school started after the summer vacation, and your brothers and sisters boarded the school bus and you looked through this window and you really looked devastated." I said, "I think what happened was that at that moment it began to dawn on you that you will never again go back to your beloved school and you will never become a teacher." I said,

"I want to ask only one question. Sometimes your teacher gives very tough assignments to some students." It was in the back of my mind that she was an honor student. I said, "Does she give these assignments to her lousy students? Does she give it to everybody in the class without discrimination, or does she give it to a very few of her hand-picked, chosen students?" Then her face lit up and she said, "Oh, she gives it to very few of us." I said, "Since God is also a teacher, do you think He gave you a tough assignment? Or an assignment he could give to any child?"

What she did then was symbolic language. At first she didn't answer me in words. Ever so slowly she looked down at her belly and her arms which were no thicker than my thumb, and her belly full of cancer. She very slowly looked down her body and then she looked at me and said, "I don't think God could give a tougher assignment to any child."

She died about two and a half or three days later. My last communication with her was totally nonverbal and to me very beautiful because I knew that it helped her. I thought at that time she was in a coma and I came then so as not to disturb the family in the last day or two. I stood in the doorway and took another look at her and she suddenly opened her eyes. She couldn't speak anymore at that time. And she looked down at her belly and her legs and she had a big smirk on her face. And I nodded. She knew what I talked about and I knew what she talked about. It was totally nonverbal. It was very beautiful.

I learn always from dying patients. Instead of always looking at the negative, what you see is the uniqueness and strength in every single human being. I have patients who never share, never communicate. They live a very bland life and anybody who looked at them would say, Is this all there is to it? and then you really get to know those people. There is a beauty in them that very few see. And all you have to do is look.

Dying patients look back at their lives and they review and evaluate what they would do over again if they had a second chance, and that's very instructive because dying patients throw overboard all the following: they don't have to impress you anymore, they do not have to pretend. They're not interested in material things. They have no secondary gains except to honestly share what life is all about and what lessons they have learned too late. And they pass it on to you and I pass it on to others so they don't have to wait until they're on their deathbed and say the same thing. Dying patients literally teach you about life.

You cannot convince people of this by talking. You can only convince them by experiencing it, and that's what my workshops are all about. You can never feel another person's pain. You cannot feel another person's grief unless you yourself have a pool of unshed tears inside you, of unexternalized pain. If your own pool is empty, if you've screamed out all your screams and shed all your tears, then your pool is empty, only then can you work eighteen to twenty hours a day with the greatest tragedies, which I do, day after day, without getting burned out.

We can help a lot of people because of the pain we have gone through. My biggest gift was that I was born a triplet. When you grow up, your mother and father don't know whether they hold you or your sister, and you never even have a lap of your own. Grownups are often so dishonest that they don't even admit that they don't know whether they talk to you or to your sister. You never have a pair of shoes or a dress or a doll or a grade card that is yours. I only was either very good or very bad at school. I only deserved A's or F's in an attempt to make my teachers at least know that I was Elisabeth. And my triplet sister, who was totally identical, was very good in everything that I was bad at and vice versa. And the teacher gave us both C's, because he didn't know who was who and he thought to be fair, so he gave us average grades. It didn't even pay to be very good or very bad because nobody there cared anyway. My sister's earliest memory was that my father gave her a bath twice and skipped me. When we were about fifteen and a half my sister had a date. She couldn't go and she was just heartbroken, so I said very casually, "If you really can't go, I'll go for you and he'll never know the difference." And I went; he never knew the difference. And I was totally devastated.

Because of that heartbreak I left home and it was the biggest gift of my life, because that's what took me to Majdanek, the concentration camp, and through postwar Europe, organizing typhoid stations, seeing what life is all about, what we do to our fellow man, all the inhumanity of man to man. Then your own tragedy becomes very little.

I had everything material when I was growing up. We had parents who loved us. We lived in a gorgeous home, in a dreamland, Switzerland, an island of peace during the war. I had everything but I had absolutely nothing. I could have dropped dead and there would have been a cloned other me. Do you understand what that was like? I needed that experience. I had to grow up that way because after that I worked with blind, retarded, multihandicapped children who had no identity. They were numbers in institutions. I swear I knew every child, their individuality and their inner beauty. I looked for it and I found it.

And then I worked with chronic, hopeless schizophrenics. They were treated like animals, much worse than any pet in this country. It was a snake pit if I've ever seen one. It was the worst thing I experienced in my entire life. To me, even worse than Majdanek is how we used to treat our mentally ill patients in our state hospitals. I knew every single patient of mine and I loved them, and they got well. I was not the psychiatrist. I was just an old-fashioned Swiss country doctor who really loved my patients. My patients knew it because I knew them as individuals, not "that schizophrenic in Room 73." And they got well because I loved them, I know that. It certainly isn't electric shock that makes a patient well.

My dying patients also had no identity. You understand that all the hardships of life are a gift to you. You can turn anything negative in your life into a positive learning and growth experience. I could have become very bitter, you understand. Both my sister and I who had the same fate in a way, the same tragedy in a wonderful home, are now caring for people of no identity. She became famous the same day I became famous, November 21, 1969, for caring for old people in Switzerland. You can turn anything into a blessing if you are willing to get rid of your resentment, your bitterness, your pain and your grief. Then you can take the best part out of it and use the positive to help other people, and prevent other people from living through the same nightmares.

It was Majdanek, the concentration camp, that helped me more than anything else. There were 960,000 children killed in Majdanek. There was a Jewish girl who lost her entire family in the gas chamber and she survived. She believed that if she would now go out in the world and share the horrors she had lived through and use revenge and hate, that she would not be any better than Hitler. But if she could accept that this happens and that there must be some reason why she survived, she believed that if she would touch one single human life and turn it from negative to positive, then her life would have a purpose and meaning. Together, she and I went into the wooden barracks in Majdanek and looked to find out if we could find clues as to how 960,000 children march into a gas chamber, five-, six-, seven-year-olds, and that's where we found the butterflies scratched into the wooden barrack walls with fingernails. I said, "My God, they draw a butterfly and march into a gas chamber. What do they know that I don't?"

Now, twenty-five years later, I work with dying children and they always draw butterflies. Dying is nothing else but a butterfly coming out of a cocoon. That's what death is all about. You see, I didn't understand that, but they were my first teachers. If it hadn't been for Majdanek, I would have never gone back to Switzerland and studied medicine and gotten into this work. Last year we had 125,000 courses on death and dying in this country alone. It all started in Majdanek.

You understand, God doesn't create Hiroshimas and Nagasakis and Vietnams and Majdaneks. We do. But we can acknowledge the Hitler in us, get rid of it. We don't need to perpetuate the negativity. We can only stop the negativity for our next generation's children by being blunt and honest with our own Hitler in us and getting rid of it.

Working with dying children like I do, day after day after day, made me want to know what death is. What bothered me was that a physician can do so many incredible things—transplants, it's really a mind-blowing thing when you think of it, but we don't know what death is. We have existed 47 million years and every instant a human being is dying, and we're so smart and have so much money and so much brains that we can bring a man to the moon and walk around up there and collect rocks and bring them back, and we don't know what death is. I mean, that to me is inconceivable. So one day I said, "O.K., that's going to be my goal. I'm going to research until I know what death is."

What I began to realize, what slowly and gradually dawned on me, is that it is only a death of a physical body. Then the question comes: And what are you besides a physical body? The moment we ask the question, the answers come back—and I mean that in a very concrete sense. Ask and you will be given. Within five days I had the first patient who shared with me the near-death experience, the kind that Raymond Moody explains in his first book, *Life After Life.*

Human beings exist in four quadrants, a physical and an intellectual and an emotional and a spiritual quadrant. When the physical quadrant begins to deteriorate and you're open with patients intellectually and answer their questions and don't play games with them, and you help them in the emotional quadrant to shed their tears and express their anger, any negative, unnatural emotion, help them get rid of it—then their spiritual quadrant begins to compensate and unfold, like a blind person has much better touch, or more acute hearing. Then if you get in touch with the spiritual quadrant of that person, that person knows everything, absolutely everything. They know that when you shed the cocoon that you are in an existence where there is no space and no time. A child who dies in an accident two hundred miles from here, the second they shed their body all they have to do is think "Mommy" or "Daddy" and they're with Mommy or Daddy because space and time do not exist.

And then you begin to do research on that, both in the laboratory and clinically, and then you get the answers in no time. Anybody can get these answers. You don't have to be a physician. I've studied children who were in family car accidents, and I sit with the little children before they die. Children before they die become very quiet, and then I ask if they can share with me what they experience. That's when their own spiritual quadrant begins to unfold. And then they always tell me the same story.

One whose mother was killed at the scene of the accident, whose brother was critically ill, whose father was in the intensive treatment unit, said to me: "Everything is all right now, Mommy and Peter are already with me, waiting for me." I knew about Mommy, but Peter wasn't dead. So I sneaked out, called the other hospital. "Oh, strange that you should call just now, we wanted to call you. Peter died ten minutes ago." For twelve years, not one child has ever made one mistake, not one mistake; not one child has ever mentioned somebody who didn't precede them in death, even if it was only by a few minutes.

There was an American Indian woman who was killed by a hit-and-run driver. And this stranger stopped to help her and she told him, "There's nothing else you can do for me except one day maybe you could visit the Indian reservation and visit my mother and give her a message"—and the message was that she should not be sad, she was O.K. She was not only O.K., she was very happy because she was already with her dad. And then she died in the arms of the stranger. This man was so touched, he drove seven hundred miles out of his way to the Indian reservation and he found the woman and told her, and she told him very calmly that her husband had died one hour before the car accident of a coronary. You can collect a thousand cases like that, if you are not afraid of the truth.

To know there is life after death is an extra bonus. It is an extra bonus because it helps me tremendously to help parents whose children are murdered, and mutilated and raped and killed and shot. To know that this life and the physical is such a short span of your total existence, and to know for certain, not just believe, that they will be together again, to be able to convey that to these parents is very beautiful. I don't just give them a schmaltzy sermon because one ought to say that. I know beyond a

shadow of a doubt and my patients know that I know and they know that
I'm not just saying that to put the Band-Aid on them.

Once you have experienced it yourself, then you know it. Then it
doesn't bother you anymore that the society in which you live tries to tear
you to pieces, tries to discredit you, tries any means to destroy your
credibility. If you have no fear or guilt you can't even be offended. People
who criticize me unjustly are people who project their own filth. I could
tell them so much filth about themselves that they would think I was the
greatest psychic in the world, because you never criticize anyone for
anything if it doesn't touch on your own pool of repressed shame, guilt or
fear. That's why it's so good for people like me, who work with tragedies
daily, that you have an empty pool, because if I would not be empty or I
would be afraid or if I had anything to be ashamed of, all this publicity
would destroy me. You could not tolerate it. I would either get physically
sick or emotionally sick, to the point where I couldn't function anymore.

I feel very blessed that I am able to do this work. Physically tired, yes,
most of the time, but it's the most gratifying work there can be. I have
blues like everybody else and when I'm in my blues I wonder if it's all
worth it. You fall into that pitfall of self-pity: poor me, I'm so alone in
spite of the constant crowds. I'm at Kennedy Airport and I've just signed
three hundred books and I barely make it to the bathroom before the
plane takes off. I sit down on the toilet and then a hand comes under the
door. "Dr. Ross, would you mind . . . ?" There are times when you feel like
screaming. There's no place where I feel I have a private spot, a private
life, I'm sure when I die there'll be a TV crew who takes pictures while
Kübler-Ross dies. So you give up a lot when you become a public
commodity. God, I could never have a love affair. It's impossible. A
magazine would come and offer them $50,000 for a dirty article. There are
many times when I feel, Why can't I just have a little fun, have a shoulder
to lean on? I just cannot have it. You have to accept that nobody has
everything. I surely have more than most people. I'm loved by thousands.
I can help more people . . .

I was born in the mountains and my father took us mountain climbing,
traversing glaciers, and I hung on the ropes in crevices as a child when I
was ten years old and I learned how to get out of it. Little did I know that
my whole life I would fall into crevices and have to climb out. But I still
come out climbing and I still love to cross glaciers and I will always do so.
It's a very high-risk, high-gain life. You just put everything into it and if
you lose it all, at least I can say, "I've tried."

I felt like nothing when I grew up. If your own parents don't even
know who you are, then you are nothing, totally nothing. I could have
disappeared and no one would have known which one was missing. And
that was a gift, to be able to move out, to search and to find the answers—
most of all to help others to live until they die.

# Judianne Densen-Gerber

*Judianne Densen-Gerber (born 1934, New York City) is a psychiatrist who in 1966 created Odyssey House, a drug treatment program based on the idea of a therapeutic community which provides group therapy and individual counseling. The program operates chapters in the United States, Australia and New Zealand. In the early 1970s she brought the problem of the sexually abused child to public awareness. She is responsible for the federal legislation which set up the National Center for Child Abuse and Neglect in 1974, and for one federal and thirty-seven state statutes prohibiting child pornography.*

I HAVE NEVER LOOKED FOR AN ISSUE. It literally hit me on the head. I never sought a cause. They've always knocked at my door. I started Odyssey House in 1966 because a group of my drug-addicted patients wanted to be drug free. Previously, I had promised them that if they kept the faith, I wouldn't abandon them. So when New York's Metropolitan Hospital turned them out, they appeared on my doorstep. I did not have an ethical choice. Truly, I didn't run out there to crusade with a lantern. I had given my word, and therefore my own sense of integrity was involved.

Two years before, I had trained with Dr. Efran Ramirez, who founded a therapeutic community for drug addicts in Puerto Rico. My work modified his method for treating character disorders and incorporated many of the ideas articulated by Maxwell Jones, the originator of the therapeutic community movement for English schizophrenics.

At this time, people considered drug addicts little better than garbage. Of course, when someone is told that he or she is garbage, then he or she will act accordingly. Similarly, if you tell people they have potential, that they can walk forward instead of being crippled, they will walk forward. People usually try to live up to reasonable expectations. Odyssey House offers such expectations.

The Odyssey concept is about people, a group of people, who always make room for another at their table. Each brings a pair of hands along with a hungry tummy. Odyssey grows and grows because people build, believe, create and do—together. Odyssey grew from a starting capital of $3.82, fourteen years ago, to a worldwide organization. The method of open, honest confrontation and peer-group pressure to change works for some, not for all. It worked for me and brought me much satisfaction, tremendous self-actualization and a deep sense of self-esteem.

I am very proud of Odyssey. Our work has traveled far beyond the initial drug-abuse program. Odyssey developed and worked for the passage of the federal bill which created the National Center for Child Abuse and Neglect in 1973, and the act now funds a significant part of child abuse and neglect programming within the nation. Odyssey also participated in the writing of one federal and thirty-seven state statutes on child pornography. I testified and assisted in the passage of such laws in England and Australia as well.

Odyssey Houses now exist in six states in America, two cities in Australia, and shortly, more will open in New Zealand and Israel. These centers treat drug-addicted persons, child-abuse victims and their parents together, and provide juveniles an important alternative to incarceration.

If you ask what is the thread running through my career, I would say I help people in tremendous pain, I guide them to focus on their strengths, or the positive aspects of their lives which can be reinforced. We face the pain together, cut out the emotional cancers and build on health. At Odyssey, patient and therapist form a forward-going, problem-solving team. This process challenges their habits of wallowing in what is not right. I often remark to patients: "Sure, lots of things are not right. You can curse the sky, or curse your parents, but the fact remains that when you get up off the couch, you have to adopt a 'So what, now what?' attitude. You cannot allow the past to inhibit the present, nor prevent the present from slowly building toward a positive future."

Recently, I saw an eleven-year-old who had been prostituted for several years after she had been sold to a pimp by her own mother. Shortly before the sale, her mother completed a jail term for having shot the child's father. The courts then returned the child to her custody. To treat this youngster who had been so violated, we did something very simple. We drew a circle around her bed. The circle visually symbolized an external protective barrier. Anyone who wanted to get close to the bed needed to ask permission: "May I enter the circle?" For the first time in her life, this eleven-year-old felt, and saw, her right to privacy. Previously, adults had invaded even her inner bodily territory. This child desperately needed to know that no one would be allowed to trespass against her any longer.

True, these sound like simple symbols, and they are. But, these real actions provide real security to real people. Simple truths make sense. It would, however, be grandiose and unrealistic to think anyone will always win the battle of curing patients, particularly those who are as hell bent on self-destruction as addicts. Physicians learn that death always competes against the healer. Death remains as the final adversary in medicine, and death is ever present.

When I became involved in challenging child prostitution and child abuse, it was because my work showed me things from which I could no longer hide. In 1969, Walter Vandermeer died of a heroin overdose shortly after his twelfth birthday . . . three days, to be exact. All his life, he had been horrendously abused and neglected. My husband, Michael, was the New York City medical examiner on the case. He came home from the death site in a Harlem hall bathroom with a little T-shirt and he threw it down . . . it was a size eight! A picture of Snoopy on the front said, "I wish I could bite someone to relieve my nervous tension." I looked at this T-shirt and grasped this child's tragedy.

Denial didn't seem a possible defense mechanism because I had been profoundly influenced by a scholarship I won in 1952 to study restoration and reconstruction after World War II. In Europe, I talked to the Germans about the Holocaust, the camps and the atrocities. One after another, they defended themselves by repeating, "We didn't know." I suppose in my work the thing that happened is that I kept learning of these denials. Once you knew a certain problem, you had the choice of not facing the reality and walking away, or squarely facing the issue no matter how difficult or unpleasant. I guess my nature was such that I wouldn't walk away.

I realized thousands of other children under sixteen did not have a single place to go for treatment. Within the next four years, we learned there were thirty thousand children addicted to heroin in New York City alone. We had thought there were three to four thousand. We all must face the question: "Does one have an investment or responsibility for the quality of life in one's community?" We all have a responsibility to say what we see, as we see it. This doesn't mean that we always have to be right. People confuse their need for being right with the need for internal honesty.

Many, many times I say things that are not right in the absolute, but they are what I believed at the time and they're what I felt to be the best I could do at that time. That's all you can expect of any person. None of us is omnipotent, or omniscient. We're not gods.

I am not the most maternal person. Of course we can never totally see ourselves. I would prefer recognition of my medical and professional "capacity" than that of nurturing. I am an extraordinarily private person who is primarily committed to the world of ideas and issues, although I don't feel particularly strong about crusading. I would not go out and scream and carry on about prostitution, but when in 1973 the late Governor Rockefeller requested an opinion about potentially legalizing prostitution in New York State, I arranged to see a "house" in Nevada. Initially, I opposed legalization because my work had taught me about the great unhappiness of thousands of prostitutes. I had never met a "happy hooker" though I had treated literally thousands of such women. During this visit, the protection and greater safety of the women within the brothels amazed me, and I returned believing prostitution should be legal.

It wasn't until 1977, when I received a letter from Senator Birch Bayh about child sexploitation, that I was out there crusading about child prostitution. He asked for comment on a book written by Robin Lloyd, *For Love or Money—Boy Prostitution in the United States.* The author, a reporter, projected that adult Americans were sexually exploiting more than one million children. I was outraged!

It was then that I visited an Adult Bookstore for the first time and saw there were sixty-four films showing the sexual abuse of children. Subsequently, I learned the United States has well-organized political pressure groups such as the North American Man-Boy Love Association and the René Guyon Society, whose motto is "Sex by Age 8 or It's Too Late." Too late for what? To say no to Daddy, or the teacher, or the Boy Scout leader or even the clergyman?

In 1979, American teenagers gave birth to over one million babies.

Eighty thousand girls fourteen and younger, and nine thousand girls eleven and younger became mothers! VD spread at epidemic rates and annual teenage suicides increased astronomically. Today, Odyssey continues to advocate the protection of children and their right to innocence.

My husband teases me for my ever-present sense of moral outrage. I have two things, two qualities, the sense of moral outrage and the ability to make an effective fuss which he calls my E.F.I., "Effective Fuss Index." These traits surface whenever I learn of injustices.

People often asked why I am not afraid of tackling horrendous problems. Independent wealth is one reason. I never underestimate its role. Not worrying about having money to eat is very liberating and I'm free to "say it as I see it." One part of me has always rationalized, If worse comes to worst, you can always stay home, take care of the children and do the wonderful things that so many of the other women in your social group do.

Being female also freed me from the pressure males face. They often believe they must succeed by doing in order to have self-esteem. In fact, the combination of marriage, children and a full-time career for a woman can be construed by some to be culturally deviant, and even perhaps unacceptable. At any time, had I decided to return to the home to be the primary caretaker of my children, many would have applauded the act as one of coming to my senses and doing the right thing.

When my mongoloid child was born, people said, "Now you're going to stop working, aren't you?" I can't describe their well-meaning cruelty. Of course I knew that mongolism is something that happens at the moment of conception and obviously I had no control, nor was I working at that moment; the egg which had an extra chromosome had really nothing to do with whether or not I was a physician or a housewife doing the dishes . . .

I'm extraordinarily independent. I don't work at it, that's just the way my drummer is put together. Furthermore, I need to move freely. Constraints of any kind are abhorrent. Even a girdle is objectionable. I would have gone braless long before it was fashionable, if Nature had permitted me. Intellectual restraints annoy me equally. I don't see things in set, bound, narrow frameworks. I see things as explosive really, not implosive. At the same time I am always ordering chaos, but I'm not uncomfortable in chaos. I love multistimuli and am endlessly restless.

Being the third generation of liberated females in my family has made for a very unique imprinting. My maternal grandmother chained herself to the White House for the vote. My other grandmother, who was self-supporting with eight children, sold real estate in the early 1900s. My mother, now in her seventies, was a corporate attorney and one of the first women to appear before the Federal Communications Commission. When other women weren't working with the commission, my mother did a great deal of negotiating with them. My father, also an attorney, always considered and treated her as an equal. Most significantly, I didn't grow up with the concept "Women couldn't do," or that having a career meant doing without husband and/or children. I saw none of the limitations so many young women today sadly still accept.

Having attended only women's schools, it wasn't until 1956, when I entered Columbia Law School, that I ever knew of prejudice. I really didn't. It was there I first encountered male chauvinism, male prejudice, male inadequacy and downright male fear. At first I didn't recognize it. Then I didn't believe it. Then I felt anger, and more anger. When I say anger, it wasn't really anger, it was rage!

For example, the boys, so-called men, in their twenties, would trip a girl on the way to her auditorium seat, cause her notes to scatter and force a commotion that would annoy the professor. The bathroom was another example. While the men's rooms were on every floor, women's facilities were confined to the basement. Since the classroom doors were locked before class began, and there were only ten-minute breaks, it was hard to get to the bathroom between classes. If you were pregnant, as I was, it was really torture. I still don't donate to their alumni appeals when they are addressed "Dear Brothers-in-Law."

The atmosphere concerning the position of women is getting worse, and with the economic realities the 1980s promise a tremendous backward movement. The only way you can balance unemployment and the economy is to put us women back in the home. Much is happening, particularly in the media, to suggest that women belong in the home and that working women account for much of the world's ills. Frequently women are so masochistic that they accept such irrational blame.

There are very few women at the top, but there are lots of women in the middle. It is still felt in the power establishment that women don't belong in conceptualization, they don't belong in policy making, they don't belong in making determinations as to the direction the nation is going to take. Women just don't seem to belong. There probably still aren't enough bathroom facilities at the top. Often, I wonder if there are sufficient provisions in heaven.

When women do succeed, the common thread is that such women believe they can succeed, and possess adequate self-esteem. Yet most women think, conceptualize and feel differently than men. One of the saddest things I see in the liberation movement is the confusion of some women who believe they must become pseudomen in order to succeed. The last thing in the world I want is to be a pseudoman or even an actual male in the sense of having to play by the concepts they have. They face unreal, exhausting pressures and are too distant from contact with, and expression of, their feelings. In classic analytic terms, "penis envy" is merely a drive to have power. I believe "womb jealousy" is probably a more prevalent dynamic. We envy their power, they our life-giving creativity.

Since human beings are basically herd animals, we only know ourselves in relationship to other people, to certain roles, or in the context of a particular status. A woman knows herself in relationship first to herself, second to her mate, third to her children, fourth to her career and, finally, through her relationship to other women.

I feel a very deep commitment to the concept of what's going to happen to other women. Every woman must be concerned enough to feel that every injustice to a woman, because of her sex, is an injustice to us all. Only when women as a group accept the responsibility for the way prostitutes are treated, for the woman who works below the minimum wage, or for the college-educated woman who gets paid the same as a man with an eighth-grade education, will we begin to solve our problems. Women truly have tremendous power. This fact makes us different from every other second-class, persecuted group, because the governing power, the male establishment, cannot create another generation without us!

There's nothing more important to mankind than the family, but the factors which constitute the healthy family must be defined and understood. Family is the essential social unit and is indispensable to the production of happy, functioning human beings. Since the thirties we have defined family as nuclear—one adult male and one adult female, chained to 2.4 mewling and puking infants! But the nuclear family, a structure mankind has only suffered under since the Industrial Revolution, is an aberration in the history of the human family. It is a prison for women. It is isolated, nonfulfilling, and sets its members up to fail. It produces divorce, promiscuity, venereal disease, child abuse, drug addiction and alcoholism, to name but a few of its effects. It is a nonfunctioning institution. But the nuclear family is well off compared to the single-parent family unit, which is even more destructive.

What human beings need is to live in groups of commonly committed persons, not the least of whose tasks is the rearing of dependent young. Family is better conceived of as a multigenerational, value-oriented group of persons sharing common life experiences and directed toward mutually acceptable goals. With such a family, there can still be the sexual exclusivity of one man and one woman. My grandmother lived with her parents, sisters, brothers and the maids. A trip to the country was an astonishment. It became a major production and took a week to pack everybody up. We were like a wagon train. It is only since the thirties that the Western world has become so isolated. People don't flourish in this kind of isolation. People flourish in communities.

The extended family system is what the Odyssey House therapeutic community experience provides. The danger in the communes of the sixties was that they did not distinguish between common goals, mutual task sharing and the need for sexual exclusivity. I think breeding couples, not a terribly romantic term but appropriately descriptive, should remain basically faithful. Sexual play, promiscuity, the back and forth, causes confusion and destruction. The stability of the family comes from couples who remain basically faithful. When my husband Michael and I were married, we made a deep commitment to each other. Both of us have divorced parents. We affirm time for "his thing," "my thing" and "our thing." We underlined the "our thing" as a commitment to the marriage and to giving up a certain amount of individual freedom for the greater good, and for the stability of a nurturing soil upon which our children would grow.

Michael and I have truly been lucky, phenomenally lucky. We've had rough times too . . . but we both have been absolutely committed to the concept of building a family foundation and basically loving each other as more important than anything else. My greatest pride is my success at combining marriage and career, and children and career, and in all three areas I've been marvelously fulfilled.

In the future I believe one of my priorities will be the examining of the nature of the family and what will be the healthy alternatives for the eighties and nineties. So many wonderful women have not been able to combine marriage, children and career. There's only a handful of women who've been able to do it. The enemy of self-actualization for women today is that we have to give up one or the other. But I know that a woman can be very happy and be married to a very independent, strong and self-actualized person who is not a patsy or a milquetoast. She can also have four children whom she guides through a world that is chaotic and teach them to be committed, happy individuals who are also their own people. It can be done!

I have often felt I see things other people don't. Often I predict or articulate things that come true, that people had pooh-poohed. I don't know why. Of course it would be foolish to deny intelligence. I also have had many experiences most other people don't have, particularly among people of my circumstances, a milieu of great comfort, the power establishment. Like them, I rejoice in creature comforts. I'm not Mother Teresa. I'm a hedonist who likes good food, good wine, good parties and beautiful things. I want my children to know these luxuries and I have no desire to give up anything.

But I also have a desire to be meaningful and other-directed. I have a desire to remain internally honest, saying loud and clear what I believe to be right or wrong, and articulating my views even if it takes feisty, abrasive tones to convey the urgency of what I believe must be changed.

I have a gift of gab. I think it's genetic, inborn. My father had a tremendous gift of gab and so did my grandfather. People say, when I walk into a room, they feel this commanding presence. I have been blessed with a quality of charisma which makes people listen, believe and follow. Charisma is a gift from God; its weight and responsibility are frightening.

Risk-taking is always part of my future. I suppose I'll always be taking leaps. Before, I didn't know enough to be afraid, now I know difficulties are ahead; but I will still go forward and every step of the way I'll continue at the pace of the reluctant dragon. Will it be alone? No. Michael and many others share the Odyssey dream.

# Ernesta Drinker Ballard

*Ernesta Drinker Ballard (born 1920, Wynnewood, Pennsylvania) is a horticulturist who has challenged the notion of horticultural societies as the exclusive domain of the wealthy. As chief executive of the Pennsylvania Horticultural Society from 1963 to 1980, she initiated an ambitious urban gardening program that has become the prototype for other cities, expanded the annual flower show to make it the largest of its kind and showed that a horticultural society could be profitable.*

I GOT INTO HORTICULTURE when I was thirty because I wanted something to do. I wanted to have a career. I had no education. I had no work experience. I was married when I was nineteen. I had four children and I lived this stereotype for ten years. Then my life just went to pieces. This was thirty years ago, before Betty Friedan or her book or before any of the things that have happened in the last fifteen years, to the world and to the women's movement. I suddenly had to have something for me.

What do you do when you're thirty and you've never been to college and you have no work experience of any kind? There was a school nearby that I could get to in twenty minutes that taught horticulture. I didn't have a strong interest in horticulture but anybody who's kept house for ten years—suburban house, that is—and enjoyed being in a garden club has had that interest; 99 percent of suburban people do. If it had been a textile school or a computer school close to me, that might have been it.

I could have just started out and gone to college, and that would have been what a lot of people would have done, but as I saw it, that was four years and I would have a college degree. Well, that's nothing. Even thirty years ago a college degree didn't guarantee you anything. You still had to go on to go into medicine or law. It was too far away. I wanted a profession and I wanted it right away. I knew I could do more than I was doing: so I went to horticultural school for two years.

At that time the school was called the Pennsylvania School of Horticulture for Women. It had been founded by Louise Bush Brown, a famous horticulturist in Philadelphia. They were training women to be people's gardeners, to go out and weed the flower beds. It was an acceptable thing for girls to do. There were some women there who did want to make horticulture their profession, but nobody expected to pay them more than about three dollars an hour, which was a very, very high wage for a woman who could tell you how to lay out a rose garden, or keep your flower border in bloom for eight months of the year.

Horticulture is thought of as the occupation of garden club women. Horticulture is a science. It's mostly about ornamental plants but includes the growing of fruits and vegetables commercially and every other way. If you're professionally involved with horticulture, usually you've had some formal training and you're paid. Whereas if you're in a garden club, you're a volunteer. When I graduated from horticultural school thirty years ago, there was no place in the Northeast where you could buy houseplants. This is hard to believe now, but the rage had not hit then. It really hadn't. I had the feeling it was an interest whose time was coming.

Next door to our house there was an acre of land and it happened to have a fifty-year-old commercial greenhouse on it. The land came up for sale. My father bought the land in order to build a house on it for my mother and him to move into in their old age so they'd be close to me. My husband happened to sit on the board of the company that owned the greenhouse. At one board meeting they announced, "Oh, we have great news, the lot down there has been sold and the new owner plans to tear down the greenhouse, and we don't have to do it." My husband heard this and he came home and told me. I immediately went to see my father and I said, "Do you care about that greenhouse?" And he said, "Oh it's terrible, I'm going to tear down the whole thing." I said, "Well, I want it." And so I got the greenhouse. Immediately upon graduation, I started a commercial greenhouse business, raising and selling houseplants.

I was all alone in this. I was considered very queer. I was virtually regarded as a traitor to my class. People would say to me, "Why do you want to work? You don't have to work." From a financial point of view, I didn't. It really had nothing to do with that.

I come from a very high-achieving family. We're the Drinker family, an old Philadelphia family. We've been here since before William Penn. My father's family were incredible people . . . artists, writers, doctors, lawyers. Everybody had always done something in that family. The women not so much as the men, although he had two sisters who had professional careers. One was the writer, Catherine Drinker Bowen. There were people around me who were doing things and who had done things and I needed to accomplish something. But my parents didn't expect me to do anything commercial or professional. That was part of the problem. Their attitude was that women should be very talented in the old-fashioned accomplishments—play the piano beautifully, paint beautifully, or write a novel or be an author—which could be done at home. It was a very nineteenth-century idea.

My father was a lawyer and when I was about twelve years old I told him I wanted to be a lawyer. I remember him telling his friends how that was just so cute and great, "She wants to be a lawyer." But he didn't take it at all seriously. He was an amateur musician of some note and he wanted me to learn how to play the piano. When I was thirteen, that was the winter he was going to teach me to read music. I had to have had my breakfast and be downstairs at quarter past seven every morning, and until eight-thirty we did Schubert songs. Schubert wrote about seven hundred songs. My father played them and I sang them and I learned to read music. Oh, I hated it. He wanted to be able to say, "I've taught my daughter all Schubert's songs, she can read anything," and I could. By the end of the winter, I could read any music and he was very proud of that.

I got married when I was nineteen because I fell in love with somebody and there was no reason not to. My parents thought it was great. That's what they expected. Fifteen years later when I went into the plant business, my mother thought that was great too. She had become a feminist herself. Just about the time I began, she began to write a book about women and music. She was very supportive. My father was amused.

Anyway, I learned all about houseplants. The second year that I ran the greenhouse, I got an opportunity to put an exhibit in the big Philadelphia flower show because an exhibitor dropped out at the last minute. Only someone with a greenhouse could fill the space at such short notice because individual exhibitors have to force their material and have to plan ahead. Somebody said, "Well, Ernesta Ballard sells houseplants. Why don't you call her?" They called me and said, "Could you fill four hundred square feet?" And I did. I used the idea of a room with a sunny window and a shady window. It won the big prize.

As a result of that exhibit, I got a call a few weeks later from a friend of mine who worked for Harper & Row, Publishers, whose wife I went to school with. He said, "I've just been appointed nature and outdoor editor, and they told me I have to do a book on houseplants." People were beginning to pay attention and be interested in houseplants. He said, "I don't know anybody who knows anything about houseplants. Would you like to write a book for Harpers?" I said, "Sure, of course."

I'd never written much of anything before. My husband is a lawyer but he's really a frustrated English teacher. So we wrote the book called *Garden In Your House.* I wrote it and he made it read right. It was published in 1958 and it's still in print. It had fantastic sales and I made some money on it. When the book was published, I took a copy over to my father. I saw him a few days later and he smiled very sweetly, the way he always did, and said, "I turned every page."

I was lucky, I had a lot of breaks. I ran that houseplant business for ten years. It didn't make any money but it didn't lose any either. It was a learning process for me, and during that time I really learned about plants and I learned about running a business. After ten years I became bored with it. I love plants and all that, it's my life and I'm good at it. I'm a very good grower, but I really needed something more. Something bigger.

Then this job at the Pennsylvania Horticultural Society opened up— executive secretary. That was in 1963. I applied for the job; at that time the society was in the Suburban Station office building in Philadelphia. The society had four employees and an operating budget of seventy thousand dollars. I was offered the job at seven thousand dollars, which was two thousand less than the man I was replacing earned. Their argument was: (a) I didn't need the money and (b) I didn't have any experience. So I said, "O.K., I'm sorry I can't consider it unless I get the same salary he was getting." After three or four weeks they agreed.

Now, almost twenty years later, we have a budget of a million and a half dollars and we have twenty-five employees, and my salary has risen considerably. I still don't get paid as much as my successor will get paid, but I understand that. You have to go as the organization goes and grows. During all this time I feel I've been making a statement to my colleagues and friends and relations and everybody else about women and about women's ability to be aggressive and successful.

I have to generate that $1.5 million every year. About half of it comes from the flower show. We take it in from various phases—tickets, selling trade space, we give a benefit opening dinner to which eighteen hundred people will come and pay a hundred dollars each. We also have about eight thousand members in the society who pay dues. The membership has doubled since I took over, but that's not terribly big for this kind of organization. The Horticultural Society in London has seventy thousand members. I'd like it if we had about ten thousand. If you compare it to the Philadelphia Museum of Art and the Philadelphia Orchestra and the Academy of Natural Sciences, that's about what a nonprofit organization with member benefits should have. The members get a magazine which we started since I've been here, and we have special activities for them. They also get a preview ticket to the flower show. We have outreach programs, helping inner-city people grow vegetables in parks and plant street trees. We get a federal grant to do that, through the Philadelphia Office of Housing and Community Development. We have nine people whose only job is go out and help city people. We've been cited as a model for the entire country. It used to be a one hundred thousand dollar program, now we have a four hundred thousand dollar program, and I got that money. So those are the kinds of things I do.

I don't do any horticulture between nine and five. I do it in my spare time, which is weekends basically. I do it as a hobby, not as a profession. My husband and I are totally involved in horticulture together. He does bonsai and he's very good. I got him started and he's one of the best in the country now. He participates in the flower show as an exhibitor. I like to exhibit plants. I think it's fun, so I'll knock myself out and put in twenty or thirty or forty entries during the week of the flower show; I'll get in there at six-thirty in the morning before I have to start to work at the show. I don't win as many prizes as I used to because in order to win you have to spend hours, clean every leaf, get off every little speck and put new sieved soil around and scrub the stems. I don't have the time.

Good horticulture is actually a combination of art and science. There are an awful lot of people who don't see the art side, and I think that's what I've contributed. I try to teach people that it's not enough to keep the plant alive, plants should have beauty and style. The people who arrange flowers understand this. They understand you have to have line and color and the proper relationships. I feel the same way about a plant. You can achieve the same effect with pruning shears and by the way you grow the plant. When you look at the whole composition it should be beautiful. I don't tolerate ratty-looking plants. One of the things we've done at our flower show is raise the standard of how plants look. No one can believe that we can get a thousand entries in there that are all so beautifully grown and beautifully presented. We've done that over the years by refusing to admit those that don't meet our standards.

A few years ago at the Philadelphia Museum of Art, the director asked me to come over and take a look at their plants. They kept them in the basement and brought them out when they needed them for exhibitions. I looked at them and I said, "They're awful, they're offensive to me in this beautiful place with all these beautiful works of art." He didn't see it. He didn't see that the pots were dirty, that the leaves of the plants were dirty, that they needed grooming. It was as though blinders went on just because they were plants.

I think that a large part of my success at the society is in putting on the biggest flower show in the world. We have two hundred thousand people in eight days who will pay $4.50 to come. It's a fantastic thing and it's dependent on mobilizing a thousand garden club volunteers. I get along very well with the volunteers. We admire each other for what we can do.

I've always tried to be fair and not give volunteers the feeling I am scornful of their way of life. I really am a very strong believer in people's right to choose, and not just what happens to their own bodies but what happens to their lives. But I also know, and it's hard for me to say this, that women like our volunteers don't always have a fair choice. A lot of them were brought up to live a certain kind of a life and it never occurs to them that they can break out of it until they get to be an unemployed homemaker. And that's happening to more and more of them. This nice, ideal life for ten or twenty years and then all of a sudden it's over. They're widowed or they get divorced or the children are gone. They have no preparation, nothing to do, no way of breaking out and finding a satisfactory solution. Some become financially impoverished. Others are left at loose ends, and many turn to drink or drugs. It's a pathetic situation.

Our social structure is based on two and two and two. That's why it's so tragic when women get left. I've had women tell me when they've been divorced, that it's suddenly like they'd been dropped off the edge of the earth. Nobody asks them to do anything. That could not possibly happen to me because I liberated myself at the age of thirty. I found a way to make money, to make enough so that I'd always be able to support myself. I happened to have a little money but I came very early to the realization that I could only achieve happiness and satisfaction if I knew that I could be independent.

Now that's not to say that I don't really value my family and my marriage. I'd be miserable if my marriage ended, but at least I was able to make these choices early enough in life, which an awful lot of my friends couldn't do. I'm sixty years old. In my generation, there were loads of women who got educated and who went and got advanced degrees and became professionals, but not very many of them are also married and have families and children. There weren't an awful lot of men in my generation who would tolerate that, who could handle it. The men need, or think they need, a woman to help them and support them in order to get ahead. I could never have done without a very supportive husband.

There have never been any conflicts between us. Oh, in the very beginning, maybe there were adjustments, but I say to my husband, "You're at least as much of a feminist as I am." My husband now is the chairman of the board of an academic medical center. At least once a month there's a social function connected with it. I get many invitations from the faculty wives and trustees' wives. From the beginning I said, "Let's have it understood; I think it would be much better if I just didn't participate in those affairs." He said fine, he didn't care. It was perfectly all right with him. Well, I never go except maybe once a year. The other trustees think it's very queer, very queer. I don't think Fred cares, I really, honestly don't think so, and it obviously hasn't hurt his situation because he was elected chairman. He gets the feeling that maybe they're afraid to ask about me because they think maybe we've gotten divorced. On the other hand, he has never participated in horticultural affairs. He seldom goes to my dinners with me.

My son, who has the same name as my husband, was divorced eight years ago. It got back to me that people thought that Fred and I were the ones getting a divorce. And there were some people who were glad. They were saying, We told you so, you can't lead that kind of life and get away with it. You can't treat a man that way and get away with it. So society still wants to punish women who want to lead an independent life.

None of my childhood friends has the kind of career that I've had and it's not expected of them. It's not particularly understood. Now I think in the next generation, my daughters' generation, this will be different. When I went to work, my friends thought I was really very peculiar. And then when I began to be an activist in the women's movement . . . I don't talk about it with my old friends. We can't talk about it. If I ever say anything to them about the ERA or that I'm going to the National Convention of NOW, or the Women's Political Caucus, I mean talk about an iron curtain; it's a freeze that comes over them.

I have made many wonderful new friends, people in the women's movement, wonderful people whom I never would have known if I'd gone the other route. Being the wife of a corporation lawyer, I never would have met this kind of woman. I have my old friends and my life with the people I've worked with for years, then I have my life as a liberal and a women's activist, and really the two don't cross.

You pay for all this. You pay for it by stomachaches and headaches. Nobody can lead this kind of life, I don't think, and not pay a price. I virtually have no conventional social life, which I don't care about because I'd rather lead the kind of life I do. My husband and I don't ever go on vacations. We've only been on one trip together, but he doesn't really like to go away and neither do I.

I will be leaving this job at the end of the year. Seventeen years is long enough. I'm tired of it, and the organization deserves a change. I've done all I can here. I want to do something else. We have a good organization.

We have a fantastic show. We have good people connected with it. I think I've been good at pulling it all together, being the catalyst for it. This job has been a soapbox. It's been a way for me to use the talent I have for the betterment of a lot more than just horticulture.

Of all the things that I've done, I've wanted to do something more. I think I'm a leader, a civic leader in Philadelphia. I'm a member of the Philadelphia Partnership, a group of about ninety people who are heads of companies, community leaders, business leaders. They have to have a few women so they have me. I have three other activities already that I spend much of my time doing. I've worked on the CETA board for Philadelphia, appointed by the mayor. I'm a member of the board of directors of one of the biggest corporations in the country, I'm their— guess what?—token, and I've served as president of the Greater Philadelphia Cultural Alliance. So I have plenty to do. I'm not really worried because I'm a good administrator. I'm a good executive. But still I have never really succeeded in convincing or showing a great number of people that I have a job.

I sit on a board of a local corporation in Philadelphia, and recently I was talking during lunch with one of the other board members who's active in a lot of liberal causes. He said he had something he wanted to bring me and asked when was I in town. I said, "Joe, I'm in town every day. I work." He said, "I had no idea you *worked* at the Pennsylvania Horticultural Society." After seventeen years at this organization, there are still people who don't understand that I work, that I have a job. I don't know whether it's because it's a horticultural organization or because it's a nonprofit organization, or that they simply cannot get it through their heads that I, a woman, work.

I think one reason things have worked out pretty well for me is that with my abilities and background, I've been able to bring connections and ideas into the field of horticulture that weren't there before. There aren't very many people like me in horticulture. I felt vulnerable because of my lack of a college education. I saw my colleagues in horticulture jealously comparing their academic credentials and boy, did they make a big deal of the fact that I didn't have any . . . how can you do anything without a Ph.D. in horticulture? And yet I've written a best-selling book on horticulture, which a lot of them haven't, and I've got a job with an organization that's in the black and most of theirs are in the red. But I wouldn't qualify for my successor's job here. We would not hire anybody to replace me who was a housewife running a little retail plant business.

# Dede Allen

Dede Allen (born 1923, Cleveland, Ohio) is the first film editor to bring attention to the film-editing process as an art. She is known for the innovative editing technique she devised for Bonnie and Clyde in 1966, as well as her work in Rachel, Rachel (1968), Alice's Restaurant (1969), Little Big Man (1970), Slaughterhouse-Five (1972), Serpico (1973), Dog Day Afternoon (1975) and Slapshot (1977). Working in New York with a specialized group, able to handle the entire postproduction film process, she has helped contribute to the revival of New York as a film production center. She is one of the first editors in the industry to receive star billing.

# Joan Ganz Cooney

*Joan Ganz Cooney (born 1929, Phoenix, Arizona) is head and cofounder of the multimillion-dollar, nonprofit Children's Television Workshop, producers of* Sesame Street, *which developed advertising techniques for the first time in the medium of television to teach preschool skills to millions of children around the world. Books, records, toys and other* Sesame Street *products generate the capital for research and development. In 1971, CTW produced* The Electric Company *for seven-to-ten-year-olds and in 1980, 3-2-1 Contact for eight-to-twelve-year-olds. The first Sesame Play Park for age three and up was opened in 1979.*

I DON'T KNOW WHAT MADE *Sesame Street* so successful. I can give some hypotheses, but there is certainly no single answer. The idea was to teach preschool skills to all children but particularly to disadvantaged children. It was a great idea that came up at a time when both the American public and the United States Government believed in preschool education. It was the Head Start period; the accent was on poverty and the educational disadvantage of poverty. That meant the money was available. There is no point in having a good idea if it cannot be executed.

The idea was so big, so idealistic, that we were able to attract the largest talents in children's television, as well as some of the largest talents in adult television. They were people who knew entertainment. Very fine talents came to the project for less money than they would have made on commercial television. That was a big factor.

I suppose having a leader who had vision and an idea and who could keep it on the track was an enormous advantage to the project. It would not have worked without the proper leadership. That leadership was not just myself, it was also Lloyd Morrisett, who was chairman of our board and one of the founders with me, and Gerald Lesser, who is an educational psychologist at Harvard, one of the leaders in the field. He organized the research and curriculum development side of the project. So from the academic arena and the entertainment arena we were able to attract the very best. The idea was an idea around which everyone could coalesce. I was the keeper of the flame, if you will . . . to make sure we stayed on the track throughout.

The show wasn't born overnight. I was a producer at Channel 13, the PBS station in New York. The Lloyd Morrisetts and Lewis Freedman, who was my boss at Channel 13, were at my house for a dinner party in 1966. Lewis, who is a very dramatic, stunning man, was talking about the future of television and its untapped potential as an educator. Lloyd was financing research in preschool education at Carnegie Corporation and it clicked in his mind: Why not preschool education on television? So he called the next day and asked if I would be willing to do a study for him and I said, "You bet." I had been interested in having more power, moving up in my job as producer and having some influence over the kinds of shows we were doing. I saw right away how interesting the idea was.

I had three or four months to do a study on the viability of educating children via television. I wrote my report in 1966 and we all liked it, including the government and the foundations, and we felt there was more than a germ of an idea there. Then I had another year to develop a full-scale proposal for Carnegie and, with Lloyd, get it funded.

I didn't suddenly get a powerful idea. It evolved very slowly. I never felt overwhelmed by it or even that it was a particularly large challenge. I felt it was highly doable and I was the person to do it. The commercials for short spots was an idea that I got while I was doing the study, because parents kept telling me how compelled their children were by commercials. I put that very interesting piece of data into the report and then into the proposal. Then someone came up with the idea, just en passant, of doing commercials for letters and numbers. That's how it started. The fun and the challenge were to use television in a new and highly specific and purposeful way. That was very exciting. My passion was to do something on television that would benefit poor children. I would have to say all of that was very thrilling.

Most educators think we are successful, most parents appreciate the show, and we are one of the most acclaimed and honored shows in the history of American television. In ten years we've slowed down the pace of the show and greatly increased the curriculum, adding bilingual and bicultural education; retarded children are part of the show; we do prereading skills, reasoning skills; we have dealt with sibling rivalry, pre-science, health, safety, nutrition. We add a new curriculum every year.

I don't feel surprised to be doing what I'm doing now but twenty years ago I would have been very surprised. When I first got involved with the Carnegie study, being a woman didn't matter because I was working on an idea that no one else was working on, I wasn't in competition. And I had the right kind of forces working with me, the United States Government, the Ford Foundation and Carnegie Corporation. So there was no way of stopping us once we got rolling. I suppose along the way they wondered about a woman heading the project, but the project was in my head, it wasn't on a piece of paper, so they didn't have much choice. There wasn't any real candidate other than me.

I had to learn to run a business. I'm not a savvy businesswoman in the sense that an MBA from Harvard is. I struggle with complicated business concepts and numbers because I wasn't brought up with them. I had to learn, and surround myself with good people I trust. Once we were successful, which was as of November 20, 1969, then we had to figure out how to keep going. I had to start a products business—books, records, toys—keep the government involved, raise new money, get a new show going. Then the Ford Foundation gave us money for investment purposes to try to stabilize the organization so it wouldn't be so dependent. I had to learn fast if I wanted to stay at the top of CTW.

I could have abdicated at that point and let somebody come in and do it, but it was my baby and I wanted to bring it up. Just as when you give birth, you don't say, "How am I going to cope with a five-year-old or an adolescent?" It just happens. I'm a lot more confident now than I was ten years ago, but there is still a lot I don't know. Now I'm a director on corporate boards and that has been extremely useful as a way of learning about business.

I majored in education in college, but I really wasn't interested in teaching. It was something that girls of my generation did because teaching was very acceptable, especially for married women. One's mother said, "If your husband should die and leave you with little children, your hours would be the same as the children's if you had to support them." So a lot of girls of my generation went into education. After I graduated, I worked for the government for a year in Washington and then went into journalism. I wanted to be in communications.

I was brought up a Catholic; Christianity was always important in my life. I was idealistic as a child. My parents didn't sit around talking idealism in the living room, but I was very influenced by my religion and wanted to do good in the world. In those days, there was this powerful idea that one person could change the world. My friends and I always talked about it, that we had to do something. You never hear that now.

One of the great influences on my life was a Catholic organization, Father Keller's Christophers. His message was that mass communications media were so powerful, idealistic people were needed to go into them and shape them; that if right-thinking people didn't get into mass communications, the other kind would.

I became very interested in public television. In 1962 the New York public television station, WNET, opened. I thought public television offered me a lot more opportunity to do serious work in the medium. I got a job as a producer in news and public affairs and produced debates and documentary films. I did a documentary about education for preschoolers in poverty areas, and that's how I discovered programs in compensatory education for poor children before Head Start had even begun.

My father died when I was twenty-six. He was very proud of me for coming to New York and working. I think my mother was absolutely stunned in one way, but pleased in another. When I left Arizona, she said, "You know you are a big fish in a little pond in Phoenix; why do you want to be a little fish in a big pond?" I said, "How do you know I won't be a big fish in a big pond?" I didn't really believe I would be, but I remember feeling rather feisty about it. She was always anticipating, not that her children were not going to succeed, but she could not imagine big success; it was out of her ken.

It was out of my ken, too, when I was younger, because I assumed when I came to New York I would marry young. I was twenty-three at the time and I assumed by twenty-five or twenty-six I'd be married. But I didn't marry until I was thirty-four, and I don't think that was because I was in a career. In my generation it was not frowned upon for the girls to work and try to get ahead as long as they were single. It was assumed if they got married, they'd quit, and I suppose that did postpone marriage in my mind. But until I established myself in a career I really couldn't get married, because, I suppose, I'm just figuring it out now, but I felt it was important for me to get set up for what I was going to do, in case I dropped out for a while. Then I'd have something to go back to. I never thought I'd try to do both at once. In fact, it was when I started doing work that I adored, producing shows at Channel 13, that my work made me feel happy enough and competent enough to finally get married.

I don't think my marriage suffered because of my work. My husband sort of became more passive with my success, but I think if it hadn't been my work it would have been something else. That was the trigger. He loved it, and in many ways I think my success kept us together longer because I was focused on work, not on the personal, and he was supportive.

My husband was a radical feminist before the women's movement started, so that I was very used to that in the home. You see, he'd given up paid work to do unpaid work in the civil rights movement. He saw women's rights as civil rights. We had a relationship with an inner-city kid who he met in 1961. Our relationship with the child had to do with our interest and commitment to civil rights. He found the boy wandering around in the ghetto and then we got to know the grandmother. My husband had that need for a child, he really almost adopted him. We had him with us quite a lot and then I got him into a boarding school in Westchester for children whose parents really cannot take responsibility for them, for one reason or another. It was a very fine boarding school, good nurturing. When he was thirteen he went to live with his grandmother and went to public school. He's now eighteen. I don't see him often but my ex-husband stays in touch with him.

If I had had children at the time I started Children's Television Workshop they would have been very young preschoolers, so that I probably would have thought it isn't fair for me to travel. I don't think you can be a good mother if you're not available a good deal of the time. I don't mean working. I mean being away for two weeks or more at a time. With one crisis after another at CTW, I could not have managed without shortchanging the children or this job. It seems absurd in a way because men don't have to make that choice.

In the seventies women thought they could have everything and they were knocking themselves out trying to have it, and now they're saying, "Oh, come on." That period is over and Betty Friedan is leading the crusade back to the family, thank heavens. I argued about it enough to have a little influence, I think. The NOW Legal Defense Fund organized a Future of the Family Conference because many of us felt we were going to lose the best and the brightest as mothers if we didn't encourage those women who wish to be full-time homemakers to do so; and those who are in careers and have children, to believe they can exercise a range of choices without neglecting the children. Women lawyers and women doctors really frequently have a choice because many of them work fewer hours when their children are little and then expand their schedules as the kids get older. It's harder in other kinds of work. A woman producer can't just say, "I'm going to work part-time." The show won't get done.

My primary role right now at CTW is both to come up with new ideas and to run the organization. I have help, I have an executive vice president and a senior vice president. We sort of divide the work up. My preference is to be on the creative side in the early stages of a show, in conceptualizing what the show will be, but I like the business side also. I like to make the two work together finding markets and who you sell to. It's a refined sort of selling, sophisticated, talking to people about ideas. I don't feel like I'm selling myself, I'm selling the idea. It's not difficult if it is a good idea. If they say no, I don't feel like they are rejecting me.

At CTW we still feel the need to pioneer and set an example. It is very hard to equal or top a show that is as successful and famous as *Sesame Street*. But we still try. Unfortunately, we are often held to that standard by the reviewers. We take on enormously difficult assignments in order to keep trying to do something new. Change can be brought about but it is very hard. When we started out it was considered a phenomenon that $8 million was raised for a children's program. Nobody was spending that on children. Today that would be equivalent to $16 or $20 million. You can imagine seeing "$20 million for children" on the front page of the *New York Times*. You'd say, "What are they talking about?" But we did it.

Television should pay a lot more attention to children. This society is the only society I know in developed or less-developed countries that has permitted such laissez-faire policies in organizing the three networks. Most countries regulate how much the networks have to do for children. With cable TV coming on the horizon I think it will change here. For reasons of competition I think there will be more for children, I hope higher quality. You may say, "Who is going to decide what is quality?" The answer is, there has always been a consensus on this question.

I like to feel I am a hardheaded businesswoman, but I suppose underneath it all I am a crusader. I would like to bring about change for the better. CTW is not a democracy. It would be all over the lot if there were not a few of us with a vision who say no. I say no a lot. It's not much fun because there are many ideas that are brought to me that are good in and of themselves. I just don't think they are right for this organization any more than Shawn necessarily would think any article was right for *The New Yorker* even though it had merit. He's looking for a certain kind of article and I'm looking for a kind of project that fits with what I feel our mission is: educational television and high-quality children's programming. Everything we do, we do because we want to do it. First we ask, "Is it consistent with our mission?" Then we ask, "Can we raise the money to meet the budget?" The two things have to go together.

I think the women at the top, I wouldn't want to put this on myself, are often of superior quality to the men on the top. They had to have more to begin with and perseverance has kept them there. It would be very hard to find a group of men comparable to the women chosen for this book across as many fields. Of course, men might articulate it differently, but I think women, to have had the courage to crack male bastions, had to have a sense of mission and an idea bigger than themselves, because a woman runs a risk of a more humiliating defeat. Women don't allow that, so women have to bring a greater passion to their work to crack through.

I read a quote of mine recently that I think the writer embellished, because I don't think I ever said it as cleverly as that. "If you travel the road to the top you don't travel many other roads." That was in answer to the question of what sacrifices I had made, for my career. It has been said in a business magazine that I made great sacrifices, for example, my first marriage ended in divorce, as if that's never happened to a man. But in fact I have entered a new marriage, and there are stepchildren involved, so now I have a large family plus a career. The story is not over until it is over.

My answer is, a woman raising two or three little children is making sacrifices to do that job. But no one ever asks her, "What sacrifices are you making?" If she's working outside the home, and is successful, the tendency is to assume she is making sacrifices. But my observation is that successful men make a lot of sacrifices too; you can't do everything. So if you're obsessed with an idea, or you are obsessed with being successful, as I think more men are than women . . . in either case, you have to be pretty obsessive about it. In that sense I guess sacrifices are made.

I think there are seasons of life. I've gone through very austere periods where I've just worked, and then less austere times when I felt I could let up and concentrate more on my personal life.

It is simpler, much simpler, to deal with one thing or the other, not both. That's why I think I concentrated only on work for four years, after my separation and divorce. I had a major illness just after my separation, and it was very simple for me to bury myself in work and not think about life-and-death issues, which now I don't have to think about anymore. I wasn't sure at the time.

I thought my illness would give me more perspective and I would have more balance, but it had the opposite effect, which is that I wanted to prove how well I was to myself and to others, so I worked all the time. My work was the only thing I had, really. It was O.K. for a while, but one day I just ran out of gas and said, "Gee, this isn't the way to live. I can start delegating if I want to." I've done much more of that in the last two years. I want both work and personal life. Gosh, I'd consider myself having lost some human trait if work were enough. The secret to a happy life is finding some balance between work and emotional relationships.

When people said to me, "You don't have any personal life," I would always say, "If I met the right person I would change that." The truth is, it doesn't exactly work that way. You have to be ready for it to happen. I was lucky enough, not soon, not right away, but within a short time after my divorce to meet the right man. The youngest child in this new marriage is eleven, the oldest is twenty-six. The two that I see most, and who will be living part of the time with us, are the youngest boy, ten, and a girl, fifteen. They are both great kids and I have a good relationship with both of them and enjoy watching them develop.

Now everything is on the upswing again and it makes me feel absolutely ill. I guess I'm very superstitious. I have a lot of anxiety and when things are going too well, the anxiety gets worse and then I make up problems as if burning incense to the gods. It is very hard on one's loved ones if things are going well, you create worries and problems. My youngest stepchild calls me "W.W" for worry wart.

I think luck is a very large percentage of how things turn out. You have to take advantage when you see a break, but boy, you have to have the breaks. I'll tell you, when people say you have to make your own breaks, that just isn't true. I knew nothing about children's programming. It's got to to be a break that I knew Lloyd Morrisett at Carnegie and that he trusted me and didn't want an expert. The kinds of people we got to work for us was a break. The idea was big enough to attract The Muppets. Jim Henson did not want to do children's shows, had never done them, never wanted to. That he would pause in his career at that time to do educational, nonprofit television was a miracle. If he hadn't, we wouldn't have been viable because it's merchandising The Muppets that keeps the income coming in here. I had something to do with it but I'll tell you, it was a piece of luck.

I'm pretty satisfied with my life; I think I've had a very good ride. I have done work that meant something to a lot of people throughout the world; I think that I did work that affected the lives of children in a very real way. We affected broadcasting by getting on the air at all. We affected education. Certainly, kindergarten teaches stuff that they never dreamed of teaching. *Sesame Street* is always cited as the reason that they had to change curriculum. I became head of my own company. Thus I have not had a boss, which means a great deal to me, a great deal. I've had enormous applause and enormous rewards, like being asked to be on the boards of large companies. That came from being a successful woman in this time. The women's movement made me ten times more visible than I think I would have been otherwise. So I had many, many breaks.

# Lucy Jarvis

*Lucy Jarvis (born 1919, New York City) is a television producer whose documentaries for NBC News during the 1950s and 1960s, on subjects that had never before been filmed, demonstrated that television could be educational, receive wide critical acclaim and still be popular. The public saw the Kremlin in 1963, the Louvre in 1964, the Ming Tombs of the Forbidden City in 1973 and the virtually unknown kidney dialysis machine in "Who Shall Live" in 1965. She was the first woman producer in network prime-time programming and currently heads her own production company.*

OVER THE PERIOD OF SIXTEEN YEARS that I was in the news department of NBC, I produced many different kinds of television programs—interviews, debates, etc.—but finally I was put in charge of cultural documentaries. During that time I initiated and produced well over one hundred different programs in about twenty countries. I became known as the whirlwind of Rockefeller Plaza because I was bringing television crews into places that never before permitted cameras. Among them was the Kremlin. I was the only producer allowed in to the Kremlin with cameras, and since then, I understand nobody has been allowed back.

That was in 1962, and I accomplished that feat with the help of President John F. Kennedy, through the cooperation of Pierre Salinger. I got in touch with the president at the White House and told him I wanted to go to Vienna with the presidential party, not as a reporter (because NBC had already filled their quota) but because I wanted to meet Khrushchev personally in order to explain to him why I wanted to do a film on the Kremlin. JFK wrote a note to the president of NBC and said, "I would like to give Lucy Jarvis permission to accompany us on the trip to Paris, Vienna and London as a guest of the White House," and that's how and when I met Khrushchev.

You must remember that this was following the McCarthy era, a period of ugliness, fear, suspicion and even hate. So many of these fears, I had the feeling, came from ignorance. We are full of fears and hate because we suspect evil of those we do not understand.

I was convinced that in spite of all the progress we had made in international communications, we still knew so little about the other peoples of the world—even in 1962! Further, I believed that the factor which was keeping the world from achieving real peace had to do with our ignorance of the differences which existed in heritage, history, traditions, customs, as well as language. If I could show the American public that the Russian people had an incredible history of their own in art and music, that they had great sensitivity, which was reflected in their literature; if I could show their architecture, show that the Kremlin was not a dungeon, a fortress, into which people were thrown never to be seen again, but on the contrary, was a series of exquisite palaces that were created long before Communism came to Russia; if I could use the exact locations in the Kremlin to dramatize on film the anecdotal material we so painstakingly researched, and re-create the life and times of the Russians, starting with the year 1142 when the Kremlin was first built, then our American viewers, learning more firsthand, would perhaps develop a different feeling about the Kremlin itself and the people whose lives were inevitably interwoven with those buildings and their histories.

President Kennedy was a great student of history, and was convinced that only through a thorough knowledge and understanding of history could we have any chance of building a solid and peaceful future. Believing that as well, I took off for Moscow. I was there five months, during which time I overcame the summer heat, my ignorance of the language, the monotonous diet, the bureaucracy, the fear and suspicion of the Russians who were assigned to me. I even survived the Cuban missile crisis, which was played out while, undaunted, I was leading my camera "troops" through the Kremlin, filming every nook and cranny.

But I never overcame the Russian telephone! Russia was, and may still be, a country of unlisted telephone numbers. You couldn't call anyone specifically—in fact, there weren't even any general numbers. You could not call, for example, the minister of culture, or even the ministry. Every time I wanted to make an appointment with someone, I'd have to go there. I developed the habit of walking into an office, going to the man's desk, looking at his telephone and writing down his number. I collected one of the great private phone books of all times. By the way, this book disappeared or was stolen three months later. It mysteriously appeared again by way of an English tourist. Two weeks after the book disappeared, the Englishman came to Moscow on business. "They" planted the book on him and he couldn't get "them" to understand that it didn't belong to him, that it obviously belonged to somebody whose name and address was clearly marked on the front page—somebody named Lucy Jarvis. They refused to believe that and continued to plant the book in his hotel room. Finally he took it back to England and sent it to my husband, whose card was also in the book. My husband had it delivered back to me in Moscow.

When I finally did meet Khrushchev again it was at the Austrian Embassy in Moscow. There was a big party. I invited myself to the party—marched up to Mr. K. and took off in my fractured Russian. After much haggling he said. *"Potchamu Niet?"* (Why not?). I said to Khrushchev, "Why did you keep me waiting for two months to give me permission to do this Kremlin film? You knew why I was coming here." He said, "My dear, there is a man from CBS who has been trying to get in the Kremlin for two years. He would have kissed my hands if I let him do that TV program, and you think two months is a lot of time!"

Well, I guess he liked women, he was fascinated by the idea that I came to Moscow and that I "crashed" his party to meet him, and most of all he was touched that I studied his language—the CBS guy couldn't even say *"Niet."* Also, Khrushchev knew that I was not going to leave until I got that permission, until I did that film. I would stay there and dig my heels in and NBC would keep making money available—until I realized my "coup!" So after two months, I finally got the contract signed.

It took us three months to complete the filming inside Russia, and three months more on the outside to finish. We were very careful to keep politics out of it. Instead, we put our emphasis on history, art, music, architecture and stories, even when we brought it up to modern times. The cinematography was very beautiful, the music superb. It was a film the public could not resist. It was a first, and it was just beautiful. NBC was delighted that I had pulled it off. It was the beginning of great adventures for me, the first of my big coups.

As for the Russians, within weeks after it was shown, the Soviet Union was bombarded with visa requests. They had almost a million tourists over the next two years, from all over the world. That was a phenomenal thing to have happen. Russians who had been away for thirty or forty years, and second-generation Russians whose parents had escaped during the Revolution, all felt that they could take a chance and go to Moscow— nothing bad would happen there.

Now, if you know me, you'd know why I was able to accomplish what no other producer could. First, I believe very strongly in the responsibility that the television industry has to the American public—to entertain, of course, but most of all to dare, to be imaginative, to create, to stimulate the mind and to overcome man's inhumanity to man by depicting not his ugly, violent nature but his beautiful, creative one.

I'm the kind of person that if I believe in what I can do, I just don't let anything stop me. I started out in life a home economics major at Cornell. I went away to school, which was unheard-of. I was one of the few of my set who did. Now, of course, it's an everyday thing. But in those days, there was one coed for every ten men at Cornell. My brother was studying engineering and going into advanced work, getting his master's and Ph.D. It was expensive sending two kids away to college at that time, joining sororities and all the things we had to do, so the fact that I went into home economics was a great help because it was a scholarship class. I had to earn it, I had to be eligible for it. I had to have the kind of graces and background, whatever it was they demanded. I spent all my extra time in the dramatic club and as the advertising manager of my college humor magazine. So you see, communications was my bent then, as well.

I graduated in 1938 and I became a food editor at *McCall's* magazine two years later. That's where I got a taste of television. I traveled around the country, making speeches and appearing as a guest on many television shows, and I was fascinated by the whole medium. I then realized that no matter how successful I might be in the written media, I could still only reach a handful of people. If I really wanted to make an impact, if I really wanted to bring something to the attention of the public, then television, was, and is, the way. I mean, *millions* in one night. I had something I wanted to bring. I wanted to bring peace, I wanted to bring understanding. I wanted women to show what they can do. I wanted to be an example. Looking back, it seems like I couldn't have been anything, absolutely couldn't have been anything else but a producer.

As food editor of *McCall's* I dreamed up a television show that became "The Home Show." It was a kind of magazine show. I couldn't go ahead with it because I was having a baby and my husband was insistent that we move to Connecticut, so that our children would grow up in the country. We built a house in the suburbs and both children were born there. I did not go back to the marketplace until Peter went away to prep school at the age of sixteen and Barbara was in high school. She didn't want to go away to school, and I didn't think it was necessary for a girl to go away to school. By then the children had full lives of their own. Those years that I spent at home with my children were years I enjoyed enormously. I always tried to be available for them and I never regretted it. I felt that was their due. The children were, in a way, a production of mine, as well as of ours, my husband's and mine. I would say to any woman today that I would have done it exactly the same way. I think women should give those years to their kids.

I spent whatever free hours I had at that time doing charity work. I was never involved in bringing clothes and food to people. I was very active in an international organization that gave scholarships to gifted musicians, singers, actors and painters. Three extraordinary young men, who now perform all over the world to great acclaim, were helped by our scholarship fund: Itzhak Perlman, the violinist; Pinchas Zukerman, the cellist; and Daniel Barenboim, the pianist.

To raise money for this scholarship fund, I arranged a dinner at the Waldorf Astoria. We were charging five hundred dollars a couple (which was unheard-of at that time) and that meant the evening had to be extraordinary. I had one office worker to help me. It was then that I knew I'd be a producer. I had to provide the menu, the decor, the publicity, the entertainment. So I went to a friend and I said, "Listen, I need good entertainers and I can't spend a lot of money." She said, "Come with me, I'm auditioning some people in an empty nightclub."

I went with her, we auditioned this comedy team, a man and a woman. They were marvelous! So funny they had me on the floor. They were just getting started and needed a large, sophisticated audience to try out their material. I immediately hired them. I told them I could only pay seventy-five dollars for the act. They were crestfallen. "O.K., I'll pay you seventy-five each, but that's it. I have very little money to spend on entertainment . . . but I don't believe in asking performers to work for nothing, even if this is a charity." That left the sum of seventy-five dollars for a singer, and I think it was three hundred dollars for a twelve-piece orchestra. For the singer I got a girl who was performing at the Waldorf, in the Empire Room, to sing for us between performances. It was Diahann Carroll! The orchestra was Meyer Davis's and the comedy team was

Elaine May and Mike Nichols. They got a standing ovation. I realized that
I must have that touch or that smell or whatever it is that successful
producers have. I went back into the marketplace in the late fifties.
Actually, it was my husband who arranged it. He introduced me to the
husband of Martha Rountree. She was the woman who originated and
developed the program *Meet the Press*. She was starting a new show and I
became her coproducer. Then David Susskind took me to CBS and
introduced me to a genius named Irv Gitlin, who immediately took his
entire team, including me, to NBC. That's the whole evolution.

At NBC I proved that programs can be informative, stimulating,
prestigious, intelligent, literate and at the same time exciting and
commercial. I tried to make NBC understand, in all the arguments I used
to have with them, why I needed big budgets. I said, "We're not an
educational institution; we are in the entertainment business. Just because
we're doing these shows in the news department doesn't mean they have
to be skimpy and the bitter pill the public has to swallow in order to get
sitcoms. The ratings and multiruns prove that I can make documentaries
as appealing as any high-rated show."

In 1976, after sixteen years, I left NBC and started my own company. It
was time to go. Documentaries were splintering into more commercially
geared magazine shows. NBC was no longer going to do the big cultural
shows. I had the rights to the Mexican Anthropological Museum and I got
into a big hassle about it. NBC didn't want to put any time, money or
priorities into that kind of programming.

When Barbara Walters left NBC to go to ABC in 1966, she came to me
and said, "You have always said you want to do new things—drama, etc.
Well, this is it. C'mon, it's time you left." We'd been friends for twelve
years. She wanted company on the outside. It was lonely and cold out
there. I said, "That's easy for you to say, you'll get a million dollars a year.
But I'm going to go out there without that." She said, "I'll guarantee you'll
do my programs. Not my news shows, but I'll do four entertainment
shows a year, interviews with rock stars and movie people, and we'll
travel; we'll have a great time." I said, "What if it doesn't work out?" I
said, "We'll do one at a time. If the first one doesn't work out, I'll give
notice. The most important thing is that we own these shows, then we can
sell them over and over again. It's income for years."

When I left NBC, it was a big step. It was a hard thing to do. There was
not one other woman I knew who had done this. Just as I was the first
woman producer in the network on a major level, for prime-time
programming, I was going to be the first woman to get out there and start
her own production company and go around hustling and selling. That's a
lot different. I mean, I couldn't just sign a voucher for my telephone bills
and throw it into the out box anymore.

When I told NBC I was leaving, the president said, "Oh, you and
Barbara won't get along." They'll say anything. They were hoping. I said,
"We know all about that. We'll take our chances." I had six months to go
on my contract. They made a deal with my attorneys and I left within a

month. They said I could take my whole office with me—the desk I'd had for fifteen years, all my furniture. Fifteen years of putting out and putting out and putting out. They said, "If you and Barbara don't make it together, or if you decide you want to do something else, you have an hour of prime time here for your first show."

When I went to work with Barbara I discovered that because ABC was paying her so much money, they would not allow her to own her own programs. They would only allow her to own a portion of her programs and the network owned the rest. That let me out altogether. So there I was back again, working hard on the two shows I did with her, one with Barbra Streisand and Jon Peters, the other with the Carters. I made as much money on each of those two shows as I made in a year at NBC, but I still didn't own anything. So I said to Barbra, "It's not going to work out. Now that I'm out of NBC and you've given me this chance, I'm going to try and do with drama, with fiction, what I did with documentaries."

Look at the fun I'm having. I can do almost anything. I've got the value of having people who are great writers and directors, and wonderful performers, whose world is fiction. Many of them have really turned their faces away from television because they consider it demeaning. But because I have worked in documentaries, they trust me to appreciate and understand their great talent and protect their integrity, and I've had a parade of writers come through my office who wouldn't normally work for television, Joe Heller, Peter Matthiessen, Peter Maas, Isaac Singer.

Whatever I'm doing now is based on reality, just as it was when I was doing documentaries. All of the things I'm preparing, for drama, for series, for movies, are all based on reality. For example: My first big project is called "Family Reunion." "Family Reunion" was developed originally by the *Ladies' Home Journal.* I have an arrangement with them whereby if they have something very interesting, they give me first refusal on it. The editor, Lenore Hershey, came to me and said, "We're going to do a study on why there is an increase in the phenomenon of families coming together in America for annual reunions, from fifty people to fifteen thousand people." These families are a microcosm of America. They go from the very poor to the very rich, from the ditch digger to the professor. Some of them take the Astrodome in Dallas for this meeting, or take a hotel in Florida. Why do they do it? What is this need that people have? It's not a search for roots. That's not what it's about. It's the feeling of belonging somewhere, of being with people you trust, the feeling that they're family, that they love you, they will not betray you, they'll give you the best advice. It may not be true. Some families have terrible feuds, and terrible competitive feelings and sibling rivalry.

We sent out questionnaires to eight hundred families. The information that came back was overwhelming and dramatic and exciting. What we then did was to create a fictional family, out of these eight hundred. We're doing a story about three hundred people, most of whom are perfect strangers to each other, who live over America, who do all kinds of things, who are all kinds of people, who come together on the old family property. The original piece of the house is still there, but it's been built onto and onto and onto since 1796. We'll show who the family members are and what they mean to each other; what their needs are for each other and what their stories are; and how the family as a whole either helps or rejects. We'll explore what it is that's happening in America today that creates a tearing apart of the fabric, through the dispersion, through people moving away from their origins.

I grew up in a family in which aunts and uncles and cousins and grandparents were all within a mile of each other. We fed into each other. There was an enormous amount of goodwill and guidance. When you became a parent, you knew that you had somebody who was a parent successfully, to whom you could go to for guidance, because there was a lot of love. Even through friction, there was learning.

There were only two children in our family. My brother is much older than I am. He was the first grandson and when I came along I upset his applecart. He had the run of the house and the run of the world. He was the cock of the walk. Everybody made a big fuss over him, all those aunts and uncles and grandparents and parents, and along comes this pain in the ass, a beautiful little girl that I probably was, with a Buster Brown haircut and fat and cute, and smiling and happy and singing and everybody making a fuss. Suddenly it was all over for him.

At the age of ten he packed his bags and left home. Where did he go? Well, to his grandparents, of course. He wasn't going to run *away*. It was easy for him. The grandparents told him how wonderful he was, and the uncles who were still living at home took him to the ball game and to the circus and did whatever had to be done for a boy to make him feel that he's a man, that he's loved and wanted. Then Friday night we all came for dinner and went home together.

Now, that doesn't happen. The grandparents live three thousand miles away. The aunts and uncles are dispersed everywhere. There might not even be any aunts and uncles. And there are no role models for marriage, so kids don't get married. The span of marriage is now seven years.

I went to a meeting of the National Assembly on the Family, sponsored by NOW, from eight in the morning until eight at night. Betty Friedan, whom I have some misgivings about, but who I think is an enormously intelligent and understanding woman, said to me, "You know, it's like Pandora's box. This whole feminine mystique was to liberate women, but I never meant it to take away from women what fulfills them as women. Now I see what it has done to my daughter. She is grown, she is married, her friends are divorced. What we have perpetrated on that generation is a whole new set of problems. We say women should have the right to determine who they are and what they are and be free to do that, but there's a lot of loneliness in that. They leave their husbands and children behind to find out who they are." I think large families used to satisfy that kind of loneliness, and provide self-definition.

At the closing session of the assembly there was a panel of four couples. Norman Lear, the television producer, and his wife Martha Lear were the moderators; and there was Eleanor Holmes Norton and Ed Norton, a wonderful black professional couple; Herman Badillo and his wife, that's the political couple; and a young couple who were the stars of a documentary called "Blue-Collar Worker," they're the blue-collar people. The title of the panel was: "How has the changing society affected your marriage, and how do you relate now to each other?"

They talked about everything: how economic gain reflected on the woman's ability to be more independent and gave her more of a sense of herself so she can have an egalitarian role in the marriage. They are now equal. Sometimes she makes more money. If she does, he compensates by doing more at home. But with all the new words like *negotiate*, which means they discuss more, not one of those people, including the moderators, used the words *love, self-respect, mutual respect, admiration, affection, warmth*; those words were not used at all, and I think those are the important words, the words that keep families together.

I was liberated long before anybody understood what the word was. I simply did as I felt I must do. I was doing it, not because I was asserting myself or because I was liberated, but because I felt that's what I wanted to do, what I felt had to be done. "What do you mean Khrushchev won't let me do the Kremlin? If I go to him, I'll convince him."

A great deal of my confidence comes from my mother, from making me feel, as she made my brother feel, that there's nothing I can't do if I really apply myself. And I believed that, totally, I accepted that. Part of my mother's pushing us must have come from wanting us to live her dreams. She really was handicapped. My mother was a very advanced woman, really, but she was born thirty years too soon. She had an enormous drive that I have inherited. She had incredible energy. She was a dynamo. She was very slim and shorter than I. She was always having me pat my chin and watch my food and do exercises. She had extraordinary taste and style. She and her sister used to draw patterns for *McCall's*, which was very unusual. Given her set and her family and the atmosphere she grew up in, women simply didn't work. Her father allowed her to work only if they did it at home. Their younger brother used to deliver the drawings and collect the check and bring it back. They were never allowed to go to the office.

My mother could sew anything in the world, sew, crochet, create, whatever. She used to make all her own clothes and designs, for herself, for me, for my cousins. Her friends were all enormously jealous and one day they said, "I know there's something you can't make, an umbrella." Well, you know, she made an umbrella. That gives you an idea of the kind of style that she had, and the kind of energies she had.

My mother gave me certain tools that I hope I gave to my kids. The tools were knowledge on various levels, and style. She used to say, "I want you and your brother to be able to walk into a room anywhere in the world and feel comfortable and be able to cope," and that is exactly what she did for me. It never occurred to me, anywhere, that I couldn't cope, never. I have never been in a situation where I was put off before I even attempted it. I simply had enough self-belief, I felt comfortable enough with myself, that even if I walked into a room where people were discussing Proust—I would still know how to handle it. I might *not* have read Proust, but at least I'd understand the abstract of what they're talking about. Or if I didn't, I wouldn't feel inadequate about it. I'd listen and ask questions.

My family loved music and always lived with paintings. We read a great deal, we talked, we studied, we always went to museums, we always understood, we had that kind of education. It gives you an understanding of the next thing, it's like putting a puzzle together. I began to see things differently than most children do. That's what education should be on any level, it should be something that stimulates fantasy and excitement and gives you a feeling of opening up a world. It should be entertainment.

It breaks my heart to see what's happening with families. It breaks my heart to see kids joining communes because what they're really looking for is a family. You can't carry a family with you all the time in this moving, changing society, but you've got to give that to kids. The Catholics know what they're talking about. They say, "Give us the child for the first six years and we'll have him forever," because they have inculcated what they want. But you can inculcate that child with anything, with the love of human beings, with the love of life, with the love of beauty. I carry that right through into my work.

I'm really interested in making an impact on the largest number of people. I feel that the programs I did created an understanding about other parts of the world and other people of the world that made this a better place, made peace more possible. Now that's a big thing for one person to have the arrogance to say, but it was my doing and whatever other people did that fed into the situation that made it happen. It was what I did with Kennedy and Khrushchev through Pierre Salinger that made that film possible. That wasn't my motive. My motive was bringing people together through their history and their culture and their language and their music and their feeling for each other. I wanted to get there first and do it first, because I wanted to be able to show it as I saw it, unadulterated by everyone else's impression or opinion, or even expertise. That's ego, I guess. I have to do what I believe in. That's the only way I can have enthusiasm.

# Denise Scott Brown

*Denise Scott Brown (born 1931, 'NKana, Zambia) is an architect, urban planner, teacher and writer who has influenced both the practice and teaching of architecture with her insistence that social, economic, political and aesthetic concerns be viewed as a whole. In her role as urban planner, she has placed special emphasis on the importance of preserving our existing architectural heritage. As a partner in one of the world's leading architectural firms, Venturi, Rauch and Scott Brown, she has worked on many of the firm's pioneering revitalization projects including South Street, Philadelphia (1968); Jim Thorpe, Pennsylvania (1979); and Washington Avenue, Miami Beach (1979). She is the author, with her husband, Robert Venturi, and Steven Izenour, of the influential work on design,* Learning from Las Vegas *(1972).*

**W**HY WHEN PEOPLE INTERVIEW MY HUSBAND don't they ask him: What's the reason for your great passion for architecture? His passion for his work is taken for granted, but perhaps women who stick with it and struggle through need more passion than men because many women have an escape hatch, or they have had. They could marry a man and be supported while they raised children, although I don't believe that marriage and child-rearing are an escape hatch.

My husband knew when he was four years old that he was going to be an architect; I did too. At about five I knew I was going to be an architect because my mother had studied architecture. I thought that was women's work. I had a proprietary feeling about architecture. I could own it because my mother owned it. At six, I was going to be a teacher because I thought highly of my first-grade teacher, and at twelve, I wanted to study languages. At fourteen I wanted to write because I so enjoyed English classes; I've had a whole lot of interests. A few years ago I compared those early aspirations with the direction my career had actually taken and realized that I have, after a fashion, done all those things.

There are many ways to be an architect, but the way I've chosen is not the most usual one. Even now, I have a diffused and uncertain identity in my profession. I've chosen to be an architect with a second profession in urban planning. I'm an architect and a planner, or an architect-planner. To span these two fields, I must range from the social sciences and law through architecture, interior design and the arts. Within this broad field that I've assigned myself, I operate as a professional, an academic, a theoretician, a writer and an educator. It's very difficult for me to define my focus exactly, because I seem to specialize in the linkages.

I didn't exactly choose this career, it chose me. I just found myself doing it. I was born in Zambia in 1931. After two years, my parents moved to South Africa where my father was born. I grew up there and started my architectural training at sixteen at the University of the Witwatersrand in Johannesburg, a rigorous, practice-oriented South African school that stressed technical competence and good drafting. In my fourth year I traveled to London to work, as the school required, in an architectural office, intending to return to South Africa for my fifth and final year. I found myself a job in the office of Frederick Gibberd, a London architect. But I also took the entrance examination of the Architectural Association. Before I left South Africa, I had been fascinated by this school and its reputation for generating both hot air and architectural radicalism. When I was admitted, fate seemed to be pushing me to stay in London. I'd left a friend behind finishing architecture school in South Africa. I thought, How can I possibly leave him and home and everything? But there I was; it seemed too good an opportunity to miss.

In this way, at twenty, I left my home, family and country for good without actually realizing I had, but it dawned on me about a year later and I developed lots of confidence problems. An old professor, Arthur Korn, a Bauhaus refugee, rescued me. We would have coffee together once a week. I would talk about a "need for structure in my life" and he about the November group. When I averred that I could never teach because I was too afraid, he said, "You shouldn't even think of it in that way. You have been very lucky. You have been given a great deal, you have a duty to pass it on." I think this gave me the courage to begin. I finished my training in London and my friend, Robert Scott Brown, joined me. We worked together in England for a while, were married in 1955, traveled, worked and studied in Europe and Africa for the next three years and arrived in Philadelphia in 1958.

We came to America because our English training taught, and our European friends agreed, that all good architects should be concerned with what they called town planning (I would now call it architectural urbanism). There were no good schools of town planning in England at the time. The best were known to be in America. Also, Robert and I felt a strong affinity for the ideas of a group called the New Brutalists. The New Brutalist movement started when I was a student in England in the 1950s. We found the Brutalists' reassessment of current architecture, their critique of the Modern Movement of the thirties and forties and their search for social involvement through architecture—for an "active socio-plastics"—to be very sympathetic to our (perhaps African) view of architecture, just as we found ourselves at odds with the ways many other architects were thinking.

In England there was enormous scorn for American architects, but in the mid-fifties Young Brutalists at the Architectural Association found illustrations of a building that looked much like the work we were interested in doing. We'd never heard of the architect. He hadn't been published before although he was quite old. I mean, he was in his fifties. We were in our twenties. The difference seemed immeasurable.

The building was the Trenton Bath House and the architect was Louis I. Kahn. So Robert and I decided to try to study in America with Louis Kahn. We applied from South Africa to the University of Pennsylvania where Kahn was teaching. We could learn little about the school from the catalog tear sheets Penn sent us, but we gathered that we needed to send drawings to enter the architecture department but not the city planning department. We applied to city planning because there was no time to send drawings.

We arrived in Philadelphia in September 1958 during a heat wave. As an African, fearing the cold, I had come prepared in a fur coat and warm hat. My suffering from the American hot weather began that day. We slept on a friend's floor and looked for an apartment. Our faculty adviser, David Crane, broke the news to us that Louis Kahn taught in the architecture department, not in city planning, at Penn, but added, "You will learn many things that will interest you here and I'll help you to get the best out of Kahn as well."

During the first semester in planning school, we studied housing, economics, urban land economics, urban sociology and statistical analysis. Robert and I didn't know what had hit us, but went twirling around in a whirl of intellectual excitement. We didn't know how we could have lived our life till then without all that information.

In the late fifties, planning was beginning to reverberate, earlier than most fields, to the incipient civil rights movement. A course in urban sociology with Herbert Gans opened our eyes to issues of urban democracy, and to social questions in planning. His thought and that of other social scientists and activists at Penn contributed to the social planning movement that dominated urban planning in the sixties. Social planners were critical of the role architects had played in urbanism. They were, I believe, overcritical but their argument was challenging. They accused architect planners of being arrogantly insensitive to the needs of people different from themselves. They argued that Modern architecture's best urban ideas had been socially harmful in their execution in American cities.

I became deeply involved in the debate between architects and planners, fighting arduously on both sides. Since that time I have felt like a circus horse rider spanning two diverging horses and trying to bring them together. I usually operate at the nexus between architecture and planning. For example, in an article called "On Architectural Formalism: A Discourse for Radical Chic Architects and Social Planners," I try to show planners why they can't afford to ignore architects' aesthetic preferences, and architects why planners find them socially irresponsible. Fighting both sides, I try to find a middle position. This makes my own situation ambiguous. It's difficult for planners to think of me as other than an architect and for architects to think of me as other than a planner.

At the end of our first year at Penn, my husband, Robert Scott Brown, was killed in a motor accident. In a state of emotional eclipse, I went back and finished my second year because I couldn't think what else to do.

*Scott Brown*

313

Returning looked brave but actually I had no alternative. The place where my intellect and passion were—where his had been—was the right place to be. Carrying on our work was the right thing to do.

At the end of my training, I noticed there was a course in the department, an introduction to urban design for nonarchitects, that had no instructor. My adviser arranged my appointment, and there I was, twenty-eight and an instructor, teaching at the other end of the studio from where I'd been a student the semester before. Soon I began to teach, as well, a course on theories of city planning, architecture and landscape architecture, to architects. So I was teaching architects about urbanism and urbanists about architecture. At twenty-nine, I became an assistant professor. It was a pleasant, symmetrical existence and a good way to get through my years of sorrow. Teaching kept my heart involved.

I took to teaching like a duck to water. I felt as if it was something I'd been doing all my life and, as an oldest sister, perhaps it was. It helped to comfort and console me too. Obviously the students were substitutes for the family and children I didn't have, but, in that, they were lucky I think. My confidence as a teacher came from my belief in the importance of what had been taught me and from Arthur Korn's admonition that I should pass it on.

The art of getting into people's heads something that wasn't there before has always fascinated me. Architects, because they can do harm, must learn to be open-minded. As urban designers they must be especially sensitive to social questions. But many students of architecture don't want to read. They would rather draw; and they certainly don't want to read sociology. How boring! Many urban architects, who really need to be aware of the problems of people who live in cities, think that urban sociology is not pertinent to them. How do you teach them in such a way that they'll want to find out this information?

Teaching a group of architecture students is like pat-a-cake, the baby's game. I get a rhythm going and persuade the child to join in. At first she follows by eye and meets my hands with help, suddenly she catches the rhythm and can do it herself. Eventually she teaches someone else. One of my ways is to set students problems that they find challenging but that depend on the information for their solution. One such problem could be the design of housing for low-income families. In order to solve the problem—and they really want to solve it because it's something they feel strongly about—they have to know how poor families live and, in the end, they have to read about them. To solve their creative problem, they need information.

One semester I audited a course on theories of architecture taught by a young architect who was thought dull by some people (but not Lou Kahn) because he was really interested in history; he was the only instructor who would give the course. That was Robert Venturi. The next two years I ran the seminar and workshop for his course. The two of us had a great deal in common. We were both mavericks in some ways, though we eventually found others in the school, like us, who didn't exactly agree with what was going on: Paul Davidoff, the planner; Angelo Savelli, the painter; and Malcolm Campbell, the historian. We became good friends.

In his lectures, Bob would take an element of architecture, say lighting, and show how the need to light buildings was dealt with by different architectural generations with different attitudes—Gothic architects one way, Renaissance another, Mannerist a third and Modern yet another. In this course Bob considered the history of architecture as a practitioner rather than an academic. He compared historical buildings in a nonchronological way to help would-be architects develop their own designs and theories. This professionalizing of academic knowledge was very interesting to me. It paralleled my attempts to help urban designers use sociology creatively, but as urban designers not sociologists. At the end of each lecture, Bob added a footnote on his own theory of architecture and that part became the subject matter for his book *Complexity and Contradiction in Architecture.*

I left Penn in 1965 because I was not reappointed. When I discovered that colleagues of similar academic standing—and indeed my own newly graduated students—were earning more than I was, I left angry. I am a feminist mainly because of such experiences in my professional life. I had been invited to U.C. Berkeley as a visiting professor, so I took a long journey west, stopping to see several cities on the way. Shortly thereafter, Bob left Penn for Yale.

I went west because I was greatly interested in western urbanization in such cities as Los Angeles, Las Vegas and San Diego. At Penn in the fifties we were taught that Los Angeles was a form of urbanism we should understand if we were to comprehend cities in the twentieth century. At Penn, and then at Berkeley, developing that reasoning, I taught that there are forces in the city—economic forces, technological forces and social forces—that shape the physical form of the city much more than do the "programs" or "functions" that architects design for. Architects say form follows function; function should determine form. They used to say it. They say it less now. But forces also determine form. Economic forces are enormously strong in directing what kinds of buildings are built and determining where they're located. I taught several courses and studio projects that I called FFF—form, forces and functions—in which we tried to analyze how the structure of society is related to the form of the city.

After one semester I left Berkeley for UCLA to help start an architecture school. I was joint head of urban design, which was the first program to be set up in the School of Architecture. Although the dean had offered me tenure, once there, I had difficulty getting it. "Join the family as an assistant professor." Can you imagine them saying that to a man?

I retired to my beach cottage in Ocean Park and said, "I'm not coming to school until I get tenure, and I'm not taking any pay at the assistant professor level either and that's all right with me. I'm going to sit here and write my book. You seem to think I should have written my book because you keep saying that if I had written a book I'd have the tenure. Meanwhile I have experience in interdisciplinary education in architecture that you won't match anywhere. Your whole program is set up for interdisciplinary studio education and I am the person who can do it. There's almost no one else. I'm surprised to be associated with an institution that takes the maxim 'Publish or perish' seriously." They were horrified.

Finally, with some help from Berkeley, a settlement was negotiated. I would be an acting associate professor, which meant I would be paid at the level of an associate professor but would not have tenure. So I accepted that, and damn it if I didn't discover they nevertheless paid me as an assistant professor for the four months we spent arguing. From such experiences I learned that if I didn't fight for my rights no one else would. I became successively more bellicose.

I had a good time at UCLA setting up the interdisciplinary urban design program. With a generous budget for visitors, I invited various colleagues to teach my students. Among these was my old friend Bob Venturi. I assigned the students a four-day sketch problem, arranged for Bob to be a member of the jury of their designs, and invited him to visit Las Vegas with me while the students worked. We rode around from casino to casino. Dazed by the desert sun and dazzled by the signs, both loving and hating what we saw, we were jolted clear out of our aesthetic skins.

By the end of all that Bob and I were in love. But I was still trying to get my tenure so I was determined to say nothing about our intentions. When I finally got my tenure, I announced my engagement. This is typically what women are accused of doing, but I felt they deserved it. For my future career, I had to leave UCLA as an associate professor and I did. Bob and I had been dating for seven years and I had been a widow for eight years when we married in 1967.

I came back to Philadelphia and joined Bob's and John's firm, Venturi and Rauch, first in an unofficial way because they needed me. I had intended to write. I felt I'd already made my way in a man's world. There's a wonderful statement by an old Canadian feminist. She said, "For a woman to succeed in a man's field she has to work twice as hard and be twice as good," and then she added, "Luckily, this is not difficult." I had been on the faculties of three first-rate schools and, from years of attending faculty meetings, I knew that I was as bright as any of my colleagues. I felt I could see things very clearly in my field. This gave me the confidence to say, "O.K., I've done that. Now I'm going to have a family and I'm also going to write a lot."

Well, it didn't happen that way. We started to try to have a family and we couldn't. I had a miscarriage and then nothing after that. I got drawn into the emergencies of a small, high-endeavor, architectural office where we were constantly wondering where the next job was coming from. At the same time, Bob and I were teaching together at Yale. We ran three studio projects. Through these we developed ideas about architecture that we shared. One project involved a study trip to Las Vegas, a repetition of our earlier visit but with students. This resulted in our book *Learning from Las Vegas.* The title doesn't reveal the fact that it's a treatise on the symbolism of architectural form and a plea to architects to broaden their sights.

We finally gave up teaching in 1970 because running our kind of practice was difficult, even agonizing. It demanded our full attention. I became a partner in 1969. I was needed to help on all sorts of levels, and although we have grown considerably since then, the same holds true today. What is the work that I do in the office? Because we're still relatively small, we all do everything. I'm involved in architectural and planning projects; as a partner, I do my share of management and development; and I spend time, when I have it, trying to relate practice to theory. Although we no longer teach, this link is still important to us.

As architects we are neither "Modern" nor "Postmodern." Although some critics place us with the Postmodernists, I feel our difference with them lies in the debt we owe to urban planning theory and to the social sciences. We depend as well on art movements and historical sources, the traditional roots of architectural theory. Bob has a far deeper knowledge of architectural history than do most Postmodernist architects. My circus-horse-riding ensures that we take a much broader view than architects usually do, on social and cultural aspects of architecture. Both positions, and their combination, make our work significantly different from that of our colleagues.

Although my span in one work day may be from the design of a teapot to the economics of a region, my particular responsibility is for urban planning and design. Since the late sixties, we have worked on small but difficult urban projects that combine 1960s requirements for social planning, democratic processes, incrementalism and pragmatism with 1970s concerns for preservation and economic viability. In small towns or urban neighborhoods, social, economic and physical problems often occur against a backdrop of once splendid or admirable architecture. We try to plan in a nurturing way to help existing occupants make economic reuse of this architectural heritage that surrounds them.

One project was for The Strand in Galveston, Texas. This old warehouse street was literally standing high and dry because the docks had moved and the warehouses had no use. We tried to plan new economic uses by following trends that were already emerging. Most of our planning has to do with seeing what's happening and helping it happen better. It's often necessary to help a small town find a new regional identity for its main street, which was once a local sales center but will never be again because the suburban malls have killed it. If the street is beautiful and historic, people from the whole region may be drawn to it to buy unusual things that you won't find in a regional shopping mall.

Our projects have been in widely different places, including Jim Thorpe, Pennsylvania; Washington Avenue, Miami Beach; Old City, Philadelphia; and Princeton, New Jersey. Each problem is different and calls for different combinations of skills and approaches. Towns that have

**317**

chosen us have probably done so for two reasons: our pragmatic approach to urbanism and our ability to get the townspeople involved. We help the local government set up a steering committee to meet and discuss with us and to talk to their constituencies about the issues so that when we hold the public meetings the public is prepared. The first public presentation tells people the findings of our survey work. At the next meeting we point out what the alternatives for development are, because it's going to be up to them to choose. We don't say, "This is the plan you should have."

We usually work with small merchants who are scared of the future and of our involvement in their business, with residents and with politicians. There's never enough money to do the work that should be done. We have to remind everybody that "rehabilitation" in their case means merchants repainting their own stores, not tearing the whole place down and building a new town.

We feel that these very real problems of small communities call for the designer's greatest imagination. How do you help an old building look mellow but not dilapidated? One way is to repaint wood trim and storefronts with dark, warm colors that tone in with the old brickwork, rather than with white paint that shows up old faults and quite soon turns yellow or gray. Also, we don't recommend "Colonializing" or "Victorianizing" Main Street, because that in itself removes part of its history. Neon signs, Art Deco storefronts and a Sunoco gas station can remain on Jim Thorpe's High Victorian Main Street, because they don't overwhelm it and they add vitality. A larger Victorian identity for the town should be achieved by reestablishing its historic link to the river and canal that formed it.

In this work there are poignant contrasts between the broad, regional, interdisciplinary vision needed to understand the problem and the constraints and limited means available for improving a single street or a few city blocks. These contrasts I find very challenging. I love the opportunity to bring all our skills to bear on one small town. Analyzing, designing, discussing and arguing, we help to get the town moving. Then we must make the physical result beautiful. The beauty that emerges from all our joint efforts may be an agonized one. Some people consider Main Street vitality to be ugly. But it can also be beautiful, with the beauty that arises from meeting hard reality.

As a planner, the vision of the world I'd like to be part of creating is pragmatic, not utopian. By understanding the forces that are shaping, or misshaping, the town or city, I hope to help its citizens use these forces to get where they want to go. This requires careful analysis and imaginative design, but it's also a teaching process, because eventually we leave town and the plan will be implemented without us, or it will be shelved.

My involvement in architecture decreases when we have planning projects. That's a pity because the part of my professional work that ends in something physical is valuable to me. If I really feel starved for designing, I start buying clothes, sometimes I buy old clothes. A while ago

I went to the Bryn Mawr Hospital thrift shop and bought two linen hand towels for three dollars. I took them to a friend, a feminist dressmaker, and she and I designed a linen jacket. We used the tatting from the towels to edge the cuffs and the front. We had such fun. I bought a skirt, too, at the Bryn Mawr thrift shop. I've learned to try the size 16s because they are usually old women's clothes, they're of good quality and they're long enough for today. I found a three-piece suit, Scottish tweed. The coat and jacket had huge, padded shoulders. The whole thing cost three dollars. I gave them back the coat and they thanked me for the donation. I tried to give them back the jacket because I knew I would have to spend a hundred dollars to have a tailor fix it. But they wouldn't take it. Therefore, I got the skirt for three dollars. The tailor fixed it for me for thirty-five dollars, so I had a beautiful Scottish tweed skirt for thirty-eight dollars. When I found a dry cleaning tag on it marked "McBride," I realized I had bought the suit of Miss McBride, the former president of Bryn Mawr College. Her three-piece tweed suits were a famous part of her identity. Mine felt like an inheritance.

In architectural design, I particularly enjoy helping to evolve what architects call the *parti,* the point of departure, of a project, basically how it should be organized. Take, for example, our firm's design for Franklin Court, Benjamin Franklin's Philadelphia home, and the houses on Market Street that he rented for income. A big red door off Market Street opened on to a passageway to the back of the lot where Franklin's house once stood. There are no records of what his house looked like.

When we were hired by the National Park Service to design a museum to Franklin on the site of his house, I suggested putting the museum underground. The exhibits didn't need daylight, and this would save ground level space for an urban park. As a planner I felt that the office workers in the dense city blocks surrounding the site would love to eat their sandwiches in a garden and that other people could wander around it or take shortcuts through it. So we reproduced Franklin's garden with modifications for public use and etched out the plan of the house in slate and marble on the ground. Then we added a beautiful "ghost" structure to suggest the frame of Franklin's house. That was Bob's idea. It was a very creative thing to have done and people love this place. It has become famous. But no one has ever noticed that I suggested the *parti.*

When we found I could not conceive, we adopted a child. I was forty. I'm now forty-nine. It's both challenging and fascinating to work in a profession and bring up a child at the same time. During my widowhood, I found my professional feet. If I hadn't worked intensively in my field for those eight years, if I'd had a child before I did, then I wouldn't have established myself professionally. Now I must put my passion into two roles—architect/planner and wife/mother. There's time for little else. Bob and I have almost no social life. We lead a guilt-ridden social existence, miss the conviviality of our friends and sorrow that we can't even answer Christmas cards.

Jimmie was six days old when we got him. Mrs. Molly Leopold, our housekeeper, arrived from Trinidad the day after Jimmie was born. I thought, "This is ridiculous, having a maid. It's a luxury." How I thought I was going to manage my career and Jimmie without help, I don't know.

Jimmie really has a third parent in Molly, and this is wonderful for him and both wonderful and hard for me. I didn't know the kind of agony I would go through, of jealousy and worry. Is he my child or Molly's child? The first word he learned to say was "Molly," and Jimmie first talked with a Trinidad accent. When he was three years old, he loved animals but asked permission to pet them by saying, "Do he bite?"

I began asking my friends. "Did you have this experience?" I particularly asked people who had grown up in cultures where there were children's nannies. I once asked a very well-known Latin-American psychiatrist, at dinner at a friend's house, "If you cut your knee, who did you go running to, your mother or your nanny?" His wife replied, "No, you don't understand. If he fell and cut his knee, seven women came running." I've settled it in my mind.

Jimmie is now nine. When we get home at night, we are grateful for a lovely supper made by Molly, and in general Molly will do what I want with Jimmie. Every now and then she will collude with Jimmie—"Don't tell your Mommy"—but I think we can keep that in manageable proportions.

I don't like the nuclear family, living in the suburbs, where Mommy stays home, Daddy goes to work and no one knows what Daddy does. We have, in a way, made an extended family around us, although Bob has few relatives here and I have none. In addition to Molly, architecture students, at the moment two, live with us, helping to restore our house and working on the yard. They become good friends to Jimmie as well as to us. Also Molly entertains her friends and we have a steady stream of out-of-town architects and relatives in the guest room.

Our house has been an odyssey for us, it's an Art Nouveau house that we are working to restore. It's emotionally very important to all of us, including Jimmie. During the Three Mile Island scare we thought of sending Jimmie to friends in Cambridge. He said, "We're not selling the house, are we?"

My mode of mothering is very much related to my mode of teaching. We say Jimmie is better than a graduate student because I went from teaching graduate students to this little man. I just love the challenge of working with him and thank God he's got a mind that's much like ours. He has a way with words. I love words and playing around with them and he does too, so does Bob. He has a great sense of humor and he's extremely interested in things mechanical, which neither Bob nor I are. So that's his identity in the family.

Jimmie identifies with the office, he calls it "our office" because he goes there a lot. He can always call us at the office. He knows that. He knows where everyone sits and where the phones are. He identifies with our professional life and I like that. We once drove by an unusual structure on Independence Mall. It was a big tent, made of canvas and guyed to form strange shapes. Jimmie said, "Do we like that, Daddy?" Bob and I, together, pointed out that he didn't have to have the same opinions as we had. But it was a lovely statement of identification.

Being too tired to play or work with Jimmie when we get home is one of our problems. He goes to bed late so he can be with us at night. We try to have the strength to read with him and watch over his homework. Sometimes I just can't. Luckily there are two of us. If I can't, Bob can. When we're too tired to do anything except lie on our bed at night, Jimmie sets up his train over the bedroom floor so he can at least be with us.

He's a difficult little demon and he's also a wonderful little angel. He's extended me. Through him, I've learned so much about myself and I've recovered pieces of myself I had ceased to know, pieces to do with my childhood that came back when I had a child around. Strange things, like songs coming back to me that I didn't remember at all, suddenly I found myself singing them.

He is also a huge slice out of my life. A while ago I was to speak at a conference in Paris. Suddenly and unexpectedly, Jimmie had to change schools. Staying home for him didn't feel like a sacrifice. I was doing what I wanted to do. We found a school, Jimmie started, it all went very well, and a few months later I flew to Zurich to give two lectures. Jimmie was a bit mad that I was away for nine days but he could certainly understand it. So I have to move over somewhat in my life for Jimmie but in general, I'm happy to do it.

The saying "Woman's work is never done" is true for me. In my professional life I can never get through all my papers. And I never get to do all the things I have to do around the house. My long-term aim now is to do some more writing. Sometimes Bob and I go away for ten days to write first drafts of articles. Then I can find the time to edit my manuscript and check galley proofs while I'm working in the office. On the other hand, Jimmie's great need for me is not going to be forever and I'm going to miss it one day, so now is the time to be a full part of his life.

Living in another culture from the one I spent my childhood in provokes a great sense of discontinuity, more than I ever thought, but having a child here helps tie me in. Jimmie is from Philadelphia and although he's only nine, he's got his coordinates in this city in a way that I will never have. But I have much more now that he's around. I feel more like a Philadelphian than I did without him.

I also retrogress happily to the children's shelves in the bookshop. I particularly enjoy buying old books for children. These books make their way into our office, and suddenly our perspective drawings show the influence of illustrations in 1910s and 1920s children's books. I think there's a nurturing outlook on architecture in our office, more than in most offices. It goes beyond having our kids here and learning from children's books. As architects, we have a strong feeling for context. We try to relate our buildings closely to their physical and also cultural contexts, siting and designing them to reveal the spirit of the place they are in, the *genius loci*. This is very creative nurturing, I think.

Also our office itself is a nurturing place. Venturi, Rauch and Scott

Brown, our name since January 1980, has about twenty-five people in all. We occupy the top two floors of an old warehouse that sits between Main Street and the canal in Manayunk, an early industrial town on the Schuylkill River and now part of Philadelphia. In addition to the partners, Bob, John Rauch and I, we have four senior associates, about a dozen architects and about six administrative people.

Most of the architects who work for us have been our students or students of our students. Everyone cares deeply about architecture and cares in the same way; all are willing to work long and hard to make a beautiful building. I think this is the key to our collaboration. Otherwise, as with every group of talented, motivated and energetic people, we could become a psychodynamic hotbed. The generosity of our associates and their identification with our aims are precious to us and make it possible to have the kind of firm we want and do the work we want. I think this too is unusual. Our employees are happy that we include their names on the attributions lists for projects they worked on. In some offices, they don't like the product sufficiently to care.

It's hard on all these people that the architectural star system operates to define the product of our firm as the work of one designer. It's difficult being an architect. Architecture is a strange profession. It's very, very macho, it's very upper class, even though it no longer wants to be. In architecture, status can be achieved only through design ability. You need talent for design and talent is not altogether definable. Because architects set such store by design and because you can't get there by measurable means—it's related to a creative process where things "just happen"—this makes designing extremely difficult for architects. Here's a parallel: Before we had navigation instruments, sailors put beautiful women on the prows of their ships and got over the water by magic. Architects, too, feel the need for magic when they confront important but intangible aspects of their work as designers. Then the temptation is great to find yourself a guru and steer your course by his magic.

Gurus have to be male because most architects are male. Also, architectural historians and critics need to crown kings to make their own careers. Can you imagine a macho architectural critic crowning a woman king? Can you imagine crowning a mom and pop king? It's not good for business. Therefore you won't hear much about me as an architect in the profession. It's Bob Venturi and then there's this woman horning in. Among architects, I am thought of as an urban planner, not an architect, and as an abrasive woman who pushes herself in where she doesn't belong. I am also considered an impediment by architectural critics wanting to establish a rapport with Bob. It's a very strange situation. It can be vicious. It means that about 100 percent of the time, in print, my work is attributed to Bob.

Just recently, *Progressive Architecture* did a teeny little paragraph on one of my projects. It labeled me a planner, leaving out my architectural career, and captioned the illustration "Venturi's Plan." This makes life hard for both Bob and me and it obscures my professional identity. It makes me angry and then I'm not always as controlled as I should be. For example, in an interview two years ago for an article in the *Philadelphia Sunday Inquirer* I asked the interviewer, "Are you going to be fair?" This angered him. He said in the article, Denise Scott Brown's "disposition suggests to the wary journalist the possibility of flying objects"; in other words, she'll easily throw a book at you. Perhaps he thought he was fair because he mentioned my attribution problem; but he depicted me as a virago and he didn't mention my work.

If architecture critics really respected me and understood my situation, they would turn away from the problem even if it makes good copy and help to solve it by acknowledging my work. In the end, the recognition of her work is the respect that should be shown a worker.

# Barbara Walters

*Barbara Walters (born Brookline, Massachusetts) is a television reporter, interviewer, writer, correspondent and producer whose reports of the day's events, and interviews with world leaders and celebrities have made history. After a fifteen-year career as a writer and later cohost of NBC's The Today Show, she became the first woman to anchor an evening network newscast in 1976. Her million-dollar-a-year contract with ABC News was the first of its kind for a woman and marked a turning point in acknowledging the valuable role women can play in the television news media.*

I'M NOT CERTAIN THAT one person's experience is necessarily of any real help to another, but let me try to think back over the years and see what I can come up with.

1. A job is not a career. I think I started out with a job. It turned into a career and changed my life. A career means long hours, travel, frustration and plain hard work and finally perhaps a realization that you can't have it all.

2. The *desire* to work is not the same as the *need* to work. During the beginning years of my "career," I had to support myself and so had to put up with jobs that were often tedious as well as demanding. I hung in there. Most men realize to get the big job, they often have to just hang in there, and do the grubby ones. Many women, especially those who do not have to work, do not know this.

3. No matter what the advances the women's movement has made, it is still very hard to work full time and have a child or children. You must want the child and the career very badly. In my opinion, and of course I can only speak for myself, neither replaces the other.

4. To feel valued, to know, even if only once in a while, that you can do a job well is an absolutely marvelous feeling.

5. To know you can support yourself is vital. Vital!

6. To sacrifice friends, love and a view of the sunset, no matter how occasional, all for a career simply isn't worth it.

7. To make it all come together somehow, sometimes, is what it's all about.

I'm still trying, still juggling, but I'm getting there.

# Betty Friedan

*Betty Friedan (born 1921, Peoria, Illinois) launched the contemporary women's liberation movement when her book* The Feminine Mystique, *published in 1963, exploded the fifties myth of the happy homemaker. As a writer, lecturer, organizer, she is the ideologue of a movement which in a few short years has changed attitudes and behavior at all levels of society. She was one of the founders of the National Organization for Women and became its first president in 1966.*

WELL, THEY SAY THE WOMEN'S MOVEMENT is the largest movement of social change of the last decades and in some ways it's probably the largest revolution of all time, though it isn't what anyone else has ever meant by revolution. You have to see it in its own terms. I think we're only beginning to see the far-flung implications of the change. Also I think the women's movement is only a step in a larger process of evolution, that it's a stage. It's been happening for a long time.

There was the great first movement for women's rights beginning with Mary Wollstonecraft, and the early suffragettes in England and America who fought for the vote, and the early rights; but that movement came to a standstill with the winning of the vote in the United States in 1920, before I was born. It didn't change the lives of women because the rights, while necessary, didn't lead to the kind of changes that are happening now. The movement was aborted, or it was asleep. There was a backlash which I then gave a name to: the "feminine mystique."

We had to break through the whole image of woman and we had to define ourselves as people; and then we had to begin a process that's still not finished, of restructuring institutions so that women could be people. The essence of the modern woman's movement is equality and the personhood of woman. That's what it is and that's all it is. All the rest of it—all the images of women's lib, the bra-burning, the man-hating, down with marriage, down with motherhood—was an expression of anger based on an ideological mistake. It is not essential. It is not a part of the whole change. The anger was real enough, but sexual politics was not what it was really all about.

The essence of what's been happening and the reason it began, as history books say, with my book *The Feminine Mystique*, was that women had come to a real jumping-off point in their identity. For generations, for centuries, women had been defined primarily in terms of their childbearing role. That was their function in society. It wasn't a mystique. They were passive to their biological destiny. The modern woman's movement did not begin because I or any other witch of Salem somehow seduced the otherwise happy housewives who'd still be having orgasms waxing the kitchen floor if we hadn't come along. It was an evolutionary necessity that came from the long years of life.

Women's life-span is now close to eighty years and women do not die in childbearing years; babies that are born are going to survive and not so many babies need to be born. We've raised the stage of technological development so that we can think of the quality of life, each individual life, not the quantity; so that we do have birth control which is technically, morally and legally a choice, and work that doesn't depend any longer on brute mastery or strength where women might not be equal to men, but depends increasingly on qualities of mind and spirit where men and women are basically equal in their potential. Then there are those particular intuitions in which women excel and which a machine may never reproduce.

So equality in society was possible perhaps for the first time for the great majority of women; but it was also necessary for a woman to move in society, to define herself as a person because she couldn't live her whole life any longer as a mother. It's as simple as that. In order to do that, she had to break through in consciousness to this definition of herself which, though it's ingrained in the Judeo-Christian tradition, had its last gasp in the post-World War II "feminine mystique."

As I defined it, the mystique defined woman solely in terms of her sexual relation as wife, mother, housewife, server of physical needs, but not as a person defining herself by her own actions in society. Until we had broken through that, we couldn't really see what our real problems or real opportunities were in this era. And once we had done that, the revolution in consciousness and the rest was clearly outlined.

It isn't accidental that the modern women's movement exploded in America because the ideology of the mainstream of the movement is first of all that women are people; and being people, they can and must demand equality of opportunity and their own voice in the decisions of society, human freedom, human dignity, all the rest that is considered our American birthright. And that's all it was. Everybody had such a hard time thinking this was a movement without an ideology, but the ideology of this movement was no more or no less than the ideology of all human revolution and of American democracy, but applied to women. That's what was unique, and it was applied to us. We did it for ourselves and not abstractly—grocery baskets to the poor for some other race.

All revolutionary movements have been made by intellectuals, the educated. It's nonsense to fool around with any silliness about whether or not the modern women's movement was a white, middle-class movement. Absolutely. It was a white, middle-class movement from the beginning, though it always had blacks in it and it always had to do with the problem of poverty, which for women cuts across class lines. The people who could articulate the philosophy of this movement were people who had education, although for some, the education had come in the labor movement and not in college. That's how movements happen.

The movement was informed a bit—our tactics, our strategy—by the

fact that it came on the heels of the civil rights movement. But the
uniqueness of this movement comes from women's own experience. It is
because we did it for ourselves, and its style and its tactics, its substance,
had to do with the concrete dailiness of life as it is lived; life in the
kitchen, the bedroom, the house and the office, and not with abstractions.
That's why it changed lives so fast. It came, it dealt with life; it was not
abstract, it was concrete.

Now you say, I am a person; woman is a person; we take ourselves
seriously. We must define ourselves, we are forced to, economically,
socially. In order to use our human energy to confront a moving society
and do its work, we must demand equal opportunity. That was the
agenda. I wrote the statement of purpose for the National Organization
for Women in 1966. The first sentence of it was: "Full equality for women
and full equal partnership with men. Take action to break through the
barriers that keep women from participating in the mainstream of
society."

It meant, first of all, breaking through sex discrimination as it was, not
only in the law, but in every field and profession in what was, at that
point, a man's world. We could see even then, or we saw it more clearly
as we went along, that it also had to mean a change, a very basic change
in marriage and in the home, which had been defined as the woman's
world. Equality for women in society had to mean, not an abolition of the
family and the home, and not "down with men."

Now the ideological mistake that crept in and really endangered the
women's movement for a while was when the anger exploded. Women
had a right to feel anger. You had a right to feel angry if you were pushed
down in the office or you were making half the pay the men were getting
in the same job, or you were keeping a patient alive as a nurse and
teaching three generations of surgeons how to do it, but you didn't have
his pay or his status. You had a right to feel angry if you were put down
on the pedestal, even in the home. But like all dependent people, the anger
was taken out on our own bodies, in self-contempt, self-hatred, self-
denigration, and it was taken out inadvertently on husbands and children.
It could feel for a while as if man was the enemy. Actually, man was the
fellow victim, although the way society was geared, the man had more
power. He had the only game in town that seemed to be rewarded.

The younger women who came out of the postwar baby boom and the
radical student movement of the sixties had cut their political eye teeth
on Marxist class analysis applied to the problems of race. Then they
began to be informed by our consciousness, the consciousness of the
people who started the modern women's movement, myself and others.

I remember at Berkeley, I tried to get the young radical women
interested in this. I went down to Atlanta and tried to get the SNCC
women and get black women organizing in the South and they said,
"We're not going to fall for that feminist bag." The position of women in
SNCC was supposed to be prone, barefoot and pregnant.

But when the young radical women did begin to become affected by things like the feminine mystique, they began to realize their own situations, you know, chicks at the mimeograph machine. The young men were just as much male chauvinist pigs as their fathers. Also it was the time that blacks were saying, "Whitey go away," and "Black is beautiful," and "separatism." The women began to make their allusions to women's liberation and they were laughed at. They walked out and started their own separate women's lib groups.

So these younger women, without very much experience in women's lives, began to apply literally the ideology of class warfare and of racial separatism to their situation of women versus men. Their terminology, and that articulated by the extremists of sexual politics, was picked up way beyond its importance by the media. This is a battle of women as an oppressed class against men as the oppressor class. Down with marriage, down with men, down with motherhood, down with sexual relations with men, down with anything that women ever did that was attractive to men. Man was the enemy. They made a whole ideology of that.

The anger was real enough but the ideology was simply a mistake. The situation between women and men is not the same as between worker and boss, it's not the same as between black and white. Sexual politics demanded that women even repudiate the sexual connection with men so that lesbianism was supposed to be the way to be, the purist form of political statement. It was too literal an analogy, and simply denied and defied actual human biological, sexual, even economic interconnection and interdependence of women and men and human reality.

Of course it was totally wrong politically and we're still paying the price for it. It would have alienated the great majority of women, who could hardly be asked to give up sex. They may have been defined too much in terms of love and marriage so that became soured for many, but most women in this society still want to marry and most do.

Women had to get to a definition of people beyond motherhood. To define them solely as mothers was making motherhood into a martyrdom, and yet motherhood is a reality for most women. Motherhood is a choice now, but most women still, I think, will continue to choose to be mothers, although maybe later in their lives than before. Those are the realities.

All this was denied by the sexual politics. It was an ideological mistake and it was also a trivialization of the gut, the essence, of the women's movement. However, even this extremist stuff articulated the anger which most women felt.

The women's movement got so large, it had so much grass roots autonomy, cutting across generations, class, economics, taking hold in the suburbs, small towns, cities, all across the country, that this movement was too big really to be contained even in any one organization. Women who never went near a consciousness-raising group or never were near a NOW chapter, identified and maybe changed their lives. It did that.

There's no question today that women feel differently about themselves than they did twenty years ago, fifty years ago. For the most part, it's been great for women to take themselves seriously as people, to

feel some self-respect as people, to feel that they do have some equality
even though we know it hasn't been completely achieved; to feel some
control over their lives, some ability to act, not just to have to wait
passively, some ability even to express their anger when they feel it. It has
given women a whole new sense of being alive. We're only beginning to
know what we're capable of.

Frankly, I think it is leading toward much better possibilities even of
sexual fulfillment for women. I do not believe that masochism is the
norm. If a woman can define herself as subject and not just object, we'll
begin to see what true sexual liberation can be for a woman. I think that
you'll have much better motherhood when she isn't so much of a martyr
to it. We're just beginning to see these things.

O.K., over the last ten, fifteen years, we have seen the breakthrough of
the women's movement which by now, in its basic sense, includes the
majority of women, and includes not only the feminist organizations like
NOW and WEAL and the others, and whatever remains of the radical
feminists, but includes the mainstream organizations. The alliance for the
Equal Rights Amendment has everybody in it from the League of Women
Voters to the Girl Scouts and the Association of Catholic Nuns, the
National Council of Churches. There has been a breakthrough in sex
discrimination in employment. Women are now in every possible
occupation. Women have become a political force. They run for office,
they are getting elected, they vote their issues on the political agenda.

Now of course there are literally millions of women living in these
terms. It's all changed terribly fast. Political scientists say that there has
never been such a change in attitudes and behavior over such a wide
stratum of society in such a few short years. But I don't think it's finished
yet. I think that the first stage has crested with the breakthrough to
woman as a person and that simple breakthrough against sex
discrimination. Now we're beginning to see, however, that the first stage
is only part of it and we have to turn a corner, a qualitative corner, to the
next stage, the second stage of the feminist movement.

We're beginning to have some new ideas about what equality really
means. It's pretty clear it cannot mean just a few women getting the jobs
that only men had before, or somehow women changing places with the
men. It has to mean a lot more than that. One of our first thrusts was for
equal opportunity in employment; we knew the equal pay for equal work
didn't do the job because so many women didn't even get a chance at
those jobs. But now we realize that most women working outside the
home are still doing the traditional work that women have done and
although this is necessary work in the society, it's not paid what it's worth
because women have been doing it. So now we see that equality really
has to mean equal pay for work of comparable value.

The goal of the next stage has got to be to make equality livable and
workable. That means that there has to be a restructuring of institutions.
Not the abolition of the home and the family. That is not what this means.
But there's got to be a restructuring of the home and the family because

it's not any longer based on the woman as the subservient, unequal housewife. Both in the couple are earning, both should have options to take leaves, or go to part-time schedules, when children are little so the woman is no longer the automatic, unpaid server in the home. But the home is still there and needs to be taken care of. Now that means not only a whole new approach to parenting, but new kinds of designs of houses, apartments, communities, new services, new appliances, a restructuring of work; because work in all the professions, all the hours of internships and residencies, is structured in terms of men and men's lives at a time when they had wives to take care of all the concrete details of life.

What we need are a whole set of options in child care, not just government funding, but preschool, after-school, in the home, funded or sponsored by unions, by industries, for profit, not for profit. Combinations of public funding, private funding, tax incentives for business to have child-care programs, tax credit for each child, whatever plans would enable one parent to stay home for a few years to concentrate on the child and be compensated for that financially, or having it to spend on child care, or take tax credit for it, plus a sliding scale with ability to pay.

We're not going to get the restructuring, the flexitime and all the rest in terms of women alone. We don't have the power to get it. You'll have men with new demands for it too. Men in their young years are going to be expected increasingly to share the parenting and the family responsibility. You're beginning to see men rebel, the quieter value revolution. They'll say, "I'm not going to live in terms of the rat race alone. I'm not going to live in terms of a definition of masculinity that makes me suppress my feelings and defines me as just an instrument, as a breadwinner, and makes me have strokes and heart attacks at age forty-five." You're seeing evidence of this all over the place. So you find that young men, and older men too, have some interest in flexitime where they won't be defined solely by the linear job career. This change coincides with changes in technology and those brought about by the energy crisis.

The changes that men are going to make are less simple because they won't come from anger. They don't have the same simple reason for anger that the women did. But if we don't move onto the second stage, we could get aborted just like the first wave of feminism. I don't think that the women's movement as such is going to be the main vehicle for the next stage of change. It may be, of necessity, still too much locked into the first agenda which isn't complete yet. We have to get the Equal Rights Amendment passed. But there are also too many women who've taken leadership in the women's movement who are still in a phase of reaction. It makes them uneasy when I talk about the family.

Young women today are showing a lot more signs of stress because they have to make decisions they never had to make before. It used to be that a young woman only had to get married. She had to find a man who would take care of her for the rest of her life. Now she has to decide, What am I going to do professionally? She still has the question of marriage and the choice of having children. With a 40 percent divorce rate, which may have affected their mothers or people they know, more and more women know in their gut that they can't look to marriage for their security. They've got to be able to earn; take care of themselves.

Also, they've been given a chance to do some work that is relatively rewarding, to go into the professions. How are they going to combine this with motherhood? They're afraid to have kids. They postpone this choice or they say, I don't want to have kids, or they have agonizing conflicts about it. You're finding women today who are living this dilemma. They don't have a free choice, a good choice yet, because to have both a career and children they have to be superwomen.

If too many women make these judgments—against marriage, against motherhood—and they look for their security and fulfillment in careers, they're going to wake up ten years from now lonely, feeling cheated, and women are going to learn what men have always known, that work is work, not play. There's a lot of drudgery to it, and there's some reward in it, but it's not all that good for men when they live for work alone. So the woman who has the strength to say no to that, plus the man who can say no to that, they will be the force for the next stage of change.

To abolish the family is not the answer. We have to come to terms with the family. There's a whole evolution of the family, no longer based on women as housewives, no longer even based on children. People need the family or its equivalent. It will take new shape. The next stage, the restructuring of work, the restructuring of family, the values revolution, will be carried out by women and men in some new alliance. And the ideology of American democracy will still be the ideology of the second stage—life, liberty and the pursuit of happiness. I don't see anything in the ideology of America that doesn't lead to this. I think that we are on the front edge of society here.

In the last year that I've been talking in these terms, I feel that young women feel a great relief. You see it would be terrible if we defined ourselves in such narrow ways that these impulses, which are very powerful in women, are denied because feminism tells them that somehow they're going to have to fulfill themselves, as opposed to having children or as opposed to marriage.

In this era of fast change in society, I think we will see an increasing value put on commitment, on long-term intimacy. We will realize its value so that "swinging" or "open marriage"—some of the things that happened as people were breaking out of a repressive sexuality and marriage—we'll look back on as cheap epiphenomena. It isn't the major thrust of the future. People want intimacy, they really do. They want structure in their lives; they want stability; they want family or the equivalent. On the other hand, it's got to be involved with reality, sharing in a new way the economic burdens, sharing in a new way the home and the family and the child-rearing or interests beyond it.

Of course it all begins with personal truths. That's what I keep cautioning. It begins with life, comes from life, and has to come back to life. I didn't know I was angry when I wrote *The Feminine Mystique*. I had no ideology for anger. It was much later, when I was living the life of the feminine mystique, that I realized that the image I called "the feminine mystique"—and was even celebrating in the articles I was writing for women's magazines—didn't explain certain things I was beginning to hear from other women, what I called the problem that has no name. That's when I wrote my new book.

How I was able to figure that out, came from everything that ever happened to me in my life, beginning with my very good education which I had never used adequately. I went to Smith College and I graduated summa cum laude in psychology. I got a psychology fellowship at Berkeley and then I won the biggest science fellowship that's given to go straight through to my Ph.D. It was the beginning of World War II and all the men were going to war. I was going out with a guy who said, "Well I'll never win a scholarship like that. It's all over." So I didn't take the fellowship. Somehow I thought if I took it I'd be a spinster. It was ridiculous, but that was the image.

I came to New York and I got a job on a newspaper. I got married—it wasn't the same guy—and when I got pregnant with my second child, they fired me. I was indignant, but I couldn't take it to the Newspaper Guild because there was no word for sex discrimination. Our contract provided for maternity leave and I got it the first time I was pregnant, but my leaving disrupted everything in the office, it cut down the staff. So the second time, they fired me.

After World War II, the career woman was an unattractive thing to be. Women would be fulfilled as housewives if only their education didn't make them neurotic, and unable to adjust to their role as women. I decided I was going to be a fulfilled woman, a mother and wife. Then I saw that it wasn't the education that made women neurotic. There was something wrong with the role as it was defined.

The shores are strewn with the casualties of the feminine mystique. They did give up their own education to put their husbands through college, and then, maybe against their own wishes, ten or fifteen years later, they were left in the lurch by divorce. The strongest were able to cope more or less well, but it wasn't that easy for a woman of forty-five or fifty to move ahead in a profession and make a new life for herself and her children or herself alone. Others succumbed to alcoholism and suicide. I think of the women that were young housewives with me, mothers with me, my social group then. One was a suicide, one was a near-suicide, one is dead of alcoholism. One, who made a very extreme feminine mystique move away from her career, was able to get back in.

And I have my scars. I haven't married again. I've been divorced ten years; I'm lonely at times, and I think I would like to get married again. But I haven't and I haven't probably for two reasons. One is, no matter what I think, I think probably there is a fear in me. It was very hard for me to get out of my marriage. My marriage was very destructive. It was much easier for me to go "Rah! Rah!" with the movement than it was to change my own life personally. I may still have a fear that I would get myself back into a terrible situation. And secondly, I have put myself into the situation somehow, willy-nilly, of being the Joan of Arc of the women's movement. That's a little threatening for a man. So in that sense I've paid some price, I suppose, for what I've done.

On the other hand, I've had a good and rich life, not just my public life which has been exciting. It's exciting to have been a part of all this and to have had a role in it. My frivolous life has been fun too. Feminism should not be all grim. And my three kids are great. Who knows? They may think I would have been a better mother if it hadn't been for the women's movement, but I don't think so. The way that you can have children now, when you've already started on your work and know what you can do, you are not subject to the guilts that women in my generation were. That was the worst, the guilts, the conflicts, the leaning over backwards against them. That put negative valences on one's own enjoyment of motherhood. It's such a short period. I wish that in the period when they were little, I wish I'd felt free to concentrate on them more. But when you're under the aegis of the feminine mystique, there was the rebellion; and then to do anything at all, you're going against the stream of society and you have your own guilts about what you're doing.

I learned as a psychologist and as a reporter, first, to really get the story, and second, to really look at your own experience and other people's experience; not through the narrow rubrics, not canned, look afresh, to spell your own name, to test it with experience, and if it doesn't fit the image, the image is wrong. You're never finished.

Today I see the same contradiction, in a way, between what almost becomes "the feminine mystique" if we get locked into the reaction, the sexual politics of the women's movement and the reality of women's lives, including my own. Don't forget that my own agony that led me to write *The Feminine Mystique* had to do with the mistaken choice: either/ or. When I see us heading toward it again, when I see us denying the basic needs of women that do have to do with love and men and children, it denies a part of me, it denies a part of my personhood and what I am as a woman. I will not deny all that I am.

"It changed my life." That's what women say about the women's movement, "It changed my life, it changed my whole life." When they said it in the beginning, they meant the book *The Feminine Mystique*. Now they mean the whole women's movement. It did change everybody's lives, including my own. But I don't want there to be any danger this time of throwing the baby out with the bath water. What I'm saying now is really unfinished. Where it seemed in the first stage that self-fulfillment for women was opposed to the family, in the second stage I think because the evolution of the family is based on the strengthened self and autonomy of women, they are not opposed. I do not think you can see a full celebration of the personhood of woman if you divorce the woman from the family. But the strengthening of the family is made possible by the new autonomy of women.

Some may think I'm a traitor for talking this way; some think I'm out ahead again.

# Index